W9-BUU-224

718-
257-
1300

UPON
THIS
ROCK

ALSO BY SAMUEL G. FREEDMAN

Small Victories

UPON THIS ROCK

THE MIRACLES OF A
BLACK CHURCH

Samuel G. Freedman

HarperCollins*Publishers*

Grateful acknowledgment is made to the following for permission to quote from copyrighted material:

"Rejoice," by Kenneth Lewis. Copyright © 1984 Arisav Music, Inc. All rights reserved. Used by permission.

"Jesus is the Light," by V. Michael McKay. Copyright © 1987 Kosciusko Music. All rights reserved. Used by permission.

UPON THIS ROCK. Copyright © 1993 by Samuel G. Freedman. All rights reserved. Printed in the United States of America. No part of this book may be used or reproduced in any manner whatsoever without written permission except in the case of brief quotations embodied in critical articles and reviews. For information address HarperCollins Publishers, Inc., 10 East 53rd Street, New York, NY 10022.

HarperCollins books may be purchased for educational, business, or sales promotional use. For information please write: Special Markets Department, HarperCollins Publishers, Inc., 10 East 53rd Street, New York, NY 10022.

FIRST EDITION

Designed by Alma Hochhauser Orenstein

Library of Congress Cataloging-in-Publication Data

Freedman, Samuel G.
    Upon this rock: the miracles of a black church/Samuel G. Freedman.
—1st ed.
        p.   cm.
    Includes bibliographical references.
    ISBN 0-06-016610-X
    1. Youngblood, Johnny Ray.   2. Baptists—New York (N.Y.)—Clergy.
3. Afro-American Baptists—New York (N.Y.) 4. Saint Paul Community Baptist Church (Brooklyn, New York, N.Y.) 5. Church and social problems—New York (N.Y.) 6. Brooklyn (New York, N.Y.) I. Title.
BX6495.Y68F74   1993
286'.1'092—dc20   92-53323
[B]

93 94 95 96 97 ❖/HC 10 9 8 7 6 5 4 3 2 1

To my father, DAVID, and my son, AARON
The guardian of conscience and the inheritor of it

Upon this rock I will build my church;
and the gates of hell shall not prevail against it.

—Matthew 16:18

CONTENTS

PROLOGUE

◎

ANOTHER BEGGAR

*T*HE FIRST AFRICAN SLAVES *arrived in the Dutch settlement of New Amsterdam in 1626. Some thirty-four years later, it is recorded, slaves appeared in the adjoining town of Brooklyn. Well before the end of the century, historical accounts tell of their presence in the expanse of flatland and estuary called New Lots, which someday would be subsumed by Brooklyn, as Brooklyn would be subsumed by New York.*

Slaves tilled the soil for corn and potatoes and wheat. They built the mills along the salt creeks. They raised the horses their masters raced for amusement. On Sundays the Dutch, believing themselves enlightened, allowed their African captives to worship in church. Christianity would keep their minds safely centered on the next world.

Still, these Africans confounded their masters, the way they clung to such strange names as Kouba and Yaft, and commingled Christianity with belief in spirits, potions, and charms. There was even a rebellion in New Amsterdam in 1712, and nine whites fell beneath hatchets and knives. Not until 150 years after slaves were first sent to New Lots did one merit burial in the yard of the Dutch Reformed Church:

SACRED TO THE MEMORY OF FLORA,
A COLORED WOMAN, WHO DIED JAN. 5, 1826, AGED 104 YEARS
STRONG FAITH, TRUSTING IN HER SAVIOR

* * *

One hundred sixty-three years later and seven blocks away, the Reverend Johnny Ray Youngblood mounts the altar of the Saint Paul Community Baptist Church to celebrate Christmas Eve. His step remains springy at the age of forty-one, his years betrayed only by a dusting of gray on each temple. He wears vestments trimmed with ebony velvet, its shade not much darker than that of his skin. Beneath the broad cedar beams of the roof, behind a lectern decorated with pin lights and evergreen sprigs, Reverend Youngblood's eyes flicker, and his high cheeks rise even higher. He is smiling at the faces before him that fill twenty-three rows of pine pews, back to the rear wall with its stained glass and tall chimes; he is smiling at the faces that stretch off to his left, claiming the metal folding chairs of the new wing. The assemblage today comes to one thousand worshipers, people who, like their pastor, descend from African chattel, who, like him, have lived against all adversity to see this holy day. Reverend Youngblood calls them "my folk."

He sees the ushers, the women in white dresses, the men in navy suits, each adorned with a medal of brass and enamel, seating the stragglers. He nods toward the wings for his childhood friend, Eli Wilson, to strike the organ chords of "For God So Loved the World." He hears from behind him the choir, bedecked in gray robes with lavender piping and a treble clef across the chest, lifting their voices into a great graceful arc. He feels on his shoulder the strong hand of Douglas Slaughter, the young minister he discovered waiting tables in Atlanta, and who now is his protégé.

And after the hymn subsides, Reverend Youngblood prays. He prays for friends and family and health; for Saint Paul is a place not only of faith but of hope. There are clipped shrubs on the lawn and poinsettias in the windows and a neon cross that bears the promise JESUS SAVES. There are a school and a bookstore and a computer system all beneath its roof. Where only eighty-four worshiped when Reverend Youngblood first was called, fifteen years ago, now the rolls tally close to five thousand. Why, in the last year alone, Saint Paul has seen the joys of 12 weddings, 16 conversions, 68 baby blessings, 275 baptisms, 620 new memberships.

But as he continues, head bowed and eyes closed, Reverend Youngblood prays also for the "enemies who give us reason to pray."

Of these, too, God has provided an abundance. Around the oasis that is Saint Paul sprawls a landscape of tenements and housing projects, of vacant lots where factories once stood, and locked and barred bungalows where decent people still try to live. It is not the places or their people that are the pastor's foes, but rather the forces of poverty and racism and industrial decline that created them, and perhaps most of all the crime that feasts upon them. In the slum called East New York, which stands on the bones of the Dutch settlement of New Lots, the last year counted the greatest concentration of violence in all New York City—90 murders, 102 rapes, robberies and assaults by the thousand. Only hours earlier on this blessed morning, a nine-year-old boy died in the neighborhood hospital, shot through the window of his aunt's apartment by a drug dealer who had mistaken his silhouette for that of a rival.

The police in this precinct wear T-shirts that say THE KILLING FIELDS. Even Saint Paul must guard its entrance with electronic surveillance and surround its parking lot with a chain-link fence topped by razor wire. Despite the activities during the week, the choir rehearsals and Bible study classes and myriad ministries, even the brawniest men would sooner double-park outside the church than turn a corner beyond its view.

It is not merely Reverend Youngblood's vanity to believe that Saint Paul is the best thing for blocks around. In the program each worshiper receives this morning, on the page labeled "Updates from 'The Paul,'" there are notices of adult education classes and sales of a videotape of a recent choir concert and the upcoming appearance by the church's youth group in a dance competition. So full of good news is the column that for one of the rare Sundays it omits Reverend Youngblood's request that parents lend him their children's report cards so that he can read their grades from the pulpit. In ways both obvious and ineffable, Sunday redeems all else.

"This is a party, y'all," Youngblood now tells the congregants, and Eli Wilson carves the deep groove of the gospel song called "Jesus Is the Light." Across the stage, his assistant, James Jones, answers on grand piano. The choir sways from side to side, hands clapping and shoulders shaking. Reverend Youngblood bounces forward on his feet, and pounds the beat into the air fist after fist, like a fighter working the heavy bag. Even the ushers, instructed to hold one hand at their sides and one behind their backs, quiver against the impossible ideal of restraint.

"Now I know we got a 'small' ensemble in the choir loft," Eli says teasingly, as he drops the volume and wipes his brow, "and I can see by the looks on your faces out there, I know what you're thinking. You think we've just come to entertain this morning. Don't you?" He lets the phrase linger. "Well, we didn't. Just because the small ensemble is in the choir loft doesn't mean you're off the hook. We came to worship. Amen?"

"Amen," one thousand voices shout.

"All right?"

"*All right.*"

Eli has a voice from an oaken cask, a voice that can inflate a bare room without effort. But now he leaps up from the organ, pulling the microphone with him, and begins to rip and tear through the song. He turns its melody into an obstacle course of grace notes and minor keys, erupting into phrases of praise, reeling back from the mike to narrow his eyes and clamp his lips in resolve, and finally pitching forward again into a fervent, shamanistic kind of call-and-response.

> *I know He'll show up*
> SHOW UP!
> *In me*
> IN ME!
> *I know He'll rise up*
> RISE UP!
> *Rise up*
> RISE UP!
> *I'm gonna praise Him*
> PRAISE HIM!
> *Praise Him*
> PRAISE HIM!

In the pews, arms swing and tilt like saplings in a strong wind. Heads bob by the score, heads in African *kufi* hats and Jamaican dreadlocks, in Madison Avenue mink and Fourteenth Street felt. Whatever the style, it is almost certainly the most elegant its owner can afford. Appearances at Saint Paul deceive. The man who wears pinstripes on Sunday may own no other suit. The woman in silk may have saved for months to buy it at the outlet mall in Reading. Yes, there are doctors and lawyers and executives, but more commonly there are packers and mailmen, secretaries and mechanics. The clue is in the hands. Saint Paul is a church of coarse hands, of oddly bent fingers and callused palms and broken nails with bruises beneath the polish, for even those hands that can now linger over a balance sheet or a computer keyboard in childhood probably picked tobacco in the Carolinas.

Normally, following the song, Reverend Youngblood would declare that each member "share the good news with your neighbor," but today the congregation needs no such cue. Instantly the sanctuary resembles an immense indoor square dance as people hug, kiss, and clutch, all the while stepping in cadence with the song. From opposite ends of the room, siblings or spouses or friends fall together in embraces so desperate and enveloping they look like newly united survivors of a shipwreck. By threes or fives, others sink to their knees in communal prayer, the urgent sound of "Bless you" rising like steam from their midst.

Steep swells of music wash forward and back. Somewhere in the maelstrom a tambourine beats. Somewhere an old man dances a jig. Somewhere a voice cries, "Thank you, Jesus." And before the last "Hallelujah" has faded, Reverend Youngblood shoots Eli a glance, and Eli deflects it toward the choir, and the next spiritual commences its slow, inexorable ascent.

From the back row of the choir, all but eclipsed by the bodies swirling around his, peeks out the white face of Tom Approbato. Between his blue eyes and his bristly red beard, his mouth opens wide in song. He rocks on his heels like the baritones beside him. He is not a white man pretending at negritude. He is just one more sinner seeking redemption.

Once, growing up Roman Catholic in the 1950s, awed by a God who could be approached only in Latin, he had thought of becoming a priest. Puberty and the English mass ended that aspiration, and slowly he drifted away from religion itself. Then one night seven years ago something terrible happened, and he found himself on his knees asking to be forgiven. And not long after that, he fell in love with a black woman, who brought his reborn faith to Saint Paul.

They laid odds, the church's ministers, on whether the white man would stay. They wondered when a visiting preacher launched a fiercely racial exegesis of the Creation. They wondered when Tom parted with his lover. Not only did he stay, he joined the choir. Not only did he stay, he volunteered to teach a night-school course. Not only did he stay, but he entered a seminary, having heard the call.

"Together," Reverend Youngblood tells the congregants, "let's sing 'Happy Birthday' to our Savior." Accompanied by James Jones on piano, they do. "And let's give God the Father a hand for sending his Son into the world." There is vigorous applause. Reverend Youngblood leans forward, both arms resting on the lectern, in a posture of intimate conversation. "You know, I have discovered there are only two good reasons why anybody should be here this morning. One is that they believe in Jesus—and all who do, may I see your hands, that you may witness." Hundreds of hands push upward. "And the only other good reason for folk bein' here is they lookin' to believe in *somethin'* and everything they got is fallin' down and crumblin' around 'em. And we just want you to know you're in the right place and you're lookin' for the right one." He straightens. "How many visitors do we have today? Could you please stand up."

A dozen people rise. The rest clap. Reverend Youngblood, as he usually does, calls on a Saint Paul member to welcome the visitors. Today he beckons Sean Blanks, the son of Rochester "Rocky" Blanks. Both men are Saint Paul success stories, Rocky a district supervisor for the Chock Full o'Nuts coffee company before becoming financial manager of the church at a fraction of the salary, Sean at age twenty-one a recent graduate of Syracuse University bound for advanced studies in hospital administration. Like most of the weekly greeters, young Blanks tells the first-timers they are attending "Church Unusual," the slogan of Reverend Youngblood's that is emblazoned on Saint Paul's stationery, bulletin boards, and vans. By "unusual," Reverend Youngblood means, don't be surprised to see cheerleaders or modern dancers involved in service, or to find dusty traditions like fried-chicken dinners absent from the calendar, or, for that matter, to observe hundreds of men like Rochester and Sean Blanks at worship.

Few members would strike a visitor as more unusual than Robert Sharper. Even some fellow congregants have whispered of him, "Why's he

wearin' those hats in the sanctuary? Why's he keepin' his hair that way?"
They refer to the knobby beginnings of dreadlocks and to the kente *hat*
from Ghana that covers them, the very elements that to Robert himself
symbolize rebirth.

More than almost anyone in the pews around him, Robert embodies
the theological idea of resurrection. In Christmastimes past, he would
have put his carpenter's pay into wine and cognac, heroin and cocaine.
And if he had already spent the money, as he so often had, then he would
have charmed some sucker into a loan or a free taste.

Even now, clean and sober for several years, he respects the tempta-
tions of what he calls "the threefold"—Thanksgiving, Christmas, and
New Year's Eve. And he worries not only about himself. Having been
saved, Robert came to understand the reason why: so that he could help
rescue others. They call themselves the Wounded Healers, and they meet
every Saturday at Saint Paul.

The powers of persuasion Robert honed in twenty years of addiction
he now devotes to teaching the twelve steps of recovery. Each week is one
step, and the cycle never ends. In this season of spiked eggnog and warmed
brandy, of plentiful excuses to indulge, Robert knows terrifyingly well the
meaning of the phrase "One day at a time."

In the church of Reverend Youngblood's New Orleans childhood, as
in so many other black congregations, the male presence consisted of
boys shy of puberty, elderly uncles and grandfathers, and gay musicians. Even the pastor was a woman. The larger part of the neighborhood's men, the robust ones, the potential leaders, ventured no closer
than the front door to drop off their women. Their sexuality made
them blasphemers, and church was for the holy.

To Reverend Youngblood, however, God needed precisely those
men. Christ's disciples, he often preached, were not sissies, and for his
own disciples he wanted men who still harbored the warrior spirit.
"This country is not going to live up to its potential," he often said,
"until the black man lives up to his." He attracted them with a concept of church rule by an all-male board of elders. He attracted them
with an all-male ministry, called Eldad-Medad after two of Moses'
aides, which combined Bible study, group therapy, and lodge cama-
raderie. He attracted them, most of all, with his distaste for moral
hypocrisy. He might be a prophet, he would have his men know, but

he was no saint, and that was all right, because the church was not a museum for saints but a hospital for sinners.

Now, with the visitors seated, Reverend Youngblood asks all the men to stand. This they obligingly do—the ushers at their stations throughout the sanctuary, the high school students in their cluster in the last few pews, the tenors and baritones and basses of the choir, the elders in their block of folding chairs just off the altar. "My men," Reverend Youngblood calls them. "My men."

One man is missing, one who worshiped last Christmas Eve and the thirteen other Christmas Eves of Reverend Youngblood's service and thirtyeight more before that, back to his own boyhood. His name was Stephen Kelly, and he was the kind of lifelong member people called a "child of the church." What absented him today was nothing less than death, death from the barrel of a police officer's gun.

It had happened about a month after the last Christmas Eve, during an argument over a parking space. Kelly was unarmed. The officer, who was off duty at the time, was forty years his junior. Still, it was said, he had pistol-whipped Kelly before shooting him. Even Mayor Koch and the district attorney made it sound like a case that would be swiftly and justly closed.

Where Kelly no longer stands, two women sit. Annie Nesbitt was Kelly's companion for the last seven years of his life. Inez Simpkins is his sister. The two hardly knew each other until that January night, but in the succeeding months they have become the closest of friends, partners for Bible class and trips to Rockefeller Center, united not only by affinity but by a kind of crusade.

They have gone to court, often with Kelly's sons, seven times since the killing, and still the prosecution seems barely to have begun. The officer remains free on bail, and the only inquiry pressed was whether Kelly was sober on the night he was shot. An insulting question, the women thought, since everyone knew Stephen Kelly never drank.

Annie had always attended Saint Paul with Kelly, but Inez had departed from the church in antipathy a generation earlier. Only when she returned for her brother's funeral did she realize how much she had missed it, and only when she heard Reverend Youngblood did she see that at least one preacher was not a fraud. Her Bible is open to Matthew this morning, but her mind, like Annie Nesbitt's, never strays far from Job.

* * *

Each Sunday at Saint Paul serves, among other things, as a town meeting. Reverend Youngblood begins it by mentioning upcoming services, events, and classes, and then he turns personal, identifying easily and intimately individuals from his vast flock. He introduces a woman turning seventy-five, and she is applauded. He points out an usher whose family is buying a low-cost home built by the coalition of Brooklyn congregations that Reverend Youngblood chairs. He announces the thirtieth wedding anniversary of one of the church elders and his wife. "You see Barbara?" he adds, referring to the elder's wife. "When she sat down, she had a look of relief. Like, 'They said it couldn't be done.'" The assemblage roars, and the pastor himself buckles with laughter. "I'm so glad I can joke with y'all," he says. "Otherwise I'd be directin' a mortuary."

Then Reverend Youngblood locates atop the lectern a letter from a vice-president of Pratt Institute, a college in a different section of Brooklyn. Before beginning to read, the pastor adds that he has never met this man, as if to validate the praise about to be heard. "'Saint Paul is the first church I have noticed, Baptist or otherwise, whose commitment to youth seems to be developing a measurable impact,'" Reverend Youngblood intones. "'I can honestly state that your work has had as much impact here in the Pratt area, by virtue of the attitude, commitment, and philosophy of your membership, as any church in this neighborhood. I salute you and your members for your commitment to youth, and for the development of a sustained emphasis on the ever-increasing need for stronger roles and higher visibilities of black men in the development of youth.... We as a community can and will reclaim our young people.'"

A stocky woman in red taffeta has reclaimed far more than her share. Her name is Kathleen Wilson, but all her grandchildren call her "Gram," the fourteen tied to her by blood and the two dozen others bound by love alone. Some stay with her for a summer, some for several years. Few have made a deeper claim on her than the teenaged boy living with her now, Ali Nurse, who was teetering on the brink of homelessness until she appeared.

She rouses him most Sundays at six o'clock for church, with the simple adjuration, "Let's get with it, Ali." He happens to be visiting relatives in

*North Carolina just now, but when he returns he will find Christmas has
been waiting. He will see how Kathleen decorated the apartment door
with wrapping paper and ribbons like a package, and beneath the tree he
will discover presents—a pair of wool gloves and a bottle of cologne and a
matching pullover and slacks.*

*Then he will return to high school and what Kathleen prays will be
his last term. The deal she made with her husband demands that Ali
graduate in June, even though that means taking twelve classes this
spring. She will support Ali but not protect him, for she is teaching him,
like all who came before, that her love must be matched by his responsibility.*

Reverend Youngblood leads another prayer, a brief one, and then
launches into a subject he dreads—debt. All his life he has nurtured a
healthy wariness of the credit system and the black family's depen-
dence on it. He remembers how the bills arrived in his parents' mail-
box each Thursday evening, because the merchants knew Johnny's
father would be paid the following afternoon. He remembers most
clearly the day two white men drove away with his father's black
Chrysler, the first car he had ever owned, repossessed because a work-
ingman fell two months behind in his payments.

In building Saint Paul to a membership of five thousand and a
full-time staff of fifty-one, Reverend Youngblood naturally enough
had to enter the mortgage and loan markets, and he always paid on
time. The church itself operated on unforced philanthropy, not only
the dollars dropped into wicker baskets at each service, but the tithes
of ten percent of their annual salaries that eight hundred members
gave. In Church Unusual, each donor even received a computer printout at year's end for tax purposes.

Recently, however, the system had fallen short. Saint Paul had
missed a $145,000 mortgage payment on the property it was buying
for a youth center, one of the pastor's central projects for the 1990s,
and the bank in turn raised the interest rate to a punishing 21.5 percent. Today Reverend Youngblood wants to cull at least $45,000,
enough to assure the bank that the church intends to meet its obligations. Beyond this immediate crisis, the pastor must collect by May
$1.5 million already pledged for the new sanctuary. All of this comes
above the donations that support a $4 million annual operating bud-

get. The business of dunning plainly pains Reverend Youngblood, but the specter of dispossession haunts him even more.

"I've made known a need to you," he tells the worshipers, "and we come today to meet that need. We have an indebtedness that must be met. We have five thousand people on our rolls, and we are the wealthiest poor people in the world." Laughter echoes from the pews. "It is not that we do not have the money. I refuse to believe black folk do not have the money." His severe tone hushes the crowd. "They just do not want to use it for the Kingdom." There are murmurs of assent. "If we would forget the Christmas trees and forget the liquor cabinets, we would have enough money to liquidate our debt."

To Eli's organ underscoring, worshipers move up the aisles to the basket before the altar. "Bless you," Reverend Youngblood says to one. And: "I like that." And: "She brought a hundred dollars from the Lindenwood Diner. Said she robbed 'em."

Then the sacrifice turns personal. Reverend Youngblood receives no set salary, only the money that members seal in envelopes marked "Pastor's Love Offering." It is his way of saying that he leads at the congregation's sufferance, of measuring in an eminently quantifiable fashion his standing. Now he asks anyone with a donation for him to contribute it instead toward the mortgage. "I have a house," he says. "I have enough food. I have folk to take care of me." He pauses, then shouts. "But we will raise this $45,000!"

A young man with thick spectacles and a morning coat made the journey to the altar both times. He is not wealthy—far from it. Hobbled by slight retardation or a learning disability, at least according to the public schools that graduated him from high school with third-grade skills, he works the midnight shift as a security guard, earning less than $250 a week, even with hours of overtime.

But Randy Murphy knows the definition of sacrifice, of struggle. He carries in his wallet a handwritten list entitled "My Goals," ranging from buying contact lenses to taking a vacation to developing discipline. Most of all, he aspires to live as he has never lived in his twenty-six years, independently.

Randy has already surprised his doubters many times, by holding a job, by helping the church, by winning the love of a college student, even if that love ended in betrayal. Still, there seems a gap between his grand

dreams and his ability to make them real, and Randy's spirit has sur-
vived only by denying that chasm exists.

As a delegation of men carries the collection into the pastor's study, Eli Wilson moves his music stand into the center aisle to conduct the choir in Pergolesi's "Glory to God in the Highest." Reverend Young-blood sinks into his chair, attending closely, moving one hand now and again as if hitting a particular chord. His eyes close in contemplation of the sermon to come and, it is hard not to imagine, in worry and fatigue. He wipes an open hand across his face, almost kneading the flesh. After a few unmoving moments he reopens his eyes, spreads his arms wide, and brings his palms loudly together. He repeats the motion twice, moves to his feet, urging on both the choir and himself.

The program in each worshiper's hand announces that today's sermon is entitled "Thank God for Joseph." Most of the listeners know it represents the final link in a trilogy of yuletide sermons, sermons that even by Reverend Youngblood standards have been bracing, controversial, and revealing.

The cycle started exactly two weeks ago, with "Christmas in the Raw." What was raw about Christmas, Reverend Youngblood declared, was that the holiday marked not simply a birth, but a pregnancy, and the sexual act that leads to a pregnancy. He knew he was treading treacherous ground, and he stopped several times to ask for prayers and amens "because there are some people out there wanna shoot me already." Virgin birth and immaculate conception, he went on, were not biblical truths, but Roman Catholic interpretations. To believe Mary had been born without original sin, to believe Mary could conceive without the act of intercourse, raised Mary to a dangerously sacred plane.

"And when they do that," Reverend Youngblood had thundered, "they take away the Gospel for the ghetto. For me, when they lift Mary to these heights where can't nobody touch her, and then they change the Trinity into a quartet—meaning the Father, the Son, the Holy Spirit, and Mary—you ladies are left out. My mama is left out! My wife is left out! And the good news of Christmas is that God got with an ordinary woman. And she conceived."

Reverend Youngblood had always appreciated the manner in which the ancient Greeks perceived their gods, as emotionally complex and physically hungry beings, and part of his intent in the sermon had been to force a freer discussion of sexuality. He wanted, too, to argue for the divinity of pregnancy, regardless of the conditions surrounding it. Mary, he reminded his audience, was an unwed teenaged mother in a religious society that forbade birth out of wedlock. The Savior was born not to the sounds of cheerful carols but amid the grunts of labor and the stirring of livestock. And if that peculiar pregnancy could bring forth Jesus Christ, then it was clear where he and Saint Paul stood on abortion.

But even that was only part of the point. For, as always with Reverend Youngblood, scriptural exegesis carried with it painful autobiography:

Don't look at me funny. Please don't look at me funny. Cause, y'all, I went to college, and I didn't spend all my times in the boys' dormitory. Oh, it's good to get this stuff off your chest. And, yes, I've had some frightening moments. And even now, when I prepare this message, I can't prepare a message where I'm clear, where I'm in the clear and I'm straight and I tell y'all what y'all oughta do.

This thing is a two-edged sword. It whips back and cuts the hell out of me and then comes forward and cuts y'all. And the truth of God's word is not predicated on my lifestyle. It is predicated on God's word itself. He sends sinful men to preach to sinful men. I'm just another beggar, tellin' other beggars where to find bread.

After the service had ended that morning two weeks earlier, Reverend Youngblood had gone directly to the telephone in his office and dialed a number in New Orleans, his hometown. "How you doin', Doc?" he had asked the man of twenty on the other end. Then he had heard a silence of surprise in the receiver, for it was usually the young man who telephoned Reverend Youngblood. "I guess you're wonderin' why I called," the pastor had gone on. "Well, I just preached a sermon, and the sermon I preached made me think of you." They had spoken for a few moments more, and before hanging up, the young man had told Reverend Youngblood, "I love you."

The young man, at least according to his mother, was the pastor's son. Reverend Youngblood, who had boys of fifteen and ten by his wife, Joyce, had floated for years in a gray zone between acknowledging and denying this child, remaining in contact with him without ever calling him "son." His mother had christened the child Johnny, although the pastor preferred to call him by his middle name, Jernell, or the endearment "Doc." But such ambivalence seemed likely to end. At Joyce's urging, he had decided to take a blood test in the coming months to settle the matter of paternity. And more than that, he was privately weighing whether to bring the young man to New York for a visit, and perhaps something more.

Reverend Youngblood knew the loneliness of a fatherless child. His own father was still married to his mother, but Palmon Youngblood, his son always felt, "gave me to my mother to raise," busying himself with the sugar-refinery job that supported the family and the outside woman who lifted his own spirits. So many times in church, young Johnny had imagined how glorious it would sound to hear his father's voice praising God in harmony with his own. It was only in the past year or two, only as he had begun to reckon with his own supposed son in New Orleans, that Reverend Youngblood had begun reconciling with his father. "My daddy," he told people now, "is a fine brother."

The week after "Christmas in the Raw," Reverend Youngblood delivered a sermon entitled "Thank God for Elizabeth." Elizabeth was the mother of John the Baptist, and the one confidante available to Mary during her own pregnancy. Elizabeth was more even than confidante, the pastor went on, for she was much older than Mary and willing to share the wisdom she had accumulated in both years and experience. When Mary found her, Elizabeth was six months into her own strange and miraculous pregnancy; until then she had assumed she was barren. Once again, the sermon had levels and more levels. Reverend Youngblood was telling the mothers and grandmothers of his congregation not to condemn the teenager who "got in trouble," and telling the teenager unprepared for motherhood to seek help from those more schooled in life. But he was also, in an elliptical way, confessing his own need:

> Mary had the Lord, but my own life in Christ forces me to confess that even when you've got the Lord, every now and then

you need somebody else. That is not against the Lord. But sometimes you need another mortal. You need another piece of flesh and blood talkin' to you. It doesn't mean the Lord is absent, but, y'all, we're just not sure angels and divinities go through what we go through.... And while "just having Jesus is enough" is a great-sounding statement, you better speak it with caution, because you may find yourself with just Him and need somebody else.

Those words echoed in several ways the pastor's own life. Reverend Youngblood had first gone to a psychiatrist twenty years earlier as a seminarian. Never before had he lived in the North and moved in white circles, and the sudden rupture with his race, culture, and value system had nearly driven him to a breakdown. He had survived the seminary, even thrived in the end, and yet now, at a time when his life appeared the definition of ministerial success, he had again sought therapy. He and Joyce saw a marriage counselor, and he himself visited an analyst.

For all Reverend Youngblood preached about the necessity for men to be strong, he strained under the demands on his own strength. He had to stand fast for five thousand congregants, for fifty-one staff members, for his wife and his sons. He had to live life against the presumption by some members that he could do no wrong and the delight of others in finding the tracks left by feet of clay. His prayer life was just fine, he told anyone who asked about his therapy, but sometimes he needed a human there just for Johnny Ray Youngblood.

He spoke often, in and out of the pulpit, of F. Scott Fitzgerald's observation, "In a real dark night of the soul it is always three o'clock in the morning." He literally walked the halls of his own home after midnight, waiting for something that might answer to the name of grace. The question that pierced him when he thanked God for Elizabeth—How can any human survive all alone?—brought him eventually to three verses in the first chapter of Matthew. These in turn formed the text for his Christmas Eve sermon:

Now the birth of Jesus Christ was on this wise: When as his mother Mary was espoused to Joseph, before they came together, she was found with child of the Holy Ghost.

Then Joseph her husband, being a just man, and not willing to make her a publick example, was minded to put her away privily.

But while he thought on these things, behold, the angel of the Lord appeared unto him in a dream, saying, Joseph, thou son of David, fear not to take unto thee Mary thy wife: for that which is conceived in her is of the Holy Ghost.

"This has been a real exciting Christmas for me," Reverend Youngblood now tells the congregation, beginning at a deceptively leisurely pace. "In terms of these passages with which we are familiar, at least the extractions of these passages, I have gotten some insights that I thank God for." His eyes lift from the page and dance. "Some of you may not thank God for them, but I thank God for them."

He quickly reprises "Christmas in the Raw" and "Thank God for Elizabeth." He remarks, as he has before, on the peculiar births chronicled in the Bible, and on his belief that Jesus' was the most peculiar of all. Had he lived in those times, the pastor says, he would have enjoyed, felt honored, to have been a wise man or a shepherd or almost any participant in the drama—except for Joseph. Yes, he would sooner have been in the mob crying "Crucify him!" than to have been Joseph. He would rather have been Judas.

"Gotta look at this thing for what it is, now," he says, opening his palms like the trays of a scale. "A man is engaged. The date for the wedding's been set. The invitations have gone out. The rehearsals have been scheduled, and one or two have taken place. The bridal party's been selected and dressed. The hope chest's been purchased with some stuff already in it." He pauses. "And the bride-to-be is lookin' strange."

He asks the congregation to imagine poor Joe Davidson, and when there are murmurs of confusion, he explains. Joseph's father, the Bible says, was David, and a man took his surname from his father. In Hebrew, then, his name would have been Joseph ben-David, and, in English translation, Joe Davidson. This etymological digression is really one more way for the pastor to make an ancient figure modern, an ancient story immediate.

"Mary's pregnancy," he goes on, "was biologically inconceivable, socially unacceptable, and historically unheard of. She talk all that 'It was the Holy Ghost. The angel gave it to me.'" He leaps from Bethlehem to Brooklyn, indignant. "I know what kinda *angel*." People howl, some in shock, some in affirmation. "Did I ever tell y'all the joke I heard about the lady who lived alone? She stood in church one day and said, 'I don't need nobody, I got the Lord, I got Jesus.' And so her house caught fire, a fella ran out the back door, somebody said, 'There go Jesus.'"

Laughter shakes the sanctuary.

"So Joseph wasn't about to talk to the brothers. *No sir.* 'Man, you know what my ol' lady told me?' *No sir.* That was one thing Joseph kept to himself. 'Cause you know what they were gonna say. They would even call somebody's name that she been with." He leans up on the lectern as if to confide. "I mean, c'mon, brothers, y'all know what it is when we sit around with other men and talk about our wives.... The brothers are out there on the street, and their wives are workin', and they got the nerve to be mad." He affects a sullen, almost drunken slur. "'Man, that woman ain't workin', she out there with somebody.' So Joseph didn't tell nobody."

"Yes sir," voices urge. "Go 'head, Rev."

"Mary and Joseph couldn't even pray. The law says they were in trouble with God. Christmas was not"—he spits out the word like chewing tobacco—"*joy* to the world until *after* Jesus was born."

"Preach it."

"Any of you know how I understand that?" Reverend Youngblood says, modulating himself from oratory to conversation yet again. "I've seen it time and again. A young woman conceives and she is not married. Her mama wants to kill her. Her daddy puts her out. They can't stand her. But as soon as the baby's born"—he turns on a proud rasp—"'Our grandchild.'" He lets the words dangle. "So when Jesus was conceived, wasn't no joy. Mary didn't go around, 'I'm expectin' for the Lord, I'm expectin' for the Lord.' No, no, wasn't none of that. Joe didn't pass out any cigars. He was burnin', but there wasn't no cigars." Laughter flows, then ebbs. "To be honest with you, in a way, for Mary and Joseph that first Christmas was hell. It was hell."

What, then, is the point of Joseph's presence? He shows, Reverend Youngblood says, that marriage is a ministry to God, a reason for devotion and sacrifice. He shows that being a man of God means being prepared for loneliness, even scorn. He shows that a man of God is a gentleman, a chivalrous man, a man who respects women. The Bible makes no mention of where Joseph stood in the community, how much education he had, how much money he earned. Only his faith mattered.

Why, Reverend Youngblood suddenly muses, are there bumper stickers about how beer drinkers, elevator operators, all kinds of men are better lovers? Where's the bumper sticker that says, "Spiritual men make good lovers"? And that means much more than sex. It means being a good listener, helping people, praying when it's time to pray. For all its levity, the notion of the bumper sticker, like the concept of "Joe Davidson," brings a distant ideal into the present moment. That bumper sticker could be the synopsis for this sermon, the core of Reverend Youngblood's ministry, one that builds a nation by building a family, that builds a family by telling a man to act like a man.

"Spiritual men are peculiar men. Spiritual men are hated and loved at the same time. Spiritual men have a potential that others are afraid of, because they don't know where it's leading." By now the pastor's voice, never classically round, sounds ragged and worn. As he shouts, one imagines blood running in his throat. "Spiritual men got somebody backin' 'em that folk can't see and don't understand. But they know they're not alone."

"Go 'head."

"I thank God that Joseph was a spiritual man," he says softly now. "What would Mary have done if that man, that kind of man, had not been in her life? Would Jesus have been born? How would she have gotten out of Bethlehem to Egypt? How would she have gotten from Egypt to Nazareth?" He pauses one final time, not for effect but in exhaustion. His voice is a hoarse whisper. "Thank God for Joseph. And remember, Joseph may not look like much while he's around. But ask any widow what it's like when Joseph's gone."

The service proceeds for another half hour, but after that sermon all else, from the call for converts to the Hallelujah Chorus, can be no more than a coda. It seems beyond imagination that in twenty minutes, at eleven o'clock, Reverend Youngblood will start all over again with the day's second service. And at eight this evening he will convene the believers yet one more time.

Now he draws breath in his study, a modest room with a door opening into the sanctuary. A telephone and a Bible rest on the glass table before him. On a smaller table to his left rise two stacks of books, from Stephen Shapiro's *Manhood* to Kwame Nkrumah's *Revolutionary Warfare*. His diplomas from Dillard University and Colgate-Rochester Theological Seminary hang on one paneled wall. A pencil drawing of a little black boy trying on a too-large wingtip shoe dominates another. "To be like Daddy," the caption explains. Above the illustration stretches a ten-foot sheet of computer paper, on which is written in huge block letters: BEYOND THE CONSPICUOUS ABSENCE AND THE CONTROVERSIAL PRESENCE OF THE BLACK MALE IN THE LOCAL CHURCH.

That is the title of Reverend Youngblood's doctoral dissertation. He shivers and coughs now with the flu he acquired while exhausting himself to meet the seminary's December 7 deadline. Standing outside City Hall in seventeen-degree weather for a half hour the other morning didn't help, either. East Brooklyn Congregations, the organization of fifty-two churches and one synagogue that he chairs, held a rally to announce it was suing the city for blocking construction of low-cost homes in the Nehemiah program. Named for the biblical prophet who rebuilt Jerusalem, the Nehemiah concept has succeeded where hundreds of public efforts have failed, in building brand-new single-family homes that working people can buy for as little as $39,000. There are nearly two thousand already constructed, and there are plans to build three thousand more. But suddenly the city seems less willing to condemn property and give away land to let the construction resume. And so a pastor with the flu marched on a frigid morn.

If not a lawsuit, something else would lay claim to Reverend Youngblood. It dawned on him a few months ago that every time he boarded a plane he was going somewhere on business. He has needed solitude so badly of late that he sent Joyce and his sons, Joel and Jason, to visit relatives in Tampa for Christmas week. Even so, there was a couple this morning asking his blessing on their engagement, an aunt seeking counseling on how best to raise her nieces and nephews, a staff member demanding that he watch the youth group compete several days hence in a "stepping" contest.

His people needed him, and not only for their temporal woes. They needed their pastor with them in their searches through life. Tom Approbato needed Reverend Youngblood in his search for holiness, Randy Murphy in his search for independence, Robert Sharper in his search for lasting recovery, Kathleen Wilson in her search for Ali's future, Annie Nesbitt and Inez Simpkins in their search for justice and a cessation of grief. What was it Inez called him? "Our Moses."

That was a frightening phrase, yet one that made its bearer proud. Reverend Youngblood had always said he wanted Saint Paul to be a "resource church," and who better than he to set the example? People understood. People appreciated. Plaques saluting him decorate an adjacent hallway. One corner of his study stores a pile of gifts from church members—a down jacket, a mahogany shoehorn, an autographed school portrait of a fifteen-year-old. Reverend Youngblood's favorite is the sweatshirt with the legend JUST DO IT.

He does. He has been doing it for decades. When did one start counting? From the day at age twelve he began preaching? From his ordination at twenty-four? From his arrival at Saint Paul some fifteen years ago? He could tell himself he had accomplished what he wanted, from building a vigorous church of his own to traveling the nation on the revival circuit to being sought out by the media for commentary on pressing events. People talked about his running for Congress, like Floyd Flake, a pastor in Queens who also served in the U.S. House of Representatives.

Then why did he feel so restless? Why did he fear he had peaked? He knew at least that elective office was not the answer; he had more latitude, he often said, as a prophet than as a politician. But what then? Would his Church Unusual fall into a tradition of its own, boring the young people as church had once so bored him? Was he, perhaps, afraid to keep changing, still hearing the voices of his past that warned not to take risks? In so many ways, he seemed still to be unearthing his past, searching through the rubble for the artifacts worth salvaging. Therapy could be the means of excavation, but not the treasure itself.

He prayed for God to speak, to direct him, to deliver him. What was the way to the Promised Land? To Calvary? He needed to know. So far the Almighty had not uttered the words.

Youngblood, a different idea dawns, an idea inspired by the Book of Joshua. This Sunday he will have the entire congregation pray for New York City, pray to redeem its promise of tolerance and opportunity, pray to be the Calebs who will conquer Canaan.

Now he moves up two flights of stairs, past an ironing board and a stack of *Ebony* back issues, and enters his study. It is a monkish domain, furnished with an empty china hutch, a metal filing cabinet, a secondhand secretary, and a small wooden chair in which Reverend Youngblood now sits. Here he often repairs to write, sometimes sermons, more often his personal fusion of journal and free verse. He inscribes these on the cardboard sheets that dry cleaners insert in folded shirts, as if remembering a time when paper was too dear to waste. The writings carry titles like "I Owe My Children," "The Purpose for Dreams," and "A Spiritual Man?" and beyond their value to Reverend Youngblood as self-therapy he hopes ultimately to have them collected and published under the rubric *Pastors Are People*.

He faces the study's northern wall, which is bare except for a painting at its base, a rendering of the Last Supper with the disciples represented by such titans of black history as Frederick Douglass, W. E. B. Du Bois, and Paul Robeson. Reverend Youngblood's mind of late has been much on legacy. He places at his feet a cardboard sheet with a list of his personal heroes, in categories ranging from the clergy (C. L. Franklin, Sandy F. Ray, Harry Emerson Fosdick) to the Bible (Jacob, Moses, Jesus) to modern history (King, Malcolm X, Robert F. Kennedy). Then he reaches to turn the sheet over, revealing an invocation of his own design. He silently reads:

> Overall consciousness of the Universe,
> Father to all mankind,
> Father to all children,
> All wise, Almighty, and Everlasting, Thou art God.
> God, Father to the Lord Jesus Christ, I address Thee this morning.
> I acknowledge Thee.
> I make myself available to be an instrument of Thy will.
> I seek to know Thy will, word, truth.
> I thank Thee for a sense of purpose—a reason for living, for being.

Moses' promise, that someday in tribute to his service a piece of Canaan would be granted him as an inheritance. The fourteenth chapter ends with Joshua bestowing on Caleb the city of Hebron, but it is several earlier verses, in Caleb's voice, that grip Reverend Youngblood:

> As yet I am as strong this day as I was in the day that Moses sent me: as my strength was then, even so is my strength now, for war, both to go out, and to come in.
>
> Now therefore give me this mountain.

A clock in the next room ticks. A train whistle sighs far off. Reverend Youngblood wraps the fingers of his left hand across his forehead, then slides back into his chair to think. His eyes trace the beams across the ceiling, then drop and meet the unwavering vision of black Jesus. He jots phrases—"never forgot whose they were," "spiritual senility," "our challenges are too small," "men and mountains." These will form the skeleton of a sermon to be delivered Sunday, and between now and then he will drape flesh on bones. It is sufficient in this moment to conceive the theme and the central event. Caleb could have died secure and fulfilled without land of his own. He could have asked for a meadow or a garden, greenery easy on an aged sovereign. But he insisted on a *mountain*. He might have been eighty-five but he demanded the challenge, for the challenge would keep him alive.

Reverend Youngblood thinks about how, when he turned forty, some friends threw him a party on the theme "Over the Hill." Their jest was a telling one. Reverend Youngblood had seen the scenario all his life: A man raises his children and retires from his job, replaces duty with ennui, then falls over dead one day at the breakfast table or in the tomato patch. So much energy wasted; so much wisdom lost. And the personal leads to the political for Reverend Youngblood. Fitzgerald's "dark night of the soul" speaks not only to his own feelings of isolation but to the weariness and drift he senses in black America in the aftermath of the Civil Rights movement. Here is New York City, Reverend Youngblood thinks, the Promised Land, the new Canaan, and all the talk is of defeat. It's unlivable; it's ungovernable; it's dying of crack and AIDS and greed. So many of his own parishioners speak of leaving New York, returning to the same South they once fled, that there is talk Saint Paul should open a branch in Atlanta. For Reverend parochial school, but the Christ he had been groping toward in his own manhood, black Jesus.

"The listening post," as Reverend Youngblood calls this ritual, is a place, a time, and, most of all, a temperament. Sometimes he reads the scriptures; at other times the text might be Ralph Waldo Emerson's essay "Self-Reliance" or Martin Luther King's sermon "Strength to Love," or Howard Thurman's book *Jesus and the Disinherited*. It was Thurman, the great theologian, who had spoken of the necessity for a believer to "center down and turn in," and it was Reverend Youngblood's own bitter joke that since so many black people prayed only when troubled, God got them in trouble at least once a day. In the listening post, he prays without agenda, converses without imperatives. He knows his wife and sons sleep safely upstairs; he knows in New Orleans his parents have not yet stirred; he knows his closest friends, Eli Wilson and Sarah Plowden and Doug Slaughter, are all safely ensconced in their own listening posts. Alone and unfettered, he aspires to a state he calls in contemplative moments "vertical consciousness" and in more colloquial ones "dialing God's 800 number."

With tea at his elbow and pen in hand, he reads carefully down the verses of the fourteenth chapter of Joshua. He sips, swallows, rolls up his collar for more warmth, eyes never leaving the page. A dog barks. A car alarm bleats. Steps click down the sidewalk toward the D train. He puts felt-tip to bond paper and softly scratches three citations. He is studying the story of Caleb, who had been one of Moses' most trusted lieutenants, one of twelve men sent to scout the promised land of Canaan. Of those dozen, ten returned with warnings of superior weapons and giant warriors, with admonitions that Moses choose some other, less daunting destiny. Only Joshua and Caleb said the land could be won.

Since he was a teenager, when he first heard the passage preached, Reverend Youngblood has considered the story of Caleb one of the seminal biblical narratives, the equal of David and Goliath or the Woman at the Well, but he has resisted sharing it from the pulpit until he could come equipped with an original lesson, a new truth. This morning he is finding it, not in the familiar account of Caleb's reconnaissance but in the details of his life forty-five years later. Moses by now is long dead and the Israelites have spent two generations in Canaan. Caleb himself is eighty-five. He is asking Joshua to honor

1

TWICE CALLED

did yo slep over?

AT THE LONG OAK TABLE OF A SLUMBERING HOUSE, a man prepares to meet his God. It is well before dawn in the first week of January, a time of year when nights are longest. Just east of Flatbush Avenue in Brooklyn, in the largest community of blacks in America, the hour belongs to delivery men flinging newspapers, to cabbies starting the five-to-five shift, to cleaning ladies waiting for the bus on a street damp as a dewy lawn. It belongs, too, to the Reverend Johnny Ray Youngblood, negotiating his path around the darkened furniture of his living room in muffled, slippered steps. He wears striped pajama pants and a terrycloth robe with a towel wrapped around his neck. On the table before him he places a legal pad, a felt-tip pen, and a Bible bound in red leather. He opens to the Book of Joshua, lays his pen in the seam of the pages. Then he folds his arms across his chest, closes his eyes, and silently prays. When he lifts his face, he gazes across six feet of wood to a bust of a gaunt black man wrapped in a cassock, sorrow in his creased face and anthracite eyes. Reverend Youngblood knew well enough the Bible's injunction against graven images, but when he had seen the statue in a Harlem market he had claimed it without hesitation. And even when he learned later that it represented Shakespeare's Othello, the knowledge did not compromise his communion. Here was his Christ, not the Christ imposed on his ancestors, not the Christ taught him in

I come before You in the prayer tradition of my fathers.

I find myself lifted from a certain depth, but not out of the mire of racism, poverty, and victimization in which all Your children of color find themselves.

I honor the spirits of those souls who You sent to pave paths, to run interference, to leave a legacy, to throw down a gauntlet.

He straightens in his chair enough to lay an open Bible in his lap. He reads from Hebrews 11 and 12 some of the most timeless verses on the subject of faith. The hour nears six-thirty. The night outside his window yields to an overcast dawn, and against the gray muslin sky appear eaves and branches and drainpipes. For the last time until he falls asleep eighteen hours later, Reverend Youngblood can encounter God on his own behalf rather than as the intercessor for his flock, the prophet for his tribe. He need not orate; he need not declaim; he need only speak in the low, hoarse voice of a middle-aged man hobbled by the flu on a winter morning. But it is this time in the sanctuary of the listening post that will gird him to carry every other petition.

"Dear God," he says, just above a whisper. "Thank You for life. Thank You for privileges. Thank You for an unfolding understanding of my reason for being and Your place in the world. Thank You for a knowledge of my weaknesses as well as my strengths. And thank You for not letting me walk alone."

Then he descends the stairs as a family man, stopping first in his bedroom to wake his wife, Joyce. "How you doin', Soup?" he asks, his hand on her shoulder. "How you doin, Sam?" These are his endearments, both drawn years ago from the baby-talk of the couple's eldest son, Joel.

"Time to get up, bro," he calls into the room of the fifteen-year-old Joel, whose sleeping form is guarded by a poster of the comedian Eddie Murphy.

"Jason," he says to his eleven-year-old, hidden beneath the covers on his bunk bed. "Jase."

"Leave me alone, Dad," a voice answers.

Often Reverend Youngblood will carry his greetings into the boys' rooms, hugging, singing, shouting, dousing them with water, playing father as fraternity brother. Too sluggish for horseplay this morning, he continues downstairs to the kitchen, fixes himself more tea, listens for a radio or a wisecrack or any sign of filial life. He marches back to the first-floor landing. "Guys," he says. "Gentlemen." His tone hardens from entreaty to threat. "Joel, you tell Jason I'm gonna run over his head if he don't get down here."

"He's gonna run over your head," a voice repeats.

Now satisfied his offspring have joined the conscious world, Reverend Youngblood showers and dresses. The house that gathers life around him is a sixteen-room Tudor that at sixty-two years of age is only months younger than the church he pastors. The immediate neighborhood, known as Lefferts Manor, was once farmland, and its development was limited by covenant to single-family homes (which were rare in Brooklyn), many of them graystones with wrought-iron filigree and bas-relief portals and sweeping bay windows. Protected now as a historical district, the homes of Lefferts Manor seemingly stand apart from the apartment blocks, groceries, bakeries, and bars that demark the West Indian neighborhood that otherwise surrounds it.

But blockbusting, speculation, and white flight more than a decade ago stripped the commercial cachet from Lefferts Manor. Its fireplace and high ceilings and parquet floors notwithstanding, the Youngblood home had sat empty for a year before the family bought it in 1983, and at $100,000 it commanded a price so low that it made sense only when racial fear was factored into the equation. Many of the nearby homeowners, Joyce Youngblood learned soon after moving in, had transformed their near-mansions into boardinghouses, often for recent arrivals from the Caribbean. One time an inspector from the Immigration and Naturalization Service came to her door searching for illegal aliens. On another occasion a would-be tenant knocked and, after being turned down by Joyce, declared incredulously, "All this house you got and you don't rent rooms? How many children you have?"

Still, the house was grand enough to embarrass the boys, who as children of a preacher wanted nothing more than acceptance as regular guys. Joel was reluctant for many years to bring friends home for fear they would contemplate the Tudor and consider him effete. (The presence of a pool table in the basement, and Reverend Youngblood's acumen on it, helped solve the problem.) Jason's most recent campaign, besides the purchase of an English bulldog, has been to transfer out of the Saint Paul Christian School, where he has heard too many teachers preface praise and reprimand alike with the words "Your father is...." Even Joyce found herself wearing jeans or sweatpants to her graduate classes at Brooklyn College, muttering her surname in introductions, trying to construct an identity beyond that of the pastor's wife.

Jason bounds into the dining room. He is an ambitious and witty child, one part drop-dead mimic and the other aspiring obstetrician, and in either guise he possesses the ease of one accustomed to sitting at the grownups' table. He wears a double-breasted sport coat, baggy cuffed slacks, and a narrow tie, his trendy concession to school dress code.

"Why isn't your shirt ironed?" Reverend Youngblood chides, for that is the latest addition to Jason's morning chores.

"It is."

"Jason, your shirt is awful. You can go like that if you want to, but I just want you to know it's not ironed properly."

As Jason ascends the stairs to the ironing board, unbuttoning himself at each step, Joel passes. He reaches the dining room already clad in down coat and wool hat for the trip to Bishop Loughlin High School, a Catholic institution that largely serves a black and Hispanic working class that has lost faith in public education. More introverted than his younger brother except when exercising his gifts behind the drum kit, Joel worries about raising his grade in sequential math and being selected for the school band and, of course, acquiring a girlfriend, which explains why he smells of his father's cologne.

A less wrinkled version of Jason returns, and the three depart, Reverend Youngblood and Jason in a Volvo sedan bound for Saint Paul, Joel on foot for Bishop Loughlin.

"I love you," Jason shouts at his brother as the car pulls away. A woman with a graying Afro, thinking the words were meant for her, glares. Father and son chortle.

The Volvo moves south on Bedford Avenue, a shopping street already bustling with delivery trucks, and then steers east on Linden Boulevard. The sturdy apartment buildings of East Flatbush, with arches and courtyards and names like Shelbourne, give way to two-family frame houses, some converted to day-care centers or television repair shops. Crossing Kings Highway, the boulevard widens to six

lanes with a service road and a concrete median, skirting car washes
and gas stations and medical offices and diners, all offering a deceptive
aura of economic stability. Behind the façade stretches Brownsville and
then East New York, a neighborhood that changed color and class
with such frightening suddenness that the commercial strip along Linden Boulevard qualifies as a kind of archaeological site.

Reverend Youngblood can only laugh ruefully to remember his
worry that, when Saint Paul moved here eleven years ago from the
corroded center of Brownsville, he would be accused of running away
from the problems. The 800 block of Hendrix Street, the church's
new home, contained only a half-dozen homes and several parking
lots. There was little traffic, and still less that was unexpected, since
the one-way street began at a T-intersection with Linden Boulevard's
service road and ended similarly at Stanley Avenue. Shops and a park,
the very amenities absent from so many poor neighborhoods, waited
within walking distance.

Yet the problems followed, and Reverend Youngblood passes evidence of each as he approaches the church today—the masonry houses
scorched from the inside out, the hillocks of garbage on vacant lots,
the knots of crack addicts around the *bodegas,* the welfare recipients
lined up to cash their checks on what is known as "Mothers' Day," the
bottles of Wild Irish Rose and Cisco wine cooler littering Hendrix
Street just feet from Saint Paul itself, some still wrapped in brown bags
of shame or discretion, some broken and jagged from a Saturday-night
fight.

Misery is not abstract or statistical on Saint Paul's block. It has a
name, a face, a history. It is Serena, the homeless woman who begs
sanctuary after the latest beating by her boyfriend, only to return to
him once her bruises have healed. It is Pearl, once a registered nurse,
now shuttling in and out of mental hospitals. It is the young man
known simply as Downhome, who one day will strut into Reverend
Youngblood's study brazen and high, announcing he has a plan the
President should know about, and the next will wail about how his
brothers got rich as rap singers and left him behind, broke in the projects.

The street, though, is peaceful this morning as Reverend Youngblood brings the Volvo to a halt. Children trudge behind mothers
toward school, their faces lost inside the periscope hoods of discount-

store parkas. The Korean grocer on the corner, crouched atop a produce crate, cleans yams for display. The damp air carries the salt tang from Jamaica Bay, once the waters where Saint Paul baptized its faithful, now the unlikely refuge for egrets and piping plovers, mere blocks from the slums.

"You ready for school?" Reverend Youngblood asks Jason.

"I thought today's the day we switch. You go to seventh grade, and I'm the preacher."

And they laugh once more as they approach the front door. Saint Paul is a low, modern building of tinted glass and tan bricks, one that could be taken easily enough for a branch library. The simple entrance belies the sprawl inside, for the rambling complex of sanctuary, chapel, offices, school, and assembly and rehearsal rooms was cobbled together from the purchase from two adjacent synagogues, one Conservative and one Orthodox. Both were built in the early 1960s by Jews who had clearly intended to stay for decades, and their abrupt desertion serves as but one more reminder of how quickly East New York, in the parlance of urban trauma, "flipped." Some in Saint Paul's congregation still speak wistfully of attending the bar mitzvahs of neighbors' children in what is now their church, of playing in the Tuesday-night bingo game that helped meet one synagogue's mortgage.

Within the walls now, preparations proceed for morning devotion, the staff meeting that begins each weekday at Saint Paul. Dee Skinner, the director of youth ministries, arrives with a bakery box of sweet rolls. Linda Rollock, a volunteer in the fiscal office, tends to the percolator, wrapping herself against the morning chill in Rochester Blank's cardigan, "Uncle Rocky" stitched in yellow across one breast. Emily Walton, one of the church's musicians, and Greta Young, a "floater" between several departments, arrange the long, narrow meeting room known as Elders Hall, drawing folding tables and metal chairs across the linoleum with a baritone rumble. The rest soon follow, bearing coffee cups and steno pads and Bibles with worn bindings, dog-eared pages, and margins thick with notes.

Reverend Youngblood enters in brown corduroys and a crimson turtleneck. In his adjoining office remain his two trademarks, a Greek fisherman's cap and a brown leather shoulder bag, so perpetually overloaded that its sides sag like an old trumpeter's cheeks.

how do you decide how much detail is too much?

An intrigued hesitancy greets him, for the staff has learned to expect anything from its pastor. Morning devotion can be a time of Bible study or political debate, of compliments or excoriation, of analysis of projects completed or implementation of ideas newly born. Whatever the agenda, it most importantly allows a pastor of myriad duties and a staff of increasing numbers and specialties a moment of direct connection. Sarah Plowden calls Reverend Youngblood "The Black Tornado" and in less charitable moments "The Exterminator." At about five-thirty one recent afternoon, while Reverend Youngblood was attending a meeting outside the church, Thenia Brandon, his administrative assistant, decided to go home. "I better leave now," she confided to Helen Parilla, the church's graphic artist, "before Pastor comes back and starts a new day." Another staff member, in backhanded tribute to Reverend Youngblood's probing nature, described him as a "nerve-plucker."

For all the kidding or criticism, it was this tornado, this exterminator, this plucker of nerves, who had drawn into this room and this church a collection of men and women who might easily have lived their lives in whiter, more secular circles. Many had done precisely that—Rochester Blanks, the fiscal manager, as a district supervisor for Chock Full o'Nuts; Leroy Howard, the church administrator, as a senior loan clerk for Morgan Guaranty Trust; Thenia Brandon as supervisor of internal money transfers for Chase Manhattan Bank; Monica Walker of the media department as a graduate student in planning at the University of Massachusetts. But that world at its best felt ineffably alien, while Saint Paul was a place people spoke of with the compound noun "church home."

For Shirley Raymond, the director of community ministries, the reasons were intimate and personal. She had grown up squirming against the strictures of a Pentecostal church that forbade dancing, bare arms, and movies on Sunday, a church whose preacher spotted her at age seventeen wearing lipstick and declared from the pulpit, "You're gonna die and go to hell, you Jezebel!" So when she left the South a month after graduating from high school, she left church, too, for the next eighteen years, consenting only to sit in the back of a Roman Catholic congregation in slacks and hair rollers while her children received their dose of reverence. Then her marriage broke up. Her youngest child and only son died in a car crash, with her at the wheel. Her ex-husband committed suicide. Sometime during that long season of heartache, she met a next-door neighbor in Crown Heights, a minister's wife named Joyce Youngblood, who invited her to Saint Paul. She walked down the aisle to join six months later, and came aboard the staff five years after that, leaving behind the work as an insurance agent that could feed but never nourish.

Charles Lewis, the church's media director, had traveled to Saint Paul along a path of political commitment. The son of a minister, he won admission to elite and overwhelmingly white Brooklyn Technical High School and from there entered the similarly rarefied engineering curriculum at City College. Shifting direction into newspaper reporting and public relations, he landed in 1981 on the staff of Howard Golden, the Brooklyn borough president. "There's only one game in town—that's politics," Charles had always told blacks skeptical of the system. "And if we don't play, we get left out." His hopes were those of a pragmatic idealist: developing affordable housing, shutting down welfare hotels, halting the pattern of dumping homeless shelters in struggling minority neighborhoods. But his talents in writing and photography carried him only to the rim of the inner circle, where he hovered in frustration. He was already attending Saint Paul, promising himself to leave Borough Hall, when circumstance made the decision for him. Using an office car for a personal errand, he had an accident and, against the advice of one colleague, told his superiors the truth. They, in turn, informed him it was best to resign. After seven years of futility in government, he joined the staff at Saint Paul, in more ways than one returning to his father's house.

Charles and Shirley, close friends, sit next to Nell Jones, the church clerk, and the first object this morning of Reverend Youngblood's curiosity.

"How's your pressure?" he asks.

"Good," she says guardedly.

"How's your diet?"

"Good."

"What you have for dinner last night?"

"Chicken backs and spinach."

"Well seasoned?"

"No."

"Does everybody else have to suffer with you?"

"Like my family?" she asks, biting the bait.

"Like visitors. Like me."

"We gotta talk about that, Pastor," she says, and Reverend Youngblood crumples over the lectern, a gassy laugh escaping from the edges of his mouth.

He straightens to lead the staff in a prayer and through a reading from Hebrews 11 and 12, the same verses he had mulled earlier in the listening post. Then he turns to the blackboard behind the lectern and writes the single word "Lineage."

"What does this mean?"

"Bloodline," Dee Skinner says.

"Kinfolk," adds Myrtis Brent, the church's prayer intercessor.

As more words emerge, Reverend Youngblood lists them— "heirs," "elders," "ancestry," "inheritance," "legacy."

"All right," he says, pivoting to face the staff. "I have been fascinated lately by the African practice of 'ancestor worship.' And I've come to recognize in my heart and mind that it's not really praying to the dead, it's *recognition* of them." He pauses. "We can be so narrow. Saint Paul is sixty-two years old, and the fifteen people who started it, we mention them maybe once a year, at the church anniversary." He points to the board. "And yet these are words that run through the Scriptures, that talk about connection across generations."

As he roams the perimeter of the room, heads swivel to follow him.

"All of us have been brought to Christ by someone. We've all inherited some ideas. We're all heirs to something—language, customs, dress. And somewhere in a corner of our brain, we believe that the people who came before us are still aware of what's going on. But we're too hung up on that *non-Christian* idea of 'When you dead, you gone.'" He pauses. "We have to connect. And you start connecting by making the phone calls."

"Excuse me, Pastor," Nell says, brow lowered. "Phone calls?"

Reverend Youngblood presses palm to palm in prayer.

"That kind of phone call. That kind of connection." He peers down the tables. "Sarah, tell me about your most important Christian ancestor."

"My godmother. Miss Lilly. She was one of my Sunday-school teachers and she lived on my road in the country. She'd let me into her house and tell me Bible stories. She told 'em out of her personality. It wasn't just soft and flowery. I had a lot of questions, and she'd answer me the best she could." Sarah halts, and resumes shaking her head slightly, a dreamy curiosity in her tone. "And you know, Pastor, I forgot her till you asked me."

"Helen?"

"Her name was Miss Denegal."

He indicates Brenda Nealy, the central office coordinator.

"Billy Sam. That's what we called him. His real name was Willy C."

"Myrt?"

"Lena Wiggins."

"Gret?"

"My uncle, Jesse Ward."

Reverend Youngblood adds the names to the board, ending with his own choice, Frank Taylor, the deacon and handyman who befriended him in his early years at Saint Paul. Just this morning, as he passed the church's guard dog, Lady, Reverend Youngblood remembered how Frank had trained her from junkyard ferocity with his voice alone. The only time many of his congregants have ever seen their pastor weep was at Frank Taylor's funeral.

"So what happens after they die?" he asks. "What happens to the stuff they were about when the material is gone? We're all here because of them, and they may not even know. With death, they lose consciousness, but in a way, so do we. And yet in the Christian perspective, they're still living. How do we see them?"

"A form of spirits or angels," Myrtis says. "You know how the Psalms say there'll be spirits watching over you."

"Our existence is not complete without them," Reverend Youngblood says, leaning on the lectern. "There's a connection we need. The Africans keep that connection. We do, too, but in a piss-poor way." He sneers. "Memorial service. Going to the cemetery. Genuflecting on the grave." He stands erect, draws breath. "And it may be that these souls are better able to make intercession for us in death than in life. You ever think about folk and then wonder why you did? This is a weird idea, but you ever think it was them trying to get in touch?"

"I'm sure all of us have the experience," Helen Parilla offers, "of thinking about someone a second before they appear or call up."

"The thing I've experienced," Greta Young adds, "is thinking about someone till it's so real it's like they're there."

"Do you entertain that feeling?" Reverend Youngblood asks.

"Oh, it scared the hell outta me. It was a very real presence. *Very real.* To the point I got up and moved away."

"We been told, 'Don't disturb the dead,'" Nell Jones says. "Someone told me in my twenties if I write a letter to a cousin who just died I would get a number." She blushes a bit. "See, I used to play the numbers then. So I wrote the letter and that night I got the number. Two-oh-five. Her house number. I was so scared I put it under my pillow."

"And what happened?" Reverend Youngblood blurts.

"The number came! The number came straight out! My brother told me to play it. But I was afraid of disturbin' the dead."

Nell's story turns the entire discussion more anecdotal, rich with remembrances of home remedies, root doctors, and, in Reverend Youngblood's case, the whisperings about voodoo that animated his New Orleans childhood. But he is careful not to depart entirely from his larger theme, so after several minutes he strides to the board and writes "S.P.C. Ministry."

"This ministry we've been entrusted with," he says, turning toward his staff, "God help us if we think it's just ours. We got the chairs, the tables, the building. But we got to remember: We caught a moving train."

Now he solicits a list of the church's ancestors, forebears like Adolphus Smith and Stephen Kelly, Wilhemina Feaster and Beulah Meadows. Then he widens the pantheon to all black America, and the nominations pour forth—King, Douglass, Malcolm X, Harriet Tubman, Mary McLeod Bethune, Marcus Garvey, Jackie Robinson, enough others to fill the board.

"In the next year," Reverend Youngblood says, "each of us ought to read one of these autobiographies. And if you read one already, you read another one." He pairs off reader and book, making history the vehicle of the Christian promise of eternal life. "We have to know these lives. We have to consider what it means if they're available to us, *really* available to us. Malcolm, Martin, Fred Douglass, Mary McLeod Bethune."

He dusts the chalk from his hand, lays his forearms across the lectern.

"There's something about a sense of aloneness that saps your strength. But there's something about togetherness that lets you keep going. And so if there are ancestors who can accompany us, I say reach for them. Because our work isn't going to get any easier."

High above the Hudson, in a chapel trimmed with teak, seventy seminarians convene for their required course on "The Church in the Modern World." Today's session will be devoted to urban ministry, a subject necessarily remote from the great majority who have never more than visited a city and whose attitudes toward the metropolis ten miles away veer from intrigue to antipathy. They appear a genial and thrifty bunch, clad in khakis and V-necks and aerobics shoes, bag lunches stowed beneath their chairs.

did you ever get bored?

All but a dozen are white, which matters only in that their guest lecturer will be the first of several black clergymen on the semester's syllabus, Reverend Johnny Ray Youngblood. The professor for this course, Dr. Craig Ellison, first met Reverend Youngblood in 1985 through a prominent Los Angeles preacher named E. V. Hill, and since then has both invited the Brooklyn minister to speak here at Alliance Theological Seminary in Nyack, New York, and has led a field trip to Saint Paul. Building such bridges is central to Professor Ellison's own faith, for he once was a strapping small-town boy who naïvely rented a graduate student apartment in the Detroit ghetto and stayed on after the cataclysmic 1967 riot to counsel and organize the remnants of a community.

At the least, Professor Ellison can depend on a captive audience for his guest speaker. What dawned as benign overcast has roiled by midmorning into gales and chill rain, suitable for little beside study and for driving least of all. Reverend Youngblood and Thenia Brandon have been advancing cautiously from East New York for nearly two hours, watching their cushion of travel time deflate. As much as he crowds his schedule, Reverend Youngblood remains finicky about punctuality. And for him this particular lecture is more than an obligation owed an associate. After so often "preaching to the choir" as the idiom has it—that is, to a congregation disposed to agree with him or at least to pretend it does—such a foreign pulpit lets him test his personal theology in a more direct and even charged way.

"I'm sorry I'm late," he says as he enters the chapel, stripping off a trench coat to reveal a dress shirt and tie from the emergency supply Thenia maintains in his office closet. "But I want you to know it has nothing to do with my race and everything to do with the roads." There are isolated and uneasy chuckles from the class. "Because there's this idea black people are always late. And like so many other beliefs about blacks, it's not true." He wipes some stray raindrops from his forehead. "I hope I can make you angry today, because if I can't, then I failed. I hope I can make you laugh, but if I can't, I don't care."

Situating himself behind the lectern, he reminds the seminarians that Professor Ellison had asked him to address a single question: Should contemporary urban ministry centrally involve advocacy for the poor? By way of answering yes, he turns to the fourth chapter of Luke for the two verses that amount to his own mission statement:

> The Spirit of the Lord is upon me, because he hath anointed me to preach the gospel to the poor; he hath sent me to heal the brokenhearted, to preach deliverance to the captives, and recovering of sight to the blind, to set at liberty them that are bruised,
>
> To preach the acceptable year of the Lord.

"So is that theological? Yes. Is it biblical? Yes. Is it scary?" His face bends into a grin, and he sways his head slowly. *"R-i-i-i-ght."* He steps before the lectern, unbuttons his collar, loosens his tie. "You have to function under the aegis of the Holy Spirit. Jesus says, 'The *Spirit* is upon me.' And the white person who ministers in the slum better not do it because you feel sorry for poor people or because you think it's the Christian thing to do or you feel some leftover liberal guilt. That will get your ass killed."

There is a stunned silence, both at the argument and the profanity that italicized it.

"We don't need any more Great White Fathers or Great White Mothers. So if you are not under the power of the Holy Spirit, then you should stick to the bucolic areas. Look at the rolling meadows. Listen to the cows moo."

Laughter, this time genuine and spontaneous, answers Reverend Youngblood. When it subsides, he repeats Christ's admonitions from Luke.

"Used to be you could get away with tellin' folk, 'It'll be all right when you get to heaven.' Don't buy that no more. If you minister to the poor, *you* help them deal with the system that keeps them in poverty, *you* deal with their shackles and chains from the inside out. Because being poor doesn't just mean not being saved. It means being economically poor, financially poor. And the church has to do more than save souls."

For the students of a seminary that serves only evangelical denominations, that prides itself on missionary work, on winning converts on distant continents, Reverend Youngblood could have chosen few more provocative words. Pens fly across notebook pages. Furtive whispers pass between rows. Heads tilt forward, rapt.

"It's blasphemous, utterly profane, for the church to tell people to turn one cheek while they're getting slapped on the other." He stops short, changes course. "How many of y'all didn't have the Dr. Spock upbringing?" About ten hands rise. "Then I know your parents had no problem whuppin' you. And the odd thing was that, when the tears were rollin' down, and your daddy put down that extension cord or strap, and had that look in his eyes and said, 'I did it because I love you.'" Suddenly that child, Reverend Youngblood shoots his eyebrows toward his scalp and opens his eyes so wide the pupils might pop loose. "And you there sayin', 'Love me? What you mean, love me?'" He breaks character, slows his delivery. "But our church needs that kind of love. We need to be on a collision course with society as we know it."

As if to anchor theory in reality, he talks about the Industrial Areas Foundation, an outfit unfamiliar to most. He explains how it was founded by Saul Alinsky, the pioneering community organizer in Chicago, how it now oversees dozens of local groups like East Brooklyn Congregations. He briefly speaks of that body's successes in building the Nehemiah homes, in winning college loans and entry-level jobs at banks for qualified high school graduates, as well as of Saint Paul's own creation of a school, a shopping district, various ministries. Finally he intones the Industrial Areas Foundation's so-called Iron Rule: "Never do for others what they can do for themselves."

"Don't do *for* us," Reverend Youngblood says, adding his own explicitly racial corollary. "Do *with* us. Don't believe what others tell you about us. Ask us. The Bible says to serve the poor, but it doesn't say to exempt the poor. The poor should still tithe. The poor should still be taking part in all the work of the church."

He recalls a young white seminarian from Alliance who was so impressed by his visit to Saint Paul that he asked to work there as a volunteer. Reverend Youngblood wanted to know if he could balance both the church work and his seminary studies. In terms of time, yes, the young man had said, but in terms of finance, probably not. He was already on the verge of dropping out for a term to earn tuition money. Reverend Youngblood proposed that Saint Paul solve the problem by paying the student's seminary fees in lieu of a salary.

"And he said no. He couldn't handle that. I think he wanted to be a Great White Father. He thought we were too poor to pay his bills!" He pauses. "So his services were refused."

Bouncing on his toes just a bit, hands on his belt, Reverend Youngblood surveys the class. Surely this was the aspect of the black church few had anticipated. The singing, the preaching, the praying, the political agitation, the plain old scaring the white man with "woofing"—those were, to some extent, the knowns. But this prideful self-sufficiency, this rigor and resolve, were to outsiders perhaps the most invisible aspect of what was called during slavery the "invisible institution."

There are more questions than time to answer them. How do you minister to the victimizers? Does educating a bigot really make a difference? What do blacks think of Asian immigrants? How do you create ties between a white, suburban church and a black, inner-city congregation? And, lastly and most candidly, why do you sound so angry?

"Do you know the etymology of that word?" Reverend Youngblood begins softly. "It comes from a Norse word, *angr,* that means 'grief.'" He drags his palm across his beard. "My brother, what we as African Americans grieve for, what we have lost in this country, is so precious. It equals out to our very identity. And we are angry. And my way of dealing with it is through Jesus."

On a steamy Sunday evening in Brookhaven, Mississippi, the 1960 conference of the United Metropolitan Spiritual Churches of Christ was drawing to a close. The choirs had been heard. The fried chicken had been eaten. The Saturday-night séance had been held in an unlit sanctuary scented with incense and oil, and those endowed with the powers of prophecy and healing had moved through the multitude, interpreting the present and foretelling the future, laying hands on the stricken and intoning at points the names of the departed. Now they sat and sweated like any other church ladies, beating the stiff August air with paper fans and handkerchiefs and awaiting the Youth Message, the final order of business.

Twelve-year-old Johnny Ray Youngblood stood at the pulpit wearing a six-dollar suit beneath his white choir robe. From prayer meetings at his own church in New Orleans, he already knew well how to please his mother and his pastor, the two dominant forces in his life. So he told his fellow children, his nominal audience, that you were never too young to devote your life to God. He told them to be obedient and avoid bad company and stay in school. "We're like crabs in a barrel," he went on, echoing one of the favorite adult maxims. "Every time one gets up, the others reach to pull him down. We've got to work together."

"Tell the truth, son," the old women called to him. "Preach your sermon, child."

His homily complete, Johnny saw a bowlegged man with salt-and-pepper hair amble toward him, carrying a certificate of some sort. He was Bishop Thomas B. Watson, the leader of the Spiritualist denomination, the man with ultimate authority for the churches and congregants gathered here from Louisiana and Chicago and California. Beaming like a new father and brandishing the document for the crowd, he announced that a preaching license was hereby awarded to Johnny ... Ray ... *Youngblood!*

The boy flinched. His breath fled. His eyes sought his mother, and he could see in her slack face a shock to equal his own. This license, he realized, could not have been the doing of his mother or Bishop Watson or even God, for he had heard nothing from God on the subject of preaching. It must have come from his pastor, the woman called Mother Jordan, who had told Johnny all his brief life how special he was, who had sculpted and glazed that specialness until it felt more like a shame, a separation, an otherness. *Now,* Johnny thought with dread, *everyone will know I'm a preacher.*

His being was marked, but it would be marked again. For the years that made the child into the man would be defined by two calls, one inflicted and one bestowed, one limiting and one liberating, one destroying faith and one restoring it. In their dialectic, both forces would inform Johnny Ray Youngblood for decades to come.

The tale of a minister twice called began long before his birth, perhaps in the late 1920s, when Fannie Bee Jordan arrived in New Orleans from Mississippi, one more black among thousands sick of cane fields and the Klan, heading for the city that promised ready jobs and softer bigotry. She earned her living at the outset as a doctor's domestic, but she felt herself chosen, granted gifts of curing and prediction. After eight years she became ordained in the Spiritualist church, one of the few that allowed female ministers, and by 1943 she was holding prayer meetings in the boardinghouse she ran to make earthly ends meet.

It was to that building at 126 Marais Street that two newlyweds came in 1947, seeking a room. Palmon Youngblood had left sharecropping and a tenth-grade education behind in Tylertown, Mississippi, to load sugar by hand at the Domino plant. His wife, Ottie Mae, had worked the fields outside Franklinton, Louisiana, from age five and had quit school after eighth grade. By early 1948 she was pregnant and showing, attracting the attentions of her childless landlady.

"Now's the time for you to pray for that child," Mother Jordan told Ottie Mae, and the young woman became a regular at the noon and six o'clock prayer meetings. Mother Jordan presided in bare feet and a white choir robe, her bearing at once both sturdy and ethereal. Ottie Mae saw her tell a worshiper who approached in a wheelchair to fold it up and walk away. She heard her share visions of tornadoes and bloodshed. She watched supplicants from throughout the city beseech Mother Jordan for potions and charms. Ottie Mae came to believe Mother Jordan was indeed blessed.

Mother Jordan drove her to Charity Hospital on the June day Johnny was born. As he grew into clothes, she bought him shirts from Krauss's department store and sewed him an overcoat of beige gabardine. By the time the boy turned four, Mother Jordan could promise Ottie Mae, "Someday Johnny's gonna carry the gospel." And who was mother or son to question the oracle, the woman who reminded her acolytes, "God told me to pray"?

So when the tremors of urban renewal reached Marais Street, on the edge of downtown, the Youngbloods and Mother Jordan alike moved four miles east to the Lower Ninth Ward. With her husband's savings from an assembly line at an insulation factory, Mother Jordan bought a lot for three hundred dollars and built a frame church for $2,500 more. She christened it Holy Family. Palmon Youngblood, meanwhile, paid eight hundred dollars for a deep, narrow patch of land on Charbonnet Street and wrought his family a house of cinderblocks and corrugated tin, pine planks scavenged from demolition sites and oak beams rescued from a ruined warehouse at work.

In those years, the early 1950s, the Lower Ninth was a wild and isolated place. The waters of the Mississippi River and two canals circumscribed it north, south, and west, and its eastern border, where New Orleans gave way to all-white and notoriously racist Saint Bernard Parish, was just as unforgiving. Vines, saplings, and marsh grass covered the land. Rabbit and deer abounded, and the occasional alligator slipped over the levee after a downpour.

Even as three-room shotgun houses rose, filling with the refinery workers and stevedores and cleaning ladies and cooks of the black working class, the Lower Ninth remained rough-hewn. The streets were paved with clamshells, their stench lingering for weeks. Crawfish swam in the gutters. Johnny's sister Betty once found a snake in the silverware drawer. And in the racial hierarchy of New Orleans, the residents of the Lower Ninth languished near the bottom. Never did the ranking become more clear than during Hurricane Betsy in 1965. With the Mississippi brimming and threatening to flood the business district and white neighborhoods, city officials chopped open the levee in the Lower Ninth. The waters surged so high that the Youngbloods took shelter on a neighbor's roof, Palmon waving a diaper as a flag of distress, and when the flood receded, it left behind mud, rot, and ruin. But it was fellow blacks, too, who scorned the Lower Ninth, most especially the *passants blancs* who attended Xavier Prep and dated only one another and patronized the Saenger Theater and Woolworth's lunch counter with their race undetected. The perverse pride of the neighborhood was distilled in the boast, "I'm a nigger from the Nine and I don't mind dyin'." One of Johnny's favorite uncles was slashed across the face in a bar fight. A high school friend's brother shot himself while playing Russian roulette. Bodies turned up periodically in the tall grass.

Palmon Youngblood lived with one foot in that world. He was, it was true, a steady provider who stayed forty-one years at Domino

Sugar, who rose before six and took all the overtime he could, who brought Ottie Mae two hundred dollars each payday. But when the working week was done, a working man wanted to relax. Staking himself to thirty dollars, Palmon drank and shot dice and played the card game called tonk on a path that wove from Red Devil's to the White Owl to the Welcome Inn. Sometimes he awakened at home without remembering how he had landed there. Sometimes he stayed out straight to Monday morning, returning only to shower before driving to work. And sometimes he kept company with a particular woman, who would ultimately bear him a son.

It fell to Ottie Mae to hold the household together with wages, hand-me-downs, and leftovers from the white families she served. She saved enough money to send Johnny, Betty, and her final child, Lionel, to Catholic school. She turned the turkey carcasses her white employers would throw away into sandwiches, salad, and stock. At times the effort abraded her cheer. "I'm out there every day wipin' these little white babies' butts," she told Johnny once, "just so they can grow up to call me a nigger."

Mother Jordan and Holy Family provided her strongest solace. Part of the appeal was the way church filled all the hours, with prayer services on Tuesday and Thursday, a choir performance on Wednesday, the Junior Missionary Society for the children on Saturday, and two services and a live radio broadcast on Sunday. But part of the appeal derived from the peculiar nature of the Spiritualist church itself.

When blacks who considered themselves educated and refined derided the Spiritualist denomination as "hoodoo," they were paying the backhanded compliment of acknowledging its African roots. For like the Haitian *voudun* and Cuban *santería* and Brazilian *candomble,* Spiritualist practice syncretized African belief and Christian ceremony. Statues filled the sanctuary at Holy Family—Saint Jude, Saint Anthony, the Blessed Mother, Jesus exposing the Sacred Heart, Lazarus with a dog licking his wounds, as described in Luke. Votive candles burned on several tables, snapshots and prayer requests placed among them, and a dish of holy water filled with good-luck coins lay before the altar.

Mother Jordan oversaw a congregation of women and children, for whom her condemnations of drinking, dancing, and cussing seemed the commonsensical ingredients of a stable home. They were called saints, Mother Jordan's faithful, and they wore robes and veils to indicate their echelon, from missionary to evangelist to reverend mother. With its singing and preaching, their Sunday service operated within the broad conventions of black Christianity, but on the weeknights there was no mistaking the Spiritualists for anyone else. The only light in the sanctuary rose from burning candles, throwing the outlines of statues against the back wall. Harsh, sweet incense hovered in the air. The organ music spread like something equally vaporous, the songs merging into a single, hypnotic melisma. In the dim light, the saints could barely be distinguished one from the next. They were a gathering of shadows and forms, voices lifting in praise, arms extending in appeal, heads lolling in reverie. Three separate times each saint moved from the cypress pews up the center aisle, once for prayer, once for anointment, once for prophecy. Under Mother Jordan's direction, the service often proceeded past midnight, and for those like Ottie Mae who fully believed, those hours redeemed all that was hard and unhappy in life.

What Johnny felt most were confusion and contradiction. The church indeed afforded a platform for his gifts as singer, speaker, leader. Worshipers awaited his solos on "God Specializes" and "He'll Wash You Whiter Than Snow." When he started "buck-jumping" during his sermons, running in place without missing a syllable, the saints agreed the spirit was surely at work. It was the boy preacher, and not Mother Jordan, who was the star attraction of Holy Family's radio show on WYLD. From a congregation of only ninety, Johnny built a youth choir that numbered thirty-five and performed as far afield as Oklahoma and Missouri. Mother Jordan rewarded him with pocket money and new clothes, with birch beer at Royal Castle and fried chicken at Dookey Chase's, the fanciest black restaurant in the city. She confided to her husband, William, that she intended for Johnny to take over the church.

But behind a demeanor of obedience and devotion, the boy's doubts were legion. The Spiritualist openness to things mystical carried with it a disdain for education or theology. Only in private moments with William Jordan, his godfather or *parrain*, could Johnny vent his vast curiosity: Is it possible to be saved without water baptism? If "God will give us the victory," who's the enemy? If the enemy is the devil, how do you fight what you can't see? Only through his mother's insistence could Johnny attend Catholic high school, earning his tuition by sweeping floors, for Mother Jordan's stated fear was not that her protégé would lose religion but that he would lose *hers*.

Among his peers, Johnny was an object of both admiration and pity. He had to sit in the front row at church while his friends clustered in the rear, plotting escape. He was forbade from joining them for movies at the Caffin. When he played football on Dorgenois Street, a neighbor yelled, "Preacher got no business playin' ball," and when he walked a girl into a grocery, the same man said, "Preacher got no business with a girl." Sometimes back home after church, Ottie Mae would send him a half-block to the White Owl tavern to buy them Barq's soda and potato chips. And for a moment Johnny would stand in his father's world, the air rich with flirtation and signifying and Irma Thomas singing, "You can have my husband, but please don't take my man." Then the bartender or some regular would notice the church boy tarrying and point him home.

"We are *supposed* to be separate," Mother Jordan often told Johnny. "We are in this world, but not *of* this world." Yet as opaque, meditative, almost otherworldly as she seemed, she acted sternly against transgression, actual or perceived. When a groom ducked out of a wedding, Mother Jordan ordered the church handyman to marry the girl; when that same handyman later resigned, she forced a teenager named Ben Warren to drop out of high school and take his job. Mother Jordan wielded a left hand that her charges talked about the way fight fans of the era talked about Sonny Liston's. And nobody suffered that left more often than Johnny. Mother Jordan hit him for talking in church, chewing gum, laughing aloud, missing assignments. Often she would note a failing with the warning, "I'm storin' it up," and a day or two later deliver the blow with the aside, "Told you I don't forget." Once she hauled Johnny before the congregation and beat him till he wet his pants. As he trembled, damp and stinking, she directed the faithful to withdraw the "right hand of fellowship" from him, and then she began to sing:

> *So sorry, so sorry to leave you*
> *I leave you in God's care*
> *I give you my hymn book and Bible*
> *I leave you in God's care*

Johnny longed for the day that his mother would tell Mother Jordan, "I don't want him there no more," or that his father would intercede, wrench him free. But all Ottie Mae said was, "Church is the best thing for you," and after Mother Jordan's assaults she would counsel, "Don't tell your daddy what happened." Without allies, Johnny himself chose the strategy of complicity, since it seemed to him Mother Jordan commanded the Holy Spirit, not the other way around.

The one friend who made Johnny feel normal was a tomboy named Jackie McDonald. They grew up together in church from age six, but Jackie enjoyed a mother more lenient than Ottie Mae, and was ousted from Holy Family in her early teens for going to parties. On her return, three years later, she shared what she had learned in the larger world with the boy who had been shielded from it. She spun like Scheherazade the plots of James Bond movies. She showed him how to catch a football, and threw passes for practice. She demonstrated the slop and the mashed potato, the dances every other kid knew, and on the night before the prom she taught him a serviceable two-step.

They attended the prom together, Johnny and Jackie, for by their late teens the tomboy had become a woman and the child preacher her beau. A modicum of approval greeted this news. Ottie Mae saw in Jackie's high-yaller tones a proven financial advantage; in color-conscious New Orleans, she could always find work if the dark Johnny had trouble. As for Mother Jordan, narcissism helped. The consensus around church had long held that Jackie resembled the pastor so closely she could have been her daughter.

The couple stayed together past high school into college, although they began to drift apart as Johnny questioned Jackie's allegiance. Then, in their sophomore year, when both were barely twenty, Jackie became pregnant. Ottie Mae guessed as much the day Jackie visited her and could not hold down any food. Mother Jordan approached the expectant mother next and, surprisingly without rancor, merely said, "We'll have to get ready for the wedding." She saved the confrontation for Johnny, finding him among some Dillard University classmates one Sunday after service.

"You gonna walk outta here like some dignitary with this girl pregnant by you?" she demanded.

"Y'all go on," Johnny quickly told his friends, few of whom had been aware of his predicament until that moment. "I'll catch up with you later."

"That's right," Mother Jordan said, pulling him out the back door of Holy Family and toward her house next door. "You come with me."

There they sat together on the porch, wordless at first, until Mother Jordan sprawled across the couch. "Oh, Lord," she bawled. "I don't know what I'm gonna do. You're killin' me. You're killin' me."

Johnny imagined the entire universe pointing its finger, pointing its finger the way his momma pointed hers at his daddy, and shouting like she did, "You low-down dirty dog." He slid his eyes toward the porch door and the street beyond. Then he gathered Mother Jordan into his arms and cried, "I'm sorry, I'm sorry, I'm sorry."

The words sounded empty as soon as he spoke them. Mother Jordan felt lifeless, like a sack of straw. How could that be? This was not merely a pastor, a prophet. This was God. She was God. It was God, all wrath and vengeance, wailing in his arms. Unless, he dared think, this God could be false. Unless this could be merely a bitter, barren woman once more exacting humiliation.

He loosened his arms.

"Go into the church," Mother Jordan said.

He opened the screen door, descended the steps, but instead of turning right into Holy Family, he went left, down Lamanche Street toward home. He would not set foot in Holy Family again for nine years, when he would deliver a eulogy for Mother Fannie Bee Jordan.

In other, less pressured circumstances, Johnny and Jackie might have wed, for they knew each other with the guileless intimacy only childhood sweethearts could share. But both also knew this looming marriage was at bottom a test of wills. To marry under the blessing of Mother Jordan would be to surrender their lives to her and to a suffocating church. Johnny was attending classes at Dillard on the day Jackie gave birth to a son named for him. Within two years she would be another man's wife, and he would be courting a Dillard freshman named Joyce Terrell.

Those were, for Johnny, the wilderness years. He had lost in Holy Family the defining element in his life. He had fled from home after a fight with his father about money for tuition. He lived like an itinerant, supporting himself with "bootleg preaching," squatting with an aunt who did not have a phone. He languished for hours in the public library, listening to records of Emily Dickinson poems, and twice each day visited the Saint Jude Catholic Church, since the patron saint of impossible cases seemed appropriate. But he could hardly frame a prayer. What did he want? For Jackie to have lost the baby? Or to have proof it wasn't his?

He found respite only with Eli Wilson, Jr., a track teammate and fraternity brother at Dillard. Eli had known of Johnny long before college from the Holy Family broadcast on WYLD, the same station on which his own family's gospel group performed. Eli's father, however, was a preacher unlike any Johnny had ever met. The self-educated son of a family of twenty-six, he balanced his mission in the pulpit with labors as a longshoreman, custodian, and cement truck driver. His wife called him Sugar. He served sweet kosher wine at holiday dinners, let his children listen to rhythm and blues, and could be overheard saying of an antagonist, "I'll knock the shit outta him."

One evening at Reverend Wilson's church, Ora Vista Baptist, Johnny came down the aisle to accept Jesus Christ anew as his Savior. A month later he was baptized, and soon afterward Reverend Wilson presented him with a Baptist preaching license and the admonition, "Man, if I had what you have, couldn't nobody touch me." Johnny had no idea what he meant. He still did not consider himself called to the ministry. He had joined Ora Vista partly in homage to Reverend Wilson and in large measure to dash the fear that if he died, Mother Jordan would perform his funeral.

With graduation from Dillard only days away, he still assumed he would become a high school teacher. The prospect had never thrilled him, though it promised a degree of security and status, and fulfilled Ottie Mae's ambition for his secular life. Hers was a generation of finite dreams, a generation that worried when its children idolized Martin Luther King, worried they too would be slain. Johnny had already broken her heart once in renouncing Holy Family. He doubted he could break it again, especially when he could offer no alternative to her aspiration.

He was walking from a dormitory to Rosenwald Hall, the administration building, when he heard the voice. It was a voice of reason and advice, a voice that made a statement as it asked a question: *Do you want to spend the rest of your life in a classroom?* He thought to himself, *Then what were these four years of college for?* and continued walking toward Rosenwald, where the dean's list had been posted.

Short of the building, he found himself turning instead into Dillard's four-pew chapel. There he dropped to his knees and prayed, "Lord, help me to find out what I'm supposed to do with my life." Then he lifted his head to the Bible open on the altar, which was giving off light, not the blaze of raging flames but the glow of a hearth. Somehow that soothing image instead filled him with anger and disgust. Here he was, a failure for all his A's, an outsider for all his charisma, a father denying his child, a child defying his mother. Where was Providence in all that?

"I tell you what, God," he said, less in the manner of a plea than of a streetcorner taunt. "I will give you one year in seminary. One year. And I expect you to take charge of my life. So that what I do will be so much a part of me, I won't think about not doing it. And if you won't take charge in one year, I still expect you to bless me. Even if I decide to become a pimp."

During commencement exercises, Johnny received the Walter J. Barker Award for Religion and Community Service. With the fifty-dollar prize, he bought a student ticket for a flight from New Orleans to Rochester, New York, the home of Colgate-Rochester Theological Seminary. And one afternoon in June 1970, he boarded a plane for the first time in his life, bound farther from home than he ever had been, holding a secondhand suitcase and two-eighty in change.

The display case just outside Saint Paul's chapel, one of the keenest barometers of Reverend Youngblood's concerns, now features a drawing of the church set against a silhouetted skyline of Manhattan. Around the sketch hang photographs and small posters of the sort usually found in airport concourses—Rockefeller Center with its art deco grace, brassy Trump Tower, the Cathedral of Saint John the Divine, Miss Liberty bearing her lamp. These images, the reminders of New York at its most grand and alluring, New York as it once beckoned internal immigrants from the Jim Crow South, appear beneath a banner declaring, SAVE OUR CITY, SO HELP US GOD, as well as a verse from Second Chronicles:

If my people, which are called by my name, shall humble themselves, and pray, and seek my face, and turn from their wicked
ways; then will I hear from heaven, and will forgive their sin,
and will heal their land.

The dozen men and women gathered in the chapel have been
humbled indeed, less by their own piety than by the wicked ways of
others. The pizza man, the greengrocer, the hairdresser, the dry
cleaner, and all the rest, everyday people in jeans and cloth coats and
wool caps, own the small businesses around the corner from Saint
Paul, in the shopping district Reverend Youngblood has dubbed
Christ Square. And there is trouble in Christ Square.

It is not new trouble. It is the same old trouble. Two teenagers
feign a fight in the Key Food supermarket, distracting a cashier, while
a third empties the till. Thieves break into the clothing store next door
overnight, carrying off costume jewelry and three hundred T-shirts.
Teachers at the local junior high school refuse to walk two blocks to
the neighborhood pharmacy, where their prescriptions can be filled
practically free under a union health plan, because they fear muggers.
No, this is not new trouble, just enough of it in a bunch to bring a
collection of Koreans, Chinese, Italians, Puerto Ricans, and Jews into
a black Baptist church seeking help.

It is only fitting they meet in a room designed for the pondering
of private miseries, a muted domain of burgundy carpet and walnut
paneling. Leroy Howard stands at the lectern in slacks and a turtleneck, his face fringed by muttonchops, his frame lean. Shirley Raymond sits in the first row facing him, a legal pad on the lap of her silk
paisley dress. She greets most of the merchants by name, for she has
worked on Christ Square since the very beginning.

That was back in 1980. From the time his church moved onto
Hendrix Street that February, Reverend Youngblood had been both-
ered by a particular irony: Saint Paul *Community* Baptist Church
could call nothing in the surrounding community its own. If anything,
the congregation was held hostage and its religious values mocked by
what happened along Stanley Avenue. Purses were snatched, chains
ripped from necks, car batteries stolen. The few legitimate stores
struggled amid the fried-chicken joint that ran numbers, the social

club that sold drugs, the boutique that offered both, the market that short-weighted old meat. One local character collected boxes of garbage at the corner of Stanley and Hendrix and stacked them into a kind of a neighborhood urinal so foul no carter would consent to remove it. The breaking point came the day a competitor set fire to the numbers spot as nearly one thousand worshiped in Saint Paul, easily within range of a spreading blaze.

A fan of westerns since childhood, Reverend Youngblood thought of Ben Cartwright in "Bonanza." Ben Cartwright owned the land. And because he owned it, he loved it. So Saint Paul would purchase an urban Ponderosa in the form of stores along Stanley Avenue, less with the idea of operating them itself than of ensuring quality and accountability from those who did. From such a base, Reverend Youngblood could press his agenda of community development in ever wider circles.

Cities, after all, were not saved in grand sweeps; cities were saved block by block. Quality of life was not defined by Trump Tower or Rockefeller Center; it was defined by being able to walk around the corner after church to buy a fresh pork chop without being propositioned or clobbered upside the head. When residents stopped feeling secure in their daily routines, they started to leave, maybe for Teaneck or Mount Vernon in the suburbs, or maybe for Atlanta.

But before Saint Paul could buy any property, Saint Paul had to determine who owned it. Not yet on the church staff, Shirley drew the assignment, and in free hours from her insurance agent's job she plunged into Brooklyn's real-estate records. She plodded through plat books for block and lot numbers, learned to run the microfiche machine that resembled a boiler, peered over the shoulders of speculators to make certain she was filling out the paperwork correctly. Once the layers of dummy corporations had been peeled away, it developed that the stores were owned by two different consortiums of whites from Long Island.

The church paid $363,000 for seven stores on Stanley Avenue just west of Hendrix Street in 1985, and $296,000 for five more one year later. The very day of the first closing, Rochester Blanks routed a crack addict from one store's basement and Reverend Youngblood invited the police to raid the bogus boutique. Within the week it was padlocked. The social club, missing several rent payments, was evicted.

A medical clinic replaced the numbers operation. A church member, Sylvia Eggleston, took over a badly mismanaged beauty salon. New sidewalks were laid and new awnings installed at church expense. To provide some measure of security around the clock, Saint Paul purchased three houses on Hendrix Street, situating in them Rochester Blanks, Sarah Plowden, and John Barber, the church custodian.

Still, improvement did not equal panacea. The liquor store and the check-cashing joint, both magnets for theft, held long-term leases and could not be ousted. A clothing store on Stanley east of Hendrix, in a block of businesses Saint Paul did not own, paid cash on the spot for gold jewelry. After the brutal attack on a jogger in Central Park, that same store began selling T-shirts emblazoned with the word *Wilding*. A delegation of men from Saint Paul bought out the inventory and informed the proprietor he would not replenish the supply.

And it was lost on no one that the man was Chinese. Absentee ownership in the ghetto was an old, sad blues, groused about and yet generally endured, but it was lately becoming the fodder for protest. Blacks in Harlem had declared a boycott of several Korean groceries, arguing they drained dollars out of the neighborhood. An even more bitter conflict was looming in nearby Flatbush over the alleged beating by a Korean grocer of a Haitian woman he accused of shoplifting. Spike Lee's film *Do the Right Thing* reached its climax when a black crowd, incensed at the slaying of a neighborhood man by white police officers, vented its rage by looting and burning the pizzeria owned by Bensonhurst Italians.

This morning, however, survival makes for common cause. The merchants need security to stay in business. The church needs decent stores to serve its people, to bolster its neighborhood. Neither merchants nor church place much faith in the police. By the standards of the Seventy-fifth Precinct, one of the most violent in New York, the area around Christ Square qualifies as a placid oasis, and it receives the inattention to match. Only after murders are officers ordered to patrol on foot. Calls to 911 often wait without response for an hour.

Since gangs roamed Stanley Avenue last Halloween, shoplifting and breaking windows at will, few businesses stay open past seven. The liquor store owner pays guards to walk him to his car with each day's cash. The dry cleaner sleeps in his shop. Rochester Blanks carries a gun when he deposits the church's Sunday offering at a bank only two blocks away.

"Everybody ready to sell?" Ernest Viscardi, who has owned the corner pizzeria for thirty-six years, jokes as the last merchants arrive for the meeting.

"Now's sure the time to buy," someone answers without levity.

Alfred Thompson, who runs a barbecue restaurant, meanwhile is speculating with several others on the price for a private security guard.

"I wouldn't walk around that block for ten bucks an hour," says Fred Wein, a pharmacist who grew up three blocks away, in the Linden projects.

"The cops could get a decoy and catch these kids," another merchant offers.

"They did, three weeks ago," says Junior Roman, a dry cleaner, "and two days later everyone they caught was back on the street."

"We need Reverend Youngblood to help us," Viscardi says, turning to Leroy Howard. "And help himself. Because if the neighborhood goes to the dogs ..."

"The neighborhood has already gone to the dogs," Leroy interjects, assuming control of the meeting. "We need to take it back from them. We can't depend on the precinct to do it for us. We can't ask them for a strategy. They've been here for years and they don't know. We have to band together. We have to come up with ideas. We need to tell them and show them what will work. It's called organizing."

"We tried that five years ago, and it didn't work."

"And things're worse now," Leroy says. "Aren't they?"

"People beg me to deliver," Wein says by way of example. "I used to when I started out. But I don't wanna send some kid into the projects with medicine. He'll get killed."

"The children, they come outta school at three o'clock," adds Viscardi, his English still thickly accented after forty years in America. "No respect. *No respect.* An old man, they hit him. And I got to stand there like stupid." He runs his hands down the sides of his flannel shirt, and then onto his pants, which are dusted with flour. "Like it's my own father."

Wein has studied the situation more closely than anyone else, logging every crime along Stanley Avenue for months, and the disease he describes is less cholera than a particularly tenacious grippe. Ten or twenty boys in their teens commit most of the crimes. With their acid-washed jeans and hooded sweatshirts and baseball caps, they can blend easily enough with the students who leave the junior high school each afternoon. They generally work in crews of three, using the projects across Stanley Avenue from the stores as their safe houses.

"They got no father at home, their mothers don't bring 'em to church," Leroy adds. "Only people they got to talk to in the streets is drug addicts."

"At that age, there needs to be a belonging," Wein continues. "It wasn't that long ago I was that age. We had the Y. These guys have nothing. We have to turn them around, get them a Guardian Angels or something."

Shirley lays down her pen for a moment.

"I get a list of all the city jobs," she explains. "I got a list of free job training. *Free.* So when they say they got no skills, tell them what-all we got at Saint Paul."

"We have to approach them very lovely," says J. T. Chun, the greengrocer and a newcomer to English. "We fight them, we get more problem."

"If I call the police," Viscardi puts in, "when they come, the kids ask, 'Who called?' The police, they say, 'The pizza man.' *No brains!* They coulda kill me and bury me before the cops come back." He looses a long, heavy sigh. "Maybe we need all get together, take some baseball bats. Vigilantes."

"We've got to be better than the criminals," Leroy says.

As he speaks, Reverend Youngblood slips into the chapel, coatless and respectfully silent. A few notice and nod, Roman saying, "Hi, Rev." Then he moves to the front and introduces himself.

"Good isn't weak," he says, picking up the argument from Leroy. "Good isn't milquetoast. Good isn't namby-pamby. Good is stronger than evil. And I can bust an ass as good as anybody on the street. So we need to do for ourselves. And then tell the cops we can work with them or without them. We need to stand together." He smiles. "And we need to get ourselves a name."

"Saint Paul Saints," offers Richard Lavecchia, who runs Stanley Avenue's second dry-cleaning shop.

"That's our basketball team."

"Saint Paul Vigilantes," Viscardi gushes.

"Well, I like that," Reverend Youngblood says, stroking his chin whiskers. "But it might not go over quite right."

Someone remembers a long-dormant outfit called the Stanley–Van Siclen Merchants Association, which even had its own checking account. Maybe the time has come to resuscitate it.

"I'm gonna be straight with you," Reverend Youngblood says. "Some of you don't live in this neighborhood. You're only partly involved. So for this thing to work, we need your whole commitment. We need to know you're here to stay."

There are nods of assent around the chapel.

The merchants all sign a new membership list. Several agree to solicit bids from security agencies, others to recruit more shopkeepers as members. A formal list of suspects in the recent crimes will be developed, and then shared with the precinct commander and the local junior high school principal. Dues are set at one hundred dollars a month, enough to pay for informational flyers and nightly guard duty.

"And I might just get me a gun," Reverend Youngblood concludes.

"Is no problem to get a gun," Viscardi says.

"I mean a *legal* gun. Because the worst thing we can do is let fear rule us."

"It's like the Bible says," the pizza man explains. "Just because someone smack you onna left doesn't mean you let them smack you onna right."

"That must be the Italian Bible," Reverend Youngblood says, shaking his head, then scanning the room to meet each man eye-to-eye. "Look, let's enjoy living in our community. Let's not be dictated to by people with no scruples or morals. And let's pray."

Night has descended on Hendrix Street and Saint Paul. A howling northwest wind has chased the day's storms out to sea and driven even the crack addicts off their corners. Corrugated steel gates guard the stores along Stanley Avenue. Ice forms in the gutters and potholes. Steam twists crookedly upward from the brick smokestack in the projects, as if the neighborhood itself were huffing frosted breath on a hurried walk home.

On the street outside the church, however, not a parking space can be found. The cars sit two abreast on the east curb with another line along the west, leaving just one blacktop gulley for the stragglers who must circle the block. A bus driver still in uniform strides into the lobby with a green beaded backrest rolled under his arm. A college student in a cardigan lugs a backpack sagging with texts. One man leans on a cane, another carries a legal pad and a fistful of pens. They clasp hands, slap backs, laugh at jokes they have told each other a dozen times, for this gathering is their welcome weekly ritual, one that climate alone cannot disrupt.

As the clock touches eight, they move into the sanctuary. On Sundays even in midwinter, the chamber can swelter with the heat of a thousand bodies, with the shouting and stamping of a service that "got good." On nights like this one, it takes on a certain slight chill. A cool film lies atop the varnish of the pews, a cool wisp brushes against bare cheeks and palms. This is the weather of football and hunting and early mornings on still water, the weather of men.

Reverend Youngblood, clad in a black sweatsuit, enters the sanctuary, and without prompting, the men join voices. Their song advances at a deliberate pace, and their tone hangs thick and musky in the air. The words can be found on page 329 of the hymnal, but few men require its assistance, for the song announces their assembly each week:

> *I am Thine, O Lord, I have heard Thy voice*
> *And it told Thy love to me;*
> *But I long to rise in the arms of faith*
> *And be closer drawn to Thee.*

Three more verses pass. The voices grow hearty and full, as if this music were not a hymn but a sea shanty. The men listen even as they sing, proudly reckoning the great sound they can make, and nodding with satisfaction as they reach the final chorus:

> *Draw me nearer, nearer blessed Lord,*
> *To the cross where Thou hast died;*
> *Draw me nearer, nearer blessed Lord,*
> *To Thy precious, bleeding side.*

That had been Reverend Youngblood's prayer, to bring a roomful of strong black men to Jesus Christ. Formally the group is called Eldad-Medad Men's Bible Study, but studying the Scriptures is in some respects the least of its elements. Just a few weeks earlier the pastor had told its members, "This is our social club. This is our fraternity. This is our basketball team. This is our family. And we're still rising. We're a phoenix coming out of the ashes."

In other religions, perhaps, such a gathering would not have seemed so innovative, so necessary, so nearly revolutionary. The Catholics had the Knights of Columbus and the Holy Name Society. Jewish men studied the Torah and Talmud and in a certain sense manhood itself in the *beit midrash,* the house of learning. The Nation of Islam made its name resurrecting convicts and criminals, most famously the hustler named Detroit Red who became Malcolm X. Yet the black church, for all the male leaders it had created over two centuries, was beyond the pulpit largely a community of women. Reverend Youngblood knew as much from childhood in Holy Family. A national survey by the University of Chicago put statistical sanction on his experience, showing that black men were less likely than black women or whites of either gender to attend church weekly. James Baldwin wrote of Harlem's men in *Go Tell It on the Mountain:*

> Not one of them ever went to Church—one might scarcely have imagined that they knew that church existed—they all, hourly, daily, in their speech, in their lives, in their hearts, cursed God. They all seemed to be saying, as Richard, when she once timidly mentioned the love of Jesus, said: "You can tell that puking bastard to kiss my big black ass."

Some of Reverend Youngblood's men had left church because they were born out of wedlock. Some had left because they fathered children out of wedlock. Some had left because if they drank or danced, fought or flirted, the pious cast them beyond the hope of redemption. Some had left because they hated the way their wives talked about the pastor until they wanted to tell the women to shut up and go ask *him* for the grocery money. Some had left because they could not worship a god of blond hair and blue eyes.

Whatever the reason, they had stayed away, stayed away in such numbers that the congregation Reverend Youngblood met upon arriving at Saint Paul counted hardly a man outside its board of deacons. And the issue in such absence was more than evangelism, more than salvation, unless one meant the salvation of an entire people. Through the 1980s, black men were increasingly missing not only from church but from college, from the workplace, from the household. Where they could be found, especially young men, was in prison or the morgue. When they considered the disease and drugs and unemployment and maleducation that had felled so many of their peers, that was reducing their life expectancy on the cusp of the twenty-first century, black men spoke of themselves as an endangered species, even as the object of governmental genocide. One need not have wholly agreed to understand the cataclysm that lent credence to conspiracy. Even Health and Human Services Secretary Louis W. Sullivan, the highest-ranking black in the Bush administration and nobody's idea of a firebrand, would say, "Not since slavery has so much calamity and ongoing catastrophe been visited on black males."

Taking up his own tiny battle in early 1984, Reverend Youngblood did away with Saint Paul's annual Men's Day, as if male presence in church were so rare as to merit a holiday. From now on, he declared, every Sunday would be Men's Day. He asked the men to stand at one point in the worship service that morning, and the handful rose among the women like oaks amid prairie grass. "I'm glad you're here," Reverend Youngblood told them. "I need you to work with me. But we need to get to know each other. Because I'm not sure I know how to pastor men. I need your help."

When they met two hours later, Reverend Youngblood carried a Bible and told a dirty joke. He could see the men waiting for lightning or brimstone or a great cosmic rolling pin to strike down the sinner. When he continued, divinely unscathed and as profane as before, the men began to share their stories. And as he heard their doubts and rage, their overarching sense of inadequacy, he wanted his church to live up to the hymn:

Just as I am
Without one plea
But that Thy blood
Was shed for me

In the next months, Reverend Youngblood launched a policy of theological affirmative action. He initiated a men's chorus and a father-son banquet, which would later be augmented by an all-male retreat. He assigned men specific tasks, some because of their urgency, others because they undercut the conventions of "man's work." The men raised the money for elementary school desks, attended the rallies of East Brooklyn Congregations, cooked and served breakfast for the church between the eight o'clock and eleven o'clock services. Convinced that the mere word *deacon* was a liability, connoting either the pastor's Jeeves or his Brutus, Reverend Youngblood reached into First Timothy for the concept of a church governed by a board of male elders. On the night of their consecration, wearing the suits usually saved for funerals and Masonic banquets, dropping onto bent knee for anointment, the first elders wept unashamedly. For the custodian and the transit cop and the gas station owner, little in life had ever offered such dignity.

Secrets die fast in black Brooklyn, and men followed the word to Saint Paul. Reverend Youngblood was no longer their wives' surrogate husband, no longer their own caricature of the "jackleg preacher," one hand in the collection plate and the other down a woman's blouse. He was "Johnny," "Rev," "Blood," their friend. One man, Arthur Jamison, presented Reverend Youngblood with a decanter of homemade wine. Rochester Blanks, perhaps the most elegant dresser at Saint Paul, gave an overcoat he had bought for himself. Joe Tarrant made the down payment on a car.

But to Reverend Youngblood the men's ministry still was not sufficient. The Sunday meetings were too truncated. The board of elders by itself could not accommodate enough men. And those it excluded might not care to join the choir or become an usher. He turned in the Bible to one of the classic treatments of leadership, the Exodus story, and he found in Numbers 11 four particular verses:

> But there remained two of the men in the camp, the name of the one was Eldad, and the name of the other Medad: and the spirit rested upon them; and they ... went out unto the tabernacle: and they prophesied in the camp.
>
> And there ran a young man, and told Moses, and said, Eldad and Medad do prophecy in the camp.

And Joshua the son of Nun, the servant of Moses, one of his young men, answered and said, My lord Moses, forbid them.

And Moses said unto him, Enviest thou for my sake? Would God that all the Lord's people were prophets, and that the Lord would put his spirit upon them!

The Israelites had their official prophets, a complement of seventy, Eldad and Medad not among them. Yet when Joshua demanded of Moses that he silence their unauthorized preaching, Moses did more than refuse. He placed his own imprimatur, and through it the Almighty's, on these two obscure renegades, never again to appear in the Scriptures. *Would God that all the Lord's people were prophets....* The parallel was clear; the paradigm was evident. If the elders were the formal prophets, then there needed to be a place for the other good men, the Eldads and Medads of Saint Paul. Men worked. Men had families. Men needed a firm schedule, with their night for spiritual fellowship as fixed as it would be for a bowling league. Since the church offices were nominally closed on Tuesday, Tuesday became the night for Eldad-Medad.

Anything might be discussed, from the previous Sunday's service to the morning news, from a taped speech by Muslim Minister Louis Farrakhan to a "Donahue" show on tension between black men and black women. There were raucous jokes about mistresses and malt liquor and masturbation. And there was safety, the safety that let men risk vulnerability. One confided the abuse of his teenaged daughter by her stepfather. Another spoke of being homosexually molested as a child. "You been told you're a dog," Reverend Youngblood said on many Tuesday nights. "But you turn *dog* around and you got *God*. And God is doing a recall on black men."

Two signs more than others augured for success. One was the coming of young men, men like Craig Campbell, a chef raising his daughter alone, and Mike Portee, a sanitation worker with the voice of Paul Robeson, and even the sullen, skeptical first-timers, like the fellow tonight with a rattail haircut and a wrist cast signed by "Cash" and "TNT." The second proof was the curiosity of women. Imagining a cabal plotting male supremacy, they would ask their boyfriends and husbands, "Is this supposed to turn us all into Stepford Wives?" Not receiving any answers, since the men held their privacy sacred, the women would walk off muttering, "Then we're just gonna have to have a group of our own. *Elmom-Memom.*"

What opens the discussion tonight, however, is not a topic of jokes but of nightmares.

"Did you see the *News* today?" asks Charles Baylor, a realtor, as he rises from his usual spot in the second row and turns to face the men behind him. Then he holds a torn page with a headline whose tall, bold typeface might normally announce a political scandal or aviation disaster: YOUNG BLACKS IN TROUBLE.

Charles Lewis meanwhile passes out photocopies of the article, and murmurs of recognition rise from the pews. The same story was all over television and radio today: A study by The Sentencing Project, a nonprofit group based in Washington, has found that twenty-three percent of black men between the ages of twenty and twenty-nine are in prison, on probation, or on parole. The proportion is more than double that of Hispanic men of the same age, and nearly quadruple that of white men. And the number of young black men already tainted with criminal records exceeds by 173,000 the number of all black men attending college.

"We've got to read it," Reverend Youngblood says, pinching his copy between thumb and forefinger. "We've got to articulate it." His voice gathers strength. "But we've got to remember this is *not* the last word. Let 'em come here on Tuesday nights and see *our* young men."

One of them, Melvin Anderson, stands to speak. At twenty, he is the junior member of Eldad-Medad, an aspiring minister in the process of transferring from community college to his pastor's alma mater, Dillard. For all that, as a black male of a certain age, with a fade haircut and a gold earring, he knows his mere presence incites people to cross streets, clutch handbags, move wallets into front pockets.

"Why do they keep writing these articles?" he asks.

"We gotta get our side of the story out," adds another young man, a bicycle messenger named Bryan Croft.

"Don't matter," someone cuts in. "Whites look at us as don't-know-nothin' folks. You can talk all you want, but the only thing you get from hittin' your head against the wall is a sore head."

The words sound alarms for Reverend Youngblood. It is difficult enough for young black men to choose the church and the legitimate world, when studying hard is derided as "bein' white," when traveling without a weapon marks you as a chump, when the girls you want to date cozy up to dealers who can drape them with "big gold." So when the pastor hears any trace of disgust or surrender, he knows it must be confronted.

"I'm here to say this article isn't the whole truth," he says with fatherly assurance. He cannot dispute the statistics, so he writes a new conclusion. "How many of you men been in jail?" Perhaps twenty of seventy raise a hand. "How many been involved in drugs?" Most of the earlier hands stay aloft, joined by ten new ones. "How many of you been redeemed?" Now every arm lifts. "I'll tell ya, I stopped givin' a damn what other folk think of me. White folk or any folk. It's what *I* think of me. It's what *God* thinks of me. And I ain't that bad." He slows the words so that each one breathes. "I ain't that bad." He repeats the affirmation a third time, spontaneously accompanied by the men. "I ain't that bad."

Now he moves toward the portable blackboard that has been placed beside the pulpit. He writes the words, "Trust God," striking so hard the chalk splinters.

"And the reason I trust God is because everything else has failed. And part of what has failed is our idea of God, that God makes everything better. God does, but not by you just sittin' there. I don't care how much you got, doctor." Suddenly he jumps in place, and the tremor of physical punctuation seems to ripple to the back wall. "Some of these dealers, you see how much money they got. But we better off. Academic degree? Doesn't mean you gonna get the job. Military? Gorbachev done fucked that up." He pauses. "You know what the two rallyin' places are for brothers? The cemetery or the penitentiary. Boot Hill or Attica. The tomb or The Tombs. So we gotta think about how we gonna get to those places, get to some of these diamonds in the rough."

He tells the story of a cop in East Flatbush who saw a black man in a store window with a gun. "Drop it!" the cop ordered. "It ain't loaded," the man replied. Once handcuffed, the suspect asked to be booked and arraigned as quickly as possible. "I gotta pitch this weekend," he told the cop, meaning in a prison ball game.

Laughter born of pain and identification rolls slowly through the sanctuary.

"So, brothers," Reverend Youngblood continues, "read these

articles, pray on 'em. Because they're tellin' us our work. They're tellin' us what we gotta do."

"A trade is very valuable," says Robert Sharper, a construction carpenter who learned his own after release from Sing Sing. "You can carry what you learn on your trade for the rest of your life. The *discipline*. Everybody's trying to explain what's wrong with the black man except us. Everything we've gone through, to still survive we must have some hell of a stuff and not even know it. So why don't we go with the strengths we have?"

"Only way you see the black man," someone adds, "he's a fool. You look at TV. The Cosby show. A sitcom. A comedy. It's a joke. And that's what our children see. In my family, I idolized my daddy. I hope that someday I can talk to my son the way he talked to me. You know, my momma still gets up at four-thirty to make him breakfast 'fore he go to work. My wife says, 'Why she do that?' Times is different now. I don't expect it."

"What the brother just said got me thinkin'," says Ron Hudson, a Marine veteran wearing the hand-tailored suit and tinted aviator glasses of his management position at The Bank of New York. "When I was growing up, my father was the king. It was a spiritual thing. My father, all the neighbors' fathers, they took their children to church, whether they went or not. When did that change?"

"We lost it," Reverend Youngblood agrees. "All our fathers at some point put their foot up our ass, and it made us mad. And it made us leave. We didn't have a place. So we made a place. Without them."

"Where we lost ourselves," Charles Lewis says, "is when we stopped looking at church for solutions. We know it's a racist society. We know it's a capitalist society. We know the pie's getting smaller. We need a system *outside* the system. And the black church is the only place."

The hour nears nine-thirty, the unofficial closing time for Eldad-Medad, in deference to men who awaken for work before dawn. As he does each week, a hospital billing clerk named Ernest Spruill rises from his seat on the aisle and moves discreetly past the pulpit to fetch a wicker basket. He travels silently through the gathering, dollar bills dropping softly into the collection, as the conversation proceeds unimpeded by his rounds.

"We want to separate ourselves, and it won't be easy," Reverend

Youngblood says, now leaning against the side of the blackboard, legs crossed. "Con Edison'll still be Con Edison. The bureaucracy'll still be the bureaucracy. We need to at least start thinking differently. And this dialogue we're having tonight is part of it." He smiles. "I mean, we must be some bad motor scooters, the way they all talkin' about us. If you look in the Bible, when God got to movin', he worked with the people on the bottom of the social order. And that's why we're here."

2

AN ACCIDENT OF MELANIN

MONDAY NIGHT IS USUALLY THE QUIETEST of the week at Saint Paul, a respite for the church to recline and exhale. The passions of Sunday morning are still fresh memories, and refrigerators swell with leftover chicken and greens. The rest of the week will bustle with adult education classes, choir and dance rehearsals, orientation for new members, and countless other gatherings until it is Sunday again. But Mondays end early. With the sun long down and their appetites stirred, the last of the church's children stop playing touch football or posing like rap singers around parked cars. By eight o'clock, the small prayer service disbands, and its thirty regulars make for home. Until daybreak Hendrix Street will belong to the wretched, sifting the trash for nickel-deposit bottles, shambling toward Linden Boulevard to wash a quarter's worth of windshields.

This Monday, the twenty-second of January, promises difference. The proof lies in the women who enter Saint Paul in threes and fours, alighting from gypsy cabs, padding in sneakers from the subway, their pumps and Bibles stowed in canvas bags stenciled with verses from John and Psalms. The proof, most of all, lies in their hats. They wear tams and pillboxes, turbans and fedoras, hats ornamented with ruffles or feathers or pins along brims that gracefully swoop. Such an exhibition could be expected on Easter and understood on most Sundays, when showing humility before God occasioned a fashion statement. But hats on a Monday night could only indicate an event of rare gravity.

Once or twice a year, Saint Paul's members convene on a Monday night to hear the initial sermon by one who has confessed the call to preach. Nothing less stands at stake than the authenticity of the revelation. In Reverend Youngblood's lifetime, he has seen men in this position quiver and stammer, the manuscripts of their addresses shaking loose from their hands. Those who succeeded, however, those who transcended the mortal pressure and uttered the immortal word, those men were said to possess "the mark." Five so far have shown it at Saint Paul, and Reverend Youngblood has welcomed them into a body of apprentices he calls "the school of the prophets."

All of them are black. This evening's prospective prophet, Tom Approbato, is the one white member of Saint Paul. The presence of just any white man at the altar would afford no cause for reverence, no cause for hats. Reverend Youngblood has opened his pulpit to the Catholic priest Leo Penta and the Lutheran minister John Heinemeier from East Brooklyn Congregations, to the evangelical preacher and fund-raising expert Van McQueen, to the Jewish rabbi Marshall Meyer, who only one week ago spoke in celebration of Martin Luther King's birthday. But Tom Approbato no longer qualifies as a novelty, a goodwill gesture, not after four years that have seen him pay tithes, sing with the choir, teach an evening course. Tonight he will claim legitimacy in the very center of black achievement, black pride, black self-determination. And nobody knows where his sermon might land in the vastness between divine ordination and blackface show.

Nobody even knows, ten minutes before the service, whether Tom will actually appear. He is sitting five miles to the southwest, stuck behind two stalled cars on the Belt Parkway. He cannot make a U-turn, because an unbroken steel rail runs down the median. He cannot pull onto the shoulder, because the shoulder consists of the beach along Jamaica Bay. The next exit waits two miles ahead, and at this rate he might reach it by midnight. "Just open the traffic, Lord," he prays aloud. "I know You can do it." But inside he worries, *Will everybody just think the white guy got scared?*

Preparing the sermon has been traumatic enough. Tom works overnight on the foreign exchange desk at Prudential Bache, and by the time he finishes scouring the Tokyo and Singapore markets for his clients, he must drive straight to New Brunswick Theological Seminary, an hour away in New Jersey. Wednesday night he teaches at Saint Paul and Thursday he practices with the choir. In a good week, he sleeps for a total of twenty hours. So he husbanded his free moments for two months, improvising a first draft of the sermon into a tape recorder as he commuted along the turnpike, practicing aloud seventeen different variations, writing out the preamble just last night, to make certain he would not turn mute. Still, there is a threshold he has never been able to cross, a passage so painful that each time he speaks it, he falls into tears.

A tow truck finally drags away one of the cars, and traffic bursts through the newly clear lane. Tom reaches Saint Paul with five minutes to spare.

"You okay?" asks Reverend Garland Ward, one of Reverend Youngblood's assistants, who has been waiting on the front steps.

"Just get me to the bathroom," Tom says.

Soon he is ushered into the pastor's study for prayer, and then he finds himself beside the altar, hearing Eli Wilson sing. His limbs feel numb, his mind preternaturally aware. How long should he talk? How long do other preachers talk? What should he do if he finishes after ten minutes? He realizes the top button has popped loose from his dress shirt. He discovers that the narrow end of his tie dangles lower than the wide one. Will anyone notice? He adds his voice to the hymn, trying to anchor himself in the familiar, but trembling legs betray him.

The sanctuary is filling with worshipers, from an initial sixty to perhaps three hundred. Four times Reverend Youngblood must pause during his introductory remarks to allow the ushers to admit the latecomers clogging the lobby. He delivers a brief biography of Tom, relaxing the congregation with a joke about his suspect sense of rhythm, and then says quite seriously, "I don't know what this is gonna come to."

Only one final song, "How Sweet His Name," separates Tom from his sermon. He moves slowly toward the pulpit, embracing Reverend Youngblood as they pass, then steadying himself one leg at a time.

"I was gonna sing 'Mama, Don't Let Your Babies Grow Up to Be Cowboys,'" he says, stepping to the altar, and the congregation roars at the implicit joke on his own whiteness. But as the laughter dies out, Tom seems uneasy. "Yeah, it's been a long time," he sighs without further explanation. Then he inhales heavily, as if preparing for a deep dive.

"I don't know how to start this thing," he says, abandoning the written introduction that was intended to prevent precisely this hesitancy. "If I could jump into a sermon, it would be okay. If I could get right into the middle and start, everything would be okay, because the spirit takes over. And the spirit will just carry you through right to the end. But it's always the beginning that's been a problem." He pauses, swallows. "So when I was in doubt where to start, I went to the Bible, which is always the best place, and I opened up to Genesis, and it says, 'In the beginning.' Well, even the Bible has a beginning. So I'm just gonna go from that. We're gonna start and we're gonna go. And we're gonna take a trip through time today, kind of jump from the past to the future back to the past."

Just past four on many afternoons, Father James D'Amato would leave his rectory and stand in the airway between that modest stone building and the Norman Gothic church it served, Saint John the Evangelist. He knew this was the hour to encounter the faithful, for this was the hour when life returned to the Sunset Park section of Brooklyn. The stevedores and welders trudged up Twenty-first Street from the Bush Terminal docks. The machinists and garment workers strode off the Fifth Avenue bus. Mothers scurried toward the corner bakery to buy fresh bread for dinner. Children chose sides for games of stickball and off-the-point.

Some would approach Father D'Amato to arrange a mass for recovery from illness or to seek mediation of a squabble with in-laws. Students might ask for help with their religion class homework. One of the neighborhood drunks might beg for loose change, and the priest would send him to Otto's Diner with a chit for a hot meal. And if Father D'Amato spotted a woman from the Rosary Society, which he oversaw, he would discuss with her its progress in creating a church library or knitting clothes for the patients of a nearby mental hospital.

There was one parishioner Father D'Amato never needed to seek out, a young man with blue eyes and a bristling crewcut who delivered the *World Telegram* after school. The rectory was on his route, near the end, and the final customers suffered, because the paperboy rarely left there before six, when the clerics took their dinner and shooed him away. His name was Thomas James Stephen Stephan Approbato, and as a teenager in the late 1950s he harbored the dream of becoming a priest.

He taught himself Latin from the missal. He lingered at the stations of the cross, prayed before the statue of the Blessed Virgin, wore his rosary beads home from catechism class, even as his friends chided, "Who d'ya think y'are? You gotta all the time show the cross? You holier or somethin'?" He was not holier, but certainly more sensitive—a wit, an A student, a lover of classical music who was sometimes derided as "Opera-bato." In a neighborhood where men generally lived by their limbs, Tom's father, Peter, worked as an accountant and supplied his six children with novels by Dickens and a Funk & Wagnalls encyclopedia.

Perhaps that was why the paperboy in jeans and the priest in the black soutane could converse with such ease. Father D'Amato was teaching psychology at a college in Brooklyn, while pursuing his doctorate at Saint John's University. He spoke German, French, Russian, and even some Japanese. So he gladly fielded Tom's inquiries. What's Purgatory? How long do you have to stay there? What does it mean to be a priest? How do you become one? Can you still go to a Dodgers game?

Then the Second Vatican Council and its liberalization brought an end to Tom's questions and his priestly plans. The first Sunday he attended the newly introduced English mass, he nearly walked out. The mystery of church, the mystery of faith, had for him been inextricably bound up with Latin. Though he knew well enough that the languages of biblical times were Hebrew and Aramaic, in his ears Latin was the tongue of Judea, Jerusalem, Calvary. Anybody down at the Three Star tavern could speak English. English was too prosaic for God. And besides, Tom had just met a girl named Louise Rouse at a recreation center. That celibacy rule was going to be tricky.

Church, however, was not the only source of values in Tom's life. His mother, Phyllis, taught him tolerance in her most homespun Brooklynese: "If you don't know somebody, how can you say they're no good?" The neighborhood seemed to prove her right. Looming above the cranes and smokestacks and grain elevators of the waterfront, Sunset Park had for decades offered home to any sailor finished with the sea, from Finns and Swedes to Peruvians and Ecuadorians. Irish and Italian immigrants settled to be near their jobs digging tun-

nels and laying roads. Russian Jews opened stores. Puerto Ricans overwhelmed by the congestion of the Lower East Side or the South
Bronx sought the neighborhood's frame houses. Blacks with enough
savings moved across the Gowanus Canal from the Red Hook projects. On the Approbatos' own block of Eighteenth Street lived families named Kilkenny, Demoratius, Rivera, Panza; one mother was a
Japanese war bride. And the entire mix, the mix that would in later
years turn volatile and even fatal in New York, was held together by
the last boom years of hard industry, when every man had a lunch pail
and a job to carry it to.

By the time the shipyards closed and the suburbs opened and
Sunset Park became a Puerto Rican ghetto, Tom was gone. After
graduating from high school, he had enlisted in the Air Force,
impressed by a recruiter's uniform. It was on his way to basic training
in Biloxi, Mississippi, that he first noticed the rest room signs: Men,
Women, Other.

Maybe he was naïve to be shocked. It was 1963. The Civil Rights
Movement had been marching for fully eight years. Yet for the Approbatos, like most New Yorkers, racism seemed a distant Southern disease. Tom had so much trouble understanding sectarian hate that, for
all his Catholic piety, he secretly thought the Crusades ridiculous.
Once on his military base, he did what felt normal, and made friends
with his bunkmate, a fellow Brooklynite, who happened to be black.

On the morning the unit received its first weekend pass, the soldiers rode a military bus to downtown Biloxi. As they stepped onto
the sidewalk, Tom asked his friend, "Where d'ya wanna go?"

"I can't walk with you."

"Why?"

"I just can't."

"Whatsa matter?" Tom said. "I got BO?"

He smelled his armpit. He had no idea.

"Because I'm Negro."

"So what? We're all American. We're all serving our country."

The friend faced Tom squarely.

"I'm Negro, and you're white," he said, "and you have to understand where we are."

Then the black airman walked away. And in the eight months he
spent in Biloxi, Tom Approbato never again accepted a weekend pass.

* * *

"So," Tom says from the pulpit, "I'm going to do my imitation of Michael Jackson with a vanilla accent." He balances on his left foot, pushes off with his right, and executes a wobbly revolution, which leaves strands of hair splayed across his forehead.

The congregation bellows and applauds, for the conceit, for the nerve, for the spectacle. Behind his own laughter, however, Reverend Youngblood frets. He had begun the evening with two fears: first, that Tom would resort to the bland, Good Samaritan, "God is love" gospel favored by white preachers in black settings, and second, that Tom would rely too greatly on his sense of humor. That wit was a blessing in moderation, the pastor believed, but in excess it would amount to condescension, intentional or not. He could not yet gauge the accuracy of his first fear, since Tom's direction remained altogether unclear. But the second, sadly, looked as if it were justified.

So far Tom has joked about how the growth of the congregation in his four years of membership "goes to show that those people came to see me." He has joked about this sermon being "a payback" for "being a token a long time." He has joked that the pastor still owes him a rose from Mother's Day of 1988, "when you asked those who had adopted children to stand, and I was there, I stood, and you ignored me." He has joked that considering the numerous duties of the position, "in order to be an effective preacher, you have to spend at least five years in a mental institution."

Until the Michael Jackson twirl, the response had been waning with each punchline. Reverend Youngblood could feel the impatience. His people wanted substance. His people wanted to see the mark. By now, Tom was giving his biography, duplicating much of what the pastor had said in introducing him. Tom was stalling.

Then, abruptly, Tom requests a moment of silent prayer, and he says something curious. He says, "Let me get your preacher for you now." He descends from the pulpit, walks before the altar, drops on both knees. The only sound in the sanctuary is that of a child unwrapping the cellophane from a package of crackers. Tom closes his eyes and clasps his hands, as if he were again a Catholic boy on a kneeler, summoning God in Latin. He prays, "I want to be heard."

He rises and starts back toward the pulpit. His walk becomes a run. And the drumming of his steps rouses the congregants from their contemplation. The man they see now stands without twitching. The ripples in his voice flatten into a plane of assurance.

"Good evening, my brothers and sisters," he says. "My name is Thomas James Approbato. A man of God. A spiritual man. The man I had before you just a short time ago was a mortal man, a physical being. I stand before you today as the spiritual part of that man and say, 'If you do not have God in you, you are not a whole being.' That is what I have done, and I think that is what we all have to do in order to become complete and whole people.

"The story that we are going to begin with today is titled 'Life, Lost, and Love.' Now, if you have life, and you have a spiritual life with God, then you are a whole person. But things happen in our lives. Burdens come upon us, and we sometimes lose sight of where we are going and we may become lost in our spiritual being. Now, in order for something to be lost, you first have to know that you have something. So if you do not know that God is a part of your life and is the center of your life, then you cannot lose what you do not have."

"Preach it," someone calls from the congregation.

"But if you have God in your life and you lose Him, you've lost something that has to be found. And if you become lost as I did at one time—there was a period of time, years, fifteen years, where I drifted. I was a man going about this world with stopped-up ears, clouded vision, no sense of right and wrong, of what I needed most in my life. I lost my sense of reality, and my sense of reality was God, because if you don't have God, then you have no reality at all."

"Yessir!" Reverend Youngblood shouts.

"And that is what I lost."

Discharged from the military in 1967, Tom Approbato went to work as a clerk for Merrill Lynch, the brokerage house, and resumed the wooing of Louise Rouse, undeterred that in his absence she had married, borne a child, and been divorced. Two years later they wed, and seven years after that they separated for the first time. By then the couple had had three children together, and Tom had legally adopted Louise's eldest.

Perhaps it was the children. Perhaps it was the church. Perhaps it was the memory of his own childhood household, the memory of his father cooking pasta and sauce every Sunday so his mother could rest, that held Tom in the marriage long after he realized it was failing. He had traveled several continents in the service and was attending college in business administration and psychology. Louise had dropped out and begun working after eighth grade, when her mother died. When Tom tuned the radio to Caruso, she asked, "How can you listen to that?" Her taste ran to Elvis. On the subject of race, both abided by the teachings of parents. Hers had warned, "They're all animals." The house the Approbatos bought together, to Tom's lasting shame, stood in a New Jersey neighborhood whose whiteness was ensured by covenant. "The only Negroes you'll see here," the real-estate agent had promised, "are maids."

In 1982, Tom moved out, the prelude to a divorce three years later. Thinking of his children, he cried every day for the first three months apart. At most, he was permitted one visit weekly, and if he arrived late, even that would be denied. Living from a single suitcase, relying on his captain's rank in the Army reserves, he migrated from an aunt's house to the barracks at Fort Hamilton to the National Guard Armory on shabby Fourteenth Street, where he slept on a couch. He tried to confide to his unit's priest and occasionally attended mass on the base, but his prayers carried no conviction. All he was doing, he had to admit, was making a show of devotion for the lieutenant colonels.

He needed a woman, well matched or not, and he moved in with Sally, a sergeant in his unit. It was a worldly time, a time of things. They launched a business selling leather goods out of their apartment. Tom bought a Lincoln Continental and, with Sally, purchased a suburban house. On visiting day with his children, he depended on a new toy or a McDonald's lunch or the rides at Rye Playland to express love. Never did he simply hold them and tell them.

All the children were struggling with the effects of separation and divorce, and Tom's namesake, his eldest, appeared the most wounded. In more than his name, Tommy reminded Tom of himself. He was a bookish child, a loner, who delivered newspapers after school and collected comic books by the thousands, as his father had once collected baseball cards. Now he seemed positively stern. As little as Louise and Tom could discuss civilly, she shared her worries about their son. Only fifteen, he had assumed the role of father, disciplining his siblings, substituting obligation for the unrestricted joy that was a young boy's birthright.

"You don't have to be so serious," Tom said on one visit. "You have your mother there, and I'm only a phone call away."

"I have to," his son answered. "Mommy's not here all the time. The kids are messin' up." Then his voice grew flinty with an anger his father would never forget. "And you're not here."

"You see," Tom continues from the pulpit, "all this time, I'm going through this world and I cannot see where I'm going 'cause I have clouded vision. But He keeps knocking on the door of my heart."

He raps the knuckles of his right hand against the oak wood, four beats in solemn martial time, then four more, an ominous underscoring.

"I cannot hear, but God never stops. You see, when I was younger, I had made a commitment to God. When I was sixteen, seventeen years old, I said, 'Lord, I'm going to take up the cross and I'm going to follow You. I want to be your son. I want to be your servant. I will do your bidding.' But this world got in the way."

In the sanctuary, women nod, their heads rocking rhythmically, wordlessly affirming Tom's truth. Men find themselves closing their hands into fists, as Tom has, and lowering them onto their thighs in cadence with him.

"And all the time," Tom says, "He's calling me. He's knocking on the doors of my heart." By now his own knuckles have reddened with the repeated strikes. "And yet I still fail to hear Him. What to do? I think about this time, the Lord said, 'I keep knocking but he doesn't hear me. What am I to do? How can I get him back?

"'Maybe I'll knock a little louder.'"

Tom has reached the threshold. He draws breath, rolls forward his shoulders, and advances in a weary, thickening voice, a voice not of deliberation but of grim reflex.

"Two o'clock one early morning, the phone rang and woke me out of a sound sleep. It was my wife. She told me, 'Your son, Thomas junior, has just tried to commit suicide.'"

A silence as thick as noise suffuses the room.

"She must've spoke to me after that. I don't know; I didn't hear her. I may have answered her. I don't know; I cannot remember. All I know is that when she told me that, my life changed. I was no longer in that darkened room answering a phone. I was at the foot of the cross." His voices hurtles and careers. "And I was back at Calvary and I was on my knees, because you can't stand up in the presence of God. You just can't stand. You've got to be on your knees."

Tom halts for a moment, trackless in unknown terrain, and then an image comes.

"I looked up and I saw my Savior there, and I saw the two crosses of the thieves that were there. But then there was a fourth cross, in the background. That was *my* cross. The one I had told Jesus I would take up and follow him on. The one that I had said, 'Lord, show me the way and I will be your servant.' The one I had forgotten about, the one that was lost in the values of this world. There was nothing there. It was my cross. *My cross.* And upon my cross hung ..."

Tom pitches forward, his mouth touching the microphone. He closes his eyes so fiercely that furrows run from brow to temple. His voice plummets into the parched whisper of confession.

"... my son."

The air has been sucked from the room, and the sanctuary is filled with the sound of gasping. White people, for so many in Reverend Youngblood's generation, seemed the paragons of "Ozzie and Harriet" or "Make Room for Daddy." White people were the ones who could move away from neighborhoods that turned rotten. White people were always lecturing them about *their* kids. And if, until this moment, they had heard a tale such as Tom's, they might well have asked, *Why would a white kid want to commit suicide? How could white folk have problems when it's their world?* A hardened handful might even have ascribed such a tragedy to divine retribution. But as the pastor surveys the congregation now, he sees handkerchiefs at damp eyes and hears the ragged murmur of heartache. *So this,* he thinks, *is where we meet.*

"You cannot know the feelings that went through me at that time," Tom continues. "You cannot understand unless you've been there, the feelings and the hurt and the pain. And I heard my son echo, as the Lord had said, 'My God, my God, why hast Thou forsaken me?' And I heard my son, Tommy junior, shout, 'Father, Father, why have *you* forsaken *me?*'

"And his words cut and pierced my heart like the spear that pierced my Savior's side. And I cried in a silent scream." He thrusts his arms outward to the edges of the cross. Grief gnarls his face. "'Jesus, save my son. Jesus, take me. Jesus, save my son.'" Now his voice falls again. "'Jesus, forgive me.'"

Tommy Approbato survived and returned home and went on to attend college and move west. But even presented with an answered prayer, his father did not resume faith. If anything, he wanted somehow to escape the implication of his spontaneous plea. He would imagine himself as a submarine that had broken the surface and now was hiding again in the depths.

Tom needed another agent of renewal, and he would find her across the hall at work. He had known Ida Fulton slightly as far back as 1973, when both worked at E. F. Hutton. Ida stayed there for years, while Tom followed promotions from brokerage to brokerage, eventually returning to Hutton in 1983 as manager of the London order desk. His room was a bare rectangle lined with glass walls, and it afforded only two views. One took in the mad dance of the sugar traders, and the other the delicate woman with dark ringlets of hair who supervised the data processors. There was little competition where Tom's bored eyes turned for revival.

He might occasionally visit Ida on the pretext of fetching telex paper or checking the transaction tickets that recorded the trades. Ida might ask him to move something heavy, since the data processors were mostly women. She noticed how Tom, unlike many others in the office, would never turn down a manual chore with the excuse, "That's not my job." She appreciated his humor, the way he dubbed the telex machine "the Green Giant." Over the course of two years, conversation edged into courtship. Tom and Ida often ate lunch together, swapping war stories of each one's marriage and pending divorce, and became partners for Broadway plays and Bear Mountain outings.

Still, theirs was a young relationship, carefully circumscribed. After Louise and Sally, Tom was wounded and wary. And besides, since he was white and Ida was black, becoming a public couple meant inviting public scorn. So they spent each Saturday together, and come Sunday morning their union separated into its parts, Tom visiting his children and Ida worshiping at Saint Paul.

Then, in late 1985, Tom left New York for an Army Reserve

training course in Kansas. He kept a taped diary of his drive west, speaking into a miniature recorder, and between describing the clouds and counting the miles and singing "Seventy-six Trombones," he longed for Ida, as unashamedly as a teenager in rapturous first love. "All I know is what I feel, and what I feel is loneliness right now," he said. "I love you, Ida, I really do. I miss you so damn bad. I want to hold you. I want to kiss you. I don't ever want to let you go."

One Saturday night after Tom's return, he turned to Ida and asked, "What do you think would happen if I went to church with you?"

He did not realize Saint Paul was entirely black. All he knew was that he had heard enough from Ida about this Johnny Ray Young-blood guy to be curious.

"You can't be serious," Ida said.

"I am," he insisted. "I need to find out what this is about."

"Are you sure?"

"I want to go," he said. "You're important to me, and everything that's important to you is important to me. I want to know."

Not yet convinced, Ida called her cousin Shirley, who also belonged to Saint Paul.

"Well, we don't have any white members," she told Ida, "but there's no sign against it."

They arrived that Sunday as a threesome, the better to obscure the romance, and slid quickly into a distant row. A few members gazed with alarm at the white man, fearing he was a bill collector or an undercover cop, but enough ventured handshakes and greetings that Tom would be struck by the welcome. The vaunted Reverend Young-blood, it turned out, was preaching elsewhere, but even without him the service left Tom overwhelmed. As much as he had embraced the mystery of the Catholic Church, he had always bridled at its rote manner of worship. Not even the "folk masses" of the late 1960s, it seemed to him, could breach the barrier separating priest from congregation, the profession of belief from the celebration of it. And here, in this black Baptist church, were people crying, shouting, leaping, singing. He envied their liberation, a liberation he could only begin to imagine for himself.

He returned to Saint Paul the next Sunday and the Sunday after that, and still Reverend Youngblood was traveling. "I think," Tom teased Ida, "this preacher doesn't exist." When the pastor returned to his pulpit, he delivered a sermon about the central importance of children, making Father God the role model for earthly Dad. The theme was a familiar one at Saint Paul, a standard, but to Tom it cut to the core of his failings. He had been, as church jargon had it, "convicted," found out by his sin, and the convicted man had only two choices, to stay or to run.

Tom stayed week after week through 1986, and as the peculiarity of his presence abated, the real questions began. The New York of Tom's childhood, the New York that prided itself on being a diverse meritocracy of pluck and elbow grease, had been replaced in the late 1980s by one that many blacks dubbed "Up South." The bitterness particularly gripped East New York. It was in Howard Beach, an adjoining neighborhood where many from Saint Paul went for new shoes or Chinese food, that a white mob fatally chased a black passerby named Michael Griffith onto the Belt Parkway. Yusuf Hawkins, the sixteen-year-old slain by vigilantes in Bensonhurst, lived in East New York, only a few blocks from Saint Paul.

The old bromides of brotherhood would not help Tom Approbato. And it was clear to the congregation by now that he was not simply a curious friend-of-a-friend or a bleeding-heart ecumenical sort. The gossip circuit knew better: He was Ida's boyfriend, Ida's *white* boyfriend. "Another fine woman done bit the dust," the single men grumbled. "Is he sincere about church?" Ida's friends asked her. "Or is he just doing it for you?"

From the pulpit as well as the pews, Tom became the subject of close observation. He did sing the hymns. He did hold hands with his neighbors during prayer. He did not aspire to be blacker than black. Tom was a cowboy hat and "How ya doin'?" not the Kangol cap and "Yo, bro" of some poseurs whom Reverend Youngblood had known. And he kept coming, kept coming, kept coming; he walked the aisle to accept Christ, attended sixteen weeks of new members' classes, and quelled his terror of water long enough to be baptized. After services one Sunday, Douglas Slaughter said to the pastor, "Looks like you're gonna have an integrated church." The talk grew so lively, the men decided to bet fifty dollars. Reverend Slaughter had Tom staying, Reverend Youngblood not. Tom's devotion to Saint Paul, he believed, would cease if his relationship with Ida did.

Tom himself yearned for permanence. In some ways he remained the naïf on leave in Biloxi, and the same ingenuous optimism that freed his spirit at Saint Paul blinded him, perhaps, to the realities of marrying across the racial divide. Yes, he and Ida trusted each other with candor, from the early days when they had commiserated over broken marriages. Yes, they enjoyed time together without an agenda, just a seafood dinner at Red Lobster or an evening of taped soap operas on the living room VCR. Tom felt so certain of their bond that he ordered a diamond from an Australian client who owned a mine, and, with the $2,500 jewel in hand, proposed. "Anytime you're ready," he told Ida, "I've already got the diamond." He opened the velvet case and let light play against the stone's facets. "You're crazy," she answered.

He would repeat the offer many more times. Ida never said no, but she never said yes. As much as she loved Tom Approbato, the person, she could not risk alienating her children with Tom Approbato, the concept, the abstraction, as her husband and their stepfather. Tom eventually put the diamond in a safe-deposit box. He still listened sometimes to the lovestruck tape from the trip to Kansas. And on the nightstand beside his bed, he placed a photograph of Ida, trim and smiling in a swimsuit.

When he called Ida his angel, he was not speaking colloquially. She was a black angel, gorgeous and evanescent, who had brought him to faith and Saint Paul and then, in a certain sense, vanished. "Once I was in the church," he would tell those who asked why he remained, "the church was in me."

He became a tither and sang with the choir. He took a course in black psychology and taught one about death and dying. When Reverend Youngblood, during a week-long revival, asked him to welcome the visitors, Tom began, "On behalf of the white minority of Saint Paul," a sure sign of his ease. And when Helen Parilla, the graphic artist, sold buttons she designed, Tom pinned on his lapel one announcing, MY BLACKNESS IS MY BLESSING.

Not every encounter, however, was so easily finessed, for Tom was making an arduous journey indeed. From slavery days through the twentieth century, blacks had depended for survival on their ability to understand the white world and intuit its ways. But rare was the white man who traveled, in W. E. B. Du Bois's phrase, "behind the veil," and there heard the words blacks shared among themselves. Reverend Youngblood had cautioned Tom at the start that sermons would not be censored in deference to his ears. And in late 1987 the test arrived in the form of a guest preacher from Detroit. What began as an explication of Genesis and the concept of chaos evolved into an attack on "Europeans" for creating every major world problem, from nuclear proliferation to drug addiction. Later the subject of black women arose. "Her master-man," the preacher declared, "used her body and abused her dignity, despoiled her integrity, and stained her innocence." Tom Approbato walked out.

But the next week he was back. His sense of mission, if anything, was deepening. Or rather it was reaching back through time to the mission once felt by a crewcut paperboy.

At work after midnight one Sunday in early 1988, Tom found a copy of the *Star-Ledger* beside the office television. That was odd. His colleagues lived in Brooklyn and Manhattan. Why would a Newark paper be around? With the markets quiet and the phones mute, he flipped through the pages, noticing as he went an advertisement for New Brunswick Theological Seminary. He returned to linger over the ad, then folded the paper and turned on the television.

The idea of entering seminary, the old and latent dream of ministry, nagged him all the next day. And when he sat down to work that night, the *Star-Ledger* was still there, although the rest of the trash had been thrown away. Within days he was formally applying for admission. He wrote in one essay of his son Tommy and Ida Fulton and Father D'Amato, and finally of himself:

> I have been going through much soul searching and feelings of unworthiness that have made me realize that the apostles themselves were not the greatest fellows in the world nor the most holy, yet Jesus chose them. I do not know if I will ever be a great preacher or even a good one. I only know that I feel maybe 30 years ago I was called but I didn't hear, or maybe He waited till I changed to Baptist because that is what was in His plan all along. The Lord will make pastors after His own heart.

"That was my direction," Tom says from the pulpit. "I did not hear it until a year ago. It came to me in the form of a newspaper. And one thing else that the Lord did, he put sandals on my feet. He said, 'It's gonna be a rough road out ahead of you. It's gonna be winding and twisting. You're gonna find burdens, and soon you're gonna have a mountain in front of you.'" He pauses and resumes with an echo of Reverend Youngblood's sermon on Caleb. "And I pray that when they give me that mountain, they give me the rugged side."

Shouts shake the room. Women wave handkerchiefs. Men twirl their fists. The black congregation is "bearing up" the white man, seconding him and stoking him with its collective will. There are few truer barometers of preaching success.

"You see, those sandals God gave me before, they're Italian sandals." Now comes the full laughter of catharsis, of tension and release. "Anybody have Italian shoes? The pointy shoes? We call 'em roach killers. Because they get the roaches in the corner." He mimes such an assault. "You see, when you get on the mountainside, you're gonna find crevices and sometimes you're not gonna be able to get your foot in the crevice if you got a regular sandal. But if you got an Italian sandal, one kick down there, you got a foothold. And soon, soon you're gonna get to the top." He pauses to admire the imagined vista. "And then you're gonna look out and see what God has out before you, and you're gonna praise Him.

"Saint Paul, you're a blessing unto me. And I thank you. I thank you from the bottom of my heart. And as Gerry Cooney found out when they had 'The Puncher and the Preacher'"—Cooney's heavyweight fight against George Foreman, an ordained minister—"you can't fight God. Gerry Cooney, you were the last Great White Hope. But guess what? The only hope the white people gonna have is standing on the word of God. And when the whites, and they're my brothers, when they learn that Jesus is alive, then we will hold hands as Martin Luther King wants us to do, and our children will walk side by side, and this thing called racism will be dead and buried, and there ain't gonna be no resurrecting racism once God takes over this world."

This is not the Good Samaritan sermon Reverend Youngblood had dreaded. This is a brotherhood earned by a man whose whiteness was not a cloak of privilege but an accident of melanin. Reverend Youngblood thinks of Paul's Epistle to the Hebrews, when he describes Christ as being "a man of sorrows, acquainted with grief."

And the pastor is not alone in the epiphany. In the next few weeks a woman will approach Tom. He will not know her name, but he will recognize her face, for she sits every Sunday in the third row, directly facing his position in the baritone section of the choir. "I want you to forgive me," she will tell Tom, "because I used to hate you because you were white. Now I know you are human." But that moment is yet to come. For now, there is time only to end the sermon.

"See," says Tom, his tie askew, his button undone, his hair strewn loosely, his serenity manifest, "I came here tonight, and I was saying, 'Will I be successful or will I be a failure?' You see, to fail is easy. You say, 'I gave it my best shot, and now I can sit back and relax.' But if I succeed, then my road is just starting."

3

◎

FLESH AND FANTASY

S KIDDING DOWN A STREET GLAZED BY MARCH SLEET, Reverend
Johnny Ray Youngblood leads a motorcade of his staff members
toward an uncommon retreat. Three or four times each year, he
gathers his aides for several days of secluded and candid evaluation,
like a round-the-clock version of morning devotion. And generally he
rewards their efforts with congenial environs, convening at a resort in
the Poconos or at a bungalow colony upstate or, at the very least, in a
Holiday Inn conference room with silver cutlery and a mural of Paris.
This morning, however, the pastor takes his group no farther than
seven miles from Saint Paul, to the Queens neighborhood of East
Elmhurst. Down the hill from the coffee shops and Laundromats of
Northern Boulevard spill two-family homes sheathed in aluminum sid-
ing, and among them sits the low, narrow brick storefront that houses
the Alpha Missionary Baptist Church, lent to Saint Paul as a favor
between preachers.

Reverend Youngblood opens the door into a shallow front office
and within several strides enters the sanctuary, its cinder-block walls
covered by wood paneling, its storm windows fitted for godly purposes with triangles of stained glass. The room is set for his arrival,
with folding chairs arrayed around three long tables and a blackboard
screening off the altar and organ. Between the footfalls of the colleagues behind him, Reverend Youngblood can hear the metallic

shriek of planes descending into La Guardia Airport, mere blocks away. There is something appropriate about this prosaic setting, something well suited to the self-examination about to unfold. For if Saint Paul inclines toward the black church at its most grandiose and institutional, then plain Alpha, on its side street, attests to the tradition from which Saint Paul grew.

And for Reverend Youngblood that tradition serves simultaneously as comfort and threat, a force at once to be embraced and avoided. How could he feel certain of tradition when he was not always certain of his church or himself? Was Saint Paul growing too large? Were its ways becoming too rote? Was he himself losing touch? The pastor held both a passion for risk and a terror of failure, and while the war within never paralyzed him in the face of action, it left him uneasily awaiting the consequences. Youngblood the innovator once designed a commemorative plate showing the modest building Saint Paul then occupied in Brownsville and asking in bold letters, "Where do we go from here?" That Youngblood thrived on defying the conservatives who counseled, "Well, that's not the way we used to do it." Youngblood the fatalist had seen imaginative clergymen felled by hidebound congregations, and had been similarly ousted from his very first pulpit. That Youngblood would often stop during his most penetrating sermons to plead, "I wish I had somebody prayin' for me."

Nothing stilled the doubts. Just three Sundays ago, Saint Paul celebrated its sixty-second anniversary. The sanctuary was so "packed out," as the church lexicon put it, that after every pew had been filled and every folding chair crammed into an aisle, scores of worshipers stood through the entire three-hour service. Hundreds in the congregation wore African garments, as Reverend Youngblood had requested, and his own father attended from New Orleans, wearing a dashiki of the same fabric as the pastor's. Surely this was the occasion for assurance, for confirmation.

Yet success itself raised the specter of failure—not the failure of vacant seats and empty collection plates, but the failure of arrogance and impersonality, the failure of surmounting an old tradition merely to settle into a new one. The inchoate fear had been made real one afternoon in December, when Reverend Youngblood went shopping with a teenager named Shawn Hunt. It seems Shawn's mother had bought the boy a Syracuse University wool cap for Christmas, and he had discovered the gift early and worn it to school. An envious and larger classmate had relieved Shawn's head of the hat, and now he needed to find a replica to slip beneath the tree. Between sallies into sporting goods stores, Reverend Youngblood detoured to an auto supply shop to get himself a license plate frame.

"Is your brother a preacher?" the woman behind the counter asked him.

"No."

"Well," she said, pursing her lips, "you sure sound like somebody I know."

"Oh, yeah?"

"Sure sound like my pastor," she continued. "You know Johnny Youngblood?"

"Yeah, I know him. I *am* him."

"Oh, my God," she said, clamping hands to temples. "My pastor."

"And who," he asked, smiling, "are you?"

"I'm a member," she said, scrambling for an alibi. "I don't come much. I work on Sundays. This is my business." She paused. "Really."

In one sense, Reverend Youngblood loved telling the story, but in another he could not laugh at its punchline. Even as Saint Paul had expanded exponentially in his sixteen years as pastor, he had prided himself on knowing its members intimately. There were few things he loved better than sighting a single worshiper from the altar and declaiming his middle initial and second cousin and Southern hometown—Slidell or Kanapolis or Hickory Valley. In return for the personal attention, Reverend Youngblood expected personal commitment in the form of tithing, Bible study, volunteer work. Since that encounter at the shop, though, both sides of the bargain had been called into question.

Perhaps that rude epiphany was the reason he had called this peculiar retreat in a chapel bound to stir sense-memory. It was certainly the reason he had decided not to preside himself. He needed someone trusted yet distant to separate Saint Paul's reality from its comforting delusions, to flay almost literally the flesh from the fantasy. For that duty he had enlisted Ed Chambers, the executive director of the Industrial Areas Foundation, the organization that oversaw, among its twenty-eight constituent groups, East Brooklyn Congregations. Chambers stands now before the blackboard, gray hair falling to horn-rimmed glasses, pot belly pushing open tweed coat, appearing as avuncular as a classics professor. His expertise lies, however, in power and clout, concepts his alliance of reformers holds as dear as do its machine foes. The son of an Irish farm laborer who arrived alone in steerage, Chambers had studied for the priesthood until the diocese expelled him from seminary for advocating the English-language mass. Two years later, in 1957, he became an acolyte of a different sort, apprenticing himself to Saul Alinsky and learning the gospel of community organizing so thoroughly that, after Alinsky's death in 1972, he would assume his late mentor's mantle. His success since then had depended not only on empowering people who thought themselves helpless but on shocking them out of any subsequent stasis. Reverend Youngblood once saw him berate a member congregation so relentlessly that its priest eventually leaped from his seat to cry, "I'm sick and tired of you coming down on us. Enough's enough."

Already this morning, Chambers has spoken of "leadership" and "relationships," two linchpins of the Alinsky philosophy familiar to the Saint Paul staff. Now he paces the front of the room, chalk pinned between two fingers like a cigarette, warming to the contest. He draws a simple chart on the board. The three columns across the top are headed "1974," for the year Reverend Youngblood arrived at Saint Paul; "1980," for the year the church moved to Hendrix Street; and "1990," for the present. Down the far left side, Chambers writes the words "Members," "Staff," "Budget." Then he lets the audience fill the grid. The church Reverend Youngblood inherited—with a congregation of eighty-four, a staff of three, and a budget of eighteen thousand dollars—has grown to five thousand, fifty-five, and four million respectively. The numbers bring smiles, sage nods. Saint Paul is growing. Saint Paul is successful. Where is the notorious Chambers temper, the tongue Sarah Plowden always remembered comparing Brownsville, her neighborhood, to Dresden? It arrives as he adds a column on the far right, labeled "2000."

"You know what's ahead," he says, voice sharpening with censure, eyes squinting with practiced reproach. "Bureaucracy! Routine! Hardening of the arteries!"

Then, evaluating the impact of his attack, Chambers scans the room.

"How many of you do three one-on-ones a week?" he asks, using foundation slang for an individual conference.

Reverend Youngblood, Reverend Slaughter, and Shirley Raymond raise their hands.

"How many do two? One? None?"

As guilty hands lift limply, Chambers directs his stare to Leroy Howard.

"How often you go to church?"

"Every day," Leroy says carefully.

"So you do that every day, but one-on-ones just aren't that important? That it?"

"The people are important to me."

Chambers pivots and stalks away, tweed sleeves slumping down toward his elbows as he hurls his arms upward in disbelief.

"'The people.' 'The people.'" He turns again to face the staff. "Don't talk about 'the people.' That's an *abstraction*. That's *sociological* talk." For the distaste on his lips, he might have been referring to syphilis or body lice. "We're talking about the *real world*. Because the one-on-one is as important as the service. We got plenty of eleven o'clock services and not enough twelve-fifteen action. We need pews that reach into the street."

"How do you define a one-on-one?" Monica Walker asks.

"You have to experience it," Chambers says with deadpan control. "You define sex to me, I'll define a one-on-one to you."

Raucous laughter rings, and Reverend Youngblood, as if liberated by the joke, jumps from his chair to run in a tiny circle, elbows tight against his sides, fists pistoning.

"Moses," Chambers intones slowly, waiting for the bustle to subside. "What's his one-on-one? The burning bush. That's the first one-on-one I know of in history. Saul of Tarsus. A Pharisee, trained as a Roman. Establishment connections. Till he had his one-on-one on the road to Damascus."

The early church is a frequent touchstone for Chambers, an archetype of his foundation's own emphasis on shared leadership and vigorous recruitment. The later church, in turn, serves as a warning of how easily those virtues can give way to the accretion of middle management and the obsession with edifice. Now he takes up another model, more contemporary and germane to his listeners, the Nation of Islam. Under Elijah Muhammad and Malcolm X, he reminds the staff, the Nation built an empire of schools, businesses, mosques. Then he wipes one hand across an imaginary surface, as if clearing a game board of pieces, and says, "Now, whew, all gone." The room is still.

"Learn what happened," Chambers declares. "Know your history. This is black history. Because Saint Paul is a little empire." He taps the board. "I'm not impressed with five thousand members. Not impressed at all. If I had fifty-five organizers, and that's what you are, I'd have a congregation of ten thousand, going on twelve."

And even five thousand, Rochester Blanks puts in, is a pretty lie. Oh, sure, there are five thousand names on the church rolls, plenty of them people who joined only because Saint Paul was "the happening church," and dozens of others probably dead by now. Rocky knows, because as fiscal manager he ordered tithing envelopes last December for only 2,200 members, and four hundred of those remain unclaimed.

Reverend Youngblood knows, too. Five thousand is a fine, round figure for impressing his peers on the revival circuit; five thousand is what preachers, chuckling among themselves, call a "ministerial estimate." The problem is that he and Saint Paul have begun to believe it. With five thousand genuine congregants, there would be more teenagers in the Yoke Fellows, more adults in the evening classes, more children in the Saturday program known by the acronym LAMBS. Most critically, had Saint Paul based its finances upon its true membership, it would not be staggering under $970,000 in loans and mortgages, and having such trouble collecting $1.5 million in pledges toward the enlarged sanctuary. Was this the same church that in 1980 had burned its Hendrix Street mortgage eight years ahead of schedule?

Just a few moments earlier, Chambers had asked if the church's school served breakfast, and the answer was no. There were feeble excuses about the difficulty of uniting the congregation on the issue, but when Chambers asked, "Why don't you just fire a couple of people and give those kids something to eat?" his common sense convicted the whole room. The choice came down to resources, not even the resources that went into Saint Paul's moderate salaries but the ceaseless siphoning of dollars into brick, mortar, and debt service. Here was Saint Paul talking about building a high school and a youth center as proof of its commitment to children, and it could not afford oatmeal and applesauce. Or, worse, it would not, because a third grader's full stomach would never be as visible a sign of success as a brand-new building. Yet losing the young people, becoming the same sort of anachronism to them that Mother Jordan had been to him, was among the greatest of Reverend Youngblood's fears. And when he voiced it once during a meeting of elders, William Brandon, a veteran of five pastors in six decades, had answered with oracular certitude, "I've seen it happen before."

"Any positive becomes a negative," Chambers says, now prowling the aisles, left hand plunged into his coat pocket, right jabbing and slicing the air. "You push any of your positives—members, money, staff—and you'll get a negative. It's like a game of cards. You put all your winnings, all your positives, on the last hand, and then you lose it. You have more of everything, but you lost church." He pauses to let the words resonate. "And you have to ask how long you want your pastor."

"Sixty-two, Ed," Reverend Youngblood puts in. "I've already announced."

"Two thousand sixty-two?" he bellows. "You'll be dead."

"No, when *I'm* sixty-two."

"That means nothing to me," Chambers answers brusquely. "How old are you now?"

"Forty-one."

"Tell me you're leaving in 1991 and that means something. Or when you're sixty-one years old, tell me you're leaving at sixty-two. That means something."

Reverend Youngblood turns to Mike Gecan, one of Chambers's top assistants, who has just entered the room. "Help me," the pastor says, as if soliciting a favored sibling's influence with their cantankerous father.

"You gotta make room at the top," Chambers continues. "Guy like Doug Slaughter, you'll lose him. We'll make room for him before you do. You can't keep that talent, that charisma, locked up under a prima donna." He slowly moves his gaze across the entire staff.

"You've gotta help your pastor. Otherwise you'll bury him in five years. And when he's gone, you'll say, 'Why'd we work him so hard?'"

After a long silence, Reverend Youngblood asks Chambers and Gecan to leave so he can debrief the staff himself. A plane roars barely above the roof. Chatter drifts from the front office, where a member has arrived with platters of cold cuts for lunch. And like clouds of road dust, Chambers's harshest words hover in his slipstream. *Hardening of the arteries ... Not enough twelve-fifteen action ... You lost church ... You'll bury him.*

"Reactions?" the pastor asks quietly, moving from a table to the blackboard.

"Challenging," says Monica.

"Prophetic," offers Doug.

"I feel motivated and energized," Brenda Nealy says, "but at the same time reluctant."

Mary McCormick, an administrative assistant to Reverend Slaughter, simply emits an exhausted moan.

"Those are not foreign words to us," Reverend Youngblood says. "They ain't new. It's just saying you got to keep your growing edge." The phrase belongs to Howard Thurman, his favorite theologian. "Did anybody feel fear?"

"It'll be twice as hard the next ten years." Leroy Howard sighs.

"I'm only a volunteer," adds Sherry Walker, who helps in the youth ministry, "and I feel tired already."

There is slow, rueful laughter.

"Ed didn't tell us anything we haven't talked about among ourselves," Reverend Youngblood says. "We suffer from a kind of organizational rigor mortis—a laziness, no desire to change. We're hypocrites, tellin' folk to do the stuff we don't want to. We've just got to be open to all God's ways of working with us."

The morning's ruthless reckoning has confirmed much for the pastor. During the New Year's Eve service, known in the church as Watch Night, he had preached the story of Gideon from the Book of Judges. It was not the man himself who interested Reverend Youngblood as much as God's use of him. First He orders Gideon to lead the Israelites, with an army of but 32,000, against the Midianites, 100,000 strong. Then, on the eve of battle, He forces Gideon to pare his own troops down to ten thousand. Then He dictates yet another cut, leaving a paltry three hundred. And then He delivers to Gideon the victory. As he taught the story in his sermon, Reverend Youngblood reminded the congregation that the Bible abounded in examples of the few defeating the many, each victory the divine reward for faith and sacrifice. It was a familiar message, so familiar that few heard its personal relevance any longer.

Until, abandoning the text, Reverend Youngblood did something startling. He dared his people to leave the church, to get up and walk out—not in the future, not at their leisure, but right then, in the middle of a service nearly equal in importance to those on Easter and Good Friday. In case anybody doubted him, thought this was just Pastor being outrageous, he returned to the challenge time after time as the sermon proceeded, his rage by the benediction softening into patronizing pity. "Be it known," he said, "that if you feel you have done all that God assigned to your hands to do, God bless you, go home. If there are those of you who feel honestly that you just can't do what the Lord wants you to do, go home. If there's those that have to leave exactly at midnight, go home. Go home. But if you understand what the call of Christ is all about, you need to know tonight that the Lord needs some soldiers."

That was the public self, the strong man, looking outward. Now, in this sanctuary of wood paneling and linoleum tile, the reminder of a past that seems capable still of devouring the present, the private self, looking inward, must answer his own question about fear.

"The thing I'm most afraid of," Reverend Youngblood tells his staff, "is that I will preside over the death of that which I gave birth to."

One morning in June 1974, on his third Sunday as pastor of Saint Paul, Reverend Youngblood was standing in the lobby after service, shaking hands with his departing congregants. As the sanctuary emptied and the receiving line thinned, he noticed a white man lurking near the radiator in the corner, dressed on this formal occasion in a windbreaker and khaki slacks.

"Who is that?" the young minister asked a deacon.

"Mr. Poulos, the contractor. He came to collect the check."

"A check for what?"

"He says we owe him a thousand dollars."

Without knowing more, Reverend Youngblood knew Saint Paul

could not pay. Already this morning he had learned that two other
checks had bounced, each for only seventy dollars and one to the
church's own musician. The chairman of the board of trustees, leading
a rebellion against the new pastor, refused even to show him the
books. Those records remained with the chairman, a man named Josh
Sanford, into whose shoe store, it was rumored, a share of the weekly
offering found its way. And now, when Reverend Youngblood asked
the contractor why he had come dunning on a Sunday, the man
replied, "Josh Sanford told me to."

Maybe he should not have felt so amazed, so appalled. He had
been warned, all right, if not about Josh Sanford, then surely about
Saint Paul. This was the church that had fallen from five hundred
members to barely eighty. This was the church that had driven away its
greatest pastor and replaced him with an assistant with a weakness for
drink. This was the church that had not even had a pastor for the past
year, dragooning reluctant applicants to its pulpit week after week.

When Reverend Youngblood had delivered his trial sermon two
months earlier, he had plotted to sabotage his own candidacy. Twenty-
six years old, and a Brooklynite for only ten months, he had intended
to wait several years before seeking any pulpit. Besides, he was already
earning nine thousand dollars annually as the assistant to Reverend
William Augustus Jones of Bethany Baptist Church, a minister of
national renown. Why trade that for one hundred dollars weekly and
the likelihood of failure? So on the day of his audition, he prefaced his
preaching by saying how very content he was at Bethany, and in case
the subtle method failed, he executed a cold and hasty exit once the
service was over. The only thing he could not bring himself to booby-
trap was the sermon itself, and his exegesis of Job won him the job.
The day the new pastor informed his mentor, Reverend Jones simply
said, "You're going to one of God's Alcatrazes."

Having been sentenced, whether by the divine hand or rotten
luck, Reverend Youngblood now had to act. He persuaded the contractor to wait until the end of the month to be paid, giving him two
Sundays to appeal to the congregation. Then he summoned Josh Sanford to a meeting of the board of trustees two evenings hence. After
songs and prayers, they faced each other across the table, the preacher
with the muttonchops and billowing Afro that advertised his youth,
the trustee old enough to be his grandfather, all gray hair and tanned-

leather skin. Reverend Youngblood had already decided on confrontation; if he was going to get fired, it might as well be now.

"How could something like this happen?" he began.

"I didn't know—"

"You didn't know?" Reverend Youngblood said, cutting off the older man.

"I thought—"

"You thought? You *thought*? How can you tell me you thought and made a mistake like that?" He was shouting and hammering the table, his fury displacing his fright. "If I'd done that, y'all would tar and feather me and ride me outta town on a rail!"

"Then I quit!" Sanford shouted back, tossing his ring of church keys across the table. The jangling ceased and the keys lay on the varnished wood, as tangible a challenge as any knightly gauntlet. Reverend Youngblood snatched and pocketed the ring before Sanford could change his mind. "Next item of business," he announced, and two more trustees resigned.

After they stalked home and the three bewildered holdovers voted to adjourn, the pastor remained in his office, free now to tremble with terror. What if this victory was only temporary? He was still a stranger to his own congregation, while Sanford was a veteran of countless coups and palace revolts. He prayed for a sign that he had acted wisely, and as he looked up from his desk he saw a deacon, Thad Johnson, passing in the hall. At Reverend Youngblood's invitation, Johnson stepped into the office, lifted his arms and started to speak, then fell mute. He tiptoed back to the door, closed it on the prying world, and said, "Pastor, we been tryin' to do that for twelve years."

It would be six months before Reverend Youngblood could believe he had exorcised Josh Sanford permanently, but he understood now that he did have allies in Saint Paul. One clearly was Thad Johnson. Another was Frank Taylor, the part-time custodian. The third and most enduring was Sarah Plowden, an outsider who would become both friend and foil. By design, Reverend Youngblood reached beyond the congregation for his assistant, because he felt he needed the loyalty of one unfettered by Saint Paul's traditions. Sarah, for that matter, rarely attended church anywhere, never having found in New York the familial spirit she remembered from the services of her Southern childhood. What she brought was a cautious nature, a qual-

ity of regarding someone sidelong even when facing him eye to eye, as
well as the varied skills of a former seamstress, nurse's aide, bookkeeper, toy assembler, and pet shop proprietor. Normally, then, Sarah
enjoyed options. But in the summer of 1974, recovering from surgery,
she was limited to part-time work within walking distance of home.
Saint Paul offered both for fifty dollars weekly, enough money for
Sarah to treat her husband to movies and her children to ice cream.
Before she even heard her new employer preach, she saw him wielding
a broom. It was an acute if unwitting metaphor for the housecleaning
endeavor she was about to join.

The Saint Paul population, small and poor as it was, had further
divided into clubs, each with its own checking account and a decided
indifference to the church's communal fortunes. There were clubs for
members from North Carolina, South Carolina, and Georgia. There
was a Floral Club. There was the Missionary Society. Voluntarism was
so rare that the handful who practiced it had their own club, the Willing Workers. The church building, as a result, suffered from neglect
and privation. Sparks shot from light fixtures. Sockets by the dozen
went without bulbs. Water poured inside one wall because a beer can
was clogging a drainpipe. The office served as an indoor Dumpster for
broken seats, stale mints, outdated bulletins, and even a concrete
planter. What was not ruined was often ridiculous, since the structure
had been planned not for praise and contemplation but for the frip-
peries of its original inhabitant, the Nonpareil Social Club. The faithful worshiped in a former theater on the second floor, with murals of
Southern belles on the rear wall and an altar assembled from bare plywood. The sanctuary could be reached only by a stairwell so narrow
that during funerals the pallbearers had to dangle their coffin halfway
out the window to negotiate one turn.

Reverend Youngblood and Sarah Plowden, marooned together,
made the only promise they felt certain they could keep: Every Sunday
there would be one improvement the congregation could see. One
Sunday the bulletin bore a handsome drawing of the church. The
next, a plain pine door boasted oak veneer. By the one after that, Bible
verses in Old English calligraphy had replaced the Southern belles.
With a new board of trustees installed, Reverend Youngblood finally
obtained the financial records, and in her inspection of them Sarah discovered the church had overpaid its utility bills by $2,300. Once

recovered, that money went to new tile, fresh paint, rewired lights, and hallway signs that said, FIND BURIED TREASURE IN YOUR BIBLE.

And who could object? In a very real way, Reverend Youngblood was giving Saint Paul something for nothing. Then, three months into his tenure, the bill came due. As the congregants entered the sanctuary that particular Sunday, they saw the pulpit laden like the pushcarts on Belmont Avenue, with ten oranges, ten apples, ten cans of yams, ten jars of jelly. All through the service the food sat inexplicably on display, until the time arrived for Reverend Youngblood's sermon. He turned to the Book of Malachi. As Bible students knew, Malachi was not the name of a prophet, but a noun meaning "message," and the pastor took his from the tenth verse of the third chapter:

Bring ye all the tithes into the storehouse, that there may be meat in mine house, and prove me now herewith, saith the Lord of hosts, if I will not open you the windows of heaven, and pour you out a blessing, that there shall not be enough room to receive it.

The lesson, reduced to its core, was as simple as "Give, and you shall receive." To lend that command specificity, Reverend Youngblood cited the verse in Numbers that set the proportion of tithing at one-tenth. Then he moved one apple, one orange, one can, one jar to the edge of the pulpit, where they would symbolically become God's. From this Sunday forward, he explained, he wanted his people to follow the same principle, not by donating their food but their salary, ten percent of their weekly income. Gross, he added, not net. God didn't pay no never-mind to union dues or withholding tax.

Beneath a surface of compliance, mutiny rumbled. "What you plannin' to do with all that money?" some members and even one deacon asked. "This a church or a bank?" One afternoon, with her own washing machine broken, Sarah visited a nearby Laundromat. As her four loads spun and churned, she heard the woman beside her grousing about a church up the hill that had a new minister. "He's takin' over," the woman said. "He's changin' everything around. Folks can't have their clubs. They gotta give all their money to church." Then she added grudgingly, "But they got a lotta young people up there."

Reverend Youngblood was at war with tradition—if not with the proud history of the black church, then certainly with the customs passed unquestioningly from generation to generation. He announced the battle in myriad ways—reading the Emancipation Proclamation from the pulpit, telling critics he shed "two tears in a bucket" for their concerns, and most of all repeating one favorite parable. A little girl sees her mother cutting the wings off a chicken she is about to roast. When the girl asks why, the mother says, "Because that's the way my momma always did it." So the girl asks her grandmother, who answers, "Because that's the way *my* momma always did it." Finally the girl asks her great-grandmother, who says, "Because my pan was too small."

Trying to unify his congregation, Reverend Youngblood collapsed the three state clubs into one, which would soon be dismantled. The Floral Club was transformed into volunteers to help Frank Taylor beautify the church. And the Willing Workers disbanded because, the pastor argued, "If you ain't willin' to work, why you here?" Even tithing, the tithing that foes claimed would take food from their babies' mouths, began to win converts. No longer did Saint Paul need to sell chicken dinners to survive. No longer did the congregation need to endure ministerial harangues, filibusters, and public shamings every time the bank balance slipped too low. People saw their tithes pay college tuition for several children and paint the entire church for Christmas. By the end of 1974, after only seven months as pastor, Reverend Youngblood had raised thirty thousand dollars, nearly twice the church's income in the previous year.

He saved part of the money, as he would each year, because he burned with plans. Why couldn't Saint Paul have a school, a credit union, a day-care center? Why couldn't it buy the vacant lot next door for a playground? Why couldn't it transport the elderly with its own vans? Reverend Youngblood would drag Sarah with him for visits to the finest black churches in Brooklyn—Concord, Cornerstone, Mount Lebanon—and across the river to the great limestone landmark of John D. Rockefeller and Harry Emerson Fosdick, Riverside Church. As they walked through the nave, surrounded by 2,500 empty seats and dwarfed by Gothic arches eight stories tall, the obscure minister told his part-time assistant, "Someday I'm gonna preach here." Sarah thought to herself, *He's hallucinating.*

Her pessimism derived from a keen sense of reality, for reality had a way of brutally intruding even on Reverend Youngblood's dreams. Every several months, thieves broke into Saint Paul, on one occasion carrying away three thousand dollars' worth of recording equipment as the Youth Choir was rehearsing unaware. Then, in 1977, an elderly and widowed member named Alice Scott was murdered, strangled with her own stocking by a junkie who made off with five dollars. Alice's apartment stood but three doors from Saint Paul, and it was Reverend Youngblood who discovered the body. He could not forget how Alice had always invited him over after Watch Night services; if a very dark man was your first visitor in the new year, black folk belief had it, he would bring you good luck.

Within the church a different kind of crisis loomed. One morning after services, a deacon pulled aside Reverend Youngblood to ask, "What are we gonna do about these two girls stickin' out pretty bad?" Sharon Reynolds was unmarried and pregnant. Faustina Johnson was both those things and more. She was a soloist in the Youth Choir, president of the Junior Usher Board, a star student in mathematics at Wingate High School—in all ways, then, a role model, an example. As if understanding the special disgrace that her maternity would bring, she had managed to hide her swelling belly for six months under floppy sweaters and crossed arms. Once she started showing, her every fear was realized. "That boy was no good," one woman told her. Another advised, "You shouldn't come to church no more." Faustina withdrew first from choir and ushering, and then began avoiding Sunday services altogether. Her friends stopped inviting her for bowling, roller skating, picnics on Staten Island. Sharon was subjected to a similar quarantine.

What indeed, as the deacon had asked, would Reverend Youngblood do? A sizable part of the congregation, it was clear, wanted the pastor to condemn the girls publicly, lest God Himself appear to sanction babies having babies. If the church would not decry this plague of ignorant mothers and runaway fathers, who in the black community would? Yet for reasons nobody in his congregation knew then, Reverend Youngblood could not fulfill the obligations of Old Testament wrath. Faustina and Sharon were Jackie McDonald, were himself. It was impossible for him also to be Mother Jordan, to order those girls as far east of Eden as he had been cast. And what would be the virtue in exile? The babies, the innocents, would be the ultimate victims.

Reverend Youngblood sought out Faustina's boyfriend, like her a lifelong member of Saint Paul, to determine his intentions. Learning they were vague, and knowing what that vaguery meant, the pastor began to weave a new family around Faustina. He encouraged the Youth Choir to throw the girl a surprise shower. On the day Faustina gave birth to a daughter named Natasha, Reverend Youngblood called her long distance from an out-of-town preaching assignment. And on a Sunday several weeks later, when both Sharon and Faustina cobbled up enough courage to attend church with their newborns, the pastor summoned them to the altar. "What does he want with us?" Faustina whispered to her friend as they crept up the aisle. "What's he gonna say?" Perhaps only now, with them visible and vulnerable, would he render his sentence. Perhaps he would drag in their boyfriends and forcibly wed both couples on the spot. With her baby in the crook of her arm, Faustina shivered and fought back tears.

Instead Reverend Youngblood reached inside the pulpit for a small jar of holy oil, blessing each baby as he touched his thumb to its forehead. Then he spoke through the mothers to the entire congregation. "I don't want nobody puttin' you down," he said. "I don't want nobody tellin' you that you done wrong. Look, God is not gonna hold against you having these babies. What God will hold against you is not giving these babies a better life than you have." When the service ended, the same people who had snubbed the girls pressed ten-dollar bills into their pockets, saying, "This is for the child." One volunteered to be Natasha's godmother.

In the years ahead, Sharon would fall away from church and into drugs, farming her child out to various relatives. Faustina's boyfriend would flee upstate, claiming he was seeking work, and never see her or his daughter again. Faustina Johnson, however, would graduate from both Wingate and a trade school, rise from typist to customer service representative at a Manhattan bank, become a tither at Saint Paul, and send to its elementary school her daughter Natasha.

But at the time of the baby blessing, in the summer of 1978, there was no school. There was no playground, no fleet of vans. There were no Yoke Fellows, no LAMBS, no Eldad-Medad, no Christ Square. These existed only in Reverend Youngblood's most extravagant imaginings. For the membership he served, Saint Paul had grown successful enough to earn its leisure. The congregation was nearing six hundred, filling the sanctuary from the choir loft to the rear windows for two services each Sunday. The church that had bounced seventy-dollar checks a few years earlier now claimed savings in the tens of thousands. The pastor was a rising star on the revival circuit.

Yet Reverend Youngblood increasingly felt not pride but disgust. One afternoon, instead of driving home for dinner, he sat in his nine-year-old Buick, staring at the church. He remembered how in his first years as pastor, trying to supplement his salary, he had performed funerals at mortuaries for thirty-five dollars apiece. And the word popped into his mind: *formaldehyde*. This building was a corpse stinking of formaldehyde. He saw only three choices for Saint Paul: expand, move, or lose him. Expansion, he already knew, was impossible, because the block narrowed to a sharp triangular corner. Moving would demand financial risk from people just learning to savor financial security. Even a collaborator as devoted as Sarah Plowden assumed the pastor was bound to exhaust his energy soon.

"Lord," Reverend Youngblood said aloud in his car, "I believe You sent me here. But You gotta show me. Can anything happen here? I can't stay if nothing can happen."

He found his response later that day in the Book of Ezekiel, a most unlikely source of practical advice. Not for Ezekiel were proverbs and parables, witticisms and wisdoms. An exiled priest, condemned to die in Babylonian captivity, he wrote of visions and phantasms that he himself seemed barely to comprehend. It was perhaps the most famous of these that drew a disconsolate preacher's attentions:

> The hand of the Lord was upon me and carried me out in the spirit of the Lord, and set me down in the midst of the valley which was full of bones.
>
> And caused me to pass by them round about: and behold, there were very many in the open valley; and, lo, they were very dry.
>
> And he said unto me, Son of man, can these bones live? And I answered, O Lord God, thou knowest.

The dry bones, which Ezekiel surely equated with the Jews who had abandoned their holy laws, Reverend Youngblood could see in the pews every Sunday. They were the people who warned, "You're goin' too fast." They were Josh Sanford delivering his parting curse, "Just wait six months and it'll all hit the fan." They were, much as he hated to admit it, a timorous and stunted part of his own psyche, which whispered after every triumph, *This far and no farther.*

At a cerebral level, Reverend Youngblood understood the scripture's reply to his dilemma. As Ezekiel prophesied, God joined the bones together, clothed the skeletons in sinews and skin, and finally breathed life into the forms until "they stood up upon their feet, an exceeding great army." But that was Ezekiel in the Bible. He was Johnny Ray Youngblood, barely thirty, in Brooklyn. He read and reread the verses, poked and pricked at them, seeking revelation, a revelation that had never manifested itself in all the times he had heard others preach the passage. Then, searching for certainty, he discovered the answer in doubt. *O Lord God, thou knowest.* Ezekiel's was the voice of an abject man, a man afflicted by apparitions, a man capable only of turning God's question back on God, and in his seeming futility making the existential leap of faith. And that was the insight Reverend Youngblood brought to the pulpit the next Sunday.

> I can hear Ezekiel sayin', "You askin' me, 'Can they live?' I don't wanna be dealin' with this in the first place. I'm not of my own mind in the first place. And then You wanna engage in a dialogue with me? You got me out here in the midst of this valley and You wanna know from me 'Can they live?'"
>
> Ezekiel didn't say yes, because he doubted. This was Death Valley, the cemetery. Couldn't say yes because of his belief. Couldn't say no because of who asked. So he took the middle ground. "Lord God, thou knowest."
>
> And I needed this word for myself. Because every now and then, I think this ministry's on me. I start thinkin' I'm supposed to have all the answers. Every now and then I become disenchanted and disgusted, and I don't know which way to go. And when I start feelin' depressed and thinking about goin' to the Big House and turnin' in my hoe, I remember what Ezekiel said: "Lord God, thou knowest."
>
> God's will is not that we be confined to ghettos and ghetto thinking. We are to look to glory and honor and majesty. We're the people of God. Our world may be a valley and we may be

dry bones, but God provides somebody in the midst. God wants us to know all of us are inextricably intertwined in the salvation process.

A few months later, in May 1979, a member named Talitha Portee, who worked in a nearby hospital, told Reverend Youngblood she had heard from a chaplain of a synagogue for sale in East New York. That September, Saint Paul made a down payment of $99,000 on the $185,000 property. And on February 10, 1980, the anniversary of the day Adolphus Smith was called as pastor in 1938, the congregation first worshiped on Hendrix Street. *Just once before I die,* Reverend Youngblood prayed to himself, *God let me fill this sanctuary.*

That plea would be granted hundreds of times, and many ministers, surveying the crowds, might well have considered their mission accomplished. But Reverend Youngblood's faith needed challenge beyond the already converted. There was still a world outside the sanctuary doors, another valley of dry bones, strewn across the land that had once inspired American dreams.

When John R. Pitkin arrived in New Lots in 1835, with money and ambition accrued as a Connecticut merchant, he found a farming district little different from the Dutch settlement it had been 150 years earlier. What he envisioned, however, was consummately urban. On the land then given to potatoes and wheat, dairy cows and swine, the land known as "the Market Garden of the United States," he would build factories and shops and homes and schools. Just to make clear whose primacy he intended to challenge, he would name his city East New York.

He bought 135 acres of land, erecting a shoe factory on one parcel, and dividing the rest into lots that sold for from ten to twenty-five dollars. He named the first new thoroughfare Broadway. And for those ignorant or skeptical of his plans, he published a monthly newspaper called *The Mechanic,* thick with hyperbole and self-promotion.

The Panic of 1837 ended Pitkin's dreams of metropolitan grandeur, reducing him to serving as the auctioneer of his own assets. But he was not without a legacy. Broadway came to bear his name. The shoe factory and the workers who built cottages around it spearheaded the area's shift from agriculture to industry. The proper name

"East New York" supplanted "New Lots" in records and on maps. And Pitkin's experience of economic cataclysm, of whirlwind change, would prove sadly prophetic.

But that reckoning lay more than a century in the future. Through the remaining decades of the 1800s, East New York grew gradually on the talents of German immigrants as brushmakers, gold-beaters, and tailors. With the installation of five subway and trolley lines between 1880 and 1922, a genuine boom began. From Manhattan's Lower East Side and the older Brooklyn district of Bushwick streamed Italians and Jews and Russians and Poles, filling tenements between the Jamaica Avenue El on the north and the Livonia Avenue trestle to the south. They bottled milk and brewed beer and stitched clothes and cast dies. Along factory assembly lines, they made products ranging from starch to fireworks, toys to torpedoes.

Rarely did East New York's families ascend above the echelon of the working poor, yet collectively they supported a vital neighborhood. They had by 1943 deposited $32 million in the East New York Savings Bank. Schools, churches, and synagogues studded Pennsylvania Avenue, the widest artery. Small businesses flourished, from the smokehouses beside the tracks that cured lox and sturgeon to Teddy's Barbershop with its tureen of steaming towels to Gertz's Girdletorium, where customers were reassured, "It's Fashionable to Be Thrifty."

The smells of East New York were of horseradish being grated fresh from the root and coal tumbling down the basement chute. The sounds were of brooms sweeping sidewalks and balls bouncing against stoops. Their elbows resting on pillows in open windows, mothers surveyed the world and found it satisfying. Yes, some of the kids drag-raced along Eastern Parkway and even stole hubcaps by night. Yes, a friend managed accounts for a bookie. But everyone knew East New York wasn't fancy like Crown Heights or Midwood. It was rich in experience, rich in family—Uncle Harry on Livonia, *Bubbe* Rebecca and *Zayde* Sam on Lott, cousins Doris and Cecile just down Blake.

Yet East New York was never quite the idyll of some expatriates' memories. A reputation for crime was born in the 1860s around its racetrack, road houses, and Civil War encampment. Arson and burglary became nearly nightly events, and gang battles turned so violent that one area was dubbed "Blood Hollow." In later decades East New York would supply a stronghold for Jewish mobsters like Abe "Kid

Twist" Reles and their Italian successors, including Henry Hill, who was raised to popular-culture celebrity by the film *GoodFellas*. Organized crime aside, what passed for prosperity in East New York depended on industrial jobs, the very jobs that from 1950 onward spun into an unending decline. Absentee landlords owned two-thirds of the neighborhood's housing. As early as 1951, a time that would be sentimentalized in retrospect, a community leader named Milton Goell was warning, "Where Brownsville meets East New York ... there is a tortured spot of the city, rampant with ugliness.... One block off busy Sutter Avenue ... is a stagnant slum, dead in the daytime and ominous at night. It sprawls, a hodgepodge of generally ancient factories and two-family shacks."

The solution that Goell and others advocated—the construction of public housing on a sweeping scale—in some ways would prove the scourge rather than the salvation of East New York. Thousands of blacks displaced by the new projects rising throughout New York City moved into East New York, where the prevalence of rental housing and the relatively liberal politics of Jewish residents eased integration, if only briefly. Their friends and relatives, part of the huge postwar black migration northward, flocked to the neighborhood from Virginia, Georgia, and the Carolinas. By the late 1950s, East New York north of the Livonia Avenue trestle was attaining a black and Puerto Rican majority. Some whites left willingly for Long Island or the new subdivisions of Canarsie, where a home could be had for less than one thousand dollars down. Many others, however, were wrenched loose by real-estate speculation, property crime, and racial tension, forces sharing a particularly insidious symbiosis.

East New York had always endured crime, but whether the work of Murder Incorporated or the Lucchese family, it had been social deviance within the ethnic and racial tribe. When it was a black or Puerto Rican who snatched a shopper's handbag or mugged a postal worker returning from the night shift, however, new and different fears arose, fears that the indistinguishable dark mass known as "they" were "taking over." It did not matter that, statistically, East New York through the late 1950s had a rate of juvenile delinquency substantially *lower* than Brooklyn's or New York City's. The social problems that had loomed over the neighborhood before the influx of minorities, from unrepaired housing to overcrowded schools to a weakening economic base, were conveniently obscured by the emotions of race. And realtors stood ready to mint money from panic.

"If you don't get out now," went their pitch to homeowners, "in a year or two it'll be worth nothing." Many brokers did more than simply stimulate the transaction; they would buy low from whites, who welcomed them as the last resort, and then sell high to blacks, who thanked them for admission to the middle class. City welfare authorities made East New York a favorite dumping ground for clients with housing allowances. Mortgage companies and corrupt public officials joined in the bonanza, inflating the incomes of black applicants so they could receive mortgages backed by the Federal Housing Administration. Once the new homeowners predictably defaulted, the company kept whatever principal and interest had already been recouped, then collected insurance from the FHA and finally resold the homes, kicking back a share of the profits to complicit housing officials.

The longtime residents of East New York, unaware of such machinations, ascribed the disaster around them to race alone. Jewish families, renters for the most part, could generally escape without great losses. But the Italians south of the Livonia Avenue trestle, the Mason-Dixon Line between white and black, would not so readily surrender the brick bungalows many had built by hand. And in July of 1966, as the profiteers of urban trauma tallied their gains, the neighborhood hurtled toward civil war.

For nearly a week, amid the summer's worst heat wave and against the backdrop of riots in Cleveland and Chicago, groups of Italians, Puerto Ricans, and blacks skirmished with guns, bricks, pipes, chains, and Molotov cocktails. On the night of July 21, about thirty young Italians claiming allegiance to a glorified gang called SPONGE—Society for the Prevention of Niggers Getting Everything—held a protest march replete with banners declaring, "Go Back to Africa, Niggers." Twenty-five blacks hurled bottles of beer and soda at them before withdrawing. Bursting through police barricades, the whites gave chase, and as the mob entered a largely black area, it came under sniper fire. None of the whites was hit, but an eleven-year-old black child named Eric Dean was struck and killed.

Once word of his slaying spread, looting and insurrection erupted across thirty-three square blocks. Where seventy-five police officers normally patrolled, one thousand were dispatched, and thousands more around the city were held at their posts in reserve. When Mayor John V. Lindsay arrived in the neighborhood to appeal for order, whites pelted his car with rocks and shouted for him, too, to go to Africa. The next morning, news of the riot shoved aside reports on the Vietnam War and the Gemini 10 space mission as the lead story in *The New York Times*. Next to the article appeared a photograph of a garbage can crashing through a butcher shop's window. On the shard of glass that remained in the window frame could be seen the Hebrew letters for the word *kosher*.

Such imagery proved nearly as destructive as the event itself. The Italian blocks south of Livonia turned black almost instantly. By the end of 1966, East New York had undergone a racial change of eighty percent in a decade. And among the greatest losers in the sudden, violent upheaval were the working-class blacks who had only sought in East New York the same modest virtues as their white predecessors. What these blacks inherited was hardly worth possessing. "In the aftermath of the riots," one account put it, "some sections resembled ghost towns. Accumulated debris lay untouched. Disemboweled cars and shattered glass blanketed the streets. There were dozens of vacated, burned-out, and destroyed homes and stores, their doors ajar, their windows smashed."

A generation later, the conditions of life were arguably even worse. The Seventy-fifth Precinct, which covers East New York, regularly placed in the top two or three citywide for violent crime. In the number of fires and false alarms, the neighborhood also excelled. Of all the community districts in Brooklyn, it counted the second-highest number of welfare recipients, foster-care placements, and cases of abused children. Barely half of its adults had graduated from high school, and four in ten households were led by a single mother. With its AIDS incidence more than doubling each year, East New York counted more cases than seventeen states. The infant-mortality rate was comparable to that of Panama.

In other eras, education and commerce had served as the social ladders for East New York's proletariat, but by the late 1980s these ladders had collapsed. Trying to control a contagion of weapons, the neighborhood's high school, Thomas Jefferson, installed metal detectors at its doors. While reading scores sank in the elementary and junior high schools, the community school board responsible for them doled out millions of dollars in patronage jobs. One particular principal, known as "the Cookie Monster," enlisted her staff to sell junk food to pupils at a three-hundred-percent markup. The local economy, which had once bristled with vigor, now belonged to a handful of Dominican or Palestinian *bodegas* and to the "gray-market" merchants who appeared unpredictably along Linden Boulevard, selling everything from couches to crabs from the tailgates of semi trailers. Only crack and prostitution could be deemed growth industries.

If any corner of the city cried for brave and decent political leadership, East New York did. And if the abrupt white flight should have left any perverse advantage, it would have been to make room for black reformers on the order of State Assemblyman Albert Vann or Congressman Major R. Owens, who served other sections of Brooklyn. Instead, the same white machine that had always ruled East New York continued to rule it through proven black allies—City Councilwoman Priscilla A. Wooten, State Assemblyman Edward Griffith, and Congressman Edolphus Towns. The organization continued to oversee the vast patronage apparatus of Community Board Five and the District Nineteen Community School Board.

With Brooklyn Borough President Howard Golden acting as his mentor, Towns had served simultaneously as Deputy Borough President and Democratic district leader for East New York, prior to being sent to Washington. Wooten was a protégé of Samuel Wright, a black councilman who, through much of the 1970s, controlled a $30 million network of schools, day-care centers, and antipoverty programs in Brownsville.* Wright, in turn, had learned at the knee of Brooklyn Democratic boss Meade Esposito, even assuming the leadership of Esposito's political club. As for Griffith, he had emerged from the John F. Kennedy Democratic Club, whose longtime leader, Mike Wollin, was ultimately rewarded for his machine loyalties with a judgeship. While Wooten and Towns sporadically drew scrutiny—she for residing illegally in a subsidized middle-income apartment, he for eliciting a $1,300 kickback from a contractor in a sting operation—Griffith glided along, genial and innocuous, running virtually unopposed

---

* Wright was eventually convicted of accepting a $5,000 bribe from a company selling textbooks to School District Twenty-three, which had the lowest reading scores of any district in the city.

term after term. (Towns avoided indictment by returning most of the money.)

Certainly the disaffection and hopelessness in East New York served all three politicians well; only twenty-nine percent of voting-age adults cast ballots in presidential elections, to say nothing of local races in off-years. But another clue to their longevity arose in February 1990, when Michael Leonard, a Saint Paul member who works as a probation officer, announced he would run against Griffith. Within days, Griffith sent a certified letter to Reverend Youngblood inviting the church to seek a state grant, with an application form attached. Thirty minutes after the missive arrived, one of the assemblyman's top aides telephoned Leroy Howard with the suggestion that seven thousand dollars was a nice round figure. This was the very same Griffith who had refused to write a recommendation in 1989 when Saint Paul wanted to build senior citizens' housing. Reverend Youngblood refused to apply for the state grant, but Michael Leonard did abandon his campaign, and soon afterward found himself invited to join a political club affiliated with the machine.

It was small wonder, then, that when Reverend Youngblood spoke of politics, he often turned to Ephesians:

> For we wrestle not against flesh and blood, but against principalities, against powers, against the rulers of the darkness of this world, against spiritual wickedness in high places.

And if he needed yet another reminder of what public service really meant in East New York, he would receive it on the morning when the brass of the Seventy-fifth Precinct came to meet with the Stanley–Van Siclen Merchants Association.

Leroy Howard leans through the chapel door to tell the merchants that the police are waiting for them in Elders Hall. This is the last moment to talk strategy. It has taken Leroy and Shirley Raymond weeks to arrange this encounter, because they would not settle for anything less than an audience with the precinct's commanding officer, Deputy Inspector Patrick J. Carroll. Between church members and shopkeepers, eighteen people will face Carroll and two sergeants, a promising ratio. And since the association has hired an overnight security guard, demonstrating its own commitment to reducing crime around Christ Square, it can approach the police with particular credibility. The pizza man, the greengrocer, the pharmacist, and the rest will ask no more of their public servants than they have already given of themselves.

Still, Leroy knows that the anger runs even higher now than it did when Saint Paul revived the merchants' group two months ago. In the past week alone, a nineteen-year-old boy was shot in a barbershop on Van Siclen, and delivery drivers were robbed twice outside Key Food. A gang burst into the waiting room of a medical clinic, forced an elderly patient to the floor, and stripped her of her jewelry; when the doctor heard the commotion and emerged from an examining room, she thought the woman was suffering an epileptic seizure.

But it is Junior Roman, the dry cleaner, who has the stories that most explain the rage. The other night, as he was sleeping as usual in his store, he heard footsteps on the roof. He called 911 and was told an officer could not be dispatched on such a flimsy tip. By the time the private guard arrived, the cash register of the Chinese restaurant next door had been emptied. And while the cops ignore him, Junior continues, the housing inspector visits plenty. All he did was cover his roof with sheet metal to stop burglars, and now he's been socked with a one-thousand-dollar fine.

"Only thing I want to know," says Richard Lavecchia, the other dry cleaner on Stanley Avenue, "is did the cops bring us bats?"

"Welfare checks are due tomorrow," adds Fred Wein, the pharmacist, "so there's gonna be a lot more predators out."

Ernest Viscardi, who owns the pizzeria, suggests putting parking meters along Stanley Avenue, which at least would force the police to appear several times daily to issue tickets.

"If we have meter there," J. T. Chun, the greengrocer, answers, "they break meter every night. There's coins there. Like telephone."

Leroy reminds the merchants that the police have only one hour. There is no point talking anymore among themselves. Be ready to compromise. Don't let the meeting devolve into a shouting match. Stick together.

The pep talk complete, he leads the merchants into Elders Hall, where they crowd around one table, leaving the three officers and a dozen empty chairs at the other. Leroy walks to the lectern at the front of the room. The soft courtliness in his voice, its nearly musical roundness, serves strangely well for confrontation.

"Since we started meeting," he explains to the police, "we've had some improvements. But lately it seems like it's getting out of hand again. We've told you how bad the numbers are. The stores are losing business on a daily basis. The parishioners are fearful of coming to church at night. And I haven't seen a lot of police activity on Stanley Avenue. I realize it's a big precinct; I realize there's a manpower shortage. But we're sick and tired of this. We want to know how you can use *us*. Tell us, Inspector Carroll, what we can do."

The commanding officer, a lean man with ruddy skin and graying hair, says that he understands there has been a problem of "harassment" by "kids." He can certainly dispatch an officer on scooter every other day. What's more, Stanley Avenue is already covered under the Community Patrol Officer Program, known as C-POP. It is the beat of Officer Zito.

"I've never met him," Wein says, and around the table the rest of the merchants shake their heads no.

"His primary job is this area," Inspector Carroll repeats. "He should be stopping in. You should have seen him."

"Is this C-POP new?" Wein asks.

"No," Inspector Carroll says, lowering his eyes to the table. The program is five years old. "I think something's wrong."

His is a rare admission to merchants who are accustomed to hearing every police shortcoming explained away with the abstractions of "budget cuts," "manpower shortage," "priorities." They grasp the moment to press their case.

"A day doesn't go by," Wein says, "when someone isn't robbed on the Ave between one and seven. If you would just put a car out there, you'd see them forming outside 640 Stanley after school. They go off in groups of three or four. They look for the easy prey." He uncrosses his legs, pulls himself to the table, lays open his palms. "You see it every day. It's so simple."

"Then they run right back into 640," Lavecchia says, completing the scenario. "It's a one-way door. They got someone to open it for 'em, then close it right up."

"I don't want this to be like 'Kojak,'" Wein resumes, "but if you put someone inside there, they'll run right to you. Give us two plain-clothesmen, we can break it up in a day."

Uncapping a pen, Inspector Carroll asks for a list of the stores most afflicted. The nominations arrive in a rush: Key Food at 655 Stanley; Wein's pharmacy at 679, because it sells Lotto tickets; the notions shop at 670 that handles jewelry; the liquor store at 681. The merchants sense progress, even victory.

But all the inspector offers in return are commonplaces and quali-fiers. Officer Zito will be more of a presence. If you see a gang of teenagers forming, call 911. We'd like to pick up truants, but the Board of Education hasn't yet agreed to cooperate. Maybe the van will be on the streets next week.

"Be like the Hasidics," Inspector Carroll concludes. "When someone hits a Hasidic business, the owner yells, and then there's fifty people in the street. That's one of the biggest deterrents. Because you know the police won't be here all the time."

For a roomful of working people already paying for security the police do not provide, and asking only to be met halfway, the sugges-tion borders on the insulting. And in a neighborhood of wartime fire-power, it strikes several as practically insane.

"These guys are *bold*," says Rochester Blanks, who had slipped into the meeting a few moments earlier. "My daughter's husband's father got mugged the other week. They punched him in the eye. Took two hundred dollars. With his four-year-old granddaughter right there." He wipes his brow with a handkerchief. "I chased one, one time, to 640. The maintenance man asked me where I'm goin'. I told him. He said, 'Don't go in there. They gonna kill you. These guys got Uzis.'" He pauses again, wags his head with resignation. "If you ain't ready to shoot first, you can't say nothin' to 'em."

"All I can tell you," Inspector Carroll answers, "is we have a worse problem on Euclid Avenue."

This old refrain brings grimaces. No matter how bad things get on Stanley Avenue, they never get bad enough. Viscardi tries to break the impasse with a practical question. He can't challenge the thugs. He's already afraid to stay open past seven. He's got the only pizza joint in Brooklyn that closes in the middle of dinner. Can't the police give the shopkeepers walkie-talkies? Citizens-band radios? Something?

There are grants available, Inspector Carroll says, and he will make certain that Viscardi receives applications. But to generate any larger reaction, he continues, the association must reach above him to the police chief, to the mayor. Having the worst crime problem does not matter; making the most noise does. The Seventy-fifth Precinct had 388 robberies last month—"*Reported* robberies," Wein inter-jects—while the 108th, in Sunnyside, Queens, had sixty. Guess who got extra officers? Guess who sent a garbage can full of petitions to City Hall?

"If I'd known that six months ago," says Leroy, who speaks with the precinct on a regular basis, "I could've been dealin' with that. How come I'm just knowin' that now?" He scans the merchants. "We know a petition is a weapon. We know how to use it." They nod vig-orously.

As if to dash the hopes he has just raised, Inspector Carroll reminds his listeners that Mayor Dinkins has delayed the admission of 1,400 cadets into the Police Academy to save money.

"You will not see a new officer here for a full year," he says, stand-ing to leave. During the round of parting handshakes, the inspector pulls Wein aside and says with a chuckle, "Freddie, if we're gonna get more cops, you gotta watch your double-parking."

Nobody else laughs.

It was not just the politicians or the police who disappointed Reverend Youngblood. It was not just a staff and congregation capable of lassi-tude. It was he himself. It was the space between his own actions and ideals, his own flesh and fantasy. He could preach with eloquence, teach with command; he could hobnob with a mayor, a bishop, a gov-ernor. But in his private dimensions as father and son, he still found himself in a lightless room, groping for the walls, the constructs of virtue.

He had formed such a pleasing portrait on Saint Paul's anniver-sary day, worshiping with his father in robes from the same cloth. Yet his father was a second choice, an understudy, offered the airplane ticket only when the man the pastor had invited, his *parrain*, William Jordan, fell too ill to travel. Accident instead of intent had brought Palmon Youngblood to his son's church. That bitter truth revealed that, for all the reconciliation effected so far, much more remained.

As for his own eldest son, Jernell McDonald, Reverend Young-blood had only begun to acknowledge him after a most public challenge. During an Eldad-Medad meeting back in December, he had begun speaking of Jernell in tortured locutions—"the young man whose mother says I'm his father," "the boy who says he's mine," "my supposed son"—when Leo Goins had halted him. Leo was a warrior with shaved head and arching shoulders, a survivor of drug addiction and hard time in prison, as fearless of his pastor as of anyone else.

"Why do you always say 'supposed'?" Leo asked as the room went silent. "Is he your son? Does he call you 'Daddy'?"

"He's been *told* I'm his father," the pastor responded sheepishly. "I'm gonna take a paternity test."

"Forget that test," Leo said. "I don't believe in denyin' no child. Whether he's yours or not."

Since that night, Reverend Youngblood had begun to call Jernell "son." But one word could hardly compensate for twenty years of evasion. He had resolved to bring Jernell to Brooklyn, into his church and his home, for the week ending in Father's Day. And what the young man's presence would surely provoke among the men of Saint Paul, so many of them the creators and creations of illegitimacy, demanded exploration. Rather than hold the discussion in Eldad-Medad, when its length would be limited, the pastor cleared an entire day. No less than sixty men answered the summons.

The last few trickle into the sanctuary now, fifteen minutes into the session, as Reverend Youngblood elicits the nickname of each. It is a painless way of achieving some intimacy, learning who are "Fuzzy" and "Footsie," "Gator" and "Lips," "Easy-E" and "Multiple Mo." When a James insists his only nickname is Jim, the pastor chides, "That's what the white folk call you. What do the brothers and sisters call you?" The man smiles and says, "Dewey."

A prayer follows, and then Reverend Youngblood draws a few personal testimonies about the ministry to men. One comes from Frank Kinard, a retired police detective who serves as an elder and sings in the choir. He talks of having learned at Saint Paul about the masculinity of God. Then he talks about King David, a sinner, a fornicator, an adulterer of uncommon cunning, yet a man in whom God still invested worth.

"That was part confession, you know," Reverend Youngblood

says, leaning against the blackboard. "And I'm glad Frank went and said it for all of us." Now he steps forward, clenching both fists and hefting them together, briefly closing his eyes. "It's like, 'Physician, heal thyself.' I can't tell y'all to do what I won't do. I had to learn to give before I taught y'all to give. I have to learn about havin' a daddy and bein' a daddy."

Without prompting the memories emerge, memories of fathers gone on gambling binges, fathers working themselves to early deaths, fathers unable to compliment or to hug, fathers leaving in their wakes anger and confusion. When one man refers to his father as a "demon," Reverend Youngblood writes the word on the board, twice underlined.

"A lot of us never had fathers," says a graying man named Kelvin. "So how can we be fathers? We don't know what a good father is."

"By doin' what we're doin' now," Robert Sharper answers. "Talkin' about what it means. Gettin' rid of all this shit we carry around."

"We gotta let it out," says Ron Hudson. "But we all have a Father. The same Father." He taps his index finger against a Bible. "And it's all right here."

Reverend Youngblood slowly strokes his beard, framing his words with delicacy.

"Ron is right," he says, voice lifting slightly, "but we have to be careful not to deal only with the spiritual. You gotta *find* your father."

"I met mine when I was thirty-two," someone calls.

"I met mine when I was twenty-eight."

"I found mine," Robert Sharper says, "in the graveyard."

"Some of us got to go to the cemeteries," Reverend Youngblood says, moving down the aisle, then stopping with arms aloft and head tilted upward to the beams. "And we got to shout out, 'Why'd you leave me?'" He waits out the echo, lowers his voice. "It's gonna be a challenge. I'm here to tell you, doctor, it's not gonna be easy. Because we *are* our fathers. That no-good dude you want nothin' to do with? Part of you. Part of you. And once you find him, you gotta raise him."

"How?"

"By bein' a friend. By not lettin' your daddy bullshit you. Because our fathers will not initiate the healing. Our fathers will live and die without things changing."

Now a very dark man in a blue suit stands in the rear of the sanctuary, his favorite place even during uncrowded gatherings. His name is Melvin Heyward, and he is well known around Saint Paul. He works on a loading dock for the phone company. He is an elder. He has a daughter named Oona who takes the solo on "Black Butterfly" with the Youth Choir. What Melvin will say now, however, nobody knows.

His mother bore Melvin when she was sixteen. He knew of his father, a man named Fred Glover, who married another woman and sired five children. In their small South Carolina town, they all attended school together, the accepted and the scorned, and Melvin played on the football team alongside the person he might have been, Fred Glover, Jr.

"You know how they looks at you in a different way in the South," he says. "You heard that expression 'black sheep.' Kids tellin' you, 'Your mother found you somewhere.' Treat you so bad you start thinkin' you deserve it." He pauses, sweat beading across his forehead. "My daddy never called me 'son.' He never talked to me. So I kept my distance. Only things I wanted to tell him were vicious. If you'da given me the chance, I'da called him anything but a child of God."

Eventually, Melvin moved north, returning to South Carolina only to visit his mother and grandfather. Sometimes he would drive a circuitous route between their homes, passing by the Glover house, hoping just to see his father waxing the car or raking the leaves. But always the old enmity reigned. When he got the news eight years ago that his father was ill, Melvin did not even ask what was the disease. Three months after that, he refused to attend the funeral.

Ten rows in front of Melvin, Tom Carter raises his hand. An elevator mechanic in the Brooklyn Navy Yard, normally clad in jeans and a sweatshirt, today he wears pressed white pants and a blue blazer. Reverend Youngblood meets his eyes and nods slightly to recognize him.

"I was also raised without my father," Tom says. "As a matter of fact, I hated my father. I got to know him two years before he died. But it didn't really hit till I came to church here, because my father was in church, he was a deacon." He pulls a hand slowly from his brow back to his neck. "And then, instead of hating him, I realized I missed him. I wished he hadn't died so young. I wished we could've got to know each other as well as God meant."

Rochester Blanks rises from his seat near the door. If anyone in the congregation seems to have been tutored and initiated by a father, it is him, for he wears his masculinity as naturally as he wears his Italian suits. He is "Uncle Rocky," giving part-time work and dollar bills to teenagers short of cash; he is "Mister Blanks," the talented and self-possessed business manager; he is "Rock," a man's man, fond of pool, Coltrane, and Appleton rum.

"I was born out of wedlock," he now admits, "and my mother never told me. To this day, she never told me who my father was. I had to find out from the kids teasing me, pointin' to this man and sayin', 'Hey, that's your daddy, boy.'"

That man's name was Calvin Lundy. The man Rocky believed into adolescence was his father, the man whose surname he carried, a military police officer named John Davis, was in fact his stepfather. And only when Rocky unearthed his birth certificate to obtain a marriage license did he discover he was actually named Blanks, his mother's maiden name.

"For a long time," he goes on, "I thought it was a disgrace. But coming together with the men here, I stopped feeling ashamed. And the last few years, when Reverend spoke about his father, I got to thinking about mine. So I called my half-sister and she give me a telephone number and an address in Baltimore. I called that number and there was no answer. But when I go south this summer, I'm stopping in Baltimore. And I am gonna find my father."

Rocky sits to applause. None has ever seen him braver.

"Our mothers and fathers are our first gods," Reverend Youngblood says, "and the painful fact is that some of us never leave them. But the Scripture says, 'The God of Abraham, the God of our fathers.' Not 'Our fathers are gods.' Not 'Our fathers are perfect.' Not 'Our fathers are divine.'"

"My daddy was a real mean son of a bitch," Rocky puts in.

"Couldn'ta been that mean," Leo Goins says. "Your momma gave him some pussy."

Some howl. Some go silent with shock. "Now I know what they mean by 'Church Unusual,'" sighs Charles Baylor. Even by the standards of Eldad-Medad, Leo has crossed the frontier. In bars and on corners, men die for making such jokes.

"That's real, y'all," Reverend Youngblood says. "Y'all left church because it wasn't in the real world. Well, that's real as it gets." He drinks now from the water goblet that had stood untouched on the lectern for two hours. "Like the folk used to say, 'Ain't nobody all halo and no horns or all horns and no halo.' I don't give a shit. No matter what your daddy did, he wasn't that bad. So go and find his halo. And if your daddy looked like a saint, he probably wasn't that good."

He was speaking, at the last, to himself. He has been the model father. He has been the pastor king. Now it is time to reach back to the Lower Ninth in New Orleans and reclaim his son and his horns.

Three banners hang from a cedar beam high above the pulpit. OBEDI-ENCE PLUS, reads the first. OPPORTUNITY EQUALS, continues the second. The third solves the equation with the words, DEBT-FREE JOY. More striking even than the declaration is the design on the final pennant, that of two manacled hands straining against their confinement until the chains burst. It is the image of Samson in the Bible; it is the image of Nat Turner and Denmark Vesey in black history; it is the image now of a campaign by Saint Paul to liberate itself from the modern bondage of loans and liens, mortgages and collateral, and, in settling those accounts, to free the weekly offering for youth programs. Which explains the standard centered beneath the other three, a depiction of black Jesus, shepherd staff in hand, tending a flock. FEED MY LAMBS, say the tall felt letters.

This fund-raising drive is led by a group of parishioners called the Gideonites. They represent, in human form, the answer to Reverend Youngblood's sermon on Watch Night, and to the withering self-examination of the staff retreat. The Sunday after that retreat, the pastor had recounted again the story of Gideon and his outmanned army, and then he had asked a question. Who were the modern-day Gideons? Who was willing to pledge a thousand dollars to save the children? Who was ready to evangelize the agnostics of the congregation? Perhaps eighty stood to answer the summons on that morning six weeks ago. By now the Gideonites number more than three hundred. And on this Sunday they will make one final appeal to the worshipers, and then they will count the money and discover whether they have succeeded or failed.

The Gideonite campaign is not the only outgrowth of the retreat. Reverend Youngblood has shifted the positions of several staff members and bestowed the formal leadership of the men's ministry and Eldad-Medad on Charles Lewis. He has assigned Helen Parilla to write and illustrate children's books steeped in religious ethics and African culture. To the consternation of even his closest aides, he has broken the custom of concluding each sermon with the invitation, "The doors of the church are now open." That made membership too public, too instant, too easy; that was how five thousand people turned up on the church rolls. From now on, those worshipers who walk down the aisle in search of catharsis and acceptance will still be heard and comforted and "witnessed to," as the phrase goes. But more than ever their membership will depend on a commitment to sacrifice.

That was where the Gideonites, Reverend Youngblood's cadres, became so necessary, and not simply to the church. East New York, like many parts of black America, had suffered a kind of demographic schizophrenia in the last twenty years. The most educated and skilled of its residents departed for newly integrated neighborhoods and suburbs, leaving behind the very population that, in its poverty and despair, most needed such role models. Seeing the painfully mixed blessings of desegregation, Reverend Youngblood and others of his generation would wistfully recall the one perverse boon of bigotry, the way it kept the doctor and the banker and the teacher living down the block from the unwed mother and her kids, rather than only appearing as Thursday-night mirages on "Cosby." The Nehemiah homes, rising from a field of ruin, were one way of reuniting a bifurcated nation; the Gideonite campaign was another, most especially for the two congregants who emerged as its leaders, Bill Scott and Muriel Richardson.

Single and slender at twenty-four, Bill had a "buppie" pedigree. An only child, he had been identified as gifted in third grade and whisked from the wretched schools of Brownsville to those in middle-class, mostly white Borough Park. His grades there earned him admission to Brooklyn Tech, one of the most selective high schools in the city, and from Tech he went on to the University of Hartford and ultimately a $29,000-a-year job as an insurance broker. His could have been the life of a Fort Greene condo, *nouvelle* soul food at B. Smith's, ballads and brandy at Sweetwaters. Instead he still lived with his grandparents in Flatbush, rode the subway to work, and saved his money for marriage. And when he measured his life against those around it, he found fresh profundity in the axiom that said, "There but for the grace of God go I."

That was most true of a buddy named Joe Rayfield. They made an unlikely pair when they first met in their teens; Bill was one of the "brains" heaped with ridicule, Joe a dropout at odds with his father and familiar with guns. During Bill's college summers, though, they discovered a mutual passion for reggae and began trading tapes; Joe asked so many questions about campus life that Bill invited him to visit, trying to make the university and the future it connoted appear attainable. And he seemed to have succeeded; Joe earned an equivalency diploma and found a job taking telephone orders in the New York Mercantile Exchange. Then he got his girlfriend pregnant and married her under duress and saw his ambitions imperiled by the simple need to cover the rent. One evening in March 1989, Joe called Bill to ask if they could meet and talk; he had just had a roaring fight with his wife, and on her birthday, no less. Bill already had a date that night, so he promised his friend, "I'll check you out tomorrow." As he was reading the *Daily News* the next morning, his eyes froze on the article about the young Brooklyn man who had slain his wife and infant son before shoving the shotgun into his own mouth. The next Sunday, which was Easter, Bill joined Saint Paul.

Muriel Richardson, too, once appeared to need little from a ghetto church. At thirty-two, she had a steady job in customer service for the telephone company, as well as a recently earned degree in financial management, *cum laude*. A sharecropping childhood had instilled in her such frugality that her boyfriend often teased her, "You could spend a dollar five times and still have change." But if Joe Rayfield had taught Bill Scott a rending lesson in humility, Muriel had learned it on her own. New to New York in her early twenties, freed from the rural proprieties of church and family, she whirled through parties, discos, and cocaine, the one thing for which she could always find money. She had been fired from her job and evicted from her apartment by the time she signed herself briefly into a hospital. And even then, she merely cut down. Only when she began attending Saint Paul in 1980 did she finally quit.

So Muriel and Bill, each with a spiritual debt to Saint Paul of which no one around them was aware, stood that Sunday in March. And when Reverend Youngblood asked later who among the eighty would serve on a twelve-member steering committee, they stood again. Then those twelve sat to study the Book of Judges, to plan their fund-raising strategy, and to pray that it worked. There were plenty of skeptics about, from tithers who griped that they had no more to give to old-timers who would donate only toward a bingo card or a fish dinner. The challenge for the Gideonites was fundamental: How do you market selflessness?

As a matter of pride, the twelve resolved not to rely on their pastor. Inspiration had been his; execution would be theirs. Shirley Tyler made sashes of royal purple with a gold sequin *G* for the Gideonites to wear each Sunday. Helen Parilla created the dramatic logo. Curtis Jones wrote a play about how Satan and Ronald Reagan were conniving to destroy black children. Bill Scott worked the lobby between services, calling above the hubbub, "Yo, you down with the Gideonites yet?" Muriel Richardson, the daughter and niece of military men, wrote a cadence call worthy of Parris Island:

God told Gideon His plan
To use a few to save the land
The crowd Gideon had was much too large
Not all of them believed in God
God said the people who have fear
Must depart away from here
Sound off
Amen!
Sound off
Amen!
Sound off
Amen! Amen! Amen!

The Gideonites held four weeknight rallies, partly to collect pledges, partly to buoy the communal will. The Yoke Fellows performed their stepping show. The cheerleaders chanted. And Randy Murphy, entrenched in his own struggles for literacy and independence, gave a testimony whose spirit would echo for weeks. He held four sheets of binder paper, crinkled with use, from the hours he and his tutor had spent honing the speech. She had corrected his spelling and grammar and carefully printed the words in large round letters with every other line blank, so Randy would not lose his place, talking in front of so many people. He turned his thick glasses toward the pages and slowly he read:

> One day I was talking to Curtis Jones and telling him about some things I wanted to buy for myself. I saw him with a purple sash and asked about it. He told me about the Gideonites. I thought about becoming a Gideonite, because I knew that Jesus made a great sacrifice for me. So this was one thing I could do for Him.
>
> I do not earn much money for my basic pay, so I worked as much overtime as I could get, and I put in for my two weeks vacation pay. I did not buy any clothes. It was hard! But I wanted to do it. Because of my faith in God I knew that I would do it.

Soon Randy reached the final page, the one his tutor had not had time to revise. And it was then, as he flung himself against his limits, that people began to praise and cry and give.

> I am in inspired to give Balck to god.
>
> in respnse To his rich and abundant Blessing on My life and family I all so response and appreciation for the great minstry of The s.p. com chuch under the Dynamite leadership of Dr. JR blood
>
> I be live that God had all so been mighty good to you because god give his own son for me i am more than willing to do anything to please
>
> My God.

The first three rallies reaped $30,000, the fourth an additional $27,000. That leaves nearly $300,000 in Gideonite pledges due today, plus whatever can be raised in a special offering from the entire congregation. The goal is made tangible in the lobby display case, where four outstanding mortgages are posted, encircled by chains made of green dollar signs. And the need is made flesh by the children themselves, as they parade their talents across the pulpit, like so many contestants on "Amateur Night at the Apollo."

Two teenagers, Ron McCormick and Michael Stone, read original poetry. Four younger boys, including Jason Youngblood, harmonize on a spiritual. Oona Heyward takes her star turn on "Black Butterfly." Malene Allen, a student in Saint Paul's elementary school, reads a "wish list" culled from her classmates: a college scholarship fund, a computer class, a gymnasium and swimming pool, "a cafeteria so we can have real food," a biology laboratory "where we can dissect a lot of things."

As the laughter at the last two items subsides, a round of testimonies begins. A seventh-grader with a flat-top haircut and a red shirt moves nervously toward a microphone taller than he is. He stretches on his tiptoes, uttering words that are instantly lost, until one of the elders, Clarence Davis, dashes from the wings to lower the mike. Then he can be heard: "I came here from public school and in the second grade I didn't know how to read or spell. My teacher here taught me how to sound out words with phonics. I sit on Miss Adele's lap every day to read for her, because when I read for my mother and make a mistake she gets mad." He is followed by another boy: "If not for Saint Paul, I might've ended up in public school with the guns, knives, and drugs." Then comes a girl with hair braided into perfect parallel rows: "I was afraid in my other school. It was all violent. When I grow up, I want to be a lawyer, and I pray to God I make it."

Reverend Youngblood, reclaiming the altar, now calls forward no fewer than fourteen children, from a three-foot-tall girl, her pigtails tied with white yarn, to Leroy Howard's strapping son Trevor. Proceeding by grade, which means roughly by height, the pastor announces the marks on each child's most recent report card, saving Trevor for the last. The young man's dream has been to attend Dillard, Reverend Youngblood's alma mater, but at times he has labored just to pass high school. So when the pastor reads his marks—including an 86 in English and a 100 in accounting, with a semester's average of 86.3—many in the congregation cheer. And when he announces that Trevor has just been admitted to Dillard, they rise in a standing ovation, for in this moment the teenager with gangly legs and blemishes is possibility personified.

"Now," Reverend Youngblood says, "I'd like to introduce one of our new-found leaders."

Bill Scott rises from his seat and moves forward on long, firm strides. He steadies himself behind the podium, fixes his eyes on a spot in the rear of the room, just as he had been taught in high school speech class. Like a practiced toastmaster, he jokes about how, after all these weeks of being pestered, folks have renamed the Gideonites the "Gimme-onites."

"Today," he says, grinning, "we have much to be happy about. First of all, self-determination. So many times we hear that we black people don't take care of ourselves and we need the help of people outside, who don't have our best interests at heart. Well, I'm here to witness, to oppose that point of view. We at Saint Paul have banded together for a purpose, using our own resources. Our purpose, to defeat debt and strengthen our future. Our purpose, to feed our lambs. And I thank God for giving us victory in this particular battle."

He brings both hands to the edges of the podium. His smile flattens.

"But please be advised that the war goes on. Because there is an ongoing conspiracy to destroy black people in this country, starting with the children." He pauses. "Our children can be saved. As long as we give them the hunger to be the best. As long as we give them a pride in being black. If we give our children an understanding of their African heritage and a knowledge of their parents' sacrifice, then they will pass this wisdom to future generations.

"There are many more lives to touch inside and outside of the church. We should carry these thoughts of pride and sacrifice into our homes and jobs. And we should remember: The victory is ours."

He is speaking, though, on faith, not figures. The collection that will define victory or defeat now will begin. Rochester Blanks and Ron Hudson place a cedar chest before the pulpit and lift open its lid. Gideonites in purple sashes stretch along both flanks. Then Muriel Richardson and her boyfriend, Richard Gaither, approach the microphone. Normally a spiritual underscores the period of offering, but on this morning the congregation will join in the "Gideonite March Song," a copy of which was stapled to each copy of the church bulletin. Trevor Howard snaps the cadence on snare drum. Larry Willis, working in the lowest range on organ, approximates a walking bass. The genre may be martial, but this song swings straight to its climax:

Gideonites are here today
Gideonites will pray and pay
Father God give us strength
To give more than just our tenth
When we do what God say do
We make one step, he makes two
Sound off
Amen!
Sound off
Amen!
Sound off
Amen! Amen! Amen!

Now the sanctuary falls silent, except for the muffled tread of heels on carpet, and the snowy rustle of envelopes drifting into the chest. Once the Gideonites have finished, Reverend Youngblood asks of the remaining worshipers, "Is there one who'll give this morning?" One comes and one hundred come and still more follow, their line stretching seventy feet down the center aisle, bending out the door and into the lobby. Checkbooks emerge from vest pockets, folded bills from wallets and purses, and the money that has been saved and budgeted for rent or groceries or Easter finery falls into the chest. Then Rocky lowers the lid and, with Ron Hudson, takes the collection into Reverend Youngblood's study to be tallied. "Pigmeat Markham used to say, 'Somebody's gonna do some time today,'" Reverend Youngblood says. "Well, I know we gonna burn some mortgages today."

As the counting proceeds in private, Eli Wilson calls for a song entitled, "I'll Say Yes to My Lord." It is an unusual piece of praise music, with its minor key, and rarer still for a Baptist church, since its variable rhythms arise from the Pentecostal tradition. Yet since Larry Willis taught it to the choir a few months ago, the entire congregation has adopted it fiercely. He starts today in four-four time, and voices join in an ecstatic litany of blessings.

He bought me out of darkness
Into the marvelous light

Placed my feet on straight street
Gave me strength to fight

He put running in my feet
Clapping in my hands
Praying on my lips
Joy in my heart

He's done great things
He's done great things
I'll say yes, yes, yes,
To my Lord

When he reaches the coda, Willis slashes the time to two-two, and the mood metamorphoses. Jubilation gives way to resolve; inventory shifts to invocation; what was spirited becomes spiritual. With each elongated "Yes," the veins rise on Reverend Youngblood's neck. Beside him, Doug Slaughter sways from shoulders to ankles. James Jones leaves the piano to bring his arms together like a falcon beating its wings in anticipation of flight. Then Leroy Howard, Leroy Howard who years ago would drop off his wife Betty at church and kill those two hours drinking beer in the parking lot of the Linden projects, Leroy Howard stands from his pew and lifts his palms in surrender and starts to weave a wobbly course through the aisles, dozens of others falling in behind him, all singing in a velvet hush, "Yes, yes, yes, to my Lord."

Saint Paul has "gotten happy," but still nobody knows how much cause for happiness there is. Behind the door of Reverend Youngblood's study, the counting continues. Two more songs cushion the wait.

"Yo, yo, yo," echoes the voice from the lobby, and as heads swivel, Rocky races into the sanctuary, holding aloft a strip of green paper representing one mortgage. "We got some burning to do." Once he reaches the pulpit, scores of Gideonites leap from their seats, each waving a similar strip, and they mass and throb around Rocky, like a football team psyched for the kickoff. As the celebration ebbs, Craig Campbell retraces Rocky's path, bearing a white strip and shouting, "We got another!" A second wave of Gideonites surges toward the front. Somewhere in the maelstrom, the symbolic mortgages are thrust into a censer and touched with flame. Slowly the smoke of victory rises.

"Hallelujah!" screams someone in the back row of the church.

"Praise God!" adds another, turning and turning in a circle of joy.

"Free!" a woman shouts hoarsely, clenching both fists. "Thank God, we're free. Thank you, Jesus. Thank you, Lord."

The next week, once all the personal checks have cleared, Rocky writes two checks from the church's account—one for $102,290.44, which settles the mortgage on four Stanley Avenue stores, the second for $146,208.33, which does the same for a house and three lots on Hendrix Street. Fully $91,000 of the money was raised on the final, furious Sunday.

In paying off nearly $250,000 of principal, Saint Paul has spared itself hundreds of thousands of dollars in interest. Those savings, in turn, can instantly help the church's youth. Some money will pay for a tour of colleges by the Yoke Fellows, all of whom are nearing the time of applying, and some will underwrite a trip to Zimbabwe this summer by an interracial group of Brooklyn teenagers, including six from the church.

But Saint Paul cannot claim to be entirely debt-free yet, and so Bill Scott will return to the pulpit one Sunday soon to announce Gideonites II. "That's right," he will say, "just when you thought it was safe to put your checkbook away." And when the knowing laughter subsides, he will add, "Our slogan is 'Keep the pressure on.' Check it out: It worked for Nelson Mandela."

4

SERIOUS

ROBERT SHARPER, A MAN IN SEARCH OF CALM, wades into the commotion that is Saint Paul late on a Saturday morning. To the beat of an Otis Redding tape and the tang of furniture polish, four custodians primp the sanctuary for tomorrow's worship service. Down the hall, the elders meet. Around the corner, amid the hum of gossip and the snap of paper bending, an assembly line of mothers and daughters folds two thousand church bulletins. Past them pad the children from LAMBS, bound for home in polyfill coats as puffy as Mylar balloons.

Steering through the obstacles, Robert arrives at Charles Lewis's desk in the media office, momentarily vacant. Robert is a slim, dark-skinned man with a full beard and new dreadlocks, and behind his horn-rimmed glasses reside eyes of particular intensity. He arranges before him a cassette recorder on which he will cue a gospel song, and a Bible in which he locates today's verse. He places beside the Bible a book called *Becoming a New Person: Twelve Steps to Christian Growth*, its cover frayed with use, its title page tattooed with names and phone numbers. Then he walks into the chapel, where he pulls a dozen chairs into a circle, setting the books and recorder beneath the seat he will occupy. He works with the efficiency honed as a construction carpenter, and learned decades earlier from his mother, who would deliver him to a playmate's three o'clock birthday party at one-thirty "to help the girl put bows in her hair."

More than force of habit, however, accounts for Robert's solitary arrival and painstaking preparations. He is answering to a sense of mission. At noon he will convene the regular weekly meeting of the Wounded Healers, a support group for recovering drug addicts and alcoholics and their families. As its leader, and as a struggling survivor himself, Robert devotes the morning to attaining peace and clarity, to "getting rid of my own bullshit so I don't bring it with me." He sips lemongrass tea and listens to an Eli Wilson tape before leaving home. He reaches church forty-five minutes before the meeting. He has anybody's frustrations—a son who needs six hundred dollars' worth of dental work, a shop steward who gives overtime only to cronies—but he cannot allow them to intrude, not on the Wounded Healers. It is he who recruited many of its members, including the dealer from whom he once bought heroin and cocaine. It is he who assists this one with an injured child, helps that one move into a new apartment, holds spending money for a third who does not yet trust himself, answers the after-midnight calls pleading, "I'm tired of this. I've tried everything. What's the use?"

Robert dims the lights and starts the tape, and the chapel fills with the Saint Paul choir performing "Precious Lord." Cushioned by its whispering tones, soothed by its words of supplication, the members begin to assemble, embracing one another at the portal, then sitting to listen and think. One man leans forward, pinching the bridge of his nose. Another drops his chin into clasped hands. A woman hugs herself across the chest. They range from their twenties to their sixties, from the illiterate and unemployed to the college-educated and professional. They wear silk blouses or sweatpants, Italian flats or scuffed sneakers. But on any topcoat one finds the same button, showing two people inside a teardrop, arms outstretched and groping toward one another. It is the Wounded Healers' insignia.

When the song ends, the members rise and join hands as Robert leads a prayer.

"We come with our ears open and our eyes wet," he says. "We pray for you to come to us, God. And we ask You to be gentle."

This morning Robert will teach the first of the twelve steps, which were developed as a program by Alcoholics Anonymous and then adapted by Philip St. Romain in his book on Christian growth. The Wounded Healers spend two weeks on each step, and when they conclude the cycle, they start it again, as if to remind themselves that recovery is never complete. They are also preparing today to testify before the entire congregation two Sundays hence, bringing their ministry outside the chapel door for the first time in its eighteen-month history. Robert asks the others to sit and close their eyes as he paces inside the circle of chairs.

"Now, don't y'all go to sleep on me now," he jokes. "First one I hear snorin', I'm throwin' the book at." Then he reads: "We admit that we cannot realize our fullest human potential by living a life of selfishness." Returning to his seat, he adds a verse of Christ's teachings from the Gospel of John:

> I am the vine, ye are the branches. He that abideth in me, and I
> in him, the same bringeth forth much fruit: for without me ye
> can do nothing.

"In reading the first step and now looking at God's word," Robert begins in his raspy voice, "we have to face the reality of the life we live. We are nothin' unless we are plugged into God. Because not bein' plugged in is bein' empty on the inside." He shakes his head. "It's like you buy a new refrigerator from Sears and Roebuck's, go out and get two hundred fifty bucks of food and fill it up, and you wake up the next morning and all the food's spoiled because the refrigerator's not working. And you call up Sears and they send the maintenance man and he comes out and says, 'Ain't nothin' wrong with your refrigerator. You forgot to plug it in.'"

He moves his gaze around the room. Between workshops on group dynamics and years of bachelor flirtation, he has learned to read body language—who crosses forearms in a resistant posture, who exposes an undefended chest in a sign of trust, who pitches forward to listen, who twiddles thumbs.

"Think about the way people look at you today, compared to the way they looked at you when you wasn't plugged into God," he continues. "You can accept that you got these selfish tendencies, but you know as long as you stay plugged into the vine, you'll find joy, peace, esteem. You unplug, you become regressed. Then you get depressed." He pauses. "Then you get the *best*."

There is the pained laughter of remembrance.

"So I ask you: Are you plugged into the vine? Do you accept that you are helpless without the vine? Are you accepting? Are you abiding with the truth of this first step?" His voice hardens. "Because if you don't get out of that denial, you gonna get high somewhere down the line." He clamps hands on hips, shrivels his nose, affects a prissy tone. "'Who's he to say that?'" He drops the character to answer the question. "Well, it's the truth. You don't believe me? Live a little while longer. Live a little while longer."

He reads aloud the verse from John one more time, lays the Bible on an empty seat, settles into his own chair, and lets silence suffuse the room. Through the closed door can be heard the faint squeals of children. Robert's eyes, again searching the faces around him, halt on a woman named Evelyn, the wife of a drug addict and an original member of the group. She stares into the carpet, arms limp at her sides.

"How you doin'?" Robert asks, as if coaxing a shy child.

"I got a cold."

"Tell me about it."

"Tell you about my cold?" she asks suspiciously.

"Yes."

"What you wanna know?" She lifts her head.

"Everything about it."

"My head's stuffed up. My throat hurts."

"I'm gonna give you a hug," Robert announces, moving across the floor.

"Then you gonna get my cold," Evelyn says, and as Robert enfolds her, she cannot suppress a smile. "You know, I didn't wanna be here today. I was drinking my tea, thinking, I'm going, I'm not going, I'm going, I'm not going. But I felt like I had to. Like I needed to."

Her admission eases something in the room. Candor encourages candor; one voice emboldens another. A woman with a graying Afro and a *Dick Tracy* T-shirt speaks next.

"I been asked to help pray for people," she says, "friends who used to know me years ago, drinkin' and all that, and they know I'm

Christian now. One lady, she's Hungarian, they believe real different from us. Her daughter is sick in her lungs. Her husband is an alcoholic. And I gave her verses to study. I'm usin' what I got here." She swallows. "And I am grateful to God for savin' my life. Because I tried to take it so many times. I still have my ups and downs, but ..." She closes her eyes, but tears squeeze through. "... ah, you know."

"You ever wonder how that comes about?" Robert says. "That's the spirit at work. It's the spirit that makes you cry. Look at the cross." He spreads wide his own arms. "When you like this, you open." Now he clutches himself into a fetal ball. "But this way, you ain't lettin' nothin' out, and you holdin' all your bullshit in. You denyin'. Like I was denyin' for twenty-two years."

Across the carpet, Tom Carter straightens in his chair. He founded the Wounded Healers with Robert, and he leads the Saturday sessions when Robert is absent. Lately, though, he has been shaken by a doctor's discovery of a growth on his lung. This week he will submit to a biopsy, which could reveal the presence of cancer.

"You know what my first thought was?" Tom says. "Go get me a eighth of cocaine, go get me a gallon of wine, go get me a pound of reefer. If I'm gonna die, I'm gonna die happy. That's what I was truthfully thinking." He spreads his legs wide before him, pins his elbows on his thighs, bows his head. "We always gonna have a fight. We always gonna have a fight. That spirit that wants to bring us down, it's always gonna come, one way or another." Now he looks up. "But I'm gonna go along with God. I'm gonna keep my faith. And what I wanna say, I just wanna say, in your prayers, say a prayer for me. So this thing'll be cleared up." His voice falls into a mumble. "Or whatever."

This recent diagnosis is Tom's personal burden, but his "first thought" is the Wounded Healers' communal one. Temptation for them will never be anything but immediate, anywhere but adjacent. Only this week Robert found out that a member named Felipe had relapsed. Another man, Delroy, has yielded two or three times in the past year. Even Robert, after four years of sobriety, will still hear a song on his car radio sometimes and think how much better the music would sound if he was high. He knows enough to confess the weakness to someone else. He knows enough to remember his final night of drugs, the night the dead were baying for him. He knows, too, the urge will return, for as he often tells the Wounded Healers, "This thing we cravin', it ain't cornflakes."

"Remember what I said before: 'Just live a little while longer,'" Robert says now, his voice low and thick. "Folk get unplugged. Folk go off. And if you pray for them, you got to be ready to be the answer to that prayer. You can't all the time be waitin' for God to pick up your friend, your husband, your whatever, just pick 'em up and dust 'em off. You wonderin' why God ain't actin', but God might be actin' through you." He pauses. "We pray for Tom. We pray that when Tom's in our presence, *we* are the answer to his prayers."

A young woman with dreadlocks and a floppy wool cardigan begins to speak. Her name is Mali James, and Robert met her in Narcotics Anonymous. Only in her twenties, she is raising seven children, four of them her brother's, and attending adult school with another Wounded Healer, learning how to read.

"When I care for somebody spiritually," she says, "it hurts. It hurts real bad. When you hold your arm out to somebody, you think, 'Dag, I got no protection.' My mother, she wrote me this letter. It said, 'Fuck you and fuck the world.' And I wanna be part of the solution for my mom and me. I wanna. But every part of my life is pain. I've been abandoned. I've run away. I'm afraid. I don't like pain. I'm the kind of person who's always cryin'. It's like I wanna come to church, but gettin' seven kids ready ... 'C'mon, y'all! C'mon, y'all!' And I ain't even got church clothes for them. So I said, okay, I can stay home and get tapes of the services and praise God that way. But it's lonely. It's so damn lonely."

Myrtis Brent opens her purse and withdraws a plastic sandwich bag filled with folded tissues. She passes them to Mali, who is now sobbing.

"I know Jesus died for me," she stammers through tears. "But I ain't that strong. I'm a human being. I'm weak. I'm not perfect." She drags a tissue across her cheeks, then fingers its texture. "And I know they's excuses."

Next to Mali sits Ike Linton, now a corrections officer, a husband, and the father of two, but in the past a cocaine dealer in the nearby projects.

"I can relate to what you say about you and your mother," he says, "because me and my father are like that. So I can *feel* your pain.

But when you stop feelin' the pain, it means you stopped growin'. You content. And when you content, you gonna go back to what you did before, gettin' high." Robert nods in agreement. "So keep dealin' with the pain, and one day you gonna claim the victory." He lifts a hand paternally toward her. "I know you gonna, sweetheart."

Danny Edmonds, a wiry man in a *kufi* hat, follows.

"It's like when we were into our drugs, and all we wanted was to hit that high," he says. "I used to see people 'round Saint Paul, singin', always happy. I was always wantin' to know how they got that way. And when I started gettin' back into real life, I found out. Now I been in Wounded Healers a year, and I relapsed once, I fell back. But today I'm here. See, this first step reminds me of a marriage. Or an engagement. You got that ring on the finger now. Ain't no backin' out."

Robert strides quietly to the door to hush some children outside. As he returns to his seat, he speaks, nominally addressing Mali, but actually intending his comments for the entire group. It is nearly two o'clock. The Wounded Healers will soon disperse. These words must last a week.

"When you tell yourself you're powerless," he says, "that's when you become power*ful*. That's when you can say no. When I was really powerless was when I thought, 'I got that little stuff under control.'" He points to an imaginary pile of cocaine. "Shit got me crawlin' around on the floor. Lookin' for people. Robbin' folks. *'Under control.'*"

He stands in the center.

"It's a struggle to get past this human shit. I know that. But, see, we ain't in the world here. We in the spirit now. When we leave outta here"—he indicates the door—"we back in the real world, but we ain't seein' it in the same way. 'Just a shot of dope. Just a hit off the pipe.'

"That shit is gone! That was just our surface. Now we down to the goddamn gravy of the situation." He mimes a hungry man hunched over the dinner table. "So grab your bread and sop it up. 'Cause that gravy's good."

On the day after his father died, Robert Sharper resolved to sneak into the mortuary. He had not seen this death, after all, but only heard in his grandmother's apartment the words *hospital, meningitis, passed away*. He would not believe it without proof. And since none of the family elders would allow a five-year-old inside the funeral home, Robert enlisted his cousin and sometime baby-sitter, Barbara, only twelve, for the secret pilgrimage.

The mortician, taking pity on their purpose, led them across the parquet floor and toward the coffin, surrounded by lilies and draped with an American flag. Barbara hoisted Robert up the side of the casket, until he could peer down at the slender cheeks, the nearly straight hair. Still, he was unconvinced. This was only half a man; he would not accept that this corpse was his father unless he saw the feet. The undertaker unhinged the lid, pushed up the trouser cuffs, untied the shoes, removed the socks. And when Robert saw those reddish, calloused soles, he ran into the street, shrieking. A few days later, after the burial, Barbara would find him bent over the ground where he normally played marbles, clawing at the dirt and promising, "I'm gonna get my daddy out."

He sought not only the man—Sonny Sharper, shirt presser, World War II veteran—but the affection and order the man meant to his only child. It was Sonny who had taken Robert to church on Sunday, Sonny who had brought him to visit relatives in Raleigh, Sonny who had led him on errands around Brownsville, where people would lift Robert into their arms and give him a quarter, just because he was Sonny's boy. And when Sonny was gone, gone except for a folded flag in a drawer and a suitcoat his widow wore for cleaning the windows, his son's life slipped from gravity's hold.

Hester Sharper tried. She set a curfew and inspected homework and demanded manners; she paid for day camp and led trips to Coney Island and Radio City. With a dollar of her salary as a presser, Robert could spend a summer day in nearby Betsy Head Park, where fifteen cents bought admission to the vast pool and another sixty-five got soda and a knish for lunch at the Jewish grocery across the street. In the Brownsville Houses, the new housing project where the family lived, there were watchful neighbors and stringent rules; merely cutting across a lawn was punishable by a fine.

So restricted in the outer world, so pampered in the household, Robert started school as a competitive swimmer and a B-plus student. He soon showed, however, a bent for classroom mayhem, from raising girls' skirts to throwing scissors, and he passed through four different elementary schools before being sent in eighth grade to a "600 school," reserved for the incorrigible. His marks there earned his return to the mainstream system, and at Tilden High School he competed as a freshman in the all-city swimming championships. But he had already found more alluring sport on the changing streets of Brownsville.

The neighborhood of Robert's childhood, a working-class district precariously balanced between Jewish holdovers and black newcomers, had evolved by his teenaged years into a notorious ghetto. Shops and synagogues and the Jews who supported them fled for the suburbs; gangs, arson, and drugs filled the vacuum. Delinquency rates quadrupled from 1951 to 1958. Lead poisoning, contracted from eating flakes of plaster or cement, had afflicted nearly half the neighborhood's children by 1969. Four of every five families in 1970 were living on welfare. If ever a son required a strong and loving father, it was in the Brownsville of Robert Sharper's coming-of-age.

Handsome and athletic, Robert kept company with boys several years his senior, who initiated him into a life of girls, nightclubs, and designer clothes. To pay for the cover charges and the alpaca sweaters, Robert began stealing paychecks inscribed with the standard weekly wage of $33.63, but not yet made out to anyone, from the youth program that employed him. An older hustler with fake ID would cash the check for a commission, leaving Robert thirty dollars' profit. When he had exhausted the supply of checks, Robert bought a pistol and began robbing supermarkets, splitting takes as high as $3,500 with three partners. Between larger operations, he once broke into a neighbor's apartment, coming away with forty dollars in cash and a television set he fenced for one hundred.

Rarely did he eat or even sleep at home, although every Sunday Hester Sharper would still cook him a supper of pot roast and cabbage, the ritual of a vanished normalcy. When he passed through the apartment one such evening, to change into his sharkskin slacks and Bally loafers for a salsa concert, she finally spoke. The time for persuasion was long past. In height as in will, the son had outgrown the mother. Her voice was of mourning.

"You don't love me," she said.

"That ain't so," he muttered distractedly. "Why you wanna say that?"

"You don't love me," she repeated.

Then he pulled on his suede jacket and swaggered into the night.

What innocence Robert still harbored was for a girl named Icie Johnson, who lived a few buildings away in the projects. With her straight-A grades and abstinent nature and stern parents, she was the neighborhood ingenue. And Robert, to her thrill, was the neighborhood rogue, yet a rogue with a leavening streak of chivalry. He courted her by telephone, after the household was asleep, and for two years in their midteens they went steady. Robert could liberate the part of Icie that loved dancing past curfew; Icie could excite Robert's intellect to purposes other than theft.

Still, this oddest of couples could not last. They drifted apart at sixteen, with Icie a virgin headed for Hunter College, and Robert a high school dropout soon to be a father and a felon. He had begun smoking marijuana and snorting heroin at thirteen, and two years later he had started shooting the drug. He indulged so heavily that, since the quinine used for cutting heroin made his skin itch, he scratched off his own eyebrows. It was robbery rather than drugs, though, that landed Robert in jail, and as his convictions mounted he proceeded from the Spofford juvenile facility to the Brooklyn House of Detention to Riker's Island to, at the age of seventeen, Sing Sing.

Only in that fortress above the Hudson, with his own street antics humbled by the murderers around him, did Robert make good on his frequent promise to reform. During his forty-six-month sentence, he learned how to operate a printing press. He read *Ebony* and Eldridge Cleaver and Mao Tse-tung. He cleansed his body of drugs. And when he returned home in December 1971, he enrolled in Harlem Prep and gained admission as an apprentice into the carpenters' union.

His life after prison would appear the very essence of rehabilitation. He earned a diploma. He found steady work as a construction carpenter. He studied the Torah with a congregation of Black Israelites. He began a ten-year relationship with an educated, employed woman with whom he shared an apartment in Bedford-Stuyvesant. He skied in New England and swam in the Bahamas, dressed as smartly as he ever had when crime bought his clothes. And amid all the seeming stability he resumed using drugs, growing more deeply addicted than ever, hiding his daily use behind the routines of legitimacy. There was invariably somebody on a construction site who sold dope, or had a friend who did, and so the more jobs Robert worked, the more connections he had. Best of all, these connections were in Manhattan, beyond the scrutiny of his family and friends.

The death of Hester Sharper on an operating table in September 1972 doubly fueled Robert's habit, providing it with both motive and means. There is a peculiar, penetrating guilt that belongs to the son who has broken his mother's heart, and Robert wanted only to obliterate it. The $75,000 he collected between pension, life insurance, and the settlement of a malpractice suit paid for a two-year binge aimed at accomplishing just that. Yet no matter how much he snorted or shot, no matter what combination he mixed, Robert could not deaden memory and conscience; it was as if the drugs themselves had lost power. And while he held his job, he lost his woman, and by the mid-1980s he was living with his cousin in a housing project in East New York.

That cousin, Gloria Burnett, worked as a substance-abuse counselor and could not be fooled by clean clothes and groomed hair and a respectable job. She knew why Robert asked for "carfare" on his salary; she knew why he gave her rent money, only to plead for a rebate; and she also knew she could not cure his disease. Only Robert could change Robert, and his only changes were for the worse.

In 1985 he took an illegal sublet in the Cypress Hills housing project, nearly a mile away, and set about breaking the cardinal rule of his hidden addiction: Don't cop where you live. Everywhere were drugs—a luncheonette on Pitkin, a basement on Montauk, a numberless apartment on Blake, a dozen other spots within five minutes of home. A dealer along Sutter Avenue, who went by the nickname Panama, advanced drugs to Robert against each Thursday's paycheck, and even then there was never enough money to quell his appetite. Robert sold a VCR so new he still had the packing box. Using forged prescriptions, he got Valium free through his union medical plan, then traded the pills for cocaine. Nothing made him stop—not convulsing from tainted cocaine, not freaking out at the wheel of a car, not waking up in the emergency room. He did pack himself off once to an ex-girlfriend in Dallas, where his version of detoxification allowed for Remy, Tanqueray, and reefer. The moment his returning plane touched down at La Guardia, twenty minutes from all the dealers, he felt the familiar anticipation fluttering in his gut.

A few weeks later, in June of 1986, Robert emerged from the subway at Euclid Avenue with seven hundred dollars in pay and the usual promises. He would pay the rent. He would pay the phone bill. He would buy food, traverse every aisle at Pathmark. And on the way he would get a half-gram of cocaine, just a little reward for his rectitude. After he cooked and smoked that half-gram, he went for another. And another. And another. Until at three o'clock in the morning, he had smoked up all but his last seventy dollars. He apportioned it with care, using fifty for a half-gram, ten for a packet of heroin, three for a bag of marijuana, the rest for a quart of wine cooler and a pack of Newports. When he returned to the apartment, he melted down all the cocaine and heroin and drew it into the needle for a single ultimate shot. Junkies called the method "gunnin' it."

As Robert worked the elixir into his vein, he heard both his parents calling. "Delanor," they cried, using the childhood endearment of his middle name. "Del, come and join us." Trying to silence the voices, he ran to the window, shoved his head into the night air, turned his eyes toward the baseball diamond below. There he saw all the friends who had died young of overdoses, of shootings and stabbings—George, Jackie, Leona, Cheryl, John. "Come on down," they were saying, beckoning him. "Come on down." Robert then noticed two paths beaten into the baseball outfield, thin dirt lines that intersected, forming a cross. *Maybe,* he thought, *I'm dead already.* And then he said aloud, "If there's a God, I wanna try him now."

He telephoned his cousin Gloria.

"I'm tired," he said.

"You're tired?"

"I don't wanna be like this anymore."

"You sure?" she persisted. "You really tired? 'Cause you been tired before."

"I'm sure."

So he gathered up his dearest keepsakes, his alligator boots and his Torah and his snapshots of Hester and Sonny, and at dawn he presented himself to Gloria. The next day he was admitted to a drug rehabilitation center.

Robert Sharper hurtles down Hendrix Street, frozen slush crunching beneath his loafers, crosswinds lifting the *kufi* hat off his dreadlocks.

He should have been here an hour ago; he would have been here an hour ago if not for the fender-bender on the way. It is already past eight on a Sunday morning, time for worship to begin, time for Robert to be ensconced as usual in the front row. And this, of course, is not just any Sunday; this is the Sunday the Wounded Healers testify.

He can see them pacing in the lobby, Tom Carter and Ike Linton. He can hear behind him the furious huffing of Terry Whitson and his mother, Georgia, who will speak. He can only hope Fred Douglas waits somewhere inside, since Fred has no telephone and did not appear at Wounded Healers yesterday. For someone clean only six months, that absence seems an ominous sign.

"How you feelin'?" Robert asks Georgia.

"Nervous."

Terry nods agreement.

"Just sit near me," Robert says.

Eli Wilson has already begun singing "Holy, Holy, Holy." The congregation, standing, lends one thousand voices of harmony. Robert leads his retinue to a few folding chairs in the sanctuary extension, far from his usual position, so reassuring in its proximity to Reverend Youngblood. His left foot beats sixteenth notes. His fingers, cold with nerves, fold and lock. A woman one row behind places her palm in the center of his back, as if buttressing an infirm wall.

"Sharp," Reverend Youngblood calls from the pulpit, "you ready?"

He nods.

"Wounded Healers," the pastor says, withdrawing.

Georgia Whitson lowers the microphone. Robert lifts a handkerchief to his eyes, too anxious to watch.

"First thing I need to do," she begins in a tremulous voice, "is just stand here and pray silently. Because I wrote out what I wanted to say, and we stopped to get gas this morning, and everything went wrong, and Terry lost my paper." She pauses, slows herself. "So I really have to go from the heart, which I needed to do from the beginning.

"About four years ago, there was a problem that hit our home. Terry went to drugs. At first, I couldn't believe it. I didn't want to believe it. And as the problem got worse and worse, it almost like, well it did, tear my home apart."

Another mother in the congregation stamps her feet, bearing witness.

"Then about a year ago, a friend of mine said, 'Georgia, Saint Paul's gonna start a drug program.' And I said, 'Oh, my God, at church?' Because this was a secret which I kept to myself. I didn't want anyone to know. I didn't even want the people on the block to know. Much less to stand here this morning, telling this story.

"But I prayed on it and I said to myself, 'If this is the way God's gonna help me, then I better go to church.'" The ripples in her voice smooth into an almost conversational ease. "So in the meantime, Terry called. We wasn't havin' too much contact with him at the time. I said, 'Terry, guess what, they're gonna start like a drug program at Saint Paul's.' He said, 'Oh, yeah? I'll see.' I said, 'Well, I need it. I'm goin'. You can meet me there if you want to.'

"I'll never forget the first Saturday. All hell broke loose. But Terry was there. And I remember that sign on the door that said, 'Wounded Healers.' Not 'Drug Abusers.' It took me three weeks to realize why. Because we're all wounded. And we all need healing. We're able to cry about it. We talk about it. We even laugh about it." She smiles at Terry in his seat beside Robert. "I already have a house. Now I've been given back a home. And I thank God for that."

As son moves toward mother, as friends and family encircle them both, the next speaker crosses to the microphone. A mustachioed man with dark skin unmarked by his thirty-five years, he wears a double-breasted blue suit, a black shirt buttoned fashionably to the collar, and one tiny diamond earring. Yet with head bowed and fingers fretfully knit, his is the posture of a chastened dandy.

His mother named him Frederick Douglas and always told him, "You gonna be somebody, now that you got this great name." He achieved greatness only in dealing drugs, at twelve selling marijuana to American soldiers, eight years later bringing his trade to New York, extending his product line to heroin and cocaine. He had lived on Fifth Avenue and he had lived on the D train. He had been thrown from a sixth-story window by rivals, breaking both legs. On the street, he was not known by the name of a black hero, or even by his social nickname of Tony; he was known by his country of birth, Panama.

"Good morning, Saint Paul, Reverend Youngblood," he says in a voice subdued and inflected with Spanish. "I wanna thank you …" He exhales heavily. "… thank you for making this …"

He halts again. Robert closes his hand around the balled handkerchief. Reverend Youngblood leans forward in his chair. Many in the congregation tilt their ears. From Tony's mouth slips a sound part grunt and part sigh. Only with effort do phrases then emerge in fragments and scraps.

"Oh, man," he says, dabbing at his eyes. "Since I came into recovery, I got very emotional, you know. Emotion I never used to feel before. Twenty-five years I been drinkin' and druggin'. I been through a lot of tribulations, you know. Once they thought I was crippled for life. But just by the grace of God, He took me outta the wheelchair. I didn't know to read or write English, you know, until I know God."

A woman in the third row, facing Tony, raises a thin arm skyward.

"You know, the Wounded Healers, they make me a new person." Again he emits that abject sound. "I never could find myself, you know. When I came to Saint Paul, it's like everything just turned, you know. I mean, my whole life just turned. I just wanna thank God and you people for being supportive to us. I really like to help anyone else walking those rooms, because I mean I was wounded. It was like a hole inside." He can barely whisper. "I just want to say thank you, Jesus. Thank you, thank you, thank you."

Tony staggers back from the microphone. Reverend Slaughter steadies him from behind. Another man, slinging his arm over Tony's shoulders, guides him to his seat as one might guide a grandfather on brittle legs. All through the testimonies, a song had been playing, repeating itself endlessly on a tape loop. It is the same song that Robert uses on his answering machine at home. And now, in the hush, its chorus can be heard:

> *Millions didn't make it*
> *But I was one of the ones who did*

From the new section walks a gaunt man in a too-large suit, the text of his speech folded over twice and shifted from hand to hand.

When he reaches the front, he braces himself, a stiff arm clutching each side of the lectern. His head falls back as if the neck muscles had suddenly gone weak, and then it rolls forward to a stop, inches from the microphone.

"Praise the Lord," he says. "My name is Roland, and I'm a dope fiend. I was asked to share what the Wounded Healers ministry has done for me. And I was thinkin', what can I say? What can I tell you people and let you feel what I felt? The pain. The powerlessness. The lack of faith I had in myself. 'Cause I tried to quit. So many times. And couldn't."

He gasps for air like a miner in a smoke-filled tunnel.

"Should I tell you about the good jobs I blown? Should I tell you about how twenty years ago I bought my first bag of heroin? Should I tell you about how my son's college money went up in a ..." His voice thickens and wells. "... a ball of crack smoke? How can I make you feel? I really don't know. But I will tell you this: I feel good today.

"For so long, I tried to quit. I been to rehabs. I couldn't quit. 'Cause I was just dealin' with the symptom. I thought my problem was drugs. It's not. I had a problem with the police *over* drugs, but my problem was never drugs, really. My problem was my attitude. The lies and deceits that built up in my character. I felt unworthy. After all I done and did, how could Jesus accept me?

"The first time I came to Saint Paul, Pastor Youngblood had preached on how God was in the salvage business, takin' and repairin' cars what was used. I thought he was just talkin' to me. 'Cause I needed a complete overhaul. And I read in the brochure 'bout the Wounded Healers meeting, and I went that Saturday."

Suddenly the words come in bursts. Perhaps he is talking to his boss. Perhaps he is talking to his son. Perhaps he is talking to himself, a middle-aged man with a college education, for whom the dated term "dope fiend" remains the harshest of judgments.

"I really tried to quit. But, you know, it's hard quittin' drugs. When you're livin' in a gallery. That's a shootin' place, where they shoot drugs. When you're half homeless and unemployed and hungry. It's hard gettin' off drugs.

"At the Wounded Healers, they taught me I am powerless over drugs, but I have a higher power, somethin' that fills the emptiness, that void I had here." He touches his heart. His voice slows. "I don't need a cure-all. I have a cure-all. And it's not easy. Jesus doesn't make it that way. You make it for yourself. The Wounded Healers were my way to *the* way."

He opens a Bible and reads from First Corinthians:

> There hath no temptation taken you but such is common to man: but God is faithful, who will not suffer you to be tempted above that ye are able; but will with temptation also make a way to escape, that ye may be able to bear it.

The last word belongs to Robert. As he reaches the pulpit, he removes his glasses and wipes his handkerchief across wet eyes. Then his back straightens and his head lifts, giving his *kufi* the semblance of an African crown.

"I thought I was finished cryin'," he says, "but don't seem like it's over yet. Right now, I'm on an emotional roller coaster. I sat there, the only thought I had was, *God is real. He is real.* In the Wounded Healers, we know that through the Lord there is hope and there is help. But we found out the only ones who get help *want* help. You can't give this to nobody. They have to come for theirselves. We also realize, as this song behind me plays, that a million didn't make it. But you have heard the ones who did. May we thank you and solicit your prayers."

When the applause finally ebbs, Eli Wilson strikes the opening organ chords of "Precious Lord," the song that will serve as a bridge between the testimonies and Reverend Youngblood's sermon. In the tenor section of the choir, Eli's younger brother, Darryl, rises for his solo on the prelude. "There's so much in my heart," he sings, "I want to say to You, Lord." Suddenly his face clenches, then falls slack with tears. Hearing his brother's distress, Eli assumes the vocals, and Darryl topples backward, arms outstretched and mouth agape, into the arms of Charles Lewis.

All through the testimonies, Darryl had listened and been convicted, degradation by degradation. He remembered the bouts of free-basing until dawn. He remembered carrying a pistol for protection when he bought. He remembered his preacher father, frightened by his excesses, counseling, "Too much of *nothing* is good for you, son." "Precious Lord" was his daddy's favorite spiritual, the one he often sang after finishing a sermon. Eli Wilson, Sr., had not lived to see Darryl return to faith and sobriety. He had died being defied by a son who, instead of attending the family church on Sunday morning, stayed home getting high.

So Darryl howls now, howls from his core. All the testimonies this morning have released his own, which takes the form not of words but of a harrowing noise. And now it runs from the choir loft through the congregation like a fast, snaking fuse.

A father leads his son before the altar to kneel in paired prayer. A woman holds both arms upright, fisting and opening her hands as if flashing a code. Across the room an usher with eyes dreamily closed sweeps her arms in perfect arcs. The aisles engorge, some people picking their way to the altar, others huddling in clusters, until only bowed heads and interlocked arms can be seen, and sobs hover disembodied in midair.

"Prayer time" is the Saint Paul term for such worship, but it is a misleading phrase. Prayer time can never be planned like a hymn or a speech; it can only arrive spontaneously, perhaps once or twice a year. And far from being about time, prayer time is about the suspension of time, from musical measures to the hour of the day. It is about the surrender of order to need.

Songs stretch and weave and merge. Voices plead and praise. Only after an hour of communal catharsis does a fatigued tranquility descend. There will be no sermon this Sunday.

One Saturday afternoon in August of 1986, on his fifty-second day of sobriety, Robert Sharper walked down Pitkin Avenue in East New York. He had been discharged a week earlier from a drug-rehabilitation program with the standard warning to the newly abstinent: "Avoid familiar people, places, and things." And he had taken the advice so seriously he barely left his cousin Gloria's apartment except to attend Narcotics Anonymous meetings, favoring those in the Bronx, as far from his old dealers and shooting galleries as the subway could carry him. But now he needed the tweed jacket he had deposited for dry cleaning months ago. In the morning he was going to church.

Then Robert saw him, standing on the curb, with the pose of practiced disinterest that actually announced he was open for business.

It was Panama. Robert's stomach started fluttering in the old, awful way. As he moved closer, he told himself, *Just get your clothes and get out.* Still, his insides rippled. He remembered what a counselor had written to him in a farewell scrapbook from the center. "Sometimes when you are alone think about the Serenity Prayer. You will need it." Until this moment, he had never understood what the man meant.

"I heard you went away," Panama said.

"Yeah, man," Robert answered, "I got tired. Now I'm not doin' that no more. I found another way to live."

He steeled himself for the sales pitch, the welcome-home present, the offer of a free taste, the three-quarters-for-the-price-of-a-half deal. *God grant me the serenity to accept the things I cannot change, the courage to change the things I can, and the wisdom to know the difference.*

"I'm glad," Panama said. "You look good. Soon as I get ready to get straight, I'll come looking for you."

As Robert hurried home with his coat, it occurred to him that Panama sounded sincere. But he could do nothing for Panama; he was still reconstructing himself; he was feeling with unsheathed nerves twenty years of aches and regrets. How often had he wept in the rehabilitation program? He had wept for old sins against his mother, wept for the waste of her inheritance, wept as he pieced together an autobiographical collage, with pictures of diving boards and basketball sneakers, symbols of a vanished grace. For the first time in years, he had felt the urge to pray for something other than strong dope and dumb cops. He recalled the verse in Proverbs that his Aunt Winifred had given him after his mother's death:

The fear of the Lord is the beginning of knowledge; but fools despise wisdom and instruction.

Robert was spending a lot of time with Aunt Winifred now, since she was Gloria's mother and lived only four blocks away. He would arrive every morning about nine, lie prone on the carpet to ease his bad back, and let his mother's sister heal him. She made him tea and grilled cheese sandwiches. She told the family history. She read from Proverbs and Psalms. And each Sunday she took Robert to the New Canaan Baptist Church, where one morning, during a sermon about

Calvary and cocaine, he walked down the aisle to accept Christ.

He did not stay long at New Canaan. Robert was playing for Narcotics Anonymous in a basketball league that started at one o'clock every Sunday afternoon. New Canaan's service, which began at ten-forty-five, made for too many close calls, so when Robert learned that Gloria's church, Saint Paul, held an eight o'clock service, he started attending with her. Immediately something informal and open struck him. The choir members could wear their own clothes instead of robes. The preacher was neither gray nor bald. The congregation was studded with old friends from Brownsville—Yvonne Ziegler, Butch Carr, Elizabeth Gray, and Icie Johnson, now working in an environmental education center and still possessed of a sleek figure and cute freckles.

Icie had actually spotted him first, when Reverend Youngblood asked all the visitors to stand, and she had thought, *Lord have mercy, what's Delanor doing in church?* She knew nothing of his drug rehabilitation or religious reawakening. The last time she had seen him, back in 1980, he had invited her home for dinner, neglecting to mention he was living there with another woman. That was the same old Del, too fast by half. She refused even to part with her phone number.

Each Sunday at Saint Paul, though, they exchanged a few more words. One week Icie watched Robert formally join the church. Another she saw him begin tithing. And another she dropped a note inside his Bible. It was, six years late, her phone number.

They arranged to meet the next weekend at a play entitled, *Yes, God Is Real*. She, who as a matter of pride had never paid for anything on a date, bought his ticket. He gave her a sweatshirt. Over the next weeks they strolled through Prospect Park, went to films in Greenwich Village, ate shrimp cocktails at Junior's. She would send him shy, girlish cards inscribed, "Thinking of you." He would squire her home, kiss her on the cheek, and leave. Now Robert realized what the Bible meant about being reborn; the father of three children by two women, neither of whom he had married, he felt, in Icie's presence, tentative and virginal.

From their separate apartments, they talked for hours on the phone, sometimes from dusk to dawn. They talked about fifty-cent movies at the Loew's Pitkin long ago. They talked about the letters she wrote when he was in Riker's Island, and how she wouldn't send photos because she thought she wasn't pretty enough. They talked about Hester Sharper, who had always liked Icie. They talked about Robert's journey to hell and back and what might lay ahead.

"I don't know how to say this," Robert blurted during one call in May 1987, "but I'm just gonna say it. You're gonna be my wife."

"I know."

Reverend Youngblood would wed them in December 1987, preaching a sermon called "Marriage Is a Ministry," but it was a question he raised during the premarital counseling that would lead Robert to his calling. "Now that I know what God saved you from," the pastor had said, "what did he save you *for?*"

Robert did not know the answer. He prayed for direction. He requested another meeting with Reverend Youngblood. As they sat down, the pastor spoke excitedly about the Help Center, a drug rehabilitation clinic in Florida funded by a church and led by a reformed dealer. "It's something we need to work with here," he went on. "But it's not my area. I need someone who can teach me." He brought his gaze to Robert. "I believe God takes our weaknesses and turns them into strengths. And it may be that's why He sent you to Saint Paul."

Robert's eyes grew large. He mulled over the words.

"If you want me to try it," he finally answered, "I'll try it."

Robert built the program over nine months, drawing on sources personal, clinical, and spiritual. From his experiences with group therapy and Narcotics Anonymous, he stressed mutual support and the twelve-step framework. After observing the Help Center, he added an overtly Christian perspective, which would complement the AA and NA programs that made only ambiguous reference to a "Higher Power." Saint Paul sent Robert to conferences on peer counseling, black alcoholism, and treating people of color. On assignment from Reverend Slaughter, he studied Henri J. M. Nouwen's book *The Wounded Healer*, which argued that only one who had suffered could minister to the suffering. The group now had its name. And Robert had an answer to the question that so plagued him: *What's my part?*

His part was to tell his tale, with blunt language and unstinting candor, and as he recounted his past, his future began to unfold. Marriage to Icie, membership at Saint Paul, leadership of the Wounded Healers—all gave Robert identity, yet even collectively their parts did not form a whole. What was missing was the defining force of a heritage, and for Robert the only clues to that heritage were some words from his grandmother. Trying to console Robert on the day Hester died, his grandmother told of her grandmother, the family's link to Africa. Two stories had survived the generations: She had once received forty lashes for resisting rape by her master. And she had been taken from West Africa on a ship with the initials "J.H.S."

Those pieces of history, laying dormant in Robert for years, reawakened the day in early 1989 he first saw a street vendor selling *kente*. The multicolored cloth from Ghana, first popularized by the nation's revolutionary founder, Kwame Nkrumah, was becoming in black America a talisman of African heritage. Robert bought a strip, which he wore that Sunday to Saint Paul. Reverend Youngblood, impressed, asked him to get one hundred more for the church's men. Searching for the lowest price, Robert found a Ghanaian immigrant named Kofi Amankrado peddling them outside a Harlem jazz concert for eight dollars apiece. With their commerce completed, Robert told Kofi the story of his grandmother's grandmother. Kofi said he would be returning to Ghana for a visit in early 1990, and he invited Robert along.

Kofi took him to the former slave prison at Elmina. He introduced him to an archivist at the national museum, and she discovered in shipping records the name of the vessel that had carried Robert's people away in leg irons and chains, the *John H. Smith*. In Kofi's home village of Asafo, with its dirt road and strange food and intermittent electricity, Robert felt almost impossibly familiar. At that dusty crossroads, he spoke aloud to God. "What are You showing me?" he asked. "What are You saying to me? I'm gonna sit still and listen."

One answer was to build a bond from Saint Paul to Asafo. But that would require more men and more time and, most important, the commitment of Reverend Youngblood. It would become Robert's project, his obsession, through most of 1990. The second answer, though, could be acted upon immediately. Robert would assume an African name. In Ghanaian fashion, his middle name would be derived from the weekday of his birth. Thus he became Yaw, "Thursday-born." His new surname, bestowed by the chief in Asafo, would be Akoto, after the twelfth chief of the Ashanti nation. And his first name would represent the dominant trait in his character. The name was Osei. It meant "serious."

*   *   *

As Friday twilight falls on Hendrix Street, the Wounded Healers climb into two church vans, bound for a retreat three hours upstate. In their previous lives, this would have been the hour of indulgence, the time to pass the quart or the vial or the pipe on the flimsy pretext of "TGIF." Now they share barbecued ribs and moo goo gai pan from the Chinese restaurant on Linden Boulevard. "You want something to drink?" Tony Douglas asks Danny Edmonds, offering a brown bag, twisted around a bottleneck. "Don't worry. You won't get drunk. Just Pepsi." They both laugh knowingly.

Five months have elapsed since the Wounded Healers gave their testimonies to the congregation. Powerful as that service was, it signaled the end of nothing. It was not a coda, but merely a crescendo, returning the Wounded Healers where they always must return, to the beginning of an unending cycle. If anything, the service placed new pressures on the ministry, and particularly on Osei Yaw Akoto. So many worshipers asked to join the group that Reverend Youngblood had to announce from the pulpit that in the fragile business of recovery the Wounded Healers could not yet bear more members. He had his worries that, faced with fifty members instead of fifteen, Osei might relapse. Osei himself, sensitive to the same risk, had resumed seeing a therapist.

There has been gradual growth and evolution in the group. Osei personally recruited Shawn Hopkins, a woman who lost a promising career in graphic design to cocaine. Tom Carter's stepson, Jim Charles, had begun attending the week before, when he was released from a rehabilitation center. Once he had been a computer programmer for a major bank, with a $40,000-a-year salary and a Manhattan co-op. Tony Douglas, meanwhile, has slowly developed into a leader. Back in the winter, he had once asked Osei, "Will I have to go to meetings the rest of my life?" To which Osei replied, "You came here from the D train and Ward's Island shelter. You can end up on the A train and Third Street shelter. You got to play the tape all way straight back to where it started." Now Tony seems at peace with that message. Just a few weeks ago, a homeless junkie had wandered into the Wounded Healers, a ragged slash above his brow, muttering about how nobody knew his pain. Tony had simply hiked up his slacks, rolled down his socks, and revealed the scars across his shins from being thrown out the window years ago. And then he had wordlessly embraced the man.

"I dunno how you were," Tony says now to Danny, "but I couldn't sleep last night, thinkin' 'bout this trip."

"And you got your first anniversary comin' up, too, right?" Danny refers not to a wedding but to Tony's first Narcotics Anonymous meeting.

"Wednesday."

"Lotta big days," Danny says admiringly. "Whew."

Then he scrapes the bottom of the Chinese food bag for two fortune cookies. Danny's cookie says he appreciates the arts, which he takes as a reference to his collection of six hundred records. Tony cracks open the other, straightens the strip of paper, and reads aloud, "'You will pass a difficult test that will make your life happier.'"

By now the van has entered the Van Wyck Expressway, crowded with traffic for the Mets game. Osei inserts a tape, which runs from the Winans, a gospel group, to the Afro-pop of Fela. Danny dozes, so Tony, too excited for sleep, introduces himself to Jim. His hair is cut nearly to the scalp. He wears a sweatsuit that fits snugly, now that cocaine is no longer deadening his young man's appetite.

"I'm ready to get back in the ball game," he tells Tony.

"Don't go too fast."

"I know," Jim says softly. "This is the first time I listened to anybody's advice. Man, when I went up there, I thought, 'Fuck this. Nobody can tell me nothin'.' Just gonna clean up, then go back, do it a little different."

Tony chuckles dryly.

"I'm a knucklehead, a real knucklehead," he says, addressing both Jim and himself. "Sometimes I think, I used to make all that money, buy anything. Now I make eighty a week. First job of my life. Livin' real humble. And I just pray to God He'll keep me in this mind. Because I know if I went back again, I won't make it alive." He turns to Jim. "You got a sponsor for NA?"

"I'm workin' on that."

"You need that person you can tell everything to," says Tony, who was sponsored by Osei. "And you got to make all your fellowship meetings. Can't go Sunday to Sunday. And after-care. You need that. I went nine to three for eighteen months. You want, I'll give you a name and number."

Jim stares at the lights of Shea Stadium. Tony indicates the highway's shoulder.

"I remember one time I ran into a pole here," he says, "with a brand new Audi. Eighty-four. Left it right there."

"Fuck it, just get another one," Jim says.

"Yeah, man. Walked away."

Jim drifts. Tony, knowing how silence hurts, keeps talking. He talks about his job, his literacy classes, the importance of filling the hours. Jim coughs hard, removes a bottle of syrup from his overnight bag. Tony leans forward for inspection. The label says, "Contains no alcohol or amphetamines."

The van finally passes the stadium, and as it scales the Triboro Bridge, traffic loosens. Marvin Gaye plays on the tape, then Joe Sample. Phil White, a member of Eldad-Medad who has volunteered to drive, pushes the speed above sixty for the first time in an hour. The South Bronx blurs past.

"Check it out," Tony says. "I'm on the freeway with jazz and I'm not high."

He mimes himself steering with one hand, lifting a spoonful of coke to his nose with the other.

"Those were the days," Jim sighs. Then he catches sight of the apartment houses perched on the bluffs north of the Deegan Expressway. "This is the place that did it to me. Thought I was on top of the world. Had my place. Had my cocaine spot. Then I got to where I thought I would die there."

Tony answers with memories of being beaten, stabbed, shot, tossed from the sixth floor, and left for dead. Those, too, were the days.

"I didn't go into detox to get well," he says. "I went in to hide. But when I came out, something clicked. I don't have to live like this. I was so scared to leave. I didn't have anywhere to go. I'd been livin' on the D train. You know those bums in Grand Central? I was one of them for a month. I was losin' my mind. I was buggin'. I'd think of all the good stuff I had and here I was, just the clothes on my back."

"I didn't know *how* to get out," Jim adds. "I didn't know what to do."

"I lived in a crack house before I hit the train. People comin' all night long."

"I used to have to leave my house to sleep. Go to a hotel. So many transactions goin' down." Jim gets a cigarette and a soda from Tony. "I saw a few of my friends die. There were contracts out on me. Soon's I left that place I was at, two weeks later they burned that house down. It's insanity."

Neither man speaks for a time. Stars prick the sky. The van glides across the Hudson on the Tappan Zee Bridge. Tony, at once worldly and simple, likens the span to the Golden Gate, but thinks the water beneath it is the Nyack River.

"This be my best year, for real," he says in a low voice, as if speaking too loudly might invite a hex. "I been to the beach. I been to Coney Island. I feel so excited. Like a kid."

It is nearly eleven when the vans reach the retreat site in Cairo, a bungalow colony that Saint Paul bought in 1986. Only with sunrise can the Wounded Healers see the pine grove and the sloping Catskills, the swimming pool and the basketball court. Before eight a game begins, with Osei putting the others at ease with his wit. "We're playin' Sing Sing rules," he announces at one point. Later, when a teammate fumbles an easy pass, he chides, "You had too many Bahama Mamas last night." After an hour, the players towel off the sweat and amble into the dining hall for grits and eggs and salmon.

Then they draw their blue metal chairs into a circle and set to the task of recovery. They discuss a Bible verse and meditate to a gospel song. Each offers a word or phrase to describe his mood—"honored," "expectant," "refreshed," "blessed," and, from Osei, "new and serene." Finally he plays tapes of the Wounded Healers' testimonies five months earlier. The last of these belongs to Roland, and Roland, as Osei explains, has disappeared.

As the hours pass, the Wounded Healers talk. And if in the van last night Jim Charles had unburdened himself, made the confession from which renewal can begin, then this morning in the dining hall is Shawn Hopkins's time.

"I feel all messed up," she says, clutching the sides of her chair as if traveling a rutted road. "There's days I think about the crack dealer on the floor under me and I think, 'Just to do it one more time. Just once.'

"And you know what stops me? When I was clean about a hundred days, I was at the bus stop with my son. He was lookin' up at the blue sky and the clouds. And you know what he said? 'If you smoke that shit one more time, you're gonna die.' God speaks through the children."

She lifts her eyes, regards the faces around her.

"I never thought I could be around church people. I never knew all those verses, all those chapters. I mean, I been doing drugs since I was eleven years old. But you know somethin'? The only way I'm gonna stay clean is to come to God as I am."

She fingers her dreadlocks, then the African bracelets around her wrist.

"I get people like me, they say, 'How you go into church lookin' like *that*? And I say, 'I don't know. I just do.' All I've ever wanted is just to be loved for what I am. So many people tried to change me, tell me what God wants, till I don't know who I am, and I think God just don't want me."

Her head slumps onto one shoulder. Her eyes glisten with imminent tears.

"And I just feel so sick now. That's how I feel about this process. I feel sick. But I thank God I don't feel so sick I'd get high."

The session, broken only by lunch, lasts until four o'clock. It is almost time to return to Brooklyn. As Myrtis Brent fries chicken for dinner, Danny Edmonds leads a last prayer. Then, as the others start for the door and the cooler air outside, he says, "I've got a lesson to teach." He speaks of Egyptian symbols, the obelisk and pyramid and finally the *ankh*, the looped cross that contains the ancient signs for man, woman, and child, that represents life itself. As he finishes, Tom Carter pulls from beneath his chair a small box wrapped in gold paper. He hands this to Osei, who opens it delicately, eyes averted from the rest. He finds inside a necklace with a gold *ankh*, which he cradles in both palms. Tom hangs it around his neck like an Olympic medal, and Osei, for a rare moment, finds himself without words.

"I personally don't want to see anyone go through what I went through," he finally says to the group. "I committed my life to this ministry. I'm willing to die for it. And being presented this today lets me know that I'm living it."

5

◉

THE OVERCOMING CROWD

D AWN DOES NOT BREAK on Easter Sunday in Brooklyn. It slowly fights night to a standoff, an overcast the shade of ashes, lit at its fringes by a streetlamp, a gas station, a diner. Rain leaves the roads slick and dark and deserted, and the heavy air holds aromas of ocean and industry. All through East New York, little life stirs. Drainwater races down the subway stanchions along Livonia. Seagulls roost on the sodden fields of Linden Park. Potting soil spills from a tray of chrysanthemums, abandoned by its peddler on a curb across the way. A gypsy cab splashes past, windows steamed, carrying home the late partiers. Two early workers meanwhile trudge toward a bus stop, this one wielding a twisted umbrella, that one wearing a plastic sack like a do-rag.

And at the corner of Hendrix and Linden, the corner nearest Saint Paul, a traffic jam builds and families flock down the sidewalk, as if this single block were living ten time zones east of its city, as if this were midafternoon. The first worshiper arrived at four o'clock, two hours before the service, with a friend who had slept on her couch. Now, an hour later, the cars stand three abreast outside the church, and a similar congestion builds up within, from lobby to coat room to lounge. There, mothers fuss one last time over daughters' barrettes, then touch up their own eyeliner and lipstick, and finally tug the pantyhose bunching around ankles in the dreaded condition known as "elephant legs."

But for this, the black church's highest day of *haute couture*, Reverend Youngblood has insisted his people dress down. He has even renamed the holiday Resurrection Sunday, trying to strip the commerce from piety. "Jesus Christ," the pastor had preached back in January, "is not about stirrup pants and patent leather shoes and curls drippin'. So when you come worship Resurrection Sunday, I don't want you so handsome you can't serve the Lord and so cute you can't shout. The people who discovered Jesus were the *ordinary* people. The muckety-mucks—they didn't get it. So when you see me, I ain't gonna be wearin' those glad rags. I'm gonna be ordinary."

He stands now at the altar, a man of his word, clad in black sneakers and a Yoke Fellows T-shirt. Eli Wilson sits at the organ in jeans and a sweater. Throughout the rows, brogans mingle with tasseled loafers, khakis with chiffon, jogging suits with pinafores and pocket squares. In the sanctuary extension, many worshipers sit in folding chairs on a concrete floor. Four steel girders, installed only last month, buttress the cedar roof. In other churches, such barren utility might seem an Easter embarrassment. Here and now it reinforces the prevailing humility.

"You might wonder why I'm dressed like this," Reverend Youngblood declares, stepping from the altar so all can see. "Because I want to be. I'm over that Easter Bunny stuff. And those four ladies who went to the sepulcher didn't have to primp. I'm here to celebrate the Resurrection. And the only person who's dressed incorrectly this morning is the person who's wearing what they didn't want to wear." He smiles. "Other than that, this is the most harmonious group you've ever seen in your life."

James Jones, on the piano, lightly strikes a melody. Then he repeats it, pressing harder on its rhythm, until the clapping begins. With two thousand palms beating four-four time, Eli bursts into a sound as clear as reveille.

> *Rejoice, come on, everybody*
> *Rejoice, come on, everybody*
> *This is the day the Lord hath made*
> *Let's be glad about it*

most ppl's lives are busy. How do you
know when its enough happiness?

THE OVERCOMING CROWD   157

As Eli opens the second verse, lifting off his seat and leaning into the microphone, Reverend Youngblood rears back his head and joins in duet. Eli possesses the round, robust voice his music professors called a "Wagnerian tenor." The pastor, self-taught, has the tense, gritty timbre of a Wilson Pickett. They sing the way long-married couples dance, anticipating each next step before it is taken. During their college years, they often spent Sundays "church-hopping," once performing at nine in a single day. There was never any money, and they usually had to pass on dinner to get to the next church. The only reward was ecstasy.

From the choir loft to the back stairs, perched on tiptoes for a view, the congregation follows their ritual of call and response. Eli soars into a single note that arches for measure after measure, effortlessly, while beneath him Reverend Youngblood punches out the bridge like percussion: "God has been so good to us! God has been so good to us! God has been so good to us!" Then, with a raised eyebrow as cue, they plunge back into the verse, trading lines, bending grace notes, driving the faithful into glorious bedlam.

Lungs bellow. Feet stamp. The very floor shakes. It is 6:07 in the morning. After a Sunday of comparable tremors not long ago, a parishioner who works in demolition told Reverend Youngblood he was worried the new concrete might buckle. What, the pastor asked, could reduce the risk? "Tell Mister Wilson," the man said, "to break up the rhythm."

"Yeah," Reverend Youngblood rasps now, as winded as a sprinter on his victory lap. "I thought I better tell y'all that on my way to church this morning I passed the worship site called Walterio's." He refers to a bar on Flatbush Avenue. "And they were havin' a good time. But I'm here today because my Lord and Savior took the sting out of death and the victory from the grave. And there's no way they're gonna have a better time than we do. No, no, no!"

"Tell it, doctor!"

"Now I want you to turn to somebody and say, 'I'm here because He got up.'"

The words, repeated down aisles and across pews, resound for nearly a minute. The embraces last well longer. It is not only Easter these people celebrate, not only the culmination of Holy Week, but the world they have made for themselves. "The glory," they will say, "goes to God." But the proof is on Hendrix Street in East New York.

A week ago, on Palm Sunday, the congregation marched 1,500 strong around Christ Square, renewing its claim against the hookers and dealers and muggers. The next morning, a busload of Yoke Fellows left for a college tour. On Maundy Thursday, the men of Eldad-Medad served communion for their families at home. Good Friday worship opened with two plays written, acted, and staged by Saint Paul's drama troupe, whose members included a recovering alcoholic and a reformed pimp. Last night, only hours ago, Eli Wilson and the choir sang at Brooklyn College. Later today the church's dance company will perform.

They are family and more than family, the people of Saint Paul. The blows that would rupture bonds of blood or friendship can somehow be absorbed by a community of faith. There was a member several years ago in the midst of a divorce. One Sunday she watched from the rear of the church as her estranged husband rose in prayer, and from the distance she made out his words. "God bless my wife," he said, "wherever she is." The woman called Reverend Youngblood that night, tearful, insisting she must leave the church. "Where else will you go?" he asked her, and ultimately she chose to stay. Even today in the choir sing two daughters of Reverend Johnny W. Walker, the church's previous pastor, while in the congregation listen the members who unseated him. The same Board of Elders contains Melvin Heyward, who went on strike against the telephone company for months this past winter, and Charles Young, who crossed the picket line as management. One parishioner, Charles Warfield, is married to the ex-wife of another, Ed Lawson. The harmony, if not easy, endures.

"Together," Reverend Youngblood says, "let us pray." Heads bow. Hands reach and clasp. Only now can the rain be heard, drumming its drone on the roof. "Father, Son, and Spirit, we thank You, we honor You, we magnify Your name. For the teachings that open our minds and our hearts. That heal our bodies. That sever bad relationships and seal the best relationships. Lord, we thank You that You serenade us again and again through Your music. We thank You for the sisters that discovered You. We thank You for the brothers that You used, beginning at Galilee. We thank You for the family of God. And this morning, we're here to take care of family business."

*   *   *

A compact woman in a navy suit and a pink flowered hat applauds. Her name is Ruth Morris. Sixty years ago, when she began attending Saint Paul, everyone knew her as Little Ruthie Meyers, the girl with braids who was best friends with the preacher's daughter. She is the church's closest link to its genesis, the deepest root of this family tree.

Her mother headed north from Richmond in 1888, alone at the age of twelve. She found her way to Harlem and then Brownsville, hiring herself out as a domestic, and bearing thirteen children, of whom Ruth was the last. They lived in a cold-water flat behind a shop, with a tub in the kitchen and a wood stove so difficult to light it reduced Ruth to tears a hundred times. In the drawer of her dresser, Ruth's mother kept the Bible in which all births and deaths were recorded.

It was not difficult to spot the black churches in Brownsville. In a neighborhood so thoroughly Jewish it was nicknamed "the New Jerusalem," there were only two, Pilgrim Baptist and Saint Paul, and the latter happened to sit down the block from the Meyers apartment. Fifteen men and women, mostly migrants from the Carolinas, had founded the church in 1927, re-creating in the strange, promising land of Brooklyn the same institution that had sustained them through slavery and sharecropping and Jim Crow.

By the time Ruth joined, in 1929, the congregation had grown toward forty and the church was on its second pastor, a gentle and heavyset man named E. L. Haywood. He presided over a converted storefront with shelfing paper covering the windows and a furnace so feeble that on cold mornings the worshipers wore their overcoats and the pastor removed his only to deliver the sermon. In fairer weather, Reverend Haywood traveled by trolley to Canarsie Beach, where he baptized the newly converted. The church's children, like Ruth, dashed between services to Pitkin Avenue for foot-long kosher hot dogs and a glimpse of the mohair jackets in Fisher Brothers' window display.

At about that time, a man named William Brandon was packing his car in the hamlet of Semora, North Carolina. He was the same William Brandon who stands beside the pulpit this morning, preparing the silver dishes with crackers and grape juice for the celebration of the Lord's Supper. No one except Ruth Morris has worshiped at Saint Paul longer.

A farmer's son, Brandon had already left the fields once, to work in a garment factory in Roanoke, Virginia. This time he would aim for Brooklyn because two older siblings lived there and told him jobs could be found. With nine dollars in his pocket, sleeping in his car, he made the three-day journey, arriving to find a city of apple peddlers and soup kitchens. Only after two months of searching did he locate work, washing cars for five dollars a week. The prospects were better, he decided, helping a friend make bootleg whiskey. A federal raid ended that aspiration, and in its wake Brandon's wife said, "Why don't we go to church?" Before long, he was the treasurer and a deacon.

The Saint Paul of that time, the mid-1930s, was growing modestly. The faithful gave fifteen cents each Sunday. The annual budget came to $480. A small radio station carried the eight-o'clock service. Reverend Haywood resigned in 1935, and his replacement, Elbert H. Hamblin, was never installed as pastor in his three years of leadership. But the great black pilgrimage northward, the pilgrimage that had brought Ruth Morris's mother and William Brandon, would soon deliver the man to mold Saint Paul.

His name was Adolphus Smith, and he served as pastor for twenty-seven years, nearly half the church's history. Except for Reverend Youngblood, no pastor before or after held the position for more than seven. Reverend Smith died in 1967, but his widow, Allie, sits this morning in her usual spot, five rows back and near the side aisle. Her presence may be the ultimate proof of church as community, for, considering all that occurred, few in the congregation ever had more reason to leave.

Adolphus Smith and Allie McCluney grew up together in Salisbury, North Carolina, a town granted moderate prosperity by its railroad switching yard, and thus a magnet for sharecroppers turned blacksmiths, mechanics, and coal haulers. Adolphus, however, was bound for more than the steady payday of manual labor. He joined the revival circuit as a seventh grader in knee pants, a preaching prodigy being groomed by Salisbury's black pastors. One of them, Reverend William Thompson, was Allie's uncle, and it was in his church one autumn evening in 1924 that she first heard Adolphus speak the word. He titled the sermon, "Sir, We Would See Jesus," and he rendered it with unerring grammar and decided charisma. "The kind of preacher my uncle was would talk a lot and say nothing," Allie would recall years later. "But this boy had points and points and points."

They courted through high school, were elected king and queen of the prom, and proceeded together to all-black Livingstone College. Buster, as friends called Adolphus, was already pastoring a church, and it was uniformly believed that a pastor ought to be married. So in December of their freshman year, he enticed Allie into a borrowed car, drove over the border into South Carolina, and found a justice of the peace. The morning after their first night together, Allie ran home. Her mother returned her to Buster. Four months later she was pregnant.

The Smiths held no grand plan to leave the South. By the standards of their time and place, they belonged firmly to the middle class. Buster was pastoring a second, larger church, which even paid him a salary. Allie worked as a substitute teacher and cared for the couple's daughter, Alfreda. Until they visited Allie's mother in New York, where she was working as a live-in housekeeper, neither husband nor wife had traveled farther north than Baltimore.

"Buster," Allie's mother said, "I believe you can make it if you stay here."

"What about me?" Allie asked.

"Your mother needs you," Buster answered. "I think we oughta stay."

They settled in Harlem and learned the first hard lessons of the North. With her teaching credentials scorned, Allie cleaned houses for twenty-five cents an hour. Buster, who had been reared among shotgun shacks with oil lamps and outhouses, became an apartment superintendent, responsible for the mysteries of boilers, plumbing, and dumbwaiters. His search for more appropriate employment took him to a packing house, where he met a butcher named E. L. Haywood, who mentioned that he pastored a church. On Reverend Haywood's invitation, Buster Smith preached at Saint Paul for the first time in 1935, and left such an impression that three years later the congregation issued him its call. Allie, who had seen nothing of Brooklyn except its raucous, stinking piers, cried the whole day.

The first years were the most thrilling. The Smiths moved into a three-bedroom parsonage, which had been vacant for several years, and the congregation set about making it into a home. Reverend Haywood's brother built a barbecue pit in the yard, which became a favored playground. The ushers painted the house and installed a telephone. A piano and a china closet arrived as donations. The new pastor was not without his critics, who whispered about his wife wearing lipstick and loudly remarked how Alfreda resembled her father, as if that should be surprising, given that he was indeed her biological parent. But in myriad ways he disarmed them.

In a decade when only one in five black ministers had attended college, Reverend Smith was a preacher of uncommon erudition. Sequestered each Saturday in his office, he would type his sermons in almost flawless detail, replete with Roman numerals and subheads, and then edit by fountain pen. Intellectual without being elitist, he could quote from Socrates or Longfellow, then compare the glittering riches of Babylon to Ebbets Field lit for a night game. His fellow pastors in Brooklyn once honored him as "Best Manuscript Minister." He was, at the same time, a forceful physical presence, as firm and broad as he had been as a star halfback in high school, and endowed with a voice to rattle rafters.

As industry awakened from the Depression to arm America for World War II, tens of thousands of blacks flocked to Brooklyn—"men with cotton-baling hooks still in their pockets," as the historian Gerald Sorin has written, "and women tired from holding their small children as they made their way in buses and railroad coach cars." Those who settled in Brownsville heard of Buster Smith and Saint Paul, and the congregation burgeoned into several hundred, overflowing the sanctuary. One Sunday in 1944, after a sermon about Nehemiah restoring the walls of Jerusalem, Reverend Smith declared, "Man's got a mind to build." Again, the critics clucked. Money was tight. Lumber and steel were reserved for the military. There could be no worse time to raise a new church. But on the pastor's prayers, Saint Paul opened its first bank account, and on Sundays each man gave fifty cents and every woman a quarter. Fried chicken was sold, bedspreads raffled off. Within two years the congregation had raised sixty thousand dollars, enough to buy a lot on Osborne Street and erect a brick church with leaded windows and carriage lamps and a steeple flecked with flagstone. A fruit warehouse next door scented the sanctuary with orange.

The new church became a monument to ambition and a growing mood of arrogance. Saint Paul prided itself on its middle-class members, the teachers and lawyers and principals and police. No man would dare worship without shined shoes and a "choked-up" tie;

women wore stockings, and the seams had better be straight. Sunday was designed so no child need leave church, progressing instead from Bible class at nine to service at eleven to fellowship at three to Baptist Young People's Union at six to evening worship at seven-thirty. And when Saint Paul would march in the annual Sunday School Union parade, Reverend Smith himself would carry a few children in his arms, striding down Stone Avenue in a panama hat and swallowtail coat.

"Y'all try to be different all the time," others would say of Saint Paul's members. "You think you're somethin' special." It was true; they did. Let these Northern blacks have their Democratic Party and their rhythm and blues. It would take a bunch of former sharecroppers to show them what praising God was all about. Besides, everyone knew Saint Paul had the prettiest girls.

But modernity, in two guises, found Reverend Smith wanting. As urban renewal swept across Brownsville in 1953, the brick church that had been erected against such odds was razed like some ramshackle tenement. Many in the congregation never forgave the pastor for selling their building to the city instead of resisting. The cash settlement, it was true, allowed Saint Paul to purchase and renovate new quarters, and still to bank a ten-thousand-dollar reserve. Yet that cushion became the excuse for many worshipers to stop giving, to stop viewing Saint Paul with enlightened self-interest.

The Civil Rights Movement, meanwhile, was severely splitting the black religious community, especially the National Baptist Convention, the single largest association of black churches, between the active and the apolitical. For Saint Paul's young people, galvanized by the protests, Reverend Smith maintained a damaging silence. Despite his many gifts as a preacher, he had always hewed to safe, predictable themes—obedience to God, stewardship, fair play, purpose in life— and against the backdrop of the Montgomery bus boycott and the *Brown v. Board of Education* case, those sermons sounded almost willfully remote. "There was nothing happening at Saint Paul," one member recalls. "Just singing and praying, and even that was dull."

As his wife and a handful of others knew, Buster Smith actually cared deeply about the civil rights crusade. He heard Martin Luther King preach in Brooklyn, and cried while watching the "I Have a Dream" speech on television. He was arrested in a protest against hir-

ing bias at a local hospital, although three hours in jail ended his taste
for civil disobedience. And as early in the movement as 1956, when
the governor of Arkansas defiantly refused to desegregate Little Rock's
Central High School, Reverend Smith delivered a sermon that captured all the indignation he had felt but rarely expressed. The mystery
is why he preached it on a weeknight to a black lodge celebrating an
anniversary, rather than on Sunday to the young adults starving for
such a word.

> Social justice, total freedom, complete equality are far overdue
> in this country.... Little Rock is not in Arkansas alone. It is
> wherever there is bigotry, demagoguery, discrimination, and
> race hatred. Little Rock is any place there is opposition to total
> integration.... The Governor of Arkansas lifted his hand and
> pledged to support the Constitution of the United States of
> America, but the shackles of segregation pulled him from that
> lofty pledge and reduced him to the miserable level of calling
> troops to defeat the law.... Little Rock could be licked if it were
> merely a city, but Little Rock is a decentralized symbol and an
> evil system....
>
> The religion we claim is geared for crisis. It was introduced
> in this world by Jesus Christ and lived in times of tension and
> upheaval. He was so rugged and reckless that His close friends
> advised against many of His decisions. His family thought He
> was mad. A distinguished leader of the highest order of the
> Pharisees had a midnight appointment with him to advise
> against His subversive teachings and dangerous actions.
>
> But He threw caution to the winds and fearlessly moved
> along the road of faith. His early disciples caught His spirit and
> launched forth into a bitter and hostile world with revolutionary
> designs. May we strive to rediscover that revolutionary faith that
> troubled kings and shook empires.

It was politics of a different, more personal sort, however, that
dominated Buster Smith's last years at Saint Paul. The issue of character was not entirely new to the pastor's tenure. During the early
1950s, a member of the congregation complained to the Board of
Deacons that Reverend Smith had taken his adult daughter as a mistress. For six months the board deliberated. "It was like a scandal, a

crime," remembered William Brandon, who was one of those deacons. Yet the pastor's accomplishments could hardly be ignored; he had, in many ways, made Saint Paul. Finally, a deacon named Clarence Davis settled the issue by reading from his Bible the story of David and Bathsheba. The king's sin had not cost him his crown, Davis argued, and neither should the pastor's cost him his pulpit.

Still, the friction between Reverend Smith and his deacons would never abate. The pastor suffered a heart attack not long after his near-removal. His wife could not sleep on the nights the board met with him. And as Reverend Smith's achievements began to fall deeper into the past, he grew increasingly vulnerable. With the rise of secular black leaders, as well as an outspoken clergy embodied only blocks away by such ministers as Gardner C. Taylor and Sandy F. Ray, Saint Paul's congregation fell from five hundred in 1953 to 150 a decade later. On the pastor's anniversary one year, the special offering amounted to a paltry three hundred dollars. The parsonage and the Buick that the congregation had bought for Reverend Smith in more favorable times now struck his critics as signs of an imperious, effete style—even though his household had also depended on Allie's income from jobs in hospitals, a wartime arsenal, and the Census Bureau.

The Board of Deacons in 1963 resolved to "retire" the pastor, offering him the rare inducement of a lifetime pension in return for his amicable departure. "We knew," Brandon recalls, "that the church was dying." Reverend Smith privately accepted the plan, but in a chaotic church meeting he instead delivered and carried a resolution to unseat five of the seven deacons. Those men, and most of the trustees, were replaced with Smith loyalists. Even the locks on the church safe were changed, and the new combination was disclosed to only three people, one of them the pastor.

So when some money allegedly disappeared from the safe in the fall of 1965, a good deal of suspicion fell on the beleaguered Reverend Smith. On the Sunday after a committee chaired by William Brandon voted to retain a lawyer to investigate, Reverend Smith delivered his farewell sermon. Some saw his resignation as a tacit admission of guilt, others as a principled refusal to be belittled any longer. His letter of retirement, written and typed as carefully as any of his sermons, quoted from Alfred Lord Tennyson.

Then Reverend Smith moved back to North Carolina, building

the first home he would ever own, and serving as temporary pastor of a country church. He died in August 1967, before he could be offered the office permanently. When she heard the news in Brooklyn, Allie wandered the midnight streets in her bathrobe. Her daughter, Alfreda, told William Brandon, "You're the cause of it."

The emotions remained nearly as raw seven years later, when Reverend Youngblood arrived. But as word of this dynamic young preacher spread, many of those who had left Saint Paul returned: Betty Staton Payne, who would become president of the Board of Ushers; Adele Toussaint, who would become principal of the church's elementary school; Bea and Jim Mackie, who would respectively become active in women's ministry and a member of the Board of Elders. But Allie and Alfreda never lost a certain primacy in Reverend Youngblood's eyes. He had seen Eli Wilson, Sr., lose a pulpit. He had lost one himself. He knew first-hand the sensation of disgrace. By his design, Saint Paul moved to Hendrix Street on the double anniversary of the congregation's call to Adolphus Smith in 1938 and its move into the brick church on Osborne Street eight years later. And when Alfreda died in 1984, leaving a widowed mother to bury her only child, Reverend Youngblood turned to Allie during the eulogy to offer financial assistance and something more. "I pledge to you," he said, "that I will be the son you never had."

By now, at seven-thirty, the rain has ceased. Through the skylight in the sanctuary extension falls morning, its color the same pale gray as the concrete floor below. With the pews already filled, another crowd forms in the lobby, awaiting the eight o'clock service, when Reverend Youngblood will preach. "All right," he says from the pulpit, indicating the gathering. "Those of you who are here for the eight, be sure not to leave with the six o'clock folk and take your offerings with you." There is laughter. "I want y'all to know I'm slick as y'all are. The Lord just saved *my* slick."

Then, as a second wave of laughter subsides, the pastor turns serious. Eli provides a melody, dreamy and wordless, needing only to be embroidered. This time Reverend Youngblood will not sing but speak.

"Is there anybody here this morning who's overcome something?" Murmurs of assent fill the air. Chair legs rattle against cement as people rise to stand in witness. "You found yourself in something you thought you'd never get out of. Going through trials. Wondering why this is happening. Knowing you couldn't take it." His words have the intense evenness of an incantation, a hypnotist's command. "Yes!" somebody screams, and then silence resumes. "Maybe there's someone sitting here this morning, heavy laden. And you know when one thing passes, another gonna come along."

Now his voice nestles and soothes.

"So you always gonna be overcoming something. Every day you gonna be overcoming. Don't know how, don't know when, but you'll overcome. Because when we follow in the footsteps of our Lord, He says whatever He has overcome, we, too, shall overcome." The pastor fists both hands, lifts his arms just slightly. "We're the overcoming crowd."

With that single phrase, improvised in an instant, Reverend Youngblood struck at the essence of the black church in America. He was alluding, in an immediate sense, to the anthem of the Civil Rights Movement, "We Shall Overcome." But the resonance rippled far beyond Selma or Montgomery, for the belief in deliverance and the expectation of justice extended back centuries, to the beginning of African bondage in the New World. Long before anyone framed the term "liberation theology," black slaves were practicing it, subverting the gospel of submission they were given, and creating instead a faith to validate their humanity and sanctify their aspirations. At times that faith would take the form of pragmatism, of building institutions and "uplifting the race"; at times it would take the form of insurrection and moral crusade; but never would the ideal of liberation be entirely absent from pulpit and pew, for it was the defining element of African-American Christianity. As C. Eric Lincoln and Lawrence H. Mamiya have written, "In song, word, and deed, freedom has always been the superlative value of the black sacred cosmos. The message of the Invisible Church was, however articulated, *God wants you to be free!*"

The message of the earliest Christian missionaries to America's African captives was, of course, the absolute opposite. Not only did God intend for blacks to be chattel, God wanted them to be better, more devoted, more docile chattel. Theologians patched together a divine defense of slavery from Ephesians 6:5 ("Servants be obedient to them that are your masters ... with fear and trembling, in singleness of

your heart), Leviticus 25:44 ("Both thy bondmen, and thy bondmaids
... shall be of the heathen that are around about you"), and a wildly
extrapolated interpretation of Noah's curse that the children of Ham
be servants. The only bondage from which a slave required emancipation, an Anglican minister named Jonathan Boucher argued, was "the
bondage of sin." Virtually every slave catechism featured a lesson on
obedience:

> *Who gave you a master and mistress?*
> God gave them to me.
> *Who says that you must obey them?*
> God says that I must.
> *What book tells you these things?*
> The Bible.

Even so, slaveholders worried about the consequences. In 1701
the British crown issued the Society for the Propagation of the Gospel
in Foreign Parts a charter to proselytize slaves; within five years, nearly
half the colonial legislatures passed laws specifying that baptism did
not change a slave's status. A Virginia minister who preached against
bondage was indicted by two courts and menaced by a mob. More
typical was the Delaware minister who warned of the "untoward
haughty behaviour" of black converts. He proved oddly prescient, for
black Christianity was bound from its origin to become a religion of
empowerment, separate and distinct from the white doctrine it osten-
sibly embraced.

The key to that seeming contradiction, to the dialectic between
acceptance and rejection, lies in the African faith the slaves carried
with them on the Middle Passage. In certain respects, traditional
African religion left slaves well disposed to adopt Christianity. Most of
their tribes, from the Yoruba to the Ibo to the Bakongo, worshiped a
supreme being, a group of ancestors, and a set of subordinate gods
known as the *orisha*. The Christian trinity, then, could be superim-
posed on the three elements of the slaves' indigenous religion. Roman
Catholic saints, in particular, could be readily equated with individual
orisha, and it was in such Catholic countries as Cuba, Haiti, and Brazil
that the syncretized result emerged as *santería, voudun,* and *candomble.*

In the colonies that would become the United States, the fusion evolved in subtler ways. Since North American plantations were smaller and more self-contained than their Caribbean or Latin American counterparts, slave culture there lost its pure Africanness to the surrounding European influences more quickly. And the Anglican faith that was dominant among North American whites, with its emphasis on formal instruction and a stultifying sense of propriety, offered black captives little of the spiritual commonality that the popular Catholicism in Spanish and Portuguese colonies did. Only with the Great Awakening of the mid-1700s did Protestants convert slaves in significant numbers, because the religion carried by circuit riders and tent revivalists spoke in unique and unexpected ways to diasporic Africans. Those itinerant preachers made preeminent the inner experience of conversion, and welcomed the outer manifestation of ecstasy. With their minds, the slaves grabbed at the concept that anyone could be "born again," implying as it did an equality of all humans before God; with their hearts and voices and limbs, they celebrated that transformation in ancient ways. "While the North American slaves danced under the impulse of the Spirit of a 'new' God," Albert J. Raboteau has written, "they danced in ways their fathers in Africa would have recognized."

Beyond theology, the Methodist and Baptist preachers who dominated the Great Awakening offered practical advantages to enslaved blacks. The Methodists opposed slavery more demonstrably than any denomination except the Quakers, requiring missionaries to free their own slaves and declaring in 1784 that the chattel system offended both the laws of God and the principles of the American Revolution. The Baptists never rose in comparable indignation, but they afforded black converts a tradition of self-government by each church. It is hardly surprising, then, that the first black church in America was a Baptist church, Silver Bluff in Beech Island, South Carolina, founded, according to various estimates, between 1750 and 1777. Black Methodists would only achieve such autonomy after Richard Allen, disgusted that he and fellow blacks were segregated from whites inside their Philadelphia church, withdrew from the congregation in 1787 to form the Free African Society. The society gradually metamorphosed into the African Methodist Episcopal denomination, which gained nearly ten thousand members within a decade of its 1816 founding.

Indeed, the same African heritage that eased the Christian conversion of slaves and black freedmen also equipped them to resist the religion's most passive, otherworldly aspects. Among the newly captured, the memory of Africa nourished the hope of freedom and return, while for later generations the North became the goal. And since most Africans believed in the active intervention of deities in daily life, the temporal and spiritual realms were potently conflated. What sounded to a planter's ears like standard prayers for heavenly rewards, fellow slaves understood to be calls for emancipation in the present tense.

The result was the development of a counter-Christianity, a reaction to the hypocrisy of the master's religion. As Frederick Douglass observed pointedly, "We have men-stealers for ministers, women-whippers for missionaries, and cradle-plunderers for church members. The man who wields the blood-clotted cowskin during the week fills the pulpit on Sunday, and claims to be a minister of the meek and lowly Jesus." White Americans saw themselves as the Israelites in the Promised Land, blacks as the Mosaic Jews slaving for Pharaoh in Egypt. Whites worshiped a Christ who taught that religion should not disturb the political order, blacks a Christ who afflicted the powerful and redeemed the oppressed. On Sundays in church, slaves heard white ministers admonish, "Obey your masters." By night in clandestine prayer meetings, they heard their own preachers declare, "Thank God, I shall not live here always!"

Those sentiments were not idle. Spirituals such as "Steal Away to Jesus" announced the clandestine departures of the Underground Railroad. Black religious leaders commanded the three most important slave revolts in American history: Gabriel Prosser's in 1800, Denmark Vesey's in 1822, Nat Turner's in 1831. The African Methodist Episcopal Zion denomination, known as the "Freedom Church," counted among its ardent followers Harriet Tubman, Sojourner Truth, and Frederick Douglass. Black troops in the Civil War called themselves the "Gospel Army."

With the Union's victory and the enfranchisement of former slaves, the black church began to surrender its primacy; of twenty black senators and representatives elected from the South during Reconstruction, only two were ministers. But once that nascent political freedom was crushed by poll taxes, literacy tests, and vigilante terrorism, all of them countenanced by Washington, the church resumed and expanded its role as the central agency of black existence. Religious groups established such colleges as Morgan in Baltimore, Fisk in Nashville, and Morehouse and Morris Brown in Atlanta. Black churchmen founded mutual aid societies—the Knights of Liberty, the Brotherhood of Liberty, the Grand United Order of True Reformers—that protested against discrimination and racial violence and operated businesses ranging from hotels to newspapers to loan associations. Starting in the early 1800s, black denominations formed their own national associations (generally titled "conventions"), which often included publishing houses and missionary enterprises. With few secular professions open to the race, ministers formed half of the black middle class in the post–Civil War South.

And if some moved toward an assimilation that eschewed spirituals and "shouting" as primitive embarrassments, then others spoke with an unstinting racial identity that anticipated the black nationalists to follow, from Marcus Garvey to Malcolm X. It was Henry McNeal Turner, a bishop in the African Methodist Episcopal Church, who declared in an 1898 essay, "God is a Negro." When a reader of the A.M.E. publication *The Voice of Missions* suggested that Turner was "becoming demented," the bishop replied with words that could have belonged decades later to Amiri Baraka: "Every race of people since time began who have attempted to describe their God by words, or by paintings, or by carvings, or by any other form or figure, have conveyed the idea that the God who made them and shaped their destinies was symbolized in themselves, and why should not the Negro believe that he resembles God as much so as other people?"

By almost any reckoning, however, the years from World War I until the mid-1950s saw a relatively subdued black church. Outspoken activists like Adam Clayton Powell and Vernon Johns were the exception rather than the rule; the most significant institutions—from the National Association for the Advancement of Colored People under the aegis of W. E. B. Du Bois to Marcus Garvey's United Negro Improvement Association—were officially secular. When the noted minister and educator Benjamin Mays analyzed sermons from black churches in the 1930s, he found three-quarters dealt with other-worldly topics. "They make God influential chiefly in the beyond," Mays wrote, "in preparing a home ... where his suffering servants will be free of the trials and tribulations that beset them on earth." The

Swedish sociologist Gunnar Myrdal, conducting research on race in America in the 1940s, discovered black clergy in Savannah *denouncing* a voter-registration drive. "All we preachers supposed to do," one explained, "is to preach the Lord and Savior Jesus Christ and Him crucified and that's all."

Looking back on this period, the contemporary theologian Gayraud S. Wilmore has argued that the black church consciously "deradicalized," that it shed its oppositional tradition in the quest for white acceptance and middle-class respectability. Lincoln and Mamiya, without dismissing that theory, suggest that the migration of millions of blacks from the rural South to the urban North forced churches to serve more as cultural intermediaries than as political advocates. Certainly the proliferation of storefront churches showed how desperately the newcomers were trying to sink familiar roots in foreign soil. But in cities like New York, with black mercantile, professional, and intellectual communities of long standing, the ministry lost its unchallenged authority.

All that changed on December 1, 1955, when Rosa Parks refused to surrender her seat to a white passenger on a Montgomery, Alabama, bus. Her arrest ignited a boycott led by the twenty-six-year-old pastor of the Dexter Avenue Baptist Church, Martin Luther King, Jr. And the boycott launched both the Civil Rights Movement and King's public life. The chronology of the movement hardly needs to be recounted here, but what is most important is understanding its black Christian nature. The image many Americans hold of a transracial, interdenominational, fundamentally political coalition is not entirely false, but it is a historical exaggeration. White liberals, Northern churches, and progressive labor unions did not join the movement in great numbers until its later stages, roughly demarked by the March on Washington in August 1963 and the Selma March less than two years later. Those whites who had worked longest and most intensively with King were marginal men in their own communities, from Will Campbell, a maverick Southern Baptist preacher, to Stanley Levison, an accused Communist Party member.

The profoundly religious quality of King's commitment derived in large part from an incident of divine revelation. On the Friday night of January 27, 1956, a sleepless King sat in his kitchen. The bus boycott seemed to be collapsing. His own life had been repeatedly threatened. Earlier in the evening, a caller had warned, "If you aren't out of this town in three days, we're going to blow your brains out and blow up your house." Then, as King later recounted:

> ... I bowed down over that cup of coffee.... I prayed a prayer, and I prayed out loud that night. I said, "Lord, I'm down here trying to do what's right. I think I'm right. I think the cause we represent is right. But Lord I must confess that I'm weak now. I'm faltering. I'm losing my courage. And I can't let the people see me like this because if they see me weak and losing my courage, they will begin to get weak."
>
> And it seemed at that moment that I could hear an inner voice saying to me, "Martin Luther, stand up for righteousness. Stand up for justice. Stand up for truth. And lo I will be with you, even until the end of the world." ... I heard the voice of Jesus saying still to fight on. He promised never to leave me alone.

King spoke often of "bearing the cross" and of the transforming power of "unmerited suffering." Far from being an endorsement of conservative passivity, these were elements of radical, direct action, which King rooted in Scripture as informed by black experience. He not only quoted the prophet Amos declaring, "Let justice roll down like waters and righteousness like a mighty stream"; he reminded his audiences that Amos had been disparaged as "maladjusted," "an extremist." Jesus, too, had been branded "a rabble-rouser," "a troublemaker," "an agitator." Responding to the pleas of eight white clergymen that he halt his protests, King wrote in his now-famous "Letter from Birmingham City Jail": "Wherever the early Christians entered a town, the power structure got disturbed and immediately sought to convict them for being 'disturbers of the peace' and 'outside agitators.' But they went on with the conviction that they were 'a colony of heaven,' and had to obey God rather than man."

Beyond King himself, the Civil Rights Movement depended on the black religious tradition. The chief organization of the movement was called, after all, the Southern *Christian* Leadership Conference; it adopted the motto "To redeem the soul of America." So central were black churches to mobilizing and motivating their communities that white foes bombed or burned down ninety-three between 1962 and 1965. Against that backdrop, active black clergymen railed against their more conventional peers, whom King ridiculed for "whooping your irrelevant mess in my face." A group of ministers led by King and Reverend Gardner C. Taylor of Brooklyn broke away from the National Baptist Convention in 1961, forming the Progressive National Baptist Convention.

Still, the most piercing voice of the era belonged not to King but to Malcolm X, the national minister of Elijah Muhammad's Nation of Islam. Malcolm may have earned his greatest notoriety for advocating armed self-defense and denouncing King as a "chump," "traitor," and "clown," but he exerted more significant and more lasting influence with his critical analysis of race and religion. The Nation of Islam offered its believers an alternative creation story, in which a mad scientist grafted from the original black men a race of inherently evil whites. Outside the Nation, however, Malcolm more often emphasized the African roots of Islam in teaching about racial pride, identity, and self-esteem. Christianity, in contrast, was "the white man's religion," "the greatest single ideological weapon for enslaving millions of nonwhite human beings." And as the son of a minister, Malcolm could attack Christianity, and particularly King's version of it, with an insider's acuity. "Nowhere in the Bible," he once said, "can you show me where Moses went to his people and said, 'Believe in the same God that your slavemasters believe in, or seek integration with the slavemasters.' Moses' one doctrine was separation. He told Pharaoh, 'Let my people go.'"

However they were presented as antagonists in life, King and Malcolm have become nearly unified in death. Spike Lee's film *Do the Right Thing* ended with quotations from both men and prominently featured a character selling copies of the photograph of their sole meeting. And the theologian James H. Cone has argued persuasively that as religious thinkers, as well as social activists, King and Malcolm served as complements and correctives for each other. It is Cone's thesis that they were moving toward a common position even while alive, with Malcolm forsaking separatism after he broke with Elijah Muhammad and embraced orthodox Islam and King viewing America far more despairingly in light of the Vietnam War and the violent resistance to integration in the "liberal" North. "I'm not for separation and you're not for integration," Malcolm X put it in one speech, as if addressing King directly. "What you and I are for is freedom.... We've both got the same objective."

What might have emerged from a collaboration between Martin Luther King and Malcolm X, from a fusion of their respective emphases on divine love and divine justice, exists in the black theology developed by Cone, Gayraud S. Wilmore, James Deotis Roberts, and others in the late 1960s. The theology itself was not wholly innovative, as its exponents themselves explained, for it drew on preaching and spirituals that were centuries old. The new element was the legitimacy this theology earned for the black Christian experience in the scholarly realm of the seminary. What formerly had been patronized as a "folk religion" was treated by the 1970s as a distinct body of religious thought—"a theology," in Cone's definition, "whose sole purpose is to apply the freeing power of the gospel to black people under white oppression." In depicting a liberating God at work in an unjust world, black theologians cited three sources especially: the Exodus account; the social justice teachings of such Old Testament prophets as Amos, Isaiah, Hosea, and Micah; and the ministry of Jesus Christ to the poor and hopeless. Harking back also to such forebears as Henry McNeal Turner, black theologians often described their God as black, employing the adjective less as "a treatise on color," as C. Eric Lincoln has written, than as an affirmation of God's commitment to the downtrodden.

For the liberal white clergy, accustomed to averting the thornier issues of race with the bromide, "We're all brothers in Christ," black theology arrived with shattering impact. Here were black ministers confronting white churches, demanding reparations for their race; here were black theologians saying urban uprisings were acts of Christian love. It was into such turbulence that Johnny Ray Youngblood plunged in 1970, when he entered seminary in search of a theology to guide his own life.

There is a story told of two men appearing before a black Baptist convention. The first, a recent graduate of seminary, takes the podium to read the Twenty-third Psalm, and his assurance and elocution earn polite applause. The second, aged and illiterate, recites the passage from memory, and the audience erupts into ecstasy. Mystified, the young man pulls the old one aside.

"What was the difference?" he asks.

"You know the poem," he is told, "but I know the shepherd."

It was a parable much on Johnny Ray Youngblood's mind as he sat in Professor Leotis Belk's classroom at Colgate-Rochester Theological Seminary. He had arrived only days earlier from New Orleans, intending to take a summer course and become familiar with the campus before September, when the real work began. Instead, he now felt dizzy with doubt. Professor Belk was black, it was true, but unlike any black Johnny had ever known. He called himself a "universal man," spoke seven languages, and favored waist sashes and gaucho hats. And what was the name of this course? "Existentialism, Black Existence, and the Ontology of Compassion." "Man," Johnny said to the professor after the lecture one day, "you got three brains."

But were three brains better than one? That was Johnny's question. Did anybody ever learn to be a stronger preacher or a kinder pastor in school? Mother Jordan's answer had been clear. There is no book but The Book; sermons are spontaneous; high school, much less anything beyond it, is a wordly indulgence. And maybe Johnny had absorbed more of Mother Jordan than he realized, more than he could consciously purge. What was the point of reading Martin Heidegger or Rudolf Bultmann, or even Howard Thurman and James Cone? If the Spirit moved you, if you "knew the shepherd," then who needed—what was that word Belk used at dinner the other night—*eschatology?*

The landscape was as strange as the lexicon. From the clamshell streets of the Lower Ninth an airplane had deposited Johnny like a paratrooper into an upstate New York city made prosperous on flour and photography, a city of mansions and art museums and lilacs by the thousand, a city that was once nicknamed "Smugtown, U.S.A." With its leaded-glass windows and Gothic bell tower, the seminary reminded Johnny of textbook pictures of Notre Dame and Westminster Abbey. Inside hung portraits of founders with gray beards and pocket watches. Oak doors opened onto easy chairs and fireplaces, their mantels etched with aphorisms in Latin.

As an epicenter of liberal Protestantism in America, Colgate-Rochester counted among its graduates such black ministers and theologians as Howard Thurman, J. H. Jackson, Samuel McKinney, and Mordecai Wyatt Johnson. But in the year before Johnny's arrival, the seminary had been jarred from its self-satisfaction. For two weeks, its handful of black students occupied the administration building, demanding a greater black presence in the faculty, student body, and curriculum. Johnny, then, arrived as part of the largest class of black seminarians to date in Colgate-Rochester's history, numbering about thirty in a total enrollment of three hundred. Most were attending on scholarship, and few had ever before lived or studied among whites. This was integration, and this was isolation.

So they clustered for identity and survival, the children of Mobile and Memphis and Lake Worth and Rock Hill sharing one long table in a cafeteria ornamented with the crests of Amherst and Harvard. Together they translated classroom philosophy into church wisdom. "How do I go back to my people," one student asked, "and talk about 'the teleological suspension of the ethical?'" And the rest answered, "Just say, 'God will give you enough rope to hang yourself.'" Beyond the official reading list, the black students consumed and discussed Frantz Fanon, James Baldwin, Eldridge Cleaver. Every Wednesday at noon they convened a chapel service, praying and shouting almost in defiance of the pipe organ and stained glass. When the work and worship were done, they might repair to Sam McCree's third-floor dormitory room, known as "the penthouse," for James Brown and Boone's Farm. And on Sunday the seminarians would be welcomed in black Rochester, preaching for the pocket money their scholarships did not provide, then washing their clothes and feasting on soul food in a dozen willing homes.

For all that balm, Johnny still suffered. His steady girlfriend, Joyce Terrell, was finishing her English degree at Dillard, 1,200 miles away. And after the first three-hundred-dollar phone bill, Johnny resigned himself to courting by mail. His letters, dense with the doings of seminary, sent Joyce to both Bible and dictionary for explanation. Yet the more Johnny studied, the more he learned, the more he lost his faith. He had always believed in a distant and lofty God; now he had a professor talking about God "sashaying through the garden in the cool of the evening." He had always believed in the Bible as the exact product of divine revelation; now he had a professor explaining that Mark's gospel was the first to be written, even though Matthew's appears before it in the New Testament. And then there was Leotis Belk, universal man, requiring Johnny to watch an X-rated movie and visit a red-light district for his course on "The Philosophy and Theology of Sexuality."

Johnny fled Rochester with two final exams remaining in his second year. When he returned in September, with an F and a D-plus to greet him, he started seeing a therapist. Only nine months short of a master's degree, he still weighed dropping out. He knew of a black pastor in Rochester who had raised a thousand dollars in a single Sunday offering—and never gone to seminary. He knew of another in Buffalo, Reverend Glenn DuBois, who had built a congregation from two to two hundred—without any formal religious training. "What do I need this for?" Johnny once asked Reverend DuBois, fully expecting his skepticism to be confirmed. Instead the minister replied, "School will do for a preacher what a grinding stone will do for an ax."

Reconciled to staying, Johnny found inspiration from two unlikely sources, Werner Lemke and Paul Hammer, professors who appeared utterly removed from the world of black ministry. Pale almost to the point of translucence, Hammer was the product of a conservative church in a Minnesota hamlet, and his original aspiration had been to pastor one just like it. A German Lutheran by birth, Lemke was a bald, stocky man, inclined toward flannel shirts and wingtips.

Intellectually, they excited and occasionally overwhelmed Johnny, with Lemke treating the Old Testament prophets as contemporary social critics and Hammer fusing history, etymology, and comparative religion into exegesis. But there was more to the men's influence than academic brilliance. Here were two of the whitest whites in the world, and yet, the black seminarians had to admit, they had soul. Johnny could see it in the way Hammer pitched forward, face reddening and arms churning the air, as he worked a verse; he could hear it when the professor declared, "Scholarship should be in the service of heartburn." As for Lemke, his ideals arose from a personal sense of penance. Growing up in Nazi Germany, Lemke had watched his father separate the practice of Christianity from the moral responsibility to oppose genocide. He had never forgotten the street sweeper with hollow eyes and ragged clothes whom he had asked, "Why are you wearing that yellow star?" When Lemke first saw the South Side of Chicago, as a postwar refugee, he had thought, *Oh, so America has its Jews, too,* and they became, in some respects, his ministry. On the night Martin Luther King was assassinated, Lemke talked until dawn with distraught black students; the next day he initiated an endowment for a King Chair in Black Church Studies, pulling six hundred dollars from his own pocket. He attended and even preached at the black students' Wednesday chapel service, in one memorable sermon evoking Ezekiel "moaning and groaning for righteousness."

With Lemke and Hammer, Johnny began to move toward a faith that could transcend race, that could embrace a broader definition of "the people of God." The segregation of New Orleans had never let him near enough to whites to see their frailty, and the credo of white supremacy had assured him none existed anyway. Now, interning for a semester as a hospital chaplain, Johnny met a white girl whose immune system had been destroyed, leaving her unable even to cuddle a baby for fear of infection. When he prayed with her family, he understood that some grief knew no color. And it was such lessons, whether learned in the classroom or the emergency room, that would years later open Reverend Youngblood to willing whites in the form of Tom Approbato and the Industrial Areas Foundation.

But in Johnny's evolving faith, fellowship had to be built on the examination of social problems, not the empty utterances of Christian brotherhood. He preached one evening during seminary at a Buffalo Baptist church in what was delicately called a "transitional neighborhood," and he struck at the euphemism with the example of Amos, arguing for the justice in genuine religion. "Look at your own congregation," he declared. "The people who used to sit next to you have already engaged in white flight." As Amos was ousted from the public life of Israel, Johnny Ray Youngblood was dispatched without a dime from the offering. He limped back to Colgate-Rochester to find a formal complaint had been lodged against him by the American Baptist Convention. Only after defending himself to the seminary's president did he escape punishment.

Forming a personal theology, however, did not complete Johnny's education. He still had to learn about the practice of ministry, and he learned more than he had ever wanted to know at Faith Baptist Church in Buffalo.

Newly ordained and just married, Reverend Youngblood assumed the position of "trial pastor" as he entered his last year of seminary. There was discord from the start. He was young, young enough to be the son of his predecessor, Reverend Roscoe M. Mitchell. He had not been born or raised a Baptist. He was too malleable, or so his critics hoped. Reverend Mitchell had founded the church and ruled it with grand autocracy, once returning a Christmas "love offering" he deemed insufficient. Now all dormant dissent erupted. When Reverend Youngblood continued Reverend Mitchell's method of having tithers make their donations before other worshipers, foes called it "segregated giving." When he proposed joining three mortgages into a single debt, several key deacons reversed their original support. One longtime member refused, as a matter of principle, to shout for anything the young minister preached, complaining, on the one occasion when he slipped, "You got me *this* time." So hostile grew the mood that one Sunday Joyce Youngblood had to scream from the pews to stop her husband from leaping from the pulpit to fight a trustee.

Six months into Reverend Youngblood's trial, the congregation scheduled a vote on his employment. Even former members, it was decided, could cast ballots if they contributed twenty-five dollars. With this version of democracy looming, Reverend Youngblood resigned. "You can't fight," his friend and adviser, Reverend DuBois, told him, "with your hands tied."

At that point, in December 1972, Reverend Youngblood stood one semester from graduation and more confused than ever. It was no longer seminary that intimidated him; it was, in the wake of Faith Baptist, the very prospect of pastoring. Then he met Reverend William Augustus Jones. The pastor of Bethany Baptist Church in Brooklyn, Reverend Jones was a visiting professor at Colgate-Rochester during Johnny's last term, teaching a course entitled "The Gospel and the Ghetto." Johnny volunteered to drive him to and from the airport each week, and he filled the twenty-minute trips with questions that required two-hour answers. What is the purpose of church in society? How is the Gospel relevant to the human condition? What is the difference between preaching as prophecy and preaching as oratory?

From those inquiries, Reverend Jones recognized in Johnny a kindred temperament, "a righteous indignation that could be a prophetic gift." And Johnny saw in Reverend Jones the answer to the dilemma that had tormented him since entering seminary: You could know the poem *and* know the shepherd; you could hold a doctorate without surrendering the earthy touch. While Reverend Jones was proud to be considered a "race man," an identity Johnny never sought for himself, he would be deeply affected by the minister's scriptural attacks on racism, capitalism, and militarism, and, most important, by his pragmatic and involved pastoral style. When Reverend Jones led Bethany through the construction of a new church, he hand-picked every element from the Ethiopian wood doors to the Dutch crystal chandeliers to the toilet paper, and he drove the congregation to retire the $1.25 million mortgage five years early. In the midst of one of New York's most depleted neighborhoods, Bedford Stuyvesant, his church operated a child-development center, an apartment house for senior citizens, and a restaurant employing dozens. "Lead by precept," Reverend Jones often told Johnny, "and lead by example."

One morning in May 1973, with two weeks left in seminary and unemployment awaiting, Johnny made his usual trip to the airport for Reverend Jones. As the car returned to campus, the pastor asked casually, "Blood, have you ever thought of coming to Brooklyn?"

By eight-thirty, sun covers the roof and pours through the skylight, turning the sanctuary as sultry as midsummer. Here and there, babies wail. Men wipe their brows. Women reach for their fans, cloth fans painted with Chinese landscapes, cardboard fans stenciled with the name of a gospel musical or a neighborhood mortician, so many fans that their communal beating resembles a flock of birds taking flight.

With a bounce that belies his own exhaustion, Reverend Youngblood steps to the pulpit. He never fell asleep last night, leaving bed well before his four o'clock alarm to read his sermon one final time. He led the six o'clock service on an empty stomach, and managed only orange juice and raisin bread before this one. A familiar weariness spreads from his back to his chest. A less common anxiety fills his thoughts.

This being the holiest day in the Christian calendar, his sermon is arguably the most important of the year, and surely the most widely heard. Surveying the congregation, he can see the audience he longs to reach, the men who consent to attend church only on Christmas and Easter. He can spot a few checking their watches, thinking about dinner tonight and work tomorrow. He can practically hear them muttering, "I'm just here 'cause my old lady asked me to come." And what must they think of him, the preacher, a figure in black life so revered and yet so ridiculed? Wear a fine suit and you're "a pimp with a license." Wear sneakers and a sweatshirt, like today, and you're a country chump. But those very men, contemptuous and just a bit guilty, live at the core of this sermon. None since "Christmas in the Raw" has caused Reverend Youngblood such worry.

"I solicit your prayers," he says, opening his Bible, and then he reads from the Gospel of John:

> And when he had thus spoken, he cried with a loud voice, Lazarus, come forth.
>
> And he that was dead came forth, bound hand and foot with graveclothes; and his face was bound with a napkin. Jesus saith unto them, Loose him and let him go.
>
> Then many of the Jews which came to Mary, and had seen the things which Jesus did, believed on him.

"I wanna talk for a little while," the pastor says, "from the thought 'Lazarus and the Black Man.'" He pauses. "'Lazarus and the Black Man.'"

There is no more important occasion in the black church than the delivery of a sermon. It is called "the preaching moment." It is called "the preaching event," like a heavyweight prizefight for which the rest of a worship service is merely the undercard. It is, as much as the shouts of ecstasy that may answer it, an act of syncretism and historical homage, returning to the African *griot,* the praise-singer, and to the slave preacher, teaching a liberation gospel after dark in the quarters. To be a preacher is to be storyteller, scholar, analyst, entertainer, political theorist, and, most ineffably, the anointed of God.

When Reverend Charles Adams of Hartford Memorial Baptist Church in Detroit is called the "Harvard whooper," or when Reverend James Forbes of Riverside Church describes himself as being a "Tillichian Pentecostal," the phrases imply the scope demanded of a black preacher. One must embrace knowledge and experience, book-learning and mother wit. One can earn a doctorate from the Harvard Divinity School, like Reverend Adams, or become an expert in the German theologian Paul Tillich, like Reverend Forbes, but one must never lose connection with the Holy Spirit. Great sermons often fol-

low a trajectory between those poles, beginning with the precise elocution, refined vocabulary, and elaborate metaphor of the academy and working their way to the vernacular language and almost physical catharsis of the black tradition. A sermon engages in another type of journey, too, migrating from biblical past to American present, from sacred to secular, "expect[ing] that the God of creation will be present to transform spoken words into deeds of liberation," as Reverend Forbes has written.

Long before Reverend Youngblood felt himself truly anointed, on that afternoon in the Dillard chapel, he had begun learning how to preach. Reverend Aubrey Watson, a Spiritualist minister who was the son of a schoolteacher, had shown him education had a place in the pulpit, even correcting young Johnny's grammar. Eli Wilson, Sr., animated Bible characters with what a literary critic might call "interior life." His Peter was a roughneck "who didn't take stuff off anybody"; his Moses was a reluctant leader, fearful his people might disobey. And Reverend C. L. Franklin, whom Johnny knew only from recordings, taught him theme and structure, particularly how to "close it out, bring it home." Decades later, Reverend Youngblood could still recite, verbatim, the culminating anecdote of a Franklin sermon that likened faith to a soaring eagle.

None of these men, however, was an overtly political preacher, and Johnny himself avoided worldly themes. Malcolm X scared him. Martin Luther King moved him, but when he exulted after watching one televised speech, "I wanna be like him when I grow up," his mother shot back, "Don't let me ever hear you say that again." (Years later, when Reverend Youngblood brought up the exchange, she explained, "I knew that white folk were gonna kill him, and I didn't want you dead.") In his "church-hopping" days during college, Johnny advanced to the point of preaching from notes and copying C. L. Franklin's delivery. But his aspirations, far from inspiring social action, went no further than exciting the amen corner with such proven lines as "Don't mess with a child of God when he's prayin'."

Only in seminary did a larger message start to emerge. Reverend Gardner C. Taylor, a guest professor at Colgate-Rochester, startled Johnny with an assignment to "exhume a biblical character, put him back together skeletally, put flesh on his bones, and breath in his mouth." That meant reading the Bible like a newspaper, realizing that

its events had occurred in actual places, timed by calendars and clocks. The writings of Howard Thurman, especially *Jesus and the Disinherited,* extended the historical perspective to Jesus, fixing him as part of a poor, oppressed minority under imperial domination. One sentence especially awoke Johnny to an immediate and applicable Christ: "If a Roman soldier pushed Jesus into a ditch, he could not appeal to Caesar; he would be just another Jew in the ditch." Then, as the assistant pastor at Bethany Baptist, Reverend Youngblood watched Reverend Jones put that real-world Jesus to work, and radically so, in government, economics, religion, and family. For a time, Reverend Youngblood modeled himself on his mentor down to his fondness for alliteration and his habit of touching his left hand to his temple. But with his own pulpit, at Saint Paul, he became his own preacher.

From those days until this one, the process of creating a sermon has been, for Reverend Youngblood, the process of uniting Scripture and social problem. Most often the problem comes first, suggesting an applicable text in much the same way, as the pastor puts it, that punching a given set of numbers on a jukebox plays a certain song. By Tuesday or Wednesday of a week, he will study the verses and start making notes on envelopes or napkins, saving every thought, as Reverend Jones instructed him. For aid in exegesis, he usually relies on *Young's Analytical Concordance; Vine's Dictionary of the Bible,* which traces English terms to the original Greek, Hebrew, or Aramaic; and Clarence Jordan's "Cotton Patch" version of the scriptures, a retelling of the gospel with everyday language and domestic geography. Werner Lemke or Paul Hammer might get a telephone call by Friday, and Reverend Jones, who lives around the block from the pastor, might hear the doorbell ring on Saturday afternoon. By that night, Reverend Youngblood will have shaped the sermon into a form ranging from detailed outline to full manuscript. And most Sunday mornings, like this one, the pressure will awaken him early for a final inspection. Always he fears failure. As Reverend DuBois in Buffalo once told him, "The people in our churches are professional listeners. If you do wrong, the littlest children gonna know it."

The risk of doing wrong seemed great as Easter approached. This was the morning to preach Jesus' resurrection, using a sturdy text like Mark 16. This was the morning to proclaim the good news of everlasting life, an upbeat message for spring, the season of rebirth. Instead,

Reverend Youngblood would be drawing on a passage most often intoned at funerals. He would be appealing to skeptics with the miracle of Christ's that "most strains modern credence," as one Bible scholar has written. And he would be examining perhaps the sorest subject in black America, the plight of its men.

In contemplating those men, he could not escape the phrase "endangered species," or the question it begged of divine absence. It was inconceivable for Reverend Youngblood to talk about Christ and His miraculous powers. That kind of preaching was what drove black men from church in the first place. Where was Jesus and his hocus-pocus when ten percent of black men were unemployed, when their average life span was declining, when the leading cause of death for the young generation was murder? *So Jesus goes into town and resurrects this dead dude,* Reverend Youngblood could imagine his listeners asking. *What does that have to do with me?*

The only strategy was to "de-miraclize the miracle," to speak less of the Resurrection than of its symbolism. Reverend Youngblood found in John 11 the analogues that could make the text contemporary. Bethany, a small and obscure town, resembled the Southern hamlets many of Saint Paul's members still considered home. The parentless household of Lazarus and his two sisters, Mary and Martha, reminded the pastor of the nonnuclear families so common in his congregation. The primacy of the sisters in dealing with Jesus struck him as akin to the overwhelming female presence in the black church, with its unspoken corollary that somehow women were closer than men to God. As for Lazarus, Lazarus was legion.

Now, standing before a sanctuary as expectant as it is overcrowded, Reverend Youngblood thinks how depressing, how disenchanting, how downright heretical the sermon may sound. That was why he solicited prayers at the outset. That is why he begins, as Reverend Jones taught him, with the safest of comparisons:

History reports that many a major event has occurred in minor places. A whole lot of famous people have come out of little-known or unknown towns. Vida Blue, onetime baseball great, was born in Mansfield, Louisiana. Never heard of it. The late C. L. Franklin, father to Aretha Franklin, was said to have been of the soil of Mississippi, a little town called Tutweiler. The late

Dr. Benjamin E. Mays, respected scholar and educator, had as
his birthplace a place called Ninety-six, South Carolina.

And I think, my brothers and sisters, we do God a disser-
vice when we stifle and smother and deny His touching down in
these obscure places, when we claim the next largest town as
our birthplace. You know what I mean. If you're from Kenner,
Louisiana, New Orleans is claimed. If one is from Tylertown,
Mississippi, Jackson is claimed. And if you're born in Mount
Vernon, New York, you still claim New York City. Stop evading
the opportunity to teach some geography and culture. Get you
a map, carry it around in your pocket if you have to. Perhaps
your town did not make you famous, but you can make your
town famous.

Do recall that God had His son born in a little town. If
God was hooked on big towns, He would've had Jesus born in
Jerusalem. But this is not the case, even with God. Jesus was
born, born, born, *born* in Bethlehem.

The incident today occurs in Bethany. A little town. It was
near Jerusalem, but it was Bethany. Neither the population, the
produce, nor the people made a difference in the usual sense
that history speaks of. No military geniuses, financial wizards,
educators or sportsmen, even clergy, became Bethany notables.
Its population was neither so large it had to be noticed, nor
really so small that attention needed to be called to it as in "O
Little Town of Bethlehem." The larger world did not profit
from nor depend on Bethany for any commodity that made life
any easier or more pleasant. Bethany's claim to fame was rooted
in a resurrection.

Reverend Youngblood recounts the story of Lazarus—his illness,
his sisters' call to Jesus, his death, Jesus' belated arrival, and finally the
resurrection. This portion of a sermon is known as the teaching, and
the sermons Reverend Youngblood heard in childhood rarely went
further, as if Bible stories were self-evident in their meaning. Only
years later, as a seminarian, did he learn from Gardner Taylor the
necessity of "swinging the pendulum from Then to Now." Bobbing
on his toes, swiveling left and right, moving his eyes from manuscript
to congregation, Reverend Youngblood almost embodies the transport through time and place. He introduces a risky set of analogies,

those involving the black family and the black church, both institutions defined by the absence of men. Then he engages the most controversial parallel of all, the one inspired by Lazarus, four days in the grave.

"Nobody today will deny," Reverend Youngblood declares, "that the black man is sick."

"Go 'head," answers a single voice, eerie in its isolation.

"In fact, if we read correctly and listen acutely, brethren, we have been diagnosed as not only sick, but they done pulled the cover up over our heads. And there's a coroner's report that we are *dead*. Prison statistics report the black male is dead. The drug epidemic reports the black man is dead. The increase of the streetcorner population reports, dead. Education dropouts, flunk-outs, and push-outs, dead. Male-less households, dead. Fatherless children, dead. There's no question relative to the black man being ill. In some instances, y'all, it may well be concluded"—his voice strains and tears—"that we are dead."

A sound gathers in the pews, something between a rustle and a rumble, ambiguous in its emotion. This had been the pastor's fear, that his version of healing would seem more like tearing scabs off sores. All the men who had returned to church under his encouragement and friendship—would they abandon it now, feel betrayed? As he had intoned every disease, from crime to drugs to ignorance to irresponsibility, he had imagined the men vanishing from one section of the sanctuary after another, until only their empty seats remained.

And now, as if the recitation of daily tragedy is not dispiriting enough, Reverend Youngblood will explore the ontological, existential issue of divine absence. It is an issue woven through the Scriptures, from Job stripped of family, fortune, and health to Jesus on the cross crying, "Father, why hast Thou forsaken me?" It is an issue central to black history in America, one of great piety coupled with great misery. It is an issue the pastor has heard women frame a dozen, a hundred, a thousand times in his life, beginning with his mother's fervent pleas for his father to come to Christ.

Let's acknowledge, y'all, that we are acquainted with Jesus' delays. Mary and Martha sent for Jesus—and he delayed. Their brother lies tormented by disease—and Jesus delays. The cold hand of death is little by little stealing its way over his chilling body—and Jesus delays. The darkness of hopelessness creeps over his sunlit skies—and Jesus delays. Ladies, sisters, I'm acquainted with the fact that a whole lotta y'all have prayed. Many of you have sent a message or two to Jesus. "Lord, save the men. Lord, save our men." And if you're honest this morning, you got to confess that the Master, just like with Mary and Martha, has delayed. Some of you have given up on your husbands. All because Jesus delayed. Sons, brothers, fathers, friends—Jesus delayed. It's not that you haven't prayed. But the reality that we struggle with is, Jesus delays.

Let's be honest in this perusal of the Scriptures. Jesus arrives in Bethany. Mary and Martha are mixed in their greeting. "We're glad you're here, Jesus, but if you'd been here sooner. If you had come when we called. If you had heeded the invitation when it was extended, Lazarus would not have died. But he's dead now. We're glad you showed up, but we've already pronounced ashes to ashes and dust to dust. He's dead."

Let me paraphrase it. "Jesus, if you'd just shown up ten years ago. Jesus, if you had shown up five years ago, one year ago, six months ago, I would not have had to give up on him. Jesus, Jesus, Jesus"—I can hear us apologizing—"don't get me wrong. We glad you here. But it doesn't matter to us anymore. If you wanna go on and raise him, raise him for his sake. But I've given up. I'm not gonna put myself in the position, Jesus, to be hurt no more. I'm not gonna put myself in the position to grieve again. I'm not gonna put myself in the position to be frustrated and angered, humiliated, disappointed. Go on and do what you wanna do if you wanna do somethin'. But I ain't got nothin' to do with it."

Sound familiar?

With that, Reverend Youngblood again leaves Brooklyn for Bethany, resuming the biblical account. Jesus asks Mary and Martha, "Where have ye laid him?" and they lead Him to a cave, already sealed by a stone. When Jesus tells the sisters to open the grave, Martha begs for Him to reconsider. Lazarus has been dead four days. His body is rotting. Still, Jesus persists, and the stone is pried free.

The pastor has come full circle, arriving at the three verses he read

at the outset of the sermon. There is, obviously, no mystery or sus-
pense in the outcome. *So Jesus goes into town and resurrects this dead
dude. What's that got to do with me?* Wrestling all week with that question, Reverend Youngblood could only find an answer in the lives of
the men around him. He remembered the day Robert Nix joined
Saint Paul, handing over his knife. He thought about Butch Carr, taking vacation days from his job to chaperone field trips from the
church's elementary school. He recalled the day he had asked James
Warren, a member of the Board of Elders, why he spoke so little.
"Pastor," he had replied, "I never thought what I had to say was
worth hearing." And behind all those men loomed Palmon Youngblood, who had tried once to accommodate himself to Holy Family,
and then left in exasperation, telling young Johnny, "There was never
any good news. It was always 'Watch your back.'"

To such men, the pastor knew, resurrection as an eschatological
concept was counterfeit money. He needed to speak of an explicit and
detailed resurrection, one that found providence in incremental effort,
one that could be experienced in life as well as death. He wanted to
tell the men what their part was in the pragmatic work of raising the
black nation.

> I've got news for you this mornin'. Brothers, I don't care who
> you are. I don't care what you done. I don't care what you ain't
> done. Jesus loves you. Jesus loves you, man. Paul said, "But God
> commendeth His love toward us in that while we were yet sin-
> ners Christ died for us." Do you know the gospel well enough to
> know that when Jesus died, he died for sinners? Mary, I know
> you sat at His feet, but are you receptive to the fact he loves
> Lazarus? Martha, I know you made sure all of Jesus' needs were
> met, but are you acquainted with the fact that Jesus loves
> Lazarus? When Jesus said, "Come unto me, all ye that labor and
> are heavy laden," He was talking to black men, too.

As Reverend Youngblood draws breath, raucous applause fills the
brief silence. An elderly woman picks her way up the aisle to pray. A
man of about twenty-five, clad in a sweatsuit and carrying his daughter, follows. The pastor jabs and points with his right hand, indicating
the men in his field of vision, as if to summon each from his grave.

Jesus said, "Loose him, and let him go." "Loose him" means "Forgive him." We've got some forgivin' to do. Take away the fetters from his hands; let him work one more time. Take the chains off his feet; let him walk one more time. Take the napkin off his face; let him see and speak one more time.

The reason we're here this morning is not just because a resurrection happened, but because there's one goin' on. Every time I see a brother come to Christ, there's a resurrection goin' on. Every time I see a man put down his bottle, there's a resurrection goin' on. Every time I see a man go back to school, there's a resurrection goin' on. Every time I see a man hug his son, there's a resurrection goin' on.

Come forth, Lazarus. Break those chains. Throw off those fetters. Remove that napkin. Son of man, stand up on your feet.

The pastor's speech bursts forth in rhythmic, syncopated segments, and at the end of each, the faithful clap two beats of punctuation. Then his voice takes on music, the words forming planes of sound, long and rippling and ragged. This is "whooping," part oratorical device, part spiritual possession. Reverend Youngblood leaps in place now, leaps again and again, and with each ascent sings out a phrase:

He rose.
He arose.
He arose.
Our heroes.
When he got up,
I got up.
When he got up,
My Daddy got up.
When he got up,
My men got up.
When he got up,
My sons got up.
Yeah. Oh, yeah.

Knees bent and heads bowed, scores of worshipers flood the narrow space between the pulpit and the front pew. The aisles engorge.

Where the carpet gives way to concrete, at the border of the sanctuary extension, Tom Carter pounds the air with his fist. "We got church today, doctor!" he shouts toward the ceiling. "We got church!"

But the realist in Reverend Youngblood will not allow Resurrection Sunday to end without an astringent. He has not been talking magic; he has been talking real life. In real life, transformations move more like glaciers than tidal waves. In real life, when the absent man returns home, home changes in unpredictable ways. Reverend Youngblood has always wondered what Lazarus thought when, after four days in the grave, he found Mary and Martha had redecorated his bedroom.

"'Loose him and let him go,'" he says softly. "When I come back to the pulpit, I wanna talk about the problems resurrections cause."

6

◉

WITH AN ASTERISK

SOME EVENINGS, EVEN NOW, SIXTEEN MONTHS LATER, Annie Nesbitt sees the shadow forming before her on the kitchen wall. It is a broad and looming darkness, and yet it does not frighten her. It brings comfort, and then sorrow, as she realizes the shape must have been formed by the headlights of a passing car or the imperatives of her own imagination.

She was standing over the sink on January 23, 1989, waiting to hear the tumblers turn in the lock, the tool box drop to the floor, the husky voice groan with the end of a day's labor. She was waiting for the shadow to appear, for the arms to encircle her waist, for the lips to kiss her cheek, for the voice to ask, "How was your day, love?"

Instead, the doorbell rang, and Annie's stepson answered. A neighbor named Claude Gray gasped, "Stuart, come with me. Your father's been shot."

ASSISTANT DISTRICT ATTORNEY ANNE SWERN: What happened after Mr. Gray advised you that your father had been shot?

STUART KELLY: After he told me that, I looked for my shoes, ran outside the building. I was looking for my father. Oh, man. Oh, man ... I didn't see him. Somebody said to me, "Look down." I looked down by my feet. My father was laying in the street, bleeding. He was lying in a pool of blood there. I looked to the corner. I saw—I saw somebody in a long black leather coat with a gun to their side. I walked up to them. The person said, "Keep away, or I will have to shoot you, too."

SWERN: Do you see that person in the courtroom today?

KELLY: Yes, I do.

SWERN: Could you please point to him?

KELLY: That's the person right there.

Testimony in the case of *People v. Radames Ortiz,* Kings County Indictment Number 1186/89, begins on the morning of June 7, 1990, in State Supreme Court in Brooklyn. Annie Nesbitt is not present. After missing a dozen days of work to attend as many false starts, after sitting through the delays caused by court vacations, misplaced exhibits, evidence analysis, conflicting trials, a change in judges, and the installation of a new district attorney—after all that, she cannot be found. She is home at a doctor's insistence, and, just as Stephen Kelly's death left her, she is alone. She is a woman of forty-eight without siblings, and with parents seventy-nine and eighty-three years old, who live five states away. She buried her first husband, and it was Steve Kelly who had courted her out of her mourning. "Now, love, you don't want to sit and cry," he would say. "Ted wouldn't want that. And if I pass tomorrow, I don't want you to cry for me. I'm just passin' through."

As a pious man, a member of Saint Paul since his childhood, Kelly must have meant for Annie to take solace in the belief that earthly life was only a prelude. Yet those words of comfort also prophesied his own sudden demise. The owner of a small construction company, he was driving home from a job site, circling the block outside his apartment, waiting for legal overnight parking to start at six o'clock. As he turned a corner in his van, an illegally parked car blocked its path. An argument ensued between Kelly and the other driver, the sort of argument that takes place harmlessly enough a thousand times a day in New York. *How do you expect me to get by? ... You almost ran me over ... Move your fucking car ... I'm not moving the fucking car.* Then the other driver pulled a gun. Kelly hurried down the street to hail a passing police car, and, having failed, returned to the dispute. The driver's sister, six months pregnant, placed herself between the men, but the driver reached over her to club Kelly with his gun butt. Kelly pushed the sister aside. One shot. A second. *Gray, get my son. I think I'm dying.* From start to finish, it had taken twenty minutes, less time than the local newscast Stephen Kelly and Annie Nesbitt usually watched together after his arrival home.

The only mercy was that the case seemed bound for a resolution as swift and decisive as the crime itself. An unarmed man of sixty-one, a lifelong church member and the father of six sons, is shot in front of eyewitnesses. True, the alleged assailant, Radames Ortiz, is a police officer, as is his sister, Nancy Silvestri. But Ortiz was off duty at the time, wearing street clothes, and behaving in a manner that could charitably be called intemperate. The police force suspended him. The Patrolmen's Benevolent Association declined to pay for his legal defense. A grand jury indicted him on five counts of murder, manslaughter, and assault.*

And Mayor Edward I. Koch, entering a reelection year with a black opponent in David N. Dinkins, all but convicted Ortiz himself. "After I met the family I told reporters that the case seemed clearly a 'bad shooting,'" he wrote in his weekly newspaper column. "Ordinarily, I would not visit the family in such a case, I continued [in the comments to reporters], but the facts were 'so compelling' in this instance that I felt an obligation to express my condolences. I said, 'Whomever is responsible, I can assure that we will pursue that person without fear or favor.'"

The mayor was not the only unusual visitor to the Kelly apartment. On the night of the shooting, two different ministers appeared to volunteer their services at "representing the family." Implied in their offer was the opportunity for the Kelly killing, like the fatal attacks by white mobs on black passersby in Howard Beach and Bensonhurst, to be brandished as proof of American race hate. One of the visitors, the pastor of a well-regarded Pentecostal church, was politely turned down. The other, the orchestrator of the Tawana Brawley affair, had the door slammed in his face.

Annie Nesbitt turned instead to Reverend Youngblood and Saint

---

*Under New York State law, Ortiz was charged with second-degree murder by intent, second-degree murder by depraved indifference to human life, first-degree manslaughter by intent, second-degree manslaughter by reckless disregard, and second-degree assault, leaving a trial jury to decide his guilt or innocence on each count separately.

Paul. In her years with Steve Kelly, she had become every bit as devoted as he to the church and its leader. "Pastor's a refrigerator," she would joke about his candid style. "He can't hold nothin'." But she knew, too, that in a crisis she could trust Reverend Youngblood to carefully, privately guide her. Faith had an interior dimension, which often involved the soothing of grief; and faith had an exterior dimension, which could press claims for justice. From Saint Paul and the pastor, Annie needed both sorts of ministry.

In the days immediately after the shooting, when the media spotlight burned hottest, Reverend Youngblood counseled a middle course, not turning the tragedy into a racial passion play, but neither trusting the public promises of swift and thorough resolution. Presiding over Kelly's funeral, he read aloud a letter to Mayor Koch and Elizabeth Holtzman, the district attorney for Brooklyn:

> *What,* possibly, *could* prevent the killer from being brought to justice?
>
> The same blue wall of silence that has obstructed the investigation into the incidents at Tompkins Square Park *could.**
>
> The inability of the two of you—the two public officials ultimately responsible for the criminal and departmental responses to Mr. Kelly's death—to work well together *could.*
>
> Turf battles between the office of the District Attorney and leadership at One Police Plaza *could.*
>
> The distractions of a season of partisan political maneuvering *could.*
>
> The tendency to overreact to critics who try to politicize this matter *could.*
>
> Sheer lack of will, or ability, or competence *could.*

The next morning, in the desired result, the *Daily News* reported the funeral under the headline: FAREWELL TO A FATHER; PASTOR CALLS FOR EQUAL JUSTICE. Lifted from the article and displayed in a prominent box was a quote from the eulogy: "We will not sit idly by in the wake of his death, caused by a man who forgot who he was." At that

---

* This referred to a riot between homeless persons, illegally squatting in a public park on Manhattan's Lower East Side, and the police officers dispatched to evict them.

moment, in late January 1989, it seemed reasonable for Annie Nesbitt and the rest of Steve Kelly's survivors to believe that without marches, without press conferences, without a special prosecutor, the system might actually work.

Then the waiting began. From 1989 through half of 1990, the trial was successively scheduled for February 10, March 20, April 19, May 5, June 7, September 11, October 26, December 4, January 9, March 26, and May 14. Annie wasted her vacation days sitting in a courtroom, seeing prisoners in handcuffs ferried in and out like cargo, watching court officers flip through computer magazines, hearing the judge chat about football, and obsessively, relentlessly, against her will, staring at Radames Ortiz, only thirty feet down the bench, wearing a cardigan sweater and silk tie, free on bail and offensively alive. "That hoodlum," she muttered one day, "that creature."

But rage, for the most part, was not Annie's way. Filling the hours until the case was called, only to have it postponed yet again, she would sift through a briefcase of faxes and charts from her job at Blue Cross. Or she would fret about being late with Christmas cards. Or she would read the Book of Job, wondering what it meant for her own affliction that God eventually restored the faithful herdsman to prosperity and contentment. She exchanged kisses and comforting words with Steve's ex-wife, Shirley, and whichever sons were attending a particular session. Annie always seated herself one row behind Shirley and the children, deferring to the bonds of blood and wedlock. In their six years together, Annie and Steve had spoken often of marrying, but had never set a date. They were decades past any youthful fantasies of gowns and cake and champagne, and besides, there was time, plenty of time.

Annie was a wife without a marriage license, until death made her a widow with an asterisk, accorded all of the pain with none of the privilege. Stoically she endured the symptoms of Steve's loss—the shadow on the kitchen wall, the solitary "pity parties," the dream of Steve returning to life. He strolled into their living room, smiling and joking, with Annie chiding, "You're talking to everybody but me." Then, as he moved to embrace her, Annie awakened. She longed for the feel of those arms, thickly muscled from a life of outdoor work, the biceps so large that paramedics could not wrap a blood-pressure strap around them on the night Steve Kelly died.

All the self-control began to break Annie down. She attended enough of the preliminary hearings in late May to comprehend just how harrowing the full trial would be. The defense attorney, Barry Agulnick, fought over every last detail, from the loss of a crime-scene diagram to the belated discovery of a second bullet hole in Kelly's coat to the payment of expert witnesses. Time after time, Agulnick and the two prosecutors, Anne Swern and Steven Schwartz, brought their arguments to the bench, leaving Annie and the Kelly family to strain forward for the loose chips of language—"legal issue," "verify," "custody," "substantial"—and try to assemble them into a coherent mosaic.

From the outset of the case, Swern and Schwartz had patiently explained each stage to Kelly's survivors, and it had won them their trust. But watching a courtroom in its full adversarial pageantry started Annie, for one, worrying. It would be Agulnick's contention that an enraged Kelly had tried to wrest away Ortiz's gun and died in an accidental discharge. And the defense attorney seemed, even in the procedural hearings, meticulous and aggressive enough to sway a jury. There was Agulnick in an Italian-cut suit with gold watch and collar bar, as Schwartz wore wingtips and poplin, the buttons missing from one suit jacket cuff. There was Agulnick wheedling and baiting, leaving Schwartz to beg the judge's intercession, as if seeking refuge from the playground bully. And who was it in the Kelly family who remembered that Agulnick had won a case like this once before? In that 1985 trial, one of the most publicized and volatile in the city, six Transit Authority police officers stood accused of beating to death a graffiti artist named Michael Stewart. Agulnick earned them acquittal on all counts, thrusting himself into the high-pay, high-profile specialty called "cop law," and gaining the nickname from admiring officers of "Get-'Em-Off Agulnick."

All through the final day of jury selection, Annie's head throbbed with the strain. Hearing Swern describe the killing in the course of a question, Annie thought of Steve's jacket, sodden with blood. Gazing at Ortiz, searching his face for any sign of emotion, she wondered how he could remain so serene when half the Kelly family had fallen into tears. The headache spread from each temple across her eyes, tightening like a belt. Her stomach clenched and rumbled with nausea. Returning home from court, she could not eat, and as she tried to sleep she was rattled by the city noises to which she was normally inured, especially the sound of firecrackers, so much like gunshots.

She gave up on rest at five o'clock this morning, made coffee, chose a somber tweed suit for court. By seven, she was working at her desk in Manhattan, opening mail and writing memos so she would not fall further behind. She swallowed two aspirin tablets with more coffee, hoping the combination would conquer her headache. Instead, she found herself mindlessly shuffling papers, thinking of Steve's corpse and Ortiz's impassive face.

Shortly before eight, a colleague named Joyce walked into Annie's office.

"Is everything all right?" she asked.

"Yes," Annie said. "Just the anticipation."

"You look all washed out."

"With all this makeup I have on?"

No amount of blusher could obscure Annie's anguish. She usually wore the crinkled smile of someone who wants to tell a joke deadpan but cannot suppress giggles at the thought of the punchline. Now her eyes were glazed, and her cheeks slumped, unable to lift her lips into even a social grin. Annie told Joyce of the headaches, the nausea, the dizziness, the sleepless night. She wondered to herself if she was having a stroke.

At Joyce's urging, Annie saw the office doctor, who found her pulse churning at ninety beats a minute. Her blood pressure, too, stood well above normal. "If it's making you this bad," he said of the trial, "I recommend you don't go."

So she called Stuart Kelly, who said, "Okay, we understand." Then she reached her friend Clarissa Rennix, a neighbor and a member of Saint Paul. Clarissa worked free-lance in telecommunications; could she skip a few days and watch the trial on Annie's behalf? Equipped with a notepad, she headed immediately to court.

Through most of the late spring of 1990, the State Supreme Court in Brooklyn had been a chaotic place, surrounded by television vans topped with satellite dishes, photographers corralled inside police barricades, riot squad officers in helmets and visors, and demonstrators chanting for justice or revenge. The Bensonhurst murder trial was being heard in one courtroom, while the assault case that had ignited a black boycott against a Korean grocery was advancing in another. All the animosity that made for tabloid hysteria and amateur sociology displayed itself on the courthouse plaza as openly as a crafts fair.

This morning the plaza is quiet. Verdicts having been rendered in both cases, the media caravan has decamped for Manhattan, where the first trial in the Central Park jogger attack will soon commence. In room 761, where the Kelly case is assigned to Judge Herbert Lipp, jurisprudence proceeds in its humdrum habit. Perhaps thirty spectators sit in four rows, working crossword puzzles and updating address books during the frequent interruptions. A retired bookkeeper and a truant yeshiva boy watch the trial for diversion. Except for the quotation from Jefferson carved into one wall, the room bespeaks bare utility. A yellowed flag dangles near a gray filing cabinet and a coat rack used to store phone books. An office-supply company's calendar hangs on the witness box, and a Tupperware water jug rests beside the judge's gavel.

"Justice sure is slow!" Clarissa writes in her report to Annie. "This seems closer to the lunacy of 'Night Court' than the efficiency of 'L.A. Law.'"

Then the testimony begins, and Clarissa can only be relieved Annie is not in court. Question, objection, ruling, answer; direct examination, cross-examination, redirect, recross. The moment of death is described and examined second by second, again and again, like a grotesque football injury repeated from every angle of instant replay.

ASSISTANT DISTRICT ATTORNEY STEVEN SCHWARTZ: How many times did the defendant hit Mr. Kelly with the gun?

CLAUDE GRAY: It was three or four times.

SCHWARTZ: And where did he hit Mr. Kelly?

GRAY: On the left side of his head....

SCHWARTZ: And then what happened?

GRAY: Mr. Kelly shoved her away. She bounced off of this van.... She grabbed her stomach and hollered that, "Don't push me that way. I am pregnant."

SCHWARTZ: And what happened?

GRAY: Mr. Kelly went into a freeze situation.

SCHWARTZ: Indicating Mr. Kelly had both hands up?

GRAY: Both hands.

SCHWARTZ: He was bent over?

GRAY: Yeah.

SCHWARTZ: Tell us exactly what happened when Mr. Kelly froze, as you described it.

GRAY: He stepped up on the curb....

SCHWARTZ: Meaning the defendant?

GRAY: Right.

SCHWARTZ: Okay.

GRAY: And he repeated what the woman said.

SCHWARTZ: What exactly did he say?

GRAY: He said, "Don't push her like that, she's pregnant." He fired one shot in the air.

SCHWARTZ: With how many hands?

GRAY: One hand. He brought the gun down, took two hands and fired the next shot. That shot dropped Mr. Kelly.

Annie Nesbitt's childhood was one of proscription—no swimming, no baseball, no field work, no summer job away from home. Even when a doctor advised an operation to correct the little girl's crossed eyes, her mother refused. It was not that Cynthia Gooch, a farm wife, was the restrictive sort by nature, but that Annie was too precious to risk. Cynthia had lost more babies in miscarriage and childbirth than she could count before bearing Annie two months premature. "You were a seven-month baby," she would later tell her only child, "and seven-month babies are hard to raise. But you're a blessed child, because you *were* raised."

Annie may have been blessed with survival, but she was cursed with an isolation few people could cure. In the tobacco belt of North Carolina, where large families worked the land together, she was limited to indoor pursuits. There were the eye exercises to right her vision, the sewing lessons from her grandmother, the stories from the issues of *True Confessions* stacked at her bedside. Cynthia Gooch dreamed Annie would become a schoolteacher, her husband Charles that she would attend college. Those were grandiose aspirations in the hamlet of Oxford in the years after World War II, where the black high school did not even offer twelfth grade since virtually every child quit before graduation to start working the fields.

The Gooches, though, owned their fifty-seven acres, and that margin of security let Annie proceed to North Carolina College in Durham. There, excited by a young student leader named Jesse Jackson from nearby North Carolina A&T, Annie hurled her energies into the Civil Rights crusade. She painted placards with slogans like "Equal Rights for All." She registered voters. She marched from the campus to the Kress store, whose segregated lunch counter was the object of a sit-in. These efforts not only politicized Annie, but opened her personal horizons too wide to be closed. In June 1965, after her junior year of college, she went to live with her Aunt Bertha in the South Bronx, and found a job for fifty-seven dollars a week answering calls from clients for Blue Cross.

The South Bronx seemed to Annie an unending sensation, from the clothing stores on Third Avenue where she spent part of each paycheck to the Italian restaurant where she ate her first slice of pizza to the Hunts Point Ballroom where she danced to the touring West Indian bands of Mighty Sparrow and Lord Kitchener. Between songs one evening when Annie was twenty-three, her cousin introduced a friend, a mail sorter named Theodore Nesbitt. He proved as outgoing as Annie was shy, taking her to clubs for soul music or calypso, making picnics on the Day Line boat cruising the Hudson. And always he impressed Annie as a gentleman, a holder of doors, a bestower of bouquets, the sort of suitor who learned his woman's favorite perfume. To this day, Annie still wears it, White Shoulders.

They married in November 1967, pursued their careers, moved to roomier apartments. They put off having children because Annie feared she would never reach her goal of a management position if she took maternity leave. Besides, she had never conceived. By 1983, with an eye toward Ted's retirement and concern about his hypertension, the Nesbitts bought land in North Carolina. There they planned to build a home with a pool and a two-car garage, all of it shaded by oaks. As they drove for a visit that June, Ted collapsed with a heart attack in the bathroom of a rest stop. He was dead by the time Annie discovered his body.

SCHWARTZ: At this point, Mr. Kelly is now on Eastern Parkway flagging down a car. Could you and your brother have left the scene? ...

NANCY SILVESTRI: Abandon my car and leave the scene?

SCHWARTZ: Well, where were the keys to the car?

SILVESTRI: They were in the ignition.

SCHWARTZ: Couldn't you have physically gone over and taken the keys out of the ignition? ... What was preventing you? ...

SILVESTRI: There were people there. It was already, so to speak, an incident. If we would have walked away, then the Police Department would have said, they would have been looking for someone and he is leaving the scene.

SCHWARTZ: Of an incident?

SILVESTRI: Of an incident.

SCHWARTZ: Would it be fair to say, if you would have walked away at that point, Mr. Kelly would be alive today?

In the months that followed Ted's death, Annie's last desire was to meet another man. A friend had a boyfriend who had a best friend who was divorced. Annie said no every time the prospect was raised. Even her friend, Mary Thomas, grew leery when she heard this eligible bachelor suffered from heart disease. "What Annie doesn't need," she said, "is to meet somebody with angina." But when Annie joined Mary and her beau, Bob Jakes, for a Broadway show one evening, she found Steve Kelly waiting. He had, it turned out, bought her ticket. Then he treated her to dinner.

He was, Annie had to admit it, a charmer, a smoothie, who abided by his own advice, "If you meet somebody, give them your smile." More important, he had substance behind the smile. He attended church. He ran his own business. He doted on elderly people. And he lived, absolutely, for his six sons. The two oldest, a lawyer and an Army sergeant, resided outside New York. But any of the others might accompany Steve on a visit to Annie's apartment. Stanford and Erik were students. Stephen junior worked for the city Department of Finance, and Stuart served as a transit police officer. That made some of Steve's friends say Stuart was the favorite, which Steve always denied. It was true, though, that Steve had always said he wanted one of his sons to become a cop—perhaps out of admiration for Bob Jakes, a detective, or perhaps for the vicarious sense of what, with fewer burdens, his own life might have been.

Steve was the twentieth of twenty-six children born to two South Carolina sharecroppers, Morgan and Jennie Kelly. When Morgan died in the fields in 1935, Jennie journeyed with the ten youngest to Brooklyn. Cleaning homes by day, selling home brew whisky by night, she managed to keep the family housed, healthy, and fed. And early on Steve emerged as the surrogate father of the home. He left high school to lay ties for the Long Island Rail Road, fittingly physical work for a teenager so brawny he resembled Jack Johnson, the black boxing champion. Steve's morality, too, was made of sturdy stuff. Neither liquor nor cigarettes nor cards sullied Steve Kelly. He enforced Jennie's curfew, chased down thieves on the street, scared the neighborhood Staggerlees away from his sisters.

When the worshipers at Saint Paul called Steve "a child of the church," they invested the cliché with an extra meaning. It was not simply that he had been a member since coming to Brooklyn at age ten; it was the way the fatherless child had become a son to his pastor, Reverend Adolphus Smith. The young man drove "Pop" to appointments and entertained him at the piano. It was uncertain what Adolphus and Allie Smith wanted more—to adopt Steve as a son or to have him marry their daughter, Alfreda. Steve and Alfreda did make a couple for a time, but he took another as his wife, a woman named Dorothy, who bore him two sons. Divorced from her, Steve met and wed Shirley Harris, who would become the mother of his four younger children. Their divorce in the mid-1970s did nothing to separate Steve from his family; when he formed his own construction company, he named it Kelly and Sons.

Those around Steve found themselves attracted by the same traits that captured Annie—the humor, the decency, the big heart. He called friends and family members "love" or "lover," a holdover from once teasing a brother about who had more girlfriends. Annie, in tribute to his paternal streak, called him "Dad." When Stuart worked night shifts with the transit police, for instance, Steve would search him out on his post, just to make sure he was wearing his warm uniform. The last construction job Steve held was located near a school, and during recess he bought the children candy and lollipops.

When Steve moved in with Annie in 1985, he brought a sense of family she never had known. His youngest son, Stanford, lived with them, and Annie indulged him with school clothes from Lord & Taylor, excursions together to museums and parks. On most Saturday mornings, Erik, Stuart, and Stephen junior would arrive for eggs and grits by the pound. And on Sunday after church, Annie would take Steve to her Aunt Bertha in the Bronx. They shared more extravagant times, too, dinner dances for which Steve waxed his Lincoln, rented a tuxedo, bathed himself in Baron cologne. "Give me my flowers now," he often told Annie, "while I can smell 'em."

> SCHWARTZ: And when that [first] shot was fired, you had your fin-
> ger on the trigger of the gun. Correct?
> ORTIZ: That would be correct, sir.
> SCHWARTZ: And when the second shot was fired, you had your
> finger on the trigger of the gun?
> ORTIZ: Yes.
> SCHWARTZ: So when Mr. Kelly was killed, it was your finger that
> pulled the trigger? …
> ORTIZ: Yes.
> SCHWARTZ: When you pulled the trigger of your gun the second
> time, the shot that ended the life of Stephen Kelly, Stephen
> Kelly did not have a weapon. Isn't that correct?
> ORTIZ: That I saw, he was unarmed.

Entering Annie Nesbitt's apartment for the first time, Inez Simpkins felt defensive, even guilty. The last time she had seen her brother, Steve Kelly, he had pleaded with her, "Why don't you come and meet Anne? You'd like her. She's different from the rest." And Inez had answered, "I'll be around," knowing she had no intention. Now, on the night of Steve's death, she would be making belated acquaintances.

Inez saw Annie's fair skin, her straightened hair, her conservative suit, and thought to herself, *Oh, Little Miss Proper. Just like a white girl.* Then, as she moved into the living room, she noticed that Annie was doing all the work. She was seating the guests, serving the drinks, busing the tables; there were a half-dozen people sitting on Annie's and Steve's bed, like it was just some couch, like this was a rent party. Only in the furtive moments between chores would Annie sit and dab at her own tears.

"Wait a minute," Inez announced to the assemblage. "Anne's gone through a terrible thing, and she's got a lot more to go through. She needs some rest. Those that's not gonna help clean, leave." Then she turned to Annie. "You sit down. You ain't supposed to be waitin' on nobody."

As the apartment emptied, Inez washed the dishes, collected the garbage, fixed Annie a cup of coffee, and sat down with her to talk.

"I heard so much about you," Annie said. "I always wanted to meet you."

"I'm sorry it had to be this way."

"Steve always used to tell me, 'I got a sister who could stop traffic.'"

"I got a backside that done stopped some traffic."

Suddenly they were laughing, laughing with fleeting relief, laughing in the birth of a friendship.

"I wish I had your nerve," Annie said wearily, thinking how Inez had cleared the room.

But what was it Inez wished from Annie's personality? "Free-hearted" was the phrase that came to her, for Inez had a damaged heart, clinically and otherwise. Her body was still recovering from an angina attack the previous year, and her spirit had just about stopped trying to heal from all the hurt it had suffered. Inez's husband had been murdered in a robbery in 1969. Her mother had died in 1983. The two grandchildren she had been raising, the ones she collectively called "my heart," had been returned by court order to their mother, a drug addict. And now her brother Steve, the only member of the family with whom she had stayed close, was gone, too.

Inez's cynicism extended to church. She had drifted from Saint Paul during Adolphus Smith's troubles, and her experiences elsewhere left her disgusted with "jackleg preachers driving fancy cars while folk go hungry and lose their lights," as she put it in typically blunt fashion. At the time her brother was killed, she was paying her tithes to Fred Price, a television evangelist. Steve's funeral marked her first visit to Saint Paul in twenty years.

Much as she had felt an instant kinship with Annie, she immediately warmed to Reverend Youngblood. They both seemed so genuine, so unpretentious. Forgoing the bombast that could have played well for the reporters in attendance, the pastor imbued the funeral with measured outrage and solemn grief. Somehow Inez ached less in its wake.

That entire week, Inez stayed in Annie's apartment, and from then on the women were partners for church. Each Sunday morning Inez rose before sunrise to drive from her home in Jersey City to Annie's apartment in Crown Heights and on to Saint Paul, staking out seats in the front center section. They followed the service with breakfast at a diner, and after Annie reached for the check one too many times, Inez kicked her in the shin—having first slipped off her shoe, so she would startle but not bruise.

Each Wednesday evening, Annie and Inez took courses together in the SPIRIT adult education program. Inez usually arrived two hours early, straight from her job as a school nurse's assistant in Queens. And it was the strangest thing: At home she could barely sleep, so plagued was she with nightmares about Steve. Sleepytime tea could not relax her, and Comtrex cold medicine could not knock her out. She was ready to ask a doctor for pills. But alone in Saint Paul's chapel, spread across three or four chairs, Inez would fall into the most effortless slumber, broken only when Annie arrived to wake her.

They were two halves of a whole. Where Annie had been the sheltered, housebound girl, Inez had grown nonstop from tomboy to knockout. Where Annie projected prim modesty, Inez was funky. Where Annie chose word and action like a natural diplomat, Inez bulled through the world brashly, whether fighting in court for her grandchildren or dancing to a soca record, sherry in hand. At such ebullient moments, Inez made Annie recall the high school friend known as "Good-Time Molly."

Annie provided Inez with trust and support in quieter ways, piercing the armor with which Inez had guarded her core. First thing in the morning and last thing at night, the two women spoke on the phone. Inez would cook and iron for Annie, straighten her apartment, kidding her all the while about being "a spoiled rich black girl." Annie introduced Inez to Broadway and Radio City and the factory outlets in Reading.

They were browsing there one weekend when Annie hesitated over a coat.

"I don't have enough money," she sighed to Inez.

"I don't wanna hear that mess," Inez erupted. "I don't care what you tell nobody else, don't tell me you got no money. Don't be gettin' to be no miser on me. I'm pissed off at you."

"Oh, Inez, don't—"

"Don't tell me 'don't.' This is what you're workin' for!"

They needed all the diversions, all the confidences, and more, as the murder trial wore on. Although Shirley Kelly kept Annie abreast of the testimony, the children rarely called her anymore. They had gathered, naturally enough, around their mother in a time of duress. Yet it also seemed, in an unspoken way, that they judged Annie harshly for not attending the trial, that they did not quite believe the severity of her condition. Only Inez, wary of exposing her own infirm heart to the trial and its torments, could understand.

Annie was far too timid to justify herself. Nor did she seek out Reverend Youngblood, not wanting to add to his workload. All her life she had been taught not to question God's ways—not when Ted died, not when Steve was killed, not when a gulf opened between her and the closest thing she had ever had to children. It took Inez to show her you could curse that goddamn God. Why had He stolen her husband and mother and brother? Why had He condemned her grandchildren to a living hell? But why, too, had He blessed her with Saint Paul and Reverend Youngblood and Annie, all in the wake of such tragedy? And why had He blessed Annie with Inez? Had that been the lesson of Job?

COURT CLERK: Has the jury agreed upon a verdict?

JURY FOREWOMAN: Yes, we have.

CLERK: Under the first count of the indictment, charging the defendant with murder, second degree, how do you find?

FOREWOMAN: Not guilty.

CLERK: Under count two, charging murder, second degree, how do you find?

FOREWOMAN: Not guilty.

CLERK: Under count three, charging manslaughter in the first degree, how do you find?

FOREWOMAN: Not guilty.

CLERK: Under count four, charging manslaughter, second degree, how do you find?

FOREWOMAN: Guilty.

CLERK: Under count five, charging assault, second degree, how do you find?

FOREWOMAN: Guilty.

*   *   *

"Just a few more minutes," says a court officer, standing in the crowded hallway outside Judge Lipp's courtroom. "We'll seat the families first, then the others." A second officer emerges, carrying a metal detector, and announces that all spectators must submit to another search, in addition to the one conducted at the elevator bank. Slowly the throng shapes itself into a funnel, and from the front periodically sounds the high shriek of the detector discovering a ring of keys.

On this, the day of sentencing, Inez has come to court. Annie should be here, too, despite her doctor's warning. Newly installed as the director of accounting operations, she had to attend a noon meeting with Blue Cross's chief financial officer. Still, she expected to reach court for the two o'clock session. But it is now two-ten, and there is no sign of her. As the Kelly children enter the courtroom, Inez peers onto the plaza, seven floors below, and Shirley rakes through the crowd, both searching for Annie.

"Is that it?" the court officer asks Shirley.

"We're still missing one. Can we get her in later?"

"We don't usually."

Shirley delays, plucking a few cousins from the line, ushering them to the courtroom door, hoping Annie will appear. At two-twenty, with the officer about to admit the general public, she concedes, taking her usual seat in the second row. Inez settles behind her, in what had been Annie's spot, and holds an adjacent space with her handbag, just in case.

Shirley passes to Inez a five-page, single-spaced letter from the prosecutors to the judge. It contains their arguments that Ortiz receive the maximum sentence, five to fifteen years for manslaughter, and two and one-third to seven years for assault, to be served consecutively. More important, it raises the matter of character. Under the rules of law, neither Stephen Kelly's personal qualities nor Radames Ortiz's could be entered into trial testimony. Only now, as the judge weighs the sentence, can the actions of a moment be placed within the context of a lifetime. Halfway through the pages, Inez halts, unable to continue.

> During his tenure as a police officer, Officer Ortiz was under investigation for drug use, for protecting drug dealers from his

fellow police officers, for his connection with missing police property, and for his false allegations of ethnic harassment to divert attention from these investigations. Officer Ortiz had been involved in a number of incidents involving allegations of brutality against civilians and against prisoners in the court holding pens. Of the six arrests Officer Ortiz has made in his career, two are under a cloud of alleged misconduct. Those arrests were made by Officer Ortiz after allegations by civilians of Officer Ortiz's misconduct. He is a police officer, who in six years on the force has failed to receive even a single commendation, whose file contains none of those informal letters of gratitude from civilians he may have assisted of the sort commonly found in the files of police officers with his years of experience.

Judge Lipp also has received six hundred letters attesting to Steve Kelly's character, 446 of them from members of Saint Paul. The campaign was designed by Charles Lewis, who often attended the trial and wrote accounts of its progress for the Sunday bulletin. From his own years in government, Charles knew the value of a groundswell. And this one attained a painfully personal tone, touching not only on Kelly himself but on the torturous relationship between blacks and the police.

From Curtis Jones: "With all the negative hype and media exploitation of African-American males in this society, it's tragic that the life of Mr. Kelly is no more. But to pour salt into the wound by not even allowing for his character to be affirmed during the trial is criminal to say the least. We miss the life and spirit of Mr. Kelly."

From Gerald Prince: "Honorable Justice Lipp, I think that NYPD's officers need to know that recklessly endangering civilian lives will not be tolerated at all. It must be the function of this city's court system to make this message clear to the law enforcement community."

From Alberta Evans: "The senseless killings in this city must stop!!!!"

Among the hundreds of letters was one from Annie Nesbitt. "Mr. Kelly was a peaceful gentle person and a gentleman who would go out of his way to assist anyone," she wrote. "A good father to his boys and a family man." Even with the privacy of a letter, she had not asserted herself, not mentioned that for six years she had shared Steve Kelly's life.

Now she stands, equally abashed, in the hallway outside the courtroom. It is two thirty-five. The meeting ran late. The subway stalled. And after all the waits and delays and postponements and interruptions she has endured with this case, the months and months of them, on this afternoon the legal system has decided to turn punctual.

"Is the Ortiz sentencing still in progress?" she asks a court officer.

"Yes."

She tries the door; it is locked.

"It's filled to capacity," the officer says.

"You mean *no one* can go in?"

"They won't permit you to stand."

Never does she tell the guard who she is. She figures it would make no difference. Besides, how do you explain an asterisk?

Annie withdraws from the door, leans against a windowsill, sharing it with a stranger.

"Are you here for the defendant?" asks the other.

"No."

"He's a cop, and I hope he gets off."

"Why?"

"Because they have such a difficult job."

Annie feels anger rising, blood surging to her face. She walks to another windowsill, this one unoccupied. A member of Shirley Kelly's church, leaving the hearing, recognizes Annie.

"They didn't let you in?"

"They told me there's no room."

"There's my seat."

They ask the officer.

"It would be disruptive."

Annie paces until her feet swell. She tries to pray, but cannot find words. The guard enters the courtroom, then returns to the hall. Annie hears someone ask how long the hearing will continue. The guard says, "It'll be a while. One of the sons is reading a letter."

Stuart Kelly is poised fifteen feet before Judge Lipp, in the zone otherwise inhabited by attorneys alone, speaking on behalf of the family. His head sags. His voice thickens. Only the handwritten text, held close to his waist, keeps him from faltering.

These last 571 days of my life have been unimaginable. From the first day to the present. Till this day I can still hear Mr. Gray telling me that my father was shot; but what hurts me even more is that I can still see him in front of me, bleeding to his untimely death.

Even though my heart had never experienced so much pain, there was a lot of happiness still in there. I was happy because Dad gave my Mom, my brothers, and myself the best years of his life. Literally!

Many people have asked me who has been my greatest inspiration in life. Without any second thoughts, I only thought of two people: my Dad, and the other great person was and is my Mom. Because of my Dad, I was inspired to become a Police Officer. Dad thought Police Officers were the greatest thing that anybody could be and because of that I wanted to show him that the man he raised was going to be one.

I myself saw something better than being a Police Officer, I saw my father. That is why I resigned as a Transit Police Officer so I could be with my father [in the construction company].

And because of a Police Officer, I stand here before you today. Dad always told my brothers and I, "What goes around, comes around, it might take a minute, it might take a week," or it might take 571 days, but it will come back to you. So treat people with the respect that you would want given to you.

So now on this day, the words of my father still speak in my heart, "what goes around, comes around." Something else I heard Dad tell every one of my brothers, including myself, "Don't worry, son, everything is going to be all right." So with God and these words in my heart, I know everything is going to be all right.

Schwartz and Agulnick address the court, with the defense attorney insulting the prosecutor a few final times. Radames Ortiz, given his chance to speak, declares that justice was not done. Then Judge Lipp delivers the sentence, five to fifteen years on the second-degree manslaughter conviction and one to three years on the assault, to be served concurrently. He makes a point of noting Ortiz's lack of remorse.

The courtroom remains oddly quiet—no gasps, no cries, only the soft padding of tissues to tears. For the Ortiz family, there is the shock of a nearly maximum sentence; for the Kelly family, there is the unaltered reality of Steve's death and the likelihood that Ortiz will appeal. As the others shuffle wordlessly into the hall, Inez remains seated, eyes fixed on the bench. She gathers herself, steps outside, sees Annie, and grasps her hands.

"Five to fifteen," Inez says. "Explain it to me."

"On good behavior," Annie adds, "he's out in five years."

Schwartz leads the Kelly family, Annie included, to a room down the hall labeled CRIME VICTIMS COUNSELING UNIT. Inez leans on a window sill, talking to Chris Harrison, an aunt on Shirley Kelly's side.

"Her heart was so broken that she couldn't get into the court," Chris says. "She deserves better. That's the worst, treatin' her like that."

"I didn't even want to come, but I knew Anne had a meeting," Inez says, gazing out the window, hands plunged into pockets. "I can't take this. I can't. I can't." She pauses. "Those who sat here every day, God bless 'em. I couldn't. When it starts killin' you, it makes no sense. Livin' it over and over and over again. I went through it once with my husband and I couldn't do it again. I know what it does to you."

After twenty minutes with Schwartz, Kelly's survivors appear from the counseling room and proceed to the elevator. A *Daily News* photographer, caught unawares, asks Shirley and her children to retrace their steps for his camera. As they oblige, Annie draws near to Inez and Chris.

"Why aren't you in the picture?" Chris asks.

Annie, ever temperate, shrugs.

"Let's get out of here," Inez says.

"Maybe I'll make you a steak," Annie says, forcing a weak smile. "I know you think I can't cook."

They ride the subway together back to Annie's apartment. Inez recounts the sentencing, but Annie's attention drifts. She remembers that night, calling the ambulance, pushing through the crowd, seeing Steve on the ground, leaning over him, clutching his hand, saying, "I'm here. Don't worry. You're gonna be all right." She remembers him smiling, strangely smiling, knowing he would die.

"The most difficult part is over," Inez says. "You can go on with your life."

"But it's something that's always gonna be there. You start a new chapter, but it's not that simple."

"I know that," Inez says. "On the top, you don't let nothin' bother you, but deep down inside, it eats you up. Then it starts to boilin' and bubblin' and you're cryin'. And who you cryin' for? You're a softie, Anne, don't you know that?"

"I just know we had a good life together," Annie says, battling back tears.

They arrive home, and Annie cooks steak, carrots, and broccoli. Then she sheds her work clothes for a housecoat and slippers, and places a tape of Eli Wilson on the stereo. His voice has soothed her often in these past weeks, his voice and a verse from Isaiah.

> Every valley shall be exalted, and every mountain and hill shall be made low: and the crooked shall be made straight, and the rough places plain....

Perhaps she heard those words first in her Civil Rights days, in a speech by Martin Luther King, Jr. Then they spoke to Annie about justice, its irresistible force. Lately they have assured her that life does go on.

So they talk, Annie and Inez, about a theater trip. They mull over Annie's plan to redecorate the apartment. They joke about who will iron Annie's dress for work tomorrow, since everybody knows spoiled rich girls don't know how. Sometime after two, Inez leaves for Jersey City, and when she arrives she phones Annie first thing.

"Okay, I'm in."

"Thanks for stayin' and all," Annie says.

"Call me in the morning?"

"Call you in the morning."

7

BLOOD TEST

IN A THIRD-FLOOR LOFT IN MANHATTAN, Reverend Johnny Ray Youngblood wipes the makeup off his face. He straightens a pin-striped suit on its hanger, carefully folds his *dashiki* and *kente* cloth. He has just posed for the first formal portrait of his life. The more prominent the pastor has become through the revival circuit and the Nehemiah housing program, the more requests Thenia Brandon has fielded for photographs, and all she had available were quick shots taken by Charles Lewis, hardly suitable for the man she sometimes called "the chairman of the corporation." So today Reverend Youngblood has obliged her with a sitting in a professional's studio, putting an official face on a public self.

Now he must drive to Kennedy Airport and confront the private self, confront it so that after twenty years of evasion he can make it one with the man in the portrait. Jernell McDonald, the son he so long denied, is coming from New Orleans. He will stay for a week, joining in Father's Day; he will sleep under Reverend Youngblood's roof; he will cause tremors, no matter how lightly he treads.

After breakfast this morning, Reverend Youngblood asked his son Joel how he felt about Jernell's visit. "It's fine," he answered. "Except what am I supposed to tell people?" And for much of last night, the pastor argued with his wife, Joyce. From the time of their marriage, eighteen years ago, she had heard him dispute that Jernell was his child, heard him declare he would submit to a blood test to settle the issue of parentage. Now he has reversed course, accepting Jernell, diminishing the test, and she was the one pressing for a scientific resolution to a matter of the heart.

None of the tension surprised Reverend Youngblood; as he had preached on Easter, resurrections not only solve problems, but create them. Still, there were less complicated times for a resurrection. It is now June 14, and the remaining days of the month rank among the busiest in the Saint Paul calendar. This weekend brings a three-day conference about black men under the title "Lazarus, Rise Up." Then comes the joint celebration of the pastor's forty-second birthday and sixteenth anniversary in the pulpit. That will be followed by a mock presidential election, complete with videotaped commercials and campaign speeches, for the congregation's teenagers. Only after the July 4 holiday and the church picnic will the pace ease. Even then, Reverend Youngblood will travel to New Orleans to preach revival in his hometown, and to resume the other reconciliation in his life, between his father and himself. Reaching across generations, one way as an absent father and the other as a neglected son, amounted to more than a personal matter. It represented, to Reverend Youngblood, an act of ministry, an example for his congregation to repair its families and so restore its nation.

He emerges now from the studio into a gray drizzle, Joel at his side. Nearing a parking lot, he hands his son the claim ticket and money for his Volvo. "I love you, brother," he says. "Really appreciate your help. It's gettin' to the point I don't know what I'd do without you." With these gestures and compliments, the pastor tries to allay the confusion at what Jernell's presence may mean. It was one thing, after all, for Joel to see movies and shoot baskets with Jernell in New Orleans, as he has done the last several summers. It is another to publicly surrender the birthright.

Driving up Third Avenue and toward the Queens-Midtown Tunnel, Reverend Youngblood indicates an Irish bar and says to Joel, "Remember when that was the Fisherman's Net?" That was the restaurant in "The City" where the pastor's family and Thenia Brandon's often ate Sunday dinner. Years have passed. Back then, Thenia was still married, with children at home; back then, the pastor had two sons by one wife, or so he liked to think.

Moving past the brick apartments of Sunnyside, past the deserted grounds of the 1964 World's Fair, closer by the moment to Kennedy Airport, Reverend Youngblood falls deeper into memory. He tells Joel about walking miles to school when he didn't have bus fare, about going through a whole year with just two pairs of pants; he tells him about not being allowed to smoke or dance or curse, like other boys; he tells him about the day Mother Jordan beat him before the entire congregation until he wet his pants.

"And if Jernell was my son," he says, "then that was proof of my manhood. And when I got cast east of Eden, that was the best exile I ever had." He pauses, shakes himself again into the present. "I told Jernell to bring his horn," the pastor says, turning a smile toward Joel. "Imagine, you on the drums, Jernell on trombone. And Jason doin' what? Backflips."

Joel laughs his easy laugh, rocking his head just a bit. "Glad you're with me, bro," Reverend Youngblood says. "Spendin' some time with your old man."

Entering the Pan Am terminal, Joel hangs on his father's arm until he spots the arrival gate on a message board. Then he sprints ahead, picking his way through baggage carts and baby carriages and garbage cans. The plane has not yet landed, so he slides into a telephone booth, unfolds a scrap of paper, and hurriedly dials, twisting the metal cord into loops.

"That Edwina?" Reverend Youngblood chides from the concourse.

"Nah," Joel says, covering the receiver with his palm. "That's Edward's girl."

Reverend Youngblood starts to laugh at Joel's evasion, then catches sight of a slender figure wearing a tie and shined shoes. "There he is," he shouts to Joel, who drops the phone and runs to Jernell, shouldering his garment bag and leading him to their father.

Reverend Youngblood looks into his face. The angle of the jawline, the square set of the chin, the almond-shaped eyes all resemble his own. The pastor no longer possesses the leanness of Jernell; but inside baggy pants and a denim jacket, Joel does. Then Reverend Youngblood spots the gold ring on Jernell's finger from Saint Augustine High School, his own alma mater, and the quarter-inch letters beside the gemstone spelling JOHNNY. That, after all, is the young man's given name.

Jernell hesitates for an instant. All through the flight he had both craved and dreaded this moment. Had his father invited him because he wanted to? Or just because he felt sorry for him? Would he be greeted or merely *met*?

"Hey, bro," the pastor says, hugging Jernell, then clasping hands. "Glad to have you here." His voice shifts from jauntiness to concern. "You okay? Were you scared? Was it turbulent?"

"I was all right."

"How you feel?"

"Just tired," Jernell says. "I been workin' on this new interstate." He pauses, slowly grins. "And I just went over."

"You pledged?" Reverend Youngblood exclaims. "What you pledge? Kappa?"

"Omega."

"Omega," Reverend Youngblood repeats with feigned disdain. "I won't hold it against you."

Groping for common ground, they talk about airline meals and Saint Augustine teachers. Joel brings up cars and basketball and college. Jernell listens attentively, answers politely, in no way imposes himself. He clutches a plastic supermarket bag, stretched thin with gifts for the Youngbloods.

They reach the car. Before the moment can become awkward, Joel takes the backseat.

"You all right?" Reverend Youngblood asks.

"Fine," Joel says, as they drive off.

Turning down Hendrix Street twenty minutes later, Reverend Youngblood says, "This is Saint Paul." The identification is unnecessary; Jernell recognizes the sprawling brick building from the church's history book and the accompanying videotape. Lent to him by Palmon and Ottie Mae Youngblood, they had tethered him to his father's world, even as he was not permitted to inhabit it. And before he had the book and tape, he had his imagination, with its picture of Saint Paul as a place of chandeliers and varnished wood and a soaring pulpit.

Now he climbs the front steps and enters the actual church—the hallway with hanging plants, the bulletin board with snapshots from Mother's Day, the sanctuary with folding chairs and a pulpit at ground level. Thenia Brandon, the first in Saint Paul to learn the existence of Jernell, hurries from the central office with a hug. Shirley Raymond follows, then Leroy Howard and Mary McCormick. "This is my son Jernell," Reverend Youngblood tells each one. Joel introduces his friend, Michael Stone, saying without pause, "This is my brother," and Michael slaps palms. Jason Youngblood, hearing the commotion, rounds a corner and races to Jernell. Naturally falling into the role of the older brother, Jernell puts Joel and Jason in hammerlocks, one inside each elbow.

Joel must remain at Saint Paul for a choir rehearsal, but Jason will ride home with his father and Jernell. The route passes the Nehemiah homes, of which Jernell has heard much, and again the imagined gives way to the real. "All the money they spent investigating Marion Barry," Reverend Youngblood says of the mayor of Washington, standing trial now for possession of crack. "If they gave that to East Brooklyn Congregations, we could rebuild this whole borough. Shows what the values are." A mile or two later, he points to Kings County Hospital, explaining it was there that Joel and Jason were born. "A county," the pastor adds, "is like what a parish is in Louisiana." Until today, Jernell had traveled no farther north than Tennessee.

They reach the Youngblood house, easily three times the size of the bungalow Jernell shares with his maternal grandparents. Joyce's niece and nephew, visiting from Pennsylvania, answer the door; she has given them the spare bedroom Reverend Youngblood had thought would be Jernell's. Looking up from a pot of sausage and corn in the kitchen, Joyce sees Jernell. She says nothing. As Reverend Youngblood moves toward her to speak, Jason leads Jernell upstairs to Joel's room, which he will share. By the time they return to the ground floor, Joyce's raised voice surges from the kitchen. Jason discreetly closes the door. Still, the voice can be heard. Jason suggests he and Jernell walk to the corner for a hamburger, and finding the restaurant closed, they wander back through the rain, prolonging the trip with slow steps.

The pastor serves the two boys dinner at the living room table. Joyce takes her dish into the adjoining breakfast nook and eats silently, watching a portable television. The only sound in the house is of cutlery touching plate.

Jason, the diplomat, moves to Joyce's table, chatting about his day in school. Jernell tells Reverend Youngblood about a New Orleans preacher who claims to collect $100,000 each Sunday from a congregation of four hundred, and they briefly laugh together. Then the pall descends again.

Drawing close across the table, Jernell whispers to his father that he can stay at a hotel, even fly back home tonight. "No, no," Reverend Youngblood answers. "It'll be all right. You're my son."

On the day in December 1968 when Johnny Ray Youngblood took his pregnant girlfriend to Charity Hospital in New Orleans, he was so distraught he misspelled the name of his own street on the admission form. How could he concentrate on details? He felt shame at having a child he could not support with a woman he no longer loved enough to marry. He felt terror that the escape from Holy Family he had so long anticipated would be halted by wedlock and fatherhood. He imagined his own picture on the posters of outlaws from his favorite westerns: Johnny Ray Youngblood, Wanted Dead or Alive.

So he made a choice that would haunt him, not visiting the hospital on the day Johnny Jernell Youngblood was born, paying only cursory calls when Jackie McDonald brought their child home, and then vanishing from the life of the flesh of his flesh for nearly fifteen years. He hedged about Jernell to Joyce Terrell, his fiancée. He disclosed nothing of Jernell to his congregations in Buffalo and Brooklyn. "Come straight out from the gate," the pastor's mother had advised him. "Tell 'em what's happening in your life." But denial had already become a habit easily repeated, and ultimately even Ottie Mae joined in the conspiracy to keep an inconvenient child offstage.

Then, six years later, Joel Youngblood was born. Joyce's pregnancy had been difficult, and the infant arrived severely ill with pneumonia. As Joel gasped for breath in an incubator, his lips turning blue, the presiding physician approached Reverend Youngblood. It would be wise, she said, to administer last rites. "Now, Lord," the pastor prayed, "You should know that we want him. We know You got the last word on everything, and if You decide to take him, You got to teach me how to teach Joyce the reason why. But if You let us have him, we'll raise him and give him back to You."

Joel recovered, and Reverend Youngblood made a compact to remain as committed a father as the one who had pleaded for a miracle. Here was this creation, unable to feed himself or turn over in his crib, able only to cry out and hope someone would answer. The picture of such helplessness made Reverend Youngblood think of Jernell, a second-grader he had last seen in diapers, a reality without a presence, a being without a face. *There's a kid out there,* Reverend Youngblood told himself. *What's he doing? Who's there for him?* If the boy grew into a derelict, it would be his father's fault. And if he succeeded, his father would not deserve to share the joy.

These spasms of conscience always passed. Colgate-Rochester, Bethany Baptist, Saint Paul—Reverend Youngblood would have lost all those things had he remained in New Orleans with Jackie and Jernell. And he could lose his pulpit still, he believed, if his secret became known. Once in a rare while, Jackie requested money for Jernell, which he provided, and his parents assisted more regularly. But soon there would need to be excuses and rationales, for Jernell was growing old enough to ask about his father.

Bitter as she may have been with Reverend Youngblood, Jackie resisted the temptation to disparage him. She told Jernell the old stories of prom night and street football. His parents had parted, in her telling, only because she wanted to stay in New Orleans while Johnny insisted on moving north. But that was a fiction that could not be sustained. Going to church at Holy Family, young Jernell heard contempt when people said, "Looks just like his daddy." And at the Youngbloods' house, only blocks from his own, his role as grandson knew strict boundaries. Most of the time he could play with his cousins around Palmon's garage, run errands, or do chores for Ottie Mae. She bought Jernell clothes for Easter, attended his school graduations. But when anybody from New York came to visit, much less Reverend Youngblood himself, Jernell was kept at a distance, described, if at all, as "a friend of the family." Otherwise, he was told, his father would surely be tossed out of his church. Jernell already suffered with unspoken guilt, believing his birth had ruined his mother's life. The prospect of causing more damage was sufficient to make him obey.

But the yearning for connection, for wholeness, would not die. While helping Ottie Mae with household duties one day, Jernell saw her throwing away a letter on Saint Paul stationery. He fished it from the garbage and carried it home, and with it he began to assemble a portrait of his father. His maternal grandmother, Jernell discovered, kept a scrapbook of clippings about Reverend Youngblood. Ottie Mae lent him cassette tapes of sermons.

In yet another way, as Jernell reached his teenage years, he sought his father. As active as he was in Holy Family—ushering, playing drums, directing the youth choir, as young Johnny Ray had done— Jernell had begun to find his life spiritually incomplete. Praying alone in his bedroom one night, he heard the divine answer, the call to preach. For the next two years he tried to ignore it, battle it back. Detached and analytical by nature, Jernell already felt painfully "set apart" from his cousins and friends. And the congregation at Holy Family, he correctly suspected, would ascribe his call less to heavenly command than to father-worship. "Little Johnny," they called him when he began preaching at fifteen. "You gonna leave us like your daddy did?" He answered with a sermon about Judas Iscariot, entitled "Saints With Sinners' Problems."

It was partly correct, and infinitely less rending, for Jernell to blame the small minds of Holy Family for having sundered his parents than to risk hating the father he adored in absentia. Sometimes Jernell envisioned Reverend Youngblood like the contestant in a televised beauty pageant and himself as the cameraman, necessary though invisible. Sometimes he found solace in the aphorism that assured, "God will make a way out of no way." But sometimes he thought of Christ on the cross, tortured and forsaken. He would dream of the day when the Youngblood family, heading north to visit Johnny, would get a last-minute call from the pastor saying, "Bring Jernell, too." His mother promised Jernell that once he turned sixteen he could travel alone to New York, but when Jernell mentioned the agreement to Ottie Mae, she warned, "You can't do that."

Then, in November 1983, Eli Wilson, Sr., died, and Reverend Youngblood flew to New Orleans to preside at the funeral. Jernell seized the opportunity, attending the service with his mother, then lingering outside the church, waiting for his father to emerge. It was a damp, clammy night, uncomfortable for idling. Trucks rumbled past on Claiborne Avenue. The sidewalk had been torn up for sewer construction. But Jernell had been emboldened, hearing his father preach in the voice he had known only from tape, seeing him weep with the face he had known only from newspaper photos. He had waited fifteen years for this moment. What was fifteen minutes more?

From the darkened street, he could not see through the church's tinted glass doors. But then he heard the voice. As he turned, he was staring at his father from only ten feet away.

"Have you seen your son?" another mourner blurted to Reverend Youngblood. "He looks just like you."

Stunned, he moved toward Jernell, appreciating the boy's height, one measure of the years of denial, and gazing into a face that seemed to ask, *Where do I stand?* Reverend Youngblood's thoughts whirled. *God, how do I talk to this kid? I can't fake my joy. I can't vent my anger.* Nor could he utter aloud his fear. He had known one day he would encounter Jernell, and in his imaginings his abandoned son was a living indictment, shouting by his mere existence, *You think you're such a big man? You think you're all that? Look at what you did to me.*

"How you doin', man?" Reverend Youngblood said stiffly. "Good to see you. How's your mom?"

Jernell could only smile, then hug him. When the embrace ended, he clung to his father's sleeve. Could he spend the night with him at the hotel? No, because the pastor was flying out early the next morning. No, too, because a Saint Paul member named Robert Graham was traveling with Reverend Youngblood, and to invite Jernell would mean either to reveal the truth of him or to cloak him in a lie. And Reverend Youngblood could not bring himself to do either.

So they parted.

Time had taught Jernell to expect nothing, lest he be disappointed. *At least this little bit,* he told himself, *is better than none at all.*

But Reverend Youngblood could not forget his son's touch, gentle and eager all at once. Far from being rejected by Jernell, he had been shown a love and respect he hardly deserved. For a man who knew theology, there was only one name for this gift: a state of grace.

Jernell talked his father's younger brother, Lionel, into providing him with the telephone number of Saint Paul. Perhaps twice a month, he would dare to dial, and it was usually Thenia Brandon who answered if the pastor was unavailable. "Could you tell him Jernell called?" he would always say. "His nephew, Jernell."

One time, after making the note, Thenia asked, "How you doin'?"

Her tone, familiar, shook Jernell.

"Do you know who I am?"

"If you mean that you're Reverend's son," she said gingerly, "yes, I do."

Thenia was the only staff member at Saint Paul, other than Eli Wilson, in whom Reverend Youngblood had entrusted the truth. He had met Thenia first as a congregant coming to him for marriage counseling, and later had hired her as his administrative assistant, and in both guises he had admired her respect for privacy. As much as faith, gossip was the currency of church, and Thenia had heard rumors of an illegitimate son long before Reverend Youngblood confirmed them in confidence. But her own sense of integrity precluded the dishing of dirt, especially when it was her boss, her pastor, her friend who would be sullied.

Jernell, knowing none of this, worried for weeks. He dreaded the call that would bear the news, "Your dad lost his church." How could he face his father then? What would become of the relationship they had so tentatively begun? Better to remain a mystery his whole life than to be acknowledged at such a cost.

But the word of Reverend Youngblood's ouster never arrived. Thenia, Jernell now realized, had honored the secret. More than that, she felt for him in a personal way. Having been divorced while the mother of two sons, Thenia understood that no matter what became of the parents' marriage, a boy needed his father. The next time Jernell called, she gave him her home phone number, if he ever wanted to talk.

Talk he did, talk and ask questions. What type of person was his father? Did he joke a lot? Was he always serious? What did he enjoy doing with his family? And how could Jernell win his attention, make him proud?

"What I'm gonna do," he said more than once, "is catch a plane up there, stay in a hotel, go to church on Sunday, then go back. Nobody would ever recognize me."

"Be patient, Jernell," Thenia answered, even as she ached at hearing his longing voice. "When the time is right, your father will introduce you. I don't think he's afraid, or he wouldn't've done some of the things he has in church."

Through the middle and late 1980s, Reverend Youngblood did draw closer to Jernell, calling often and visiting once or twice yearly, discovering a bond more important than chromosomes. Like his father, Jernell graduated from Saint Augustine and entered Dillard, giving them teachers and courses in common. More important, as an aspiring preacher, Jernell chafed under the confines of Holy Family, just as Reverend Youngblood once had. If the church ladies spotted him playing basketball, they would say, "That's really not becoming for a minister." The candles and incense and statues struck him as traditions that had nothing to do with the worship of God. If the Bible said, "My help cometh from the Lord," then why did the Spiritualists appeal through saints? And if people wept and shouted and called "Lord, Lord" on Sunday, how could they act so lowdown mean the rest of the week? Upon turning twenty, Jernell left Holy Family, joining a Baptist church and submitting to a second baptism, yet again retracing his father's path.

As Reverend Youngblood shared that past with Jernell, he was not only offering paternal advice, but explaining the forces that drove him away, and asking obliquely for forgiveness. In New Orleans, at least, Jernell could now play as a brother with Joel and Jason. Reverend Youngblood sent him money for books, clothes, and college tuition, and intervened with the Dillard registrar when Jernell's records were lost.

Still, there were limits. Having assured Joyce all these years that Jernell was not his son, welcoming him into the family seemed to Reverend Youngblood a choice between "my blood child and my legal wife." Even that thinking was a kind of displacement. Reverend Youngblood himself, for reasons of his own, still could not fully acknowledge Jernell.

The reckoning came in August 1989, when the pastor returned to New Orleans for revival. He was the star attraction, the closer three nights in a row, and each evening Jernell and his mother attended. From the pulpit, Reverend Youngblood introduced Jackie as "my old girlfriend," but he fell mute when it came to Jernell. And that silence, he knew, was the definition of sin, "an evil worse than all the evils I'd perpetrated against him."

Over the next months, no matter how often he spoke to Jernell, the shame racked him. So when Leo Goins declared that night in Eldad-Medad, "I don't believe in denyin' no child," Reverend Youngblood knew instantly the true source of the voice.

*   *   *

The visit unfolds like a vacation, a celebration, a fantasy. Twenty mothers invite Jernell for home cooking. Joel Youngblood and Trevor Howard, Leroy's son, take him to see a Schwarzenegger film and the street scene of Greenwich Village. Reverend Youngblood introduces him to both Eldad-Medad and the Sunday congregation, and he is received with warm, lasting applause. On the morning of his father's birthday, Jernell joins his brothers for a serenade:

> Happy birthday to you,
> You live in the zoo.
> You look like a monkey,
> And you smell like one, too.

But there is something unreal, or too rich, in all the giddiness. Joyce still treats Jernell coolly at best. Joel gives Reverend Youngblood a Father's Day card signed, "Your Number One Son." And until Jernell and his father find themselves alone in the breakfast nook one afternoon, their difficult history remains unaddressed.

"Let's talk," the pastor says simply.

As they take seats, Joel bounds down the stairs from his bedroom, moves to join them.

"Jernell, do you mind if Joel's here?"

"No."

But he feels the room vibrating, the very air trembling; he feels the kind of anxiety that makes him pray the hardest. With himself and his father, promises could be spoken in secret. With Joel at the table, any words will have a witness. *Will they approve of me? Will they accept me? Because if they won't, I'll never see them again.*

"Jernell," Reverend Youngblood says, "I want to apologize for the cold and distant attitude Joyce had. I hate that it happened, but I think you understand why." Jernell nods softly. "I want you always to feel welcome here."

Then he clears his throat, cups his palms, and retreats twenty-one years, speaking not only to Jernell but himself.

"The reason your mother gave you for not becoming husband and wife," he says, "is not the real reason. Remember she said I went to school in Rochester and she didn't want to leave New Orleans?"

"Yeah."

"The real reason I didn't marry your mother is I had some questions about whether you were mine. Based on some past experiences."

He mentions briefly another boyfriend of Jackie's, as if it might matter. Then, hunched forward, he unshoulders his burden.

"The main reason," he says, "was I felt if I'd married your mother, I would've been tied up, entangled, and suffocated in that community for my whole life. And there was no way I could handle that thought."

Jernell sits, wordless, composed, eyes on his father. He imagines himself a slave being freed, extending his manacled wrists to the man who holds the key, his father. This is liberation, to know at last the answer, after a lifetime of wondering, "Why?"

"It's bad now," Jernell says of Holy Family, comforting his father, seeking communion.

"And when Mother Jordan was alive, it was a thousand times worse."

"Whenever I preached," Jernell puts in, "this one lady frowned, grunted, gawked. Once she walked out on me."

The burglar alarm sounds briefly as Joyce, returning from a doctor's appointment, unlocks the front door. The conversation halts. Jernell cannot ask the last question left in his heart: *Do you love me?*

A few days later, Jernell manages to miss his flight home. He reaches Kennedy late for a replacement flight, too. Neither he nor his father wants the visit to end, but Reverend Youngblood is committed to a staff retreat upstate, and Jernell must return to his summer job to earn school money. There is just one final bit of business. So on his way to the airport Jernell stops at Downstate Medical Center in East Flatbush.

Beverly Rutherford, a member of Saint Paul, has arranged for the hospital to administer a paternity test. Every mention of it has wounded Jernell, as if the years of healing since that night outside the funeral could be undone with just one drop of blood. Walking up stairs, around corners, down halls, on the way to the room labeled Histocompatibility Laboratory, he tries to strut cockily, thinking of Mike Tyson entering the ring.

He sits in a blue cushioned chair, facing a large refrigerator filled with test tubes and jars. The doctor removes a pillow from a drawer, places it atop a table to cushion Jernell's left arm; then she taps a vein and inserts the needle. As the blood surges, he replays all the voices from his past. *You look like your Daddy. You sound like your Daddy.* He remembers the time he played a tape of one of his sermons for Ottie Mae, and even she thought it belonged to her son.

Two weeks later, after Reverend Youngblood has given his sample and the analysis has been begun, Jernell calls him.

"They haven't finished everything," the pastor says, "but what they've finished so far is positive."

"What do you hope?" Jernell asks.

"I hope everything comes back positive." Reverend Youngblood pauses. "Even if it doesn't, you're my son. Even if you're not, you are."

One evening, a few weeks before Jernell's visit, Reverend Youngblood was speaking to Eldad-Medad on the subject of fathers. "You want an excellent formula for raising your son?" he said. "Raise him the way you *wish* you'd been raised." How well he understood the emotional equation. What made it possible for the pastor to face his own failings and recognize Jernell was that he, as a son, had suffered the same wounds of paternal neglect.

There was a calculating quality to Palmon Youngblood's absence. He did not simply miss the spontaneous moments of Johnny's childhood, for those by their nature could not be foreseen, but knowingly avoided the rituals of passage. When his firstborn graduated from eighth grade, from Saint Augustine, from Dillard, from Colgate-Rochester, Palmon did not attend. When he was ordained as a minister in Buffalo and installed as a pastor in Brooklyn, Palmon remained home in New Orleans. Only under duress did he take part in Johnny's wedding.

In his early twenties, Johnny wrote Palmon a letter, steeped in guilt and want. *If I've failed you in some way I don't understand ... If I've been a bad son ... Then I'm sorry.... But there are some ways you could have been a better father.* He never received an answer. The bitterest denunciation, the crudest profanity, would have been no crueler than that silence. At least then, Johnny would have felt his existence acknowledged. Denied even that, he could think only of the spiritual:

Way down yonder by myself
And I couldn't hear nobody pray

So he resolved to make a world without his natural father. He found ministers for whom he was a "son in the gospel"—E. D. McNeely, Murphy Greer, L. T. Boyce, Eli Wilson, Sr., Glenn DuBois, whom he even called "Dad." From them he received advice and instruction, respect for his gifts of spirit and mind. Oh, he still phoned Palmon occasionally, but only when he needed money, and only to punish. "I'll see what I can do," his father would answer each request, and to Johnny's mordant satisfaction the help never arrived.

Money was always an issue between them, not for its intrinsic value as much as for its symbolism, freedom for Johnny and bondage for Palmon. "You need to get outta school, get you a job, help me pay some of these bills," Palmon said through Johnny's teens. Since neither Ottie Mae's wages as a domestic nor Johnny's after-school job sweeping classrooms paid enough for his Saint Augustine tuition, Ottie Mae would sneak bills out of Palmon's pocket when he fell asleep drunk.

"You were in my wallet," he would claim on awakening.

"You always tellin' me you don't have no money. So how could I take it?"

At one point during his Dillard years, Johnny had banked $150. When Palmon fell two months behind on the mortgage, with the bank threatening foreclosure, Johnny gave $109 of it to save the house. He had to formally declare his father's nonsupport to qualify for the loans that let him finish college. And where was the paternal pride in his achievement? Johnny had never forgotten the evening he was talking on the phone with a classmate about their philosophy assignment when Palmon lumbered in from the sugar refinery. "Get your goddamn ass off that telephone," he had bellowed, "if you can't talk right!"

What Johnny did not know, and would not know for decades, what his father was too bitter or too stoic to tell, was that Palmon was asking him to abdicate no more of his dreams than Palmon himself once had done. That was back in the Great Depression, in Tylertown, Mississippi. As the oldest of Floyd Youngblood's four children, Palmon had shared the responsibility for feeding the family. From the age of twelve, he was hired out by his father—two dollars a week for farm work, then twenty-one for cleaning stores in town, finally thirty-two for laying highway asphalt. Having sworn to graduate from high school, Palmon reluctantly dropped out in the tenth grade. He did keep his other promise, riding the highway out of "the country." But even from New Orleans, he supported the family; his father once traveled four hours to get twenty dollars.

This other Palmon, humane and engaged, did show itself in flashes to Johnny. And much as the young minister tried to forget his father, certain memories refused to depart. There was Palmon cranking his right arm until the bicep rose round and hard, and Johnny hanging from it as if from a tree limb. There was Palmon selling so many chocolate bars for a Holy Family fund-raiser that his buddies dubbed him "Candy Man." There was Palmon driving the family to his folks in Mississippi, a paper sack of fried oysters beside him. A white cop stops the car, and Johnny, terrified, leaps into the front seat. After the cop leaves, Palmon looks down and says to his son, "Man, looky here, you jumped in my oysters." Then Palmon and Ottie Mae laugh a long time, deep and rumbling and high and crinkly, like sweethearts.

So, yes, he loved his father. If only love were enough.

For the celebration of Reverend Youngblood's tenth year in the Saint Paul pulpit, the church planned an imitation of the old television show, "This Is Your Life." After receiving almost daily pleas by telephone, Palmon agreed to appear as the surprise guest. It would be his first trip in an airplane and his first visit to Saint Paul. When his moment to speak arrived, Palmon stood behind a curtain, a microphone at his lips. "Johnny Ray Youngblood is my son," he said, "if he is a minister." His son, on the other side of the divider, could not identify the voice. Only when Palmon walked onto the stage did Johnny recognize him, and then he grasped his father, sobbing, wishing he were still a little boy who could be picked up and held.

In the days that followed, several Saint Paul members told Palmon how often their pastor spoke of him. "You ought to get closer to him," they said. To which Palmon, defensive, asked, "What closer can I get?"

Back at the sugar refinery, though, he started to brag. Palmon had expected Saint Paul to be the size of Holy Family, seating maybe one hundred. No, no, he told his friends, his boy's church held ten times that. And needed two services on Sunday. And was going to expand.

"Look at your son and look at you," said one man, who knew Palmon for drinking, cursing, and dice.

"He's still my son," Palmon answered. "He ain't yours."

The object of all the pride and praise never heard it. As far as Reverend Youngblood could tell, his father's visit had been just a blip on the radar, leaving the screen quickly dark once again. Or, worse, the visit had somehow opened even more distance between them. The world of church, the pastor knew, was one in which Palmon felt censured and condemned. Church called him a sinner for indulging in the pleasures he enjoyed, that he felt he deserved. Why, Mother Jordan had once prophesied he would lose his job to a white man. Who needed a dose of that every Sunday?

Yet, Sunday to Sunday, and each day in between, church consumed his son's life. When Johnny visited New Orleans, he packed his schedule so tightly it precluded what Palmon hoped for, an afternoon of driving with no destination, a twilight on the porch, just time to talk. And, his father had to admit, half the times Johnny phoned from New York, Palmon was either drunk or sleeping it off. Drift, unspoken words, missed connections—with a son nearing forty and a father past sixty, only a fool would expect anything to change.

One morning in November 1988, passing a mirror on his way to the bathroom, the son saw the father. He saw the beginnings of a belly. He saw the low, wide nose and the curving forehead. He saw the skin so dark it was called "blue-black." He knew then he had been running from that figure, the one whose flaws had been trumpeted for so long. *Your Daddy don't handle money. He drinks, runs around. His friends matter more than his family.* And more than any other phrase, *Your Daddy don't know.* With college and the ministry, Reverend Youngblood had built a life around not being his father. Now the mirror told him he inescapably was.

He would be traveling to New Orleans in two months for a board meeting of the Progressive National Baptist Convention. The stay could be lengthened. He dressed, went downstairs, dialed New Orleans.

"Daddy," he said, "I'm comin' home and I need to spend some time with you. Because I'm forty years old and I realize I don't know who you are."

"I'll be here."

In every way, Reverend Youngblood prepared himself. He devoured books and films about fathers, sons, and manhood. He began unearthing his childhood in therapy. He shared his yearnings with the congregation. Still, he boarded the plane with an anxiety bordering on terror. It was one thing to be disappointed when you expected nothing. But to extend yourself to your father after a lifetime of caution and be thwarted again would be a kind of—what was the word in his mind?—*infanticide.*

Moving through the arrival gate in New Orleans, he spotted his father, waiting alone. That was a good sign; he had asked Palmon not to bring anyone else, anyone whose presence would blunt candor. He thanked his father and then he blundered forward.

"Everything I know about you," he said as they settled into Palmon's car, "is stuff Mama has said. I'm a man now, and I know how I feel about some stuff my wife says to my boys about me."

"Yeah," Palmon said.

Reverend Youngblood remembered that voice, vague and guarded. Was his father seconding the emotion or just being polite? There was no way of knowing. The description Reverend Youngblood had once hung on a particular preacher, "congenially aloof," suited his father as well. Palmon had once told him of working a warehouse job in his first days in New Orleans and being promoted into the office when the white manager discovered he could read and write. His friends in the back all quit in protest, and Palmon, feeling responsible, resigned in their wake. It was that day he chose to be a loner, an enigma. Sure, he was loose and funny in the barroom after work, the place he felt most at home, but even there his eyes retained far more than they revealed.

By now, Palmon had driven free of the airport and onto the expressway. It was a route he could follow half asleep, the same one he made twice daily, to and from Ottie Mae's current job as a domestic. Suburban blocks were passing in a blur; the downtown skyline was coming into sight; in ten minutes the men would reach the Lower Ninth and a houseful of relatives. The chance to speak intimately, Reverend Youngblood knew, was slipping away.

So he risked perhaps the most difficult subject, one that would either blast open a channel of communication or forever seal it off. For years Johnny Ray had heard rumors that a certain woman had been

Palmon's mistress. There were even stories that the pastor had a half-brother he had never seen.

"Did you love her?" son asked father.

He waited a long minute for the reply.

"Well, I don't know so much 'bout love," Palmon said slowly. "Treatment. It was the way she treated me. When I had to leave the job and come home to that 'yap-yap,' I couldn't deal with it."

Suddenly, no subject seemed forbidden. Palmon talked about his disdain for a religion that judged him. He talked about the resentment he felt when Johnny sent money to Ottie Mae behind his back. He talked about the qualities he most wanted his son to possess—honesty, sincerity, the bigness to forgive. And Reverend Youngblood saw that his father had thoughts and ideas, an interior life, that Daddy *did* know.

The next morning they ate breakfast together in a restaurant for the first time. The afternoon after that, Reverend Youngblood brought fifteen preachers from the Progressive Baptist meeting to the shotgun shack on the clamshell street, to meet his parents. Ottie Mae cooked gumbo by the bucket, and Palmon met the ministers neither as superiors nor as sissies, neither as objects of awe nor as butts of jokes, but as his son's friends. He felt, after so many years, included.

Then the visit was over. Before they parted, father and son struck a bargain. Reverend Youngblood promised never to send money home without checking with Palmon; Palmon promised to attend the commencement exercises when Johnny received his degree as doctor of ministry. From Brooklyn, Reverend Youngblood started calling his father almost weekly, just to listen, just to talk. He learned how to ask, without traps or rancor, for the sustenance of love.

"Daddy," he said one morning in June 1988, "I just called so you could wish me happy birthday."

"When is it?"

"The twenty-third."

"You know mine's the twenty-fifth."

And Reverend Youngblood realized he did not know. His father's birthday, in fact, had never once been celebrated.

So everyone had his bruises, even an imperfect father. So there were things for a son to learn. Reverend Youngblood learned some when Palmon came to Saint Paul in February 1990 for the church

anniversary, and learned some more when Palmon attended his doctoral graduation, three months later. Still, so much remained unspoken, undone. When Reverend Youngblood flew to New Orleans in
August, then, it was not only to preach revival, but to seal something
between himself and his father, and so to close the blood knot around
three generations, Palmon and Johnny and Jernell.

Like a battleship in a harbor of dinghies, the New Hope Baptist
Church rises in brick certainty from the forlorn landscape of New
Orleans's Third Ward. Just west of downtown, within eyesight of the
Superdome and the Hyatt Regency and the World Trade Center, the
Third unfolds in blocks shaped like triangles and trapezoids, lined with
shotgun shacks and liquor stores and a grocery touting its ninety-nine-
cent fried chicken basket as the "hard times special."

The Twenty-second Annual Citywide Revival and Congress on
Evangelism, then, arrives as an interlude from adversity. At the least,
the faithful can escape the stale heat for the carpeted, paneled, air-con-
ditioned haven of New Hope. In collective memory, too, revival
means respite. It was always in the late summer, when the crops had
been "laid by" in anticipation of harvest, when the brutish work could
cease briefly, that the itinerant preachers erected their tents for camp
meetings. Two centuries ago, the traveling ministers brought the Baptist and Methodist teachings that their enslaved listeners transmuted
into liberation Christianity. On this August evening, six hundred
descendants gather, fans in hand, to hear the word from Reverend
Johnny Ray Youngblood.

BACK BY POPULAR DEMAND, declare the posters tacked to lamp-
posts around town. The phrase disquiets Reverend Youngblood, with
its suggestion of showbiz, but its emphasis on his presence remains
accurate. For all the competition among black ministers, friendly and
otherwise, he *is* the acknowledged star of this pulpit. A baggage han-
dler at the airport recognized him this morning, and asked his advice
on pursuing a clerical career. Preaching at New Hope this afternoon,
Reverend Lloyd Blue of Oakland said of Reverend Youngblood, "I
don't expect to win the race, but I can profit by the association."

Homecoming has its joys and vindications. Reverend Youngblood, his family, and the Saint Paul choir are staying at the Clarion
Hotel on Canal Street; during his childhood, it was called the Jung

and open only to whites. He will dine at Dooky Chase's, once the restaurant of the high-yaller elite, without worrying as he had on prom night about using the wrong fork or just being too dark. And in ways both public and private, Reverend Youngblood will settle emotional accounts.

He stands now before a wooden cross as heavy and coarse as a railroad tie. The golden thread in his *kente* vestment glints in the light. He had just finished telling the women, who make up ninety percent of the audience, to bring their men here tomorrow night. He will be preaching "Lazarus and the Black Man." Before he launches into tonight's sermon, he asks Joyce, Jason, and Joel to stand, and they are warmly received. Then his gaze moves toward a young man in the fifteenth row at the side aisle, a typically inconspicuous niche.

"I want, out of my own sense of honesty, my own sense of health, to introduce you to somebody who's very important to me," he says. "I mean, well ..." Uncommonly, he stammers. "When I was growin' up here, I was courtin'. Like a lot of young men were." He draws breath. "And I did something that I thought I messed up. I was *made* to feel I messed up. But when I look today I realize I didn't mess up."

There are stirrings from the crowd.

"I have a son outside of my marriage. His name is Johnny Jernell McDonald, and some of you know him, but not as my son. He is a fine young man, and I love him, and I'll do anything for him. Jernell, will you stand?" He does, to applause. "And he wants to be a preacher." Now the clapping grows from approving to impassioned.

The following night, before preaching "Lazarus," Reverend Youngblood indicates one of the men who inspired it. Not until 1988 did Palmon Youngblood first hear his son preach at this revival, only twenty minutes from home. Now he will not miss a night.

"I'm forty-two years old," Reverend Youngblood tells the audience, "and it's only in the last two years I've gotten to know my daddy. He was in the house the whole time. But my problem is I was listenin' to what everybody else said about him without checkin' him out for myself. My daddy has become real special to me. Getting to know him has made me grow as a person and a preacher. So I want you to know in front of all these people, Daddy, I love you." Applause interrupts him. "And, Momma, that doesn't mean I don't love you. Sometimes Momma thinks I don't have enough love to go around, that if I love Daddy, I can't love her. But she had three children and loved them all the same. And I can love my momma *and* my daddy."

He can also delight in them. The next afternoon, Reverend Youngblood leads a busload of Saint Paul members to his brother Lionel's house for lunch on the scale of the Marshall Plan. Every stick of furniture has been removed from the living room and two bed-rooms, which are equipped with long tables and folding chairs bor-rowed from New Hope. From her kitchen a mile away, Ottie Mae dis-patches platters of fried chicken, macaroni and cheese, and potato salad, stockpots of both filé and okra gumbo, the product of three days' loving labor. In case any guest might depart less than bloated, one of Lionel's neighbors appears with a roasting pan of barbecued ribs, stacked like cordwood.

Along the shady side of the house, Palmon Youngblood sits talk-ing with Jim Mackie, who serves on Saint Paul's Board of Elders. At fifty-seven, Jim is virtually a peer, but he is city-born and city-bred, recently retired as a bus driver. So he enjoys hearing Palmon's wisdom on the subjects of shrimp heads (important to save for gumbo broth) and watermelons (sweeter when grown on a hillside, where they won't grow fat and bland on standing water). From his world, Jim talks about the bus passenger shot dead for resisting the theft of a transfer. As Palmon shakes his head in disgust, Reverend Youngblood walks around the corner of the house, spotting him.

"You ready, Daddy?"

"Yeah."

Then they climb into Palmon's pickup truck for a trip to Domino Sugar's Chalmette Refinery. In all the years he lived in New Orleans, in all the times he has visited since moving away, Reverend Young-blood has never seen where his father worked, and, more than that, never quite appreciated its toll on the man. Preaching, after all, was not only a calling but a profession that enjoyed respect and visibility. And Reverend Youngblood adored it. Other forces, however, gov-erned his father's working life—obligation and responsibility, danger and tedium. He stayed at the refinery for forty-one years, rising from seventy-seven cents to fifteen dollars an hour, from "working the iron," as the stevedore's hook was known, to driving a forklift so "only my fingers was workin'."

But all his family knew was that Thursday was payday. They never knew about the desperate men who lined the levee just outside the refinery gate, waiting for you to faint in the heat so they could claim your job. They never knew about the way raw green sugar clung to your sweaty clothes, attracting roaches and rats. They never knew about your pal Timothy, who got fired for reading his Bible on the job, or about the scabs who reached the plant by raft during the '53 strike. They never knew how you confronted the union about giving all the crane operator's jobs to white boys and leaving blacks to wield hooks. They never knew it was you, Palmon Youngblood, who broke the color barrier.

The truck rumbles out of Lionel's driveway. Palmon loves this heap the way a teenager loves his hot rod, with equal parts extravagance and care. Two fuzzy dice, colored orange, hang from the rearview mirror. The steering wheel is made of chain links. Just last week, Palmon installed a new engine, as the truck crossed the threshold of 200,000 miles. As he drives, he lays two packs of Salems atop the dashboard, and rolls a lit cigarette between his lips.

"Now, you started out doin' what?" his son asks.

"Hand truck. They load a sack. Sack weigh three seventy-five. You throw it on the hand truck, push it on the belt. Go back, do it again. And later I was workin' the crane, liftin' the raw sugar."

"That when that man got crushed?" Reverend Youngblood asks, recalling one of the few stories he knows.

"Somethin' fell on him," Palmon says. "That girl at church last night?" His son nods. "In the wheelchair?" He nods again. "Her daddy was the one."

Moving south on Alvar, then east on Saint Claude, they pass landmarks. Here is a police station house, improbably equipped with bay windows, the site of countless beatings. Palmon never received one, but he was dragged from home in handcuffs one day, with young Johnny watching, for overdue parking tickets. There, in a frame house, now boarded shut and stained dark with rainwater, was the loan office where Palmon paid so many bills. The last time Johnny accompanied him, nearly thirty years ago, was the day a skinny white clerk made some sarcastic comment and Palmon had to answer, "Yes, sir." No wonder it was so hard for son to venerate father; no wonder a father would feel he had nothing worthwhile to share.

Past the lumber stores and vacant warehouses, past the drugstores and auto brokerages, the road turns abruptly smooth. Palmon takes a right onto Mehle, heading toward the Mississippi River. Brick bungalows with tile roofs line the side streets, and in some yards can be seen pleasure boats on trailers. Palmon has just crossed the city line into Saint Bernard Parish, a place tolerant of blacks only as long as they promptly came and went from Domino.

Just shy of the levee, Palmon turns left, and slowly the refinery comes into view. The plant sprawls for perhaps a half-mile, from the docks through the low metal warehouses through brick factory buildings ten stories tall, all of them lashed together with conveyer belts and tubular pipes. Steam pours from stacks. A crane dips toward a freighter. A man on a riding mower trims the lawn of the management headquarters, set apart from the rest.

"That's where I started," Palmon says, pointing. "On that dock. And that's where I ran the hand truck. Inside them doors. Didn't used to be closed off."

Driving deeper into the complex, he indicates a small rail car, explaining that it is carrying refined sugar to the pier. A truck, piled high, pulls away, and Palmon says with real pride, "That's takin' that sugar to Philadelphia, Chicago, all them places." Then he draws his son's attention to a forklift, its yellow paint cracking with age, the same model he first drove. Finally he motions toward one of the tall buildings, which houses a granulating mill.

"That's where the explosion took place," he says. "Blew two women out the window." He pauses, his memory still feeling the tremors. "They washed the sugar with stuff called 'born black.' It was so black. Get you sick. You wear a mask, but when you take a bath, it come outta your ear."

Palmon drives back outside the gate, parks his truck. He and his son climb through the scrub grass to the wall atop the levee. They watch the buses arrive and depart with the three o'clock shift change. A lady drives off in a Dodge, adjusting her glasses. A young man guns his Harley, as if he could not banish the place quickly enough. Three bars wait within a half-mile.

"Forty-one years, huh, Dad?"

"Right there," Palmon says.

As they lean against the wall, backs to the river, they gaze across the road to a plantation mansion with five columns and a wrought-

iron veranda. Palm trees and manicured hedges rise from the front
lawn. This, Palmon explains, is the "White House," where the executives had their offices until the modern building next door was
erected.

"They never took anybody in there," he says, "but when I retired,
they brought me in. Took my picture. Asked me, 'Have things
improved?' I said, 'They better than when I come here.'"

They laugh dryly, father and son, at the double entendre. Then
they step into the truck and drive away, passing a small road sign with
the logo of a conquistador on horseback and the words HISTORICAL
TOUR. That much, today, is true.

By the time Palmon and his son return to Lionel's house, the
Saint Paul members have left for the hotel, sated. Ottie Mae wipes
table after table as Palmon fixes himself a rib sandwich. Across the hall,
Jernell lingers, a paper bag under his arm, the old uncertainty a hard
habit to lose. Walking like an early riser trying not to wake a sleeping
house, he crosses to his father, presents the bag, says, "This is for
you."

During his visit to Brooklyn, Jernell had proposed the gift to Joel
and Jason. As brothers, they split the cost three ways. And as the
eldest, Jernell placed the order and picked up the finished piece. Now
Reverend Youngblood withdraws from the bag an engraved plaque.

WORLD'S GREATEST FATHER
From Your Sons

The gift is dated August 24, 1990, tomorrow, the final day of the
Citywide Revival. But Jernell could not wait any longer. As his father,
too, had discovered on the drive to the refinery, after enough years,
some gestures become as imperative as breath or blood.

8

WHERE THE ROSES GROW

T HERE ARE TOWELS ON THE BATHROOM FLOOR, and Kathleen Wilson is not pleased. One of the rules of her summer cottage, one of the ways she restores the contours to misshapen lives, is by insisting that damp towels be draped across the porch railing to dry. Over the years she has passed the rules, the chores, the discipline, the punishment, and the love that accompanies them, to more than forty grandchildren, only fourteen of them genealogically her own. The three latest are about to discover you don't mess with Gramma.

"Who had this yesterday?" Kathleen declares, lifting a terrycloth portrait of Daffy Duck off the linoleum tile.

An eight-year-old girl named Temesha, her spindly shanks and groggy face protruding from opposite ends of a pink nightshirt, nods by way of confession.

Kathleen peels another towel off the floor.

"And this one, too? Why you need two? And how come you left 'em here? You know to hang 'em up."

Temesha shrugs shyly. Kathleen folds the towels and adds them to the laundry bag. Temesha's sister, Dina, wanders toward the activity. Kathleen sniffs. Dina, aged seven, has wet the bed again.

"Darlin'," Kathleen says gingerly, "why don't you take a shower? You know you ain't goin' in no pool today."

"Why?"

"It's rainin' outside."

The sky, in fact, is clearing from an overnight storm. But before Dina notices, Kathleen nudges her with firm fingertips into the shower. Then she returns to the kitchen to fix breakfast, toast and juice and milk and cereal for the children, Ultra Slim Fast for herself. She wears a flowered housecoat decorated with blooming carnations. A golfer's visor keeps her forehead dry and her braids still while she works. As the blender whirls, she removes Dina from the shower, and replaces her with Tycia, who is four. Standing in the bathroom doorway, arms crossed and head tilted, Kathleen judges the girl's technique.

"Come on, now," she finally says, rolling up one sleeve and starting to scrub Tycia herself. "You got more soap on the washcloth than on your body."

At breakfast, as usual, the children will amaze Kathleen with their capacity. The other day they inhaled her box of Teddy Grahams at snack time, then talked Kathleen's friend Liz Jones, six houses away, into opening another. In the past week, Kathleen has exhausted three boxes of cereal, four gallons of Kool Aid, six loaves of bread, one bucket of peanut butter, and fifty dollars for pizza, McDonald's, and the Laundromat. The total is not exceptional for someone accustomed to housing ten or twelve "grands" at once.

Kathleen pays the bills herself, and she is far from a wealthy woman. She resigned from the post office several years ago with a disabled leg, and since then has patched together an income as a caterer and seamstress; even now, the pink chiffon pieces for six bridesmaids' dresses are spread across two beds on the front porch. Her husband, Herbie, runs a small candy store in Harlem. They bought this cottage four years ago for eight hundred dollars, and like most of its neighbors in the summer colony called Hopewell Manor, it is a modest affair, built of fiberboard and wood paneling, raised on cinder blocks above the regular floods, spiked with saplings that grow from clogged drainpipes.

To the children Kathleen brings here, ninety miles north of New York, this is the architecture of Eden. They come to her through assorted intermediaries—in-laws, clients, friends, lodge sisters—so that she rarely knows exactly why they have come. Sometimes she will learn of a vanished father or a mother on drugs or a grandparent too weary to keep pace with a child; more often she will see the symptoms in the bed-wetting, the thumb-sucking, the desperate hugs, the way, like Temesha and Dina, they cannot even recite their home addresses, as if home were such an unfamiliar concept.

It has long been traditional for black families in Northern cities to send their children south for the summer, where they can play barefoot and harness a mule and hear tales of the spirits called "haints." And Kathleen used to regard Hopewell Manor as a similar sort of retreat, offering children bike rides and a swimming pool and glimpses of wild deer. This year, though, she has thought about the colony and her grands in a more fundamental way: *If they come here, they won't get killed.*

It is, indeed, a summer of young death in Brooklyn. Early one Sunday afternoon, a homeless man throws a three-year-old boy to his death from a housing project roof, only blocks from Saint Paul. A nine-year-old girl, asleep in the family car as it returns from an amusement park, is struck fatally by a stray bullet. The fifteen-year-old enforcer for a crack ring, aiming at a dealer who duped him out of several vials, instead shoots a three-year-old girl. Another errant shot kills a twelve-year-old girl as she braids a friend's hair on a playground, while one more claims a third-grader being carried in her mother's arms. From early July, when school vacation begins, until mid-October, when evenings turn cool, twenty-nine New York City children are shot and eight younger than fourteen are killed. The scenario eventually becomes so common that newspapers lump all but the most gruesome examples into Monday-morning wrap-ups.

The immediate cause resides in the evolving drug economy. Compared to the heroin trade, which is centrally controlled by Italian and Chinese syndicates, the more diffuse crack business lets anyone with a frying pan, baking soda, and a few ounces of cocaine set up shop, leading to incessant battles over turf and money. But, as Reverend Slaughter suggests in a sermon one Sunday, the roots of the violence lie far deeper, in a tangle of hopelessness, self-hatred, and unchecked materialism. The police, for their part, appear unable or unwilling to restore order, and they are certainly outgunned by juvenile militias with assault rifles and nine-millimeter automatics. The Dinkins administration, in its feckless fashion, appeals to criminals to surrender their weapons. The black activists so quick to organize around a Bensonhurst trial or a Korean grocery boycott, meanwhile, muster little evident outrage about the autogenocide of their own people. In East New York, only the Nation of Islam mounts a rally against black-on-black violence. Aware of Saint Paul's success with black men, the Muslims invite the church to collaborate. Charles Lewis begins his speech by selecting several boys at random from the audience to stand onstage. "They don't have to be drug addicts," he proclaims. "They don't have to be drug dealers. They can be bus drivers. They can be doctors and lawyers. But it's up to us as a community to ensure that they have a future other than drugs."

That is why Kathleen Wilson sits on the porch, beside her tape deck and sewing machine, doing Tycia's hair. She removes the blue and red pins, unravels the old braids just a bit, then rakes them back out with a long plastic comb, pausing only when she spots Temesha playing jacks.

"Are those Tycia's?"

"Yes," Temesha says, unruffled.

"What're you doin' with 'em?"

"She gave 'em to me to hold."

"That's what you always say," Kathleen says, leaning forward and hunching over one knee. "Somehow you always forget what doesn't belong to you. You have to learn how to respect other people's belongings. Right?"

"Right."

The lesson completed, Kathleen returns to Tycia's hair, which has opened into an Afro as thick and billowy as a thunderhead. To this she takes a brush, then fingers coated in lanolin, and finally the comb once again. Her dressmaker's hands dancing with swift precision, she divides Tycia's scalp into tiny interlocking triangles, and spins from each a new braid, held fast by a barrette in the shape of a sneaker. A tap on the rear end tells Tycia she is free to play.

Kathleen, though, will remain occupied all day. She must fix Temesha's hair, scour the kitchen, inspect the beds to see they were properly made. This afternoon she needs to buy postage stamps and groceries in town, before starting dinner. There is just time enough now for Gramma to wipe her glasses, sip her diet shake, and insert the tape of a favorite sermon by Reverend Youngblood. It is entitled "Children in Search of a Father."

*   *   *

By the time she turned ten in 1939, Kathleen Anfield was searching for both parents, or, more accurately, for their successors. She lost her mother to tuberculosis and cancer, death arriving one Thanksgiving afternoon. Her father fell away by increments. First his back failed and with it his business hauling coal and ice, the source of personal pride and family security. He became an embittered servant, an elevator operator for the affluent of Manhattan, forced to place his two children with relatives. And when he remarried, he chose a woman with youngsters of her own. Making her own favoritism too clear, Kathleen's stepmother took away the little girl's pinafore, left her behind on a Christmas trip south, summoned her with the salutations "bitch" and "motherfucker."

It was two grandmothers who raised Kathleen. One lived on a clay hill in Georgia, the other in a Harlem apartment. One taught school, the other could barely read. But both loved Kathleen, taught her, shaped her into a woman who would comfort without distinction the grandchildren bound to her by blood and those that serendipity left at her door.

During the years of her mother's progressing illness, Kathleen was dispatched to her paternal grandmother, Mattie Anfield, in the hamlet of Rosenall Hill, Georgia. The city girl hated the country life, hated using the outhouse, walking two miles to school, bathing in a tin tub with water left from washing clothes. And then there were the rattlesnakes. But she adored Mattie. Mattie was, in Kathleen's eyes, a "goer-getter" who taught kindergarten, delivered babies as a midwife, went door-to-door enlisting future customers for the local undertaker. She was a strict woman, fast with a hickory switch when she learned Kathleen had spent her church offering money on candy, but possessed more often of a robust laugh and a soothing alto voice.

No calamity, it seemed, could disturb Mattie Anfield. When her husband died, she took on yet another job, doing laundry by hand, and kept so much food on the family table that the first time Kathleen heard the phrase "Great Depression," she asked, "When was that?" During the hurricane that hit in Kathleen's seventh year, shattering windows, yanking oaks loose, tearing tin roofs off shacks, Mattie started churning a batch of homemade ice cream and singing "Rock of Ages." And never did she refuse refuge to the children who arrived at her back porch crying, "Miss Mattie, I don't have anyplace to stay. Miss Mattie, I don't know what to do."

With her father's remarriage, Kathleen returned to Rahway, New Jersey, and found it felt little like home. On one final visit south, she begged Mattie to let her remain. "Grandma would like to have you," she told Kathleen, "but sometimes you have to do that which is right. God will take care of you, and you'll find out life isn't as long as you think it is. You'll survive, and your time will come." It came later that year, in a sense, when fire destroyed the Anfield home, sending Kathleen to her maternal grandmother, Celester Johnson.

To all appearances, Celester seemed one of Harlem's black bourgeois, strolling 125th Street in her red straw hat, living in a building with an elevator attendant and lobby plants. In truth, she had married at fourteen and worked ever since, first as a domestic, then in a garment factory. She made the rent on her apartment only by letting four of its seven rooms to boarders. What truly sustained Celester was faith. Poorly as she read, she labored each morning over the Bible verse selected from a cardboard box shaped like a loaf and labeled OUR DAILY BREAD. She would not permit Kathleen to see the Saturday matinee at the RKO Regent, tantalizingly across the street, until the girl had memorized her Sunday school lesson. And come Sunday, she would dress Kathleen in patent leather shoes and white ankle socks and a pleated dress with red ribbons and walk her to the Mount Olivet Baptist Church, five blocks away, for a day-long dose of religion.

Kathleen's growing piety was childlike but not childish. Other youngsters, hearing the hellfire sermons, envisioned God as a cosmic truant officer, always ready to punish them for playing hooky; Kathleen had experienced something different, the grace afforded her through the vessel of two grandmothers. Her God was an elder whom one chose to respect. She could close her eyes and imagine Him next to her, a smiling figure awash in light, arm outstretched in kindness. Having felt divine presence in her own disordered youth, Kathleen could never encounter Christ's instructions to "feed my lambs," to "suffer the little children to come unto me" as mere aphorisms. They were a mission to which one aspired.

On the records of the New York City Housing Authority, she was Mrs. Kathleen A. Robinson, a divorced mother of four, paying thirty-seven dollars and fifty cents each month for her apartment in the Marcy Houses, a brick project in a working-class section of northern Brooklyn. To the children who clustered outside her first-floor window, she was "Miss Kathy" or "Amma." She curled or straightened or braided their hair; she sewed them graduation dresses or prom gowns; she jumped rope and played hopscotch and treated them to the movies, even after a day on the assembly line, napping in her seat as they thrilled to *Godzilla*.

Yes, Kathleen had dreamed of grander things. She had entered Pace University with designs on becoming an accountant, only to wind up pregnant and married by nineteen. Nine years and four children later, her husband departed. She found work not on Wall Street but in a doll factory, a sweltering place even in midwinter, attaching acrylic hair to plastic scalps for seven cents per dozen.

But at least the Marcy Houses provided a kind place to raise kids. There were lawns and hedges and playgrounds, and an array of rules and fines to ensure their protection. For years after arriving in 1951, Kathleen would sit outdoors past midnight on warm evenings, then retire behind an unlocked door and open windows. Most of all, the housing project enjoyed a style of collective parenting. When Kathleen saw her best friend's two daughters fighting, she could without hesitation impose a cease-fire. And when Kathleen had to enter the hospital for serious surgery, that same friend insisted on caring for Kathleen's four children along with her own seven.

"I can't leave my kids," Kathleen protested, trying to delay the operation.

"You gonna leave 'em anyway," her friend answered, "if you stay here and die."

Things changed toward the end of Kathleen's twenty-five years in the project. The grass was paved over. Maintenance workers were laid off. Trees that died went unreplaced. And with the forced exodus of families exceeding the income limit, and the simultaneous end to the screening of applicants, the human ecology suffered even more. The Marcy Houses, like so many other subsidized developments around the city, changed from being a community of the working poor to a catchbasin for the welfare-dependent. When longtime tenants hung curtains and arranged plants in the hallways, newcomers stole them overnight. As Kathleen slept one evening, a thief entered her apart-

ment through an open window and hauled away her stereo and vacuum cleaner. The new version of communal child-rearing was embodied by the mother who walloped Kathleen's twelve-year-old son for
scrapping with her daughter, then pretended to speak only Spanish
when Kathleen confronted her. "You wasn't that way when you
needed to use my phone yesterday," Kathleen was left to mutter.

So in 1976, Kathleen and her second husband, Herbie Wilson,
moved into a sprawling if aging apartment on the border between the
Haitian and Hasidic sections of Crown Heights. She carried the Marcy
Houses in the form of a photograph album filled with graduation
snapshots and academic commendations and thank-you cards rendered in crayon and sparkles. Her own children had grown, married,
and begun careers in music, finance, and the military, and among her
surrogate offspring she counted a model, an assistant principal, a telephone executive. Kathleen recognized the tragedies, too—the girl shot
dead by a jealous boyfriend, the young man killed when his own gun
accidentally discharged. One of her own granddaughters violated
Kathleen's curfew so often, returning home at daybreak with addled
eyes, that she sent her packing with the suggestion, "Tell you what,
get your clothes before I hurt you."

No disappointment, however, proved so great as to extinguish
Kathleen's hope. So they came to her in Crown Heights and in
Hopewell Manor, Tamika and Keesha and Stacy, Malcolm and Mau-
rice and Tawana, and she worked her love into them like lotion into a
callus. There were four-year-olds who had learned profanity from
Harlem Nights, eight-year-olds who could distinguish the sound of
gunshots by the make and caliber of weapon. "You see that, Gram?"
one boy said to her as they drove through Brooklyn. "That's the crack
house." Sometimes she wondered about the value of PG movies and
country air. But she always remembered the little girl who, on the eve
of departing, had told her, "If I go home and my Mommy don't want
me, I'm comin' back to you."

It was Herbie who urged Kathleen to slow down. She was nearing
sixty, and she was too old to be wiping bottoms, feeding dozens,
sleeping two hours a night. "Anyone can come to you with a soft story
and you're ready," he complained. But when Kathleen's daughter
Patricia phoned one afternoon in May 1989, asking her to take in a
teenager named Ali Nurse, Herbie relented reluctantly. "This is it," he

said. "This is the last time." He paused. "You're gonna do what you're gonna do, anyway."

One afternoon in 1974, when his son was three years old, Al Nurse got a call from his ex-wife's grandmother. The old woman was minding Ali that day, and he had remarked without prompting, "Nobody loves me." Then, in his fragmentary way, the boy had told of being punished, threatened, and beaten in his mother's household. Al Nurse needed to hear no more. After having three daughters by three different women in what he called his "street days," he had sworn he would be a father to Ali, the only child of a legal marriage. Getting divorced and losing custody had only hardened his conviction. He took the next bus to the grandmother's apartment, determined to rescue his son.

"Dee-Da," Ali exclaimed on his arrival.

"Little man," Al replied, holding him. "You don't have to go back there, and I'll see to that." Then he phoned his ex-wife and said, "I ain't givin' you no more money for Ali so your people can beat on him."

A few weeks later she formally surrendered custody, and four years afterward she moved to North Carolina, seeing Ali only for Christmas. By the time the boy reached third grade, she had become disabled from a bungled brain operation, and existed for Ali mostly in the form of a monthly Social Security check. He would be his father's son, by choice and by chance.

"Your offspring," Al often told friends, "is your immortality." So he taught Ali survival, from riding the subway to cooking spaghetti to fishing for dinner in Sheepshead Bay. And to provide Ali more than subsistence, Al worked overtime on his maintenance job in a housing project, taking extra hours on weekdays and twelve-hour shifts on Saturdays and all-nighters during snowstorms. That money paid for parochial school tuition, vacations to Canada and Disney World, a tweed coat from Barney's, and copies of *The Autobiography of Malcolm X* and *Manchild in the Promised Land*, books that would infuse Ali with identity. "Sit down and read," Al would insist when Ali grew restless in their apartment. "Stop goin' outside so much."

Al's discipline proved as grand as his devotion. Violating curfew or skipping chores meant Ali would be sent to bed hungry, tethered to a radiator, or made to stand on one foot until he dropped. Rough justice, in Al's mind, prepared you for a rough world. But until he turned ten, Ali had no clue to the source of the dignity and bitterness that struggled inside his father. Only then did he discover Al Nurse could neither read nor write.

Years later, as Al described the way letters wandered and swam when he stared into a text, his problem sounded very much like dyslexia. But attending ghetto schools in the 1950s, and being an unruly sort, he had simply been categorized as slow, stupid, even mentally disturbed. He dropped out in ninth grade, worked as a delivery boy and a hospital porter, served in the Army, and eventually found municipal jobs in sanitation and maintenance. How he passed the tests for those positions he never quite understood, except that he had become an expert bluffer and a genuinely self-educated man. He frequented museums and lectures, never missed "Nova" or a National Geographic special. He navigated his car by landmarks instead of street signs, and memorized enough restaurant staples that he could scan a menu, pretending to comprehend, and order with authority. One of his girlfriends, a college graduate with a degree in journalism, never learned his secret.

But once Ali did, it vested him with more power than any child should possess—the power to sign his own report card, the power to lie about billboards and mail, the power to resent paternal sacrifice. "I took you when nobody else would take you," Al would declare in times of friction. "Nobody *made* you take me," Ali would respond. "I put you through private school." "You put me there because *you* wanted me there. I never asked you."

Their largest battles began with high school. Ali wanted to prepare for a career in law with a college prep curriculum; Al pulled strings to win him admission to a selective public school specializing in business. "You get a skill," he told Ali. "These guys make money. I want you to have things I didn't have."

However reluctant he was, Ali earned B's as a freshman. But he began failing every subject the following year, and fooling his father with imitation report cards produced on a computer by a friend. The lies might have gone undetected if not for an issue of fashion. Ali asked for money to buy his own clothes, trendy things by Calvin Klein and Ralph Lauren; Al said no. Several days later, when Ali noticed a new portable typewriter lying unattended in a classroom, he saw his wardrobe. He stowed the machine in his backpack, felt guilty, started to return it, got caught.

At a meeting with a dean the next day, Al learned about everything—the typewriter, the grades, the cutting. To spare Ali a criminal charge, Al accepted his transfer to an alternative school, which would serve Ali with nothing but glorified day care. Once home, the beating began. "Why'd you do it?" Al said as he struck. "Why'd you lie? I always told you, 'You lie, I'll tighten you up.' How could you do this to me? I thought I brought you up better than that."

Punishment bred defiance, and defiance bred further punishment. Ali spent half of the coins in Al's silver dollar collection on cigarettes. He started smoking marijuana and drinking beer. Al kicked him out for a week. And then, one afternoon in October 1988, Al's camera, Seiko watch, and videocassette recorder disappeared from the apartment the Nurses rented in a house owned by Al's aunt. Ali's version was that he had mistakenly left a window open and the burglar gate unlocked when he walked to a nearby store. He had came home to find the cops investigating—and hadn't his own Walkman vanished, too? The police, however, were telling Al's aunt that the crime suggested complicity. "This is what you do?" Al said to Ali. "This is how you repay me? By settin' up our house?"

For days a cold peace prevailed, with Ali maintaining his innocence, the aunt threatening eviction, and Al unsure what to do or whom to believe. He was confiding his confusion to a friend on the telephone one evening when Ali interrupted.

"Why you tellin' other people my business?"

"Because I'm your father, and you're my child. I say what I wanna say."

Then Al slammed down the receiver and put his hand to Ali's throat, forcing his son to the floor.

"Get off me, get off me," Ali shouted. "I'm gonna fuck you up."

"Fuck me up?" Al said, rising to his feet. He moved into the kitchen to fetch a cleaver. "I'll kill you. I'll cut your throat."

Ali stared at the cleaver, envisioning all the times his father had used it to score a steak for better marination, just as he had taught him. *He wouldn't cut me*, Ali thought, *'cause then he'd kill himself.* Al did put down the cleaver, and Ali seized the moment to shove him into the wall. As they tumbled to the floor, Ali found himself atop his father, pummeling the face that so resembled his own, screaming, "You can't beat me like you used to. I'm not afraid of you no more."

The aunt pulled them apart.

"You know you got to go now," Al said, dusting himself off. "You made your bed hard, you gotta lay in it."

"You never did nothin' for me."

"Well, if I didn't," Al answered, "I sure ain't from now on. Let that door hit behind you."

Ali grabbed his bookbag and fled. He was seventeen years old.

He spent one night in the apartment of his father's last girlfriend. Then came a few months with a friend's family, who made Ali pay for his lodging with his monthly Social Security check. That arrangement ended with another allegation of theft—three hundred dollars missing from the father's wallet. Ali was not even permitted into the home to collect his belongings; they were stuffed in a garbage bag and left on the porch. He landed for a few weeks with Patricia Cowart, the mother of his best friend, and a woman who found him responsible, polite, even "geeky" with his thick glasses and quizzical gaze. Patricia's husband, Billy, was less enthused. He considered Al Nurse a volatile man, and thought that housing Al's son invited confrontation.

"I can't put him out on the street," Ali could hear Patricia telling Billy one night several weeks into his stay. "He has nowhere to go."

The couple took their discussion outside the apartment, beyond earshot, leaving Ali to shudder. *Where'm I gonna spend the night? How long is this gonna last?* He had not attended school in months, church even longer. He missed cooking for himself, reading in solitude, seeing his father. One memory in particular tugged. It was when he was five and his stepmother had broken up with Al, moving out with her bookkeeper's salary, and somehow his father had made the rent and bought the food and covered the tuition, all on his paycheck as a porter. These days, Al would not even see Ali. The closest he came was to send him a suitcase of clothes through relatives.

Patricia and Billy returned to the apartment.

"There's some difficulties," she said to Ali. "My husband and I don't agree, and I don't want to do anything against him. We have to find you someplace to go."

Then he waited as Patricia dialed a phone number. "Hey, Ma," she said to Kathleen Wilson, "we have a problem."

*   *   *

One night was the agreement. Ali could stay one night in Kathleen's apartment, and then he had to move on. Kathleen had to contend not only with Herbie's opposition but her own agenda. Summer was coming, and summer meant traveling to Mississippi for an Eastern Star convention, sewing dresses for a dozen weddings and proms, fitting in a few weeks at Hopewell Manor. She did not want to be housebound, yet she had friends telling her not to dare leave Ali Nurse alone. "Your stuff's not safe," they warned. "He won't go to school. He's got girls layin' up in his bed." And after the experience with her own grand-daughter, Kathleen could not entirely dismiss her doubts. Besides, Ali said he might be able to share an apartment with a female friend who worked at the Brooklyn Botanic Gardens. More likely, he knew, he would sleep in a car. It would not be the first time.

But as he lugged his suitcase across Linden Boulevard, to catch a bus to Kathleen's, Ali collapsed. The meniscus of his knee had torn. Two friends carried him back to Patricia's apartment, Kathleen was summoned, and she drove him straight to the emergency room at Kings County Hospital. There they waited until four in the morning amid gunshot victims and stuporous bums and prison inmates cuffed to their chairs. Not long after they got home, the phone rang. It was Herbie, calling from Harlem.

"When is he leaving?"

"He hurt himself," Kathleen said. "He can't get hold of that lady. He can't find her. I can't throw him out."

Instead she settled Ali into her son John's bedroom. Since John traveled almost all year playing bass with jazz and salsa bands, the room became Ali's own. Kathleen cooked him steak and bought pints of his favorite ice cream, Monster Cookies. These she laid on a bedside table so that Ali need not hobble to the kitchen. Ali imagined himself as a stunt man he had once seen on television, tumbling off a cliff and through open air, only to land, laughing, in a pile of mattresses.

Still, he assumed nothing. He did not unpack his suitcase. He never posted his favorite photograph, of himself and Patricia's son Trevor exchanging a soul shake; he never displayed the teddy bear given by an old girlfriend, the one with the tiny T-shirt saying, SOME-BODY AT WASHINGTON IRVING H.S. ♥ ME. Every day, it seemed, Herbie called for word of Ali's departure, and every day Ali eavesdropped on an extension as Kathleen fended him off. *Is it this day or the next day I've got to leave?* Ali wondered, listening. *And where do I go then?*

He lasted through the summer, spending time at Hopewell Manor, and as Labor Day approached, Kathleen convened a family conference. "We givin' you one year," she informed Ali afterward. "And I expect you to go to school and graduate in June. No ifs, ands, or buts."

Ali started hugging and kissing her. Kathleen thrashed her arms like windshield wipers and cried, "Get away from me." After only three months, this routine was their private joke. Only in jest would she deny Ali a hug, for she could feel his hunger for affection.

For the first time in ten months, Ali felt secure enough to unpack. He decorated the bedroom with his snapshot and his teddy bear, bought new posters of Malcolm X and Michael Jordan. He returned to school, riding the subway an hour each way to Park West High in Manhattan. It was a vocational school, not well suited to Ali's goal of becoming a lawyer. With all the tumult in his life, however, Ali had lowered his ambitions. Now he just wanted to join the Navy. The Navy would give him a steady paycheck; the Navy would teach him discipline.

He showed enough self-discipline to raise his grades during the year. The day he received his quarterly report card in March 1990, with marks above eighty in all but one of his eight courses, he raced home, only to find Kathleen was visiting a friend.

All evening, Ali waited. Finally he placed the small printout in the bedroom, atop Kathleen's pillow. She returned home after midnight, read the results, admired Ali as he slept. Then she taped the report card on her bedroom door, next to a cartoon of Miss Piggy saying, "It's not easy being a goddess." When Ali awoke at seven, though, she played dumb.

"Well? Well? Did you see it? Did you see it?"

"Yeah," she said laconically. "I saw it. I saw that sixty."

"Gram," he pleaded. "But did you see all those eighties? All those eighties, Gram."

"I did," she said, "and they looked beautiful."

"Great, huh?"

"Not great, but better."

"Can I have a kiss?"

"This time," Kathleen said, embracing him, "you get a kiss."

"It takes a village," Reverend Youngblood often preached, quoting an African proverb, "to raise a child." In a place as physically dangerous and morally corroded as East New York, that village was Saint Paul, where college admissions were pronounced from the pulpit, where a backyard playground was protected by razor wire, where dances could be held without fear of gunplay. Literally around the corner, madness reigned.

On the night Tom Approbato delivered his sermon, for instance, a teenager named Naldo Scott was playing touch football on Hendrix Street. He walked to a *bodega* on Linden Boulevard for a soda, where he was jumped. The attackers, interestingly, stole only some of Naldo's money and left his watch on his wrist. The point of the assault, it seemed clear, was to break his will, to say, *Don't be a church boy. Don't be good.* One of Naldo's peers at Saint Paul, Raheem Warner, received so many beatings from street kids for the mere act of attending school that he began lying to his mother to save face. Arriving home covered with bruises one evening, he explained he had fallen down the stairs from the El platform. Helen Parilla's daughter, Mary, took the subway home from Hunter College as late as ten some nights. Her guarantee of safe passage between the station and her apartment was by remaining on social terms with the drug gangs who worked the territory.

Those incidents, awful as they were, pointed to larger issues—the inability of the police to secure public order, the shortage of responsible adult male leadership, and the street culture that considered achievement selling out. Early in 1990, in fact, two anthropologists, both of them black, had released a study of black high school students in Washington, D.C., that found pupils were afraid to excel for "fear of acting white."

Ali Nurse was not immune to such pressures. As much as his father had tried to protect him, Ali had seen friends drop out and start selling crack, several of them landing in jail, one being assassinated for a debt to his supplier. "You wanna make some money?" they would say to Ali. "You just carry this for me. I'll set you up with a couple of dollars." Which meant, in the drug trade's glossary, a couple of hundred.

Early on, then, Kathleen had taken Ali with her to Saint Paul. From the first Sunday, he was struck by the scores of teenagers in the congregation. All their parents, he figured, couldn't be forcing them to come. A few months later he went to the church's retreat site upstate for All-Male Round-Up, a weekend of sports and worship and teaching. There he first began to think of Reverend Youngblood as a father. He already knew how the pastor would buy a carload of teenagers Chinese food on a whim, how the church's children could appear unannounced at his house to shoot pool in the basement. But the binding moment came when Reverend Youngblood warned Ali he was "bottled up," harboring a temper that could consume him from within. That took insight; that took love.

Ali formally joined Saint Paul in November 1989, and at about the same time he pledged the Yoke Fellows in Excellence. The Yoke Fellows formed the linchpin of Saint Paul's vision of itself as an extended family, a tribal village. The title derived from a verse in Lamentations, "It is good for a man that he bear the yoke in his youth," and the structure borrowed from the fraternities and sororities so popular in black colleges. (Didn't everyone know Jesse Jackson and Bill Cosby were Alphas, William Gray and John H. Johnson, Kappas?) Reverend Slaughter, classics major that he was, even found a suitable Greek title, Sigma Mu Upsilon.

As pledgees, called Acorns, the teenagers dedicated every free hour to meeting the requirements for initiation. They received academic tutoring and SAT preparation courses on Friday nights, and physical training on Saturday afternoon; they wrote summaries of both services each Sunday, memorized such church chestnuts as the poem "Invictus," and practiced the extravagantly syncopated form of group dance known as "stepping." Their parents, too, were required to participate, checking homework nightly and soliciting monthly progress reports from school. But the surrogate parenting the Acorns received, particularly from men, was crucially important. Fewer than one-quarter of the pledgees lived with a father at home.

When Ali pledged, not only he but Kathleen had to submit a letter of intent. His focused on specific goals such as acquiring discipline and improving his marks; Kathleen's placed the Yoke Fellows in a grander plan:

Ali has only been living permanently with me since May of this year. I have seen a great improvement in his attitude and desires. But I know and he also knows that he can do better and that I expect more of him and from him.... I expect him to graduate in June and go to college. The ability is there, and also the opportunity. I expect his association with the youth of St. Paul to give him Spiritual motivation once he realizes that through Christ all things are possible and his love for God really dawns on him.

When Ali first met Dee Skinner, though, he was still talking about the Navy. As the director of the Youth Ministry at Saint Paul, Dee oversaw the Yoke Fellows program, oversaw it so personally she once broke her foot chasing an Acorn, water pistol in hand. As a former counselor of dropouts, she had a practiced eye for teenagers who thought themselves unworthy. Ali appeared intelligent, a natural leader—a young man who learned the Saint Paul computer system on his own, who tutored a fellow pledge being bedeviled by "Invictus"— except when the subject of college arose. Then his voice flattened, and his eyes fell, and she realized he considered college too good for him.

Ali was taking twelve courses in his final term at Park West just to graduate by the Wilson family's June deadline. He started at eight in the morning, continued past six at night, then rode the train ninety minutes to Saint Paul for pledging activities. More than once he fell asleep in his clothes and shoes. But he was adamant about adhering to the schedule, even refusing to consent to a knee operation until after the Acorns' stepping show.

The show fell on the last Friday in March, the prelude to an all-night hazing session and the daybreak induction of the survivors as Yoke Fellows. Several hundred parents, grandparents, siblings, and friends packed Frank Taylor Hall for the event, lining the walls three deep. First the pledgees, as individuals or in small groups, performed what would be termed the "talent" portion of a beauty pageant, from a recitation of the Gettysburg Address to an a capella rendition of "Lift Every Voice and Sing." Then the stepping commenced.

Kathleen couldn't believe it. Bad enough Ali was prancing around on a damaged leg, but there he was, second from the back in the middle row, without his glasses. He was so blind he'd probably break his other leg tripping on something. But it was too late for intervention. The crowd was standing, whistling and barking, shouting "Go 'head" and "Work it, y'all, work it out." With swinging elbows and swiveling heels, slapping hands between thighs at each stride, the pledgees moved like a fire drill reimagined by Alvin Ailey. All the while, in hoarse voices, they chanted inside jokes, their own faces impassive as informed friends in the audience convulsed. Then they withdrew behind a cloud of dry-ice vapor.

Kathleen drove home at midnight, slept for an hour, then baked one hundred eighty biscuits for the induction breakfast. By seven she returned to Saint Paul, where Frank Taylor Hall had been fitted with tables for the forty-one new Yoke Fellows. At each setting lay a baseball hat, a T-shirt, and a windbreaker, each emblazoned with the letters Sigma Mu Upsilon. When the Acorns ran the gauntlet one final time before "crossing over," Ali was limping and weary, but wearing his glasses. Tongue firmly in cheek, Kathleen asked, "Did you have a hard night, darlin'?"

On the day of Ali's knee operation, Kathleen first met his father. The introduction was one purely of necessity; Al Nurse had to provide the hospital with his medical insurance policy, which covered Ali. That duty done, he remained in the waiting room as the surgery proceeded, and slowly he and Kathleen started to talk. For her part, Kathleen knew of Al mostly through the tales of his temper; and Al suspected Kathleen had only housed Ali to get at the Social Security checks.

"He's your son," Kathleen began with a sense of reproach. "He's your responsibility. If something happens to Ali, they'll come looking for you, not for me."

Then Al told the stories Kathleen had never heard, about raising Ali from age three, about buying an encyclopedia for the household, about helping Ali once with a homework assignment about Nefertiti.

"I didn't have to take him," Al said, as if he were addressing his son directly. "I always looked out for him. I struggled a lot to get him. I love him." He paused. "And Ali's got to know that."

From then on, Al and Kathleen spoke on the phone several times each week. Learning that she charged Ali nothing to stay with her, Al offered to buy groceries, donate lump sums of cash. When Ali needed money to visit relatives in North Carolina, Al provided it. "You may think that because I'm not around you, I don't see you, I don't worry about you," he told Ali. "But I worry about you all the time. It only takes a quarter to let me know."

There was one problem, though, in permanently repairing the rift. As long as Al lived in his aunt's house, Ali would not be permitted to rejoin him, since the aunt still believed Ali had arranged the robbery. So Saint Paul became the middle ground on which father and son groped toward communion.

Church seemed a compromise to Al. The overwhelming whiteness of Christianity had driven him away decades ago, and his search for God and blackness had drawn him toward the Nation of Islam. He never joined, but he did hear Malcolm X. So he was shocked, pleasantly shocked to find so many Saint Paul members in *kufi* hats and dashikis. He appreciated Reverend Youngblood's preaching about youth. And he loved hearing the pastor read aloud Ali's March report card as Ali stood beside the pulpit. He only hoped Reverend Youngblood would never ask him to read. Even after several adult literacy courses, Al struggled with those swimming letters. If he faltered before the congregation, he knew, he would never return.

"I'm Ali's father," he told the pastor after one service. "I don't have too much book education, but I'm street-smart. And I got common sense and mother wit."

"You don't need to be ashamed," Reverend Youngblood answered. "We've got officers, the men who stand up front, and elders who have trouble reading. One of the brothers learned how to read at sixty-seven."

Then they spoke about Kathleen.

"I owe her," Al said, "more than I could ever give."

Kathleen, however, was not finished yet. There were surrogate parents who took a perverse pride in bettering biological ones, in competing for a child's allegiance. But Kathleen wanted to restore Ali to his father.

The occasion arose in the last week of June, a few days before she moved to Hopewell Manor for the summer, with the commencement exercises of Park West High School. Al spent a week's salary buying Ali a double-breasted suit from Barney's for the event. He rented an LTD to drive Kathleen and Ali to Hunter College, site of the ceremony. And he reserved a table at a restaurant on Madison Avenue.

Traffic crawled across the Brooklyn Bridge and up the FDR Drive. Al and Kathleen talked of Nelson Mandela's recent visit to New York and the upcoming African Festival in Bedford-Stuyvesant. Ali remained tense, grasping his tassel in a tight fist, as if it might otherwise flee.

"Well," Al said to him as they finally reached Hunter, extending an open palm, "congratulations, man."

"I was gettin' nervous," Ali confessed.

"Nervous? Save that for college. You're talkin' four years. Seven if you want law."

Al and Kathleen found seats in the auditorium as Ali lined up with the graduates. They found his name in the program between Xiomaras Nuñez and Howell Ogarro. They stood and shouted and shot photos when he received his diploma. They nodded in agreement as the principal spoke. "A male becomes a man," he said, "the day he accepts responsibility for his failures as well as his successes. A male becomes a man the day he realizes the knowledge he puts in his head matters more than the name on the side of his sneakers. A male becomes a man the day he realizes a cocker spaniel can father a child, but a man takes care of himself and his child."

Then it was over. Kathleen explained she had to skip dinner to resume sewing dresses for a bridal party. Al insisted on driving her back to Crown Heights, and once there, he and Ali felt too tired to double back to Manhattan. Instead of filet mignon on Madison Avenue, they ate shrimp platters at a diner in Canarsie.

But that was all right, at least to Kathleen. In part she had withdrawn from dinner so father and son could celebrate alone together. And it was true, she needed to finish the dresses. The money for them was going to pay for this summer's grands.

The afternoon passes listlessly, pale sun giving way to overcast, muffled thunder sounding in the west. Two of Liz Jones's grands, Kindra and Danielle, come to Kathleen to have their hair braided. Sweat drops from her chin and nose, but neither her handiwork nor her vigilance ceases.

"Why y'all put on white to play in the mud?" she calls to Dina. "Don't you have any other color pants to put on?"

The girl retreats into the bedroom, then appears in another pair, also white.

"You got any shorts?" Kathleen asks.

This time Dina finds something in black, and she scrambles off the porch.

Temesha, sitting on the floor near Kathleen, sticks a playing card inside her shoe.

"Gramma," she says, "you know what they call this?"

"I call that cheatin'," Kathleen replies.

Two hours after she had begun doing hair, Kathleen ties the last braid of the day.

"You're all finished," she says to Kindra, turning the girl so she faces her. "It's my beautiful child. My gorgeous, beautiful child."

A storm descends and scatters, and in its wake Kathleen piles the grands into her car for the trip to the post office and grocery store. She weakens enough to buy Gummy Worms for the children and a Lotto ticket for herself, picking 8528, from her license plate. If she ever hits, she's going to buy a new sewing machine.

Then she drives back to Hopewell Manor, passing a roadside florist. Tycia props herself onto the backrest, her face near Kathleen's.

"Gramma, I wanna bring you a rose."

"Where you gonna get roses?"

"Where the roses grow."

"I like that," Kathleen says, pulling up Ruby Lane, toward her cottage. "I like that."

9

BETWEEN MARROW AND BONE

BY EITHER CALENDAR, HOLY OR CIVIL, August should sag, the trough of the year. It lies equidistant from Easter and Christmas, stretches between July Fourth and Labor Day, the pillars of summer. It is the month, in the fiercely urban realm of East New York, of pungent reminders of the rural past—ribs roasting on an oil-drum grill outside the Linden projects, sugarcane being peddled beneath the Livonia El, watermelons arriving by flatbed truck, piled in pyramids, four dollars apiece. One morning Linden Boulevard itself smells of picnics and wears a coating of smashed rinds, as one hapless vendor, by now a mile up the road, lashes the remaining fruits into his payload.

Saint Paul, too, falls slack with the season. Its day camp dismisses. Adult evening school ends. Reverend Slaughter, Dee Skinner, and six teenagers remain on their interracial tour of Zimbabwe, the fullest reports of which originate with a lovesick girl who makes three hundred dollars' worth of phone calls to her Brooklyn beau. The Sunday pulpit belongs often to Reverend Anthony Bennett, a graduate student of James Cone's at Union Theological Seminary, whiplash thin in physique, yet endowed with a voice of sonorous bass. To those who hear him preach about Samson, under the rubric "The Tragedy of a

Bad Haircut," it is clear this young man bears "the mark." Still, so many members take vacation or just plain slide during late summer that the weekly total of tithes and offerings, normally $25,000, falls by one-third.

Appearances aside, though, these days grow fulsome with plans. Before the month ends, Reverend Youngblood and the other leaders of East Brooklyn Congregations will design a fall offensive of community organizing to mark the group's tenth anniversary. And more than mere ceremony argues for action. Even a church as energetic as Saint Paul knows the limits of autonomous effort. Its attempt last year to organize residents of two nearby housing projects collapsed in futility. Now the Christ Square merchants' association is failing—thanks, paradoxically, to its own success. As crime along Stanley Avenue has subsided briefly with the nightly patrols of a private guard, the owners of many stores have stopped paying monthly dues. So the sentry must be laid off, and burglars are bound to fill his vacuum.

Certainly, Saint Paul has learned to expect little from Mayor David N. Dinkins. Having inherited a racially divided and fiscally rickety city from Edward I. Koch, New York's first black mayor has proved in his first eight months in office no better than his white predecessors at serving neighborhoods like Brownsville and East New York. Saint Paul's grievances start with the usual bureaucratic blunders: Why is Linden Park, the only oasis for blocks around, being torn apart for reconstruction during the busiest months of summer? Why is the Sewer Department, after eighteen months, still holding up approval of the church's sanctuary expansion? Why is the mayor refusing to honor his preelection promise to meet with EBC?

Then there are issues that literally involve life and death. The new police commissioner, Lee Brown, has met with Reverend Youngblood and worshiped at Saint Paul, but resists collaborating with EBC on a community policing program. Amid the almost daily shootings of children, the mayor attends the United States Open tennis tournament, flying to Flushing by helicopter. He and Commissioner Brown do meet the media one afternoon at the Seventy-fifth Precinct, a gathering that serves less to allay doubts about public safety than to inspire them about public relations. When a neighborhood woman lobs Mayor Dinkins a question so soft that many in the audience wonder if she has been planted—"What can we, the citizens, do to help *you*?"—

he refers her to an underling. This, after all, is a *press* conference. Yet afterward, as reporters and camera crews wait, the mayor and commissioner never appear for their own photo opportunity on the block where a girl was recently shot. Meanwhile, the *bodegas* and discount stores of East New York sell a water gun shaped like an Uzi, the drug trade's weapon of choice, faithful right down to the imitation ammo clip.

The second project that looms over Reverend Youngblood's autumn is a trip to Ghana. After Osei Yaw Akoto's first visit, in April 1990, Saint Paul raised one thousand dollars for a nursery in the village of Asafo. More than that, the congregation became captivated with Osei's stories, photographs, and home videos, and with the assured sense of identity he brought back from Africa. The idea emerged for Saint Paul to form some lasting link with its heritage, in the form of Asafo. In years past, after all, the church endowed a school in Haiti. Why not create a similar touchstone in Africa? A church, a school, and a retreat site were all proposed. But proposals alone did not satisfy Osei. Phoning Reverend Youngblood at home, slipping into his study without appointments, applying all the guile honed by years on the street, he spent months persuading the pastor to travel with him to Ghana in December. And through intermediaries, he equally excited the leaders of Asafo. Which explains the letter Osei hands the pastor between services one Sunday:

> Dear Reverend in name of the Lord,
>
> How do you do? I hope by His Grace you are all fine.
>
> I thought I should send a word or two and to express how anxious our kith and kin in the village are to welcome you when you pay your visit to Ghana.
>
> A Committee has been set up to plan your welcome as well as monitor the scheme for establishing a Branch of your Church back in our little village of Asafo.
>
> We are praying that our Lord almighty in his own way give his blessing to your visit and help us to join hands with you to make your plans materialise.
>
> We celebrated our Yam Festival last—a festivity analogous to the Feast of the Pass Over in Biblical days. And may I on my own behalf and behalf of my elders and people of Asafo, by the Grace of

"Mother Earth" and the Power of our Father in the "Heavens" wish all of you over there in the states very happy and prosperous tidings.

Yours very sincerely,
Barima Asante Abedi III
Chief of Asafo

Reverend Youngblood's most immediate concern, however, is one far less concrete than either Ghana or East Brooklyn Congregations. It is, in fact, almost the private counterpoint to such public campaigns. And, as usual, the clues to the pastor's passion can be found in the lobby showcase. Beneath the single word HEALING hang three broken hearts, fashioned by Greta Young from pillow foam and bridal satin. Across the fissure in each, she has attached like bandages strips of white paper, inscribed with verses from James and Psalms, Chronicles and Colossians. The theme extends to a bulletin board in the hallway outside the media office. This Greta has decorated with snapshots of congregants and staff members. LET THE HEALING BEGIN, say letters at the top. And in the center, beside a small mirror, the sentence resumes: IN YOU.

Both displays arose from a recent series of sermons by Reverend Youngblood. In one of them, "Two Steps to Healing," he drew on the Epistle of James to plead with his worshipers to bury old grudges, even asking the entire congregation to recite aloud the signature verse:

Confess your faults one to another, and pray one for another, that ye may be healed. The effectual fervent prayer of a righteous man availeth much.

But it was a later sermon, "How to Heal the Children," that brought the pastor to the peak of his oratorical and analytical gifts. He taught Mark's version of a miracle that appears in all four of the Gospels: A man whose son is possessed by demons, rendered deaf and dumb, afflicted with seizures, asks the Apostles to cure the boy. They fail. Then Christ, returning from the Mount of Transfiguration, encounters the father, the son, and the bewildered Disciples. He exorcises the demon, and explains to his followers why they had been unable to do so, saying, "This kind can come forth by nothing, but by prayer and fasting."

The biblical story, in the pastor's telling, provided a metaphor for the black church's failures, Saint Paul's failures, his own failures:

> If Jesus came back this morning to check on our discipleship, to see what we have done, right here in our very midst, he would find failures that do not have to be. We have failed in terms of black men. And if you really want to go into the lion's den, into Satan's stronghold, we have failed our children. I don't wanna hear any garbage this morning, even in the Spirit, about "I tried." Accept, first of all, we failed. And the reason we gotta look at ourselves is because we all recognize now that the social service system is failing our children. The schools are failing our children. There are no jobs for our children. Parents are hopeless in terms of not being able to handle it by themselves.

This devastating message brought Reverend Youngblood back to the noun *fasting*. It meant, he argued, "more than staying away from food, more than turning the plate down," but rather an abstinence from old ways, traditions without utility, and a radical change in priorities. In his years at Saint Paul, the pastor had already transformed youth ministry from the familiars of Youth Choir, Junior Usher Board, and Baptist Young People's Union—the trinity that had bored into resentment and departure so many of his generation—into the Yoke Fellows, cheerleaders, day camp, martial arts classes, an elementary and junior high school. All these efforts sought to create an extended family, to build the village that would raise the child.

But healing, more than being the topic of any sermon or the goal of any program, was an ongoing and often intimate element of ministry. Nor was it exclusively devoted to children. In exposing his own flaws, in annotating his own therapy, Reverend Youngblood sought to heal by example, leaving others in their personal lives to follow his model. In the weeks after he brought Jernell to Saint Paul, for instance, two members told their wives of children they had outside their marriages, children they wished now to acknowledge. The pastor's reconciliation with his father inspired both Rochester Blanks and Reva Jamison, the director of the church's dance troupe, to search out their fathers. Within the last month, Reva found hers in a Veterans Administration hospital in South Carolina, Rocky his in a senior citizens' housing complex in Baltimore.

Beyond serving as a role model, Reverend Youngblood operated more formally as a counselor. In a typical week, he held ten sessions with various members, covering topics from incest to debt, poor grades to criminal pasts, bisexuality to spiritual despair. "Counseling folk," he sometimes joked, "takes two hours and fifteen minutes: One hour of them lyin', then one hour of them tellin' the truth, then fifteen minutes of sayin' what you got to say and figurin' out if they want to hear." More seriously, he considered the ability to intuit and ameliorate pain one of a minister's most vital skills. It was not accidental that Reverend Youngblood watched with fascination television's "Quincy," a forensic pathologist "who could use his intelligence to get a corpse to 'talk' to him," or that he often likened counseling to medicine. "Doctors work with finesse," he said once. "There's a difference between a surgeon and a butcher." Or, as he put it in "Two Steps to Healing," "God speaks between the marrow and the bone."

And in this uniquely active August, Reverend Youngblood twice found himself trying to heal just so deep a wound in so narrow a space. One incident presented itself in the form of an unsolicited letter, the other through a commotion in the coat room.

On a night that was to have been devoted to a pleasant duty, interviewing prospective teachers for the elementary school, Reverend Youngblood calls an emergency meeting of the Board of Elders. Many drive straight from work to the church, still wearing sport jackets, carrying ballpoint pens or folded eyeglasses in breast pockets. William Brandon, awaiting word that he can be admitted to a hospital for prostate surgery, leaves the telephone to attend. In time, twenty-one men arrive, filling two long tables and several stray chairs in Elders Hall, chatting anxiously about Anthony Bennett's last sermon as they wait for the pastor to explain the urgent summons.

"Now, gentlemen," he says, standing between lectern and blackboard at the front of the room, "the matter we've got to deal with is sensitive. I know the Ray Ledder matter was sensitive, but this is even more so. It is incumbent that we handle it prayerfully, with love, spiritually. And it is incumbent we do it immediately—though that's not as soon as some people want."

Glances cross the table. Eyebrows lift. Lips form questions. What could be worse than Ray Ledder? He was an elder, in his mid-forties and separated from his wife, who attracted and seemed to return the attentions of a church member half his age. When Reverend Young-blood asked him on two different occasions about the rumors, Ledder insisted, "There's nothing between us." Then, when the pastor approached him with the gossip that the young woman was pregnant, he confessed. That was back in late 1988, when governance by elders was new to Saint Paul; one man's indiscretion threatened to destroy the congregation's trust in the entire system. The only way to preserve it was to demonstrate its fairness, even if that meant the board must banish one of its own. And when the elders declared their willingness do exactly that, Ledder acquiesced and ultimately left the church entirely.

What could be worse? Reverend Youngblood, at the board, now explains. During the eight o'clock service the previous Sunday, a ten-year-old girl named Justine Redmond walked out of the sanctuary because she felt ill. She was standing in the lobby when an usher, a retired dry cleaner named Carter Naulls, told her she could not wait there. He brought her into Elders Hall, and led her to a chair. Then, according to Justine, Carter kissed her on the lips and fondled her buttocks. The girl reentered the sanctuary through the basement and found her eighteen-year-old brother, Gregory. And after the service, in the coat room off the lobby, Gregory found Carter. "Keep away from my sister," he shouted, "or I'll kick your fucking ass."

Another usher, Butch Carr, separated the two. Early the next morning, however, Reverend Youngblood received a call from Jus-tine's mother, Ella Redmond. Her ex-husband wanted Carter in jail. Ella was less certain. All she saw in the legal system was more trauma for her daughter—cops, jurors, lawyers, all of them strangers. But something had to be done by the church, something forthright and forceful, or she would have no choice but to call the police. And, as Reverend Youngblood knew, once Carter Naulls was arrested his repu-tation would be ruined forever, no matter what the ultimate verdict.

"So," he says, scanning the room, "do we have a problem?" The faces and postures give the obvious reply. Shelton Jefferson, normally ebullient, a jokester, sinks his head into two fisted hands. Charles Young removes his glasses, drops his eyes to the table. Elias Singleton rubs his fingers against his lips, his beard, his lips again.

The Redmond family has belonged to Saint Paul for more than fifteen years. Ella is a close friend of Sarah Plowden on the staff, Charles Young on the board, many others. Carter is not only an usher; he was installed on the Board of Elders only six months ago. More than a difficult personal dilemma, more than a test of the board's credibility, this case also carries a great risk to Saint Paul's ministry to youth. The church's new motto, adopted this summer, declares it to be "Child-Centered, Adult-Run, Elder-Ruled." Its logo, designed by a high school student named Craig Miller, shows two elders flanking a parent who in turn cradles an infant. This very room is decorated with young people's paintings of the Exodus story. For years, Reverend Youngblood has been recruiting men to teach LAMBS classes, to chaperone school trips, to literally embrace children, so many of whom are growing up without a father. It was not always easy. Last year, when he assigned staff members to cover elementary school classes during a teachers' meeting, several parents refused to let their children be minded by a male. And now, if one man's hug proves to have been prurient, then no man's hug will be welcomed again.

"Right here," Reverend Youngblood continues, "we're in the throes of 'good touch, bad touch.' We're in the tall grass. Maybe we need to be right here every night next week to hear evidence. Nobody now is innocent or guilty. We're not saying Justine lied, and we're not saying Carter did it. We have to be objective."

"Did Justine say they were in here alone?" asks Charles Young.

"That's what Sarah told me," the pastor answers. He entrusted Sarah Plowden to debrief Justine, believing she would speak most candidly to a woman she knew. "Carter brought her in. He *closed* the door."

Mike Portce, the father of a daughter Justine's age and the president of the elementary school PTA, speaks in the bass voice usually reserved for solos with the choir.

"We have to teach our children if anyone touches them in a way that makes them uncomfortable to tell somebody," he says. "But I've seen Carter several times hug little kids. That's his affection. I don't *think* it was meant to be sexual."

"That," Reverend Youngblood says, gripping the sides of the lectern so tightly his knuckles lighten, "is why we need to have a hearing." He scans the room, meets every face. "But we need to decide.

Do we ask him to resign, pending investigation? Or do we make him resign, pending investigation?"

"You gotta understand what he's goin' through," says Robert Graham. "We're leaving him out there."

"If we suspend him, I know Carter, he'll resign," Elias Singleton puts in. "Can't we just say we're investigating?"

Then Melvin Jones speaks. With deep-set eyes and angular beard, an almost Old Testament cragginess, intensity informs his presence. And it is he, as a SPIRIT instructor, who taught many of these elders in his class on faith.

"Anytime something shady comes up," he says, "it's got to be suspension. We're in a position of trust. If we don't do anything, it's like we're leaning toward him, an elder. If we suspend him, we're doing something. We're saying, 'We don't know what the truth is, but we'll find out.'"

Reverend Youngblood moves from the lectern down the side wall.

"Let's face it," he says, underlining Melvin's argument with his own authority. "If we don't investigate, we're fuck-ups. From where we sit, managerially and spiritually, we have no choice."

Even with that much settled, questions fly. What if the elders decide Carter is guilty? Should they have him arrested? Send him for therapy? What if Justine is lying? What'll keep others from bogging down the board with unfounded allegations? Does this mean Saint Paul can't be an affectionate congregation anymore?

Then a knock on the door silences the room. A bespectacled face, topped by gray hair, peeks inside. "I'm here," says Carter Naulls.

The elders pray. Then the questioning begins. Reverend Youngblood asks Carter simply to give his version of events.

Carter stands beside the lectern, staring directly at the pastor. His voice gathers speed. His arms move constantly, and veins slowly rise on his forehead. Another usher, he explains, told him a group of children was making noise in the lobby. He went to collect them and bring them back into the sanctuary. But one girl, Justine Redmond, said she felt poorly, so he led her into Elders Hall, putting his arm across her shoulders to guide her. Then, as he seated her, he kissed her, either on the forehead or the cheek. It was possible he brushed against her buttocks. All the while, the door to Elders Hall remained open and the ceiling light on. Several other children were watching from the portal. And that was the end of that—until, an hour later, Gregory confronted him in the coat room.

"Carter," Reverend Youngblood says, "you realize how sensitive this is?" Carter nods. "Not only in Saint Paul, but because of the times?" Again, he nods. "Any incident involving a grownup and a child. Especially a male and a female." By now Carter is hunched over the lectern, as if his legs had lost the will to support him. "Do you trust us to handle this fairly?"

"Sure," he answers. "I love you guys."

"Are you aware there might be child molestation charges?"

"Oh, yeah. It hurts. Makes me feel under a cloud. I'd like to talk to Justine myself. I'd like to get up and tell the congregation what happened."

The pastor grips a pen, one end in each hand, like a taut wire. Most of the elders lean forward, elbows planted.

"I think," Reverend Youngblood says with forced delicacy, "you might want to keep away from Justine right now. And if you tried to tell the congregation, you wouldn't be believed. Not in these times, Carter. You've just got to trust us. To be your bodyguards and your dictators."

"Whatta you mean?"

"I mean, if we tell you to stand on your head for an hour, you do it."

For now, the pastor only asks Carter to leave the room. Then he outlines on half of the blackboard the substance of Carter's testimony. In the remaining space he lists the questions that have emerged: Was the door closed? Were the lights on? Were there witnesses? What did they see? The elders, it is evident, must hear not only from Justine but from several ushers and, most important, from the other children Carter was returning to the sanctuary. This will not be resolved in a week, even meeting every night.

So, drawing on the earlier discussion, Reverend Youngblood confirms that Carter must be suspended from his positions as both elder and usher until the investigation is completed. He will be permitted to attend church, but only accompanied by several elders, partly to protect him, partly to observe him.

Carter is called back to hear the decision. He grimaces, stares into the floor, rubs his eyes. "Can I still go on the ushers' retreat?" he asks in a tiny voice.

"Sure, man," Reverend Youngblood says.

"And, Carter," Shelton Jefferson adds, "let's pray those other kids remember where they were last week and what they saw."

Well before Reverend Youngblood introduced himself to Monica Moody, waiting in line for curried goat at the bring-a-dish banquet for new members, he had heard something of her. The information had arrived in an unusually thick letter, photocopied from an original, as if the pastor were but one entry on an extensive mailing list. Yet he, by name, was the object of the communication. Are you aware, the writer wanted to know, that one of Saint Paul's men, Larry Johnson, stole my wife? Do you intend to marry them? When can we meet?

Reverend Youngblood knew Larry Johnson, and regarded him with a special satisfaction. Larry's presence at Saint Paul was literally an answered prayer. On an Eldad-Medad retreat in September 1987, his younger brother Joe had beseeched God to reclaim Larry. From the time he was eleven, and defying his father's curfew, Larry had been drawn to the streets of Brownsville. He had dropped out of school, taken up heroin, gone to prison for robbery. Paroled, he had pushed himself to earn an equivalency diploma, attend two years of college, acquire an expertise in computer operations. But well into his thirties, he was still dabbling in cocaine, still hanging out, and only when he was beaten bloody without explanation in a tavern one night did he consider it a sign that he must change. On the Sunday after attending the first of Reverend Youngblood's all-male worship services, in March 1988, he joined Saint Paul.

What had always impressed the pastor most was that, in traveling from the debauched to the divine, Larry had understood some of the old baggage was worth keeping. The way his brows lifted, the way his voice tightened, the way his eyes seemed to swell—all that told Reverend Youngblood that Larry could be as fierce about his faith as he had once been about his stash.

So he asked about the letter. And Larry's eyes, this time, rolled skyward. Yes, Monica was his girlfriend. Yes, it was possible they would marry. No, she was most definitely not married to someone else, least of all the pastor's pen pal. That guy had been Monica's companion, the father of her young son, but his cocaine addiction had driven her away. And once Monica became involved with Larry, the former boyfriend had turned vindictive. First he had gone to court seeking custody of the child, Jordan, and then he had started writing letters by the score, posing as her aggrieved husband. Monica had grown so fearful of him that on the two days each week he had Jordan—by the terms of a court decree—it was Larry who dropped off and picked up the boy.

Neither the letters nor the courtship stopped. Which brought Reverend Youngblood to this Sunday afternoon, when he will begin the premarital counseling of Monica and Larry. He harbors no small hope for this marriage. He liked the way Larry had brought Monica to Saint Paul; he loved the way Larry held Jordan, like his own child; he appreciated that Monica trusted Larry enough to let him. But there is an embittered ex afoot, and even if there were not, counseling remains mandatory for any couple being married in Saint Paul. The pastor's reasons begin with the practical; he has seen a groom unfamiliar with his vows halt the whole ceremony as he stumbled over "troth." But the premarital also serves as the preemptive, the precautionary.

"You understand part of the reason I do this," Reverend Youngblood says as he motions for Larry and Monica to sit, "is because one of the things we learn with couples in marriage counseling is that the problems were there all along. They just thought it would go away when they got married. So this way, I've been in on the relationship since the beginning." He sips orange juice, his throat frayed from two sermons. "And I hope the time will come when members like you, who know this is important, can do marriage counseling for others in the congregation."

Larry and Monica, sitting along one side of the table, hold hands. At thirty-nine, he has skin like creamed coffee, bristly hair turning gray. Five years his junior, she is caramel in color, with a model's smile and a sweep of straightened hair. There is about them a nervous quiet, a reserve beyond politeness or the usual jitters, it seems to the pastor. He can only assume the ex-boyfriend looms in their minds. The subject must be raised, but in a way that dashes the fear, eases the mood.

"Now, y'all better make sure this dude ain't comin' in here the day of the wedding," he says. "When I say, 'Is there anyone who sees fit why this man and woman should not be joined together?' I don't want this guy lettin' loose with a machine gun. I ain't gonna ask *that* question."

His own laughter unlocks theirs. Now he leans back in his chair, unbuttons his collar, flips quickly through a pile of telephone messages. Then he asks his usual opening question, about the couple's history.

Trading pieces of the story, finishing each other's sentences, Monica and Larry explain they met three years ago, while working together in the computer department of a city agency. As Monica's relationship with Jordan's father was dissolving, she discovered in Larry a confidant. She had always sworn not to date anyone from work, but they both lived toward the end of the A train, near the border of Brooklyn and Queens, and the hour's ride home from Manhattan evolved into courtship. By now they have been living together for five months, and already Monica is answering the phone, "Johnson residence." That the pastor applauds.

Finance comes next. In Reverend Youngblood's experience as a counselor, money produces more anxiety, more discord than even sex. Who, he asks, handles the household expenses? Do you have trouble managing? What debts are you taking into the marriage? The pastor arranges for Larry and Monica to meet with Sarah Plowden, to design a household budget, even a sequence for paying bills. Then he turns to the matter of Jordan, if only to confirm his favorable sense of the situation. Is Larry willing to treat the boy as his own? Is Monica comfortable allowing him?

Finally he turns to what is often the most penetrating topic of the initial counseling session: Who is your role model as a spouse?

"My father," Monica says, and although he is five years dead, she speaks of him still in the present tense. "He's West Indian, from Jamaica, and he raised five girls, and they have a tradition of watching out for their families. And that's what I see in Larry."

Wilbert Moody ran a small grocery, where his frequent assistant was Monica, his third and favorite daughter. When she started kindergarten, on the afternoon session, he kept her with him at the store until noon, then drove her miles to school. He taught her how to count by making change. Years later, adamant that she escape New York and its miseries, he scraped together the money to send her to a tiny Catholic college on the Indiana prairie.

As Monica speaks, Reverend Youngblood understands her attraction to Larry. He is a protector, a strong man, stronger for the kiln that fired him. Now it is his turn to answer.

"My mother," he says, "but not all of her attributes. I saw some ways she could've helped my father more. The kind of person my father was, he *did*. She didn't have any say-so."

The message, to Reverend Youngblood, is that Larry welcomes Monica's self-assurance. She grew up, after all, the product of a more comfortable home than he, in a West Indian culture that some American blacks consider arrogant and haughty. She holds the college degree that eluded him. For a less secure man, such ingredients could combust. But Larry seems to want a genuine partner.

As he talks more about his father, Joseph Johnson, Larry also reveals his own desires as a father, his love for Jordan. An elevator operator and janitor for *The New York Times,* Joseph was a stern, dependable, even authoritarian figure in a housing project all too depleted of such men. But he was, too, a distant, diffident parent. When Larry would attend family reunions and hear his older cousins recall fishing and hunting with Joseph, he would wonder why those binding experiences had been denied him, the firstborn child.

Time is running out. Reverend Youngblood must drive to a member's home to counsel her son, anxious about beginning college in the Midwest later this month.

"I've got an assignment for y'all for next time," he says, reaching across the table for his car keys. "Make a list. The five things you most like about each other." Monica and Larry smile, until he continues. "And the five you like least."

Even as air conditioners cool Saint Paul, the elders linger on its front steps, rolling up sleeves, wiping brows. There is a scientific calculation for the combination of heat and humidity, a measurement known as the "discomfort index." But even a stagnant August twilight, all jaundiced sky and exhaust fumes, feels preferable to the emotional climate that awaits within. Tonight the elders will hear from Justine Redmond.

Four days ago, after Sunday services, ten of them and Reverend Youngblood met informally with Ella Redmond. She recounted the incident between her daughter and Carter Naulls. More important, she said that she had taught Justine to be aware of a sexual type of touch, and that after the encounter with Carter, Justine had told her, "It was like you said, Mommy." There were just two more questions. Yes, Ella said, she would abide by the elders' disposition of the case. And no, she had no doubt Carter was guilty.

Now Ella leads Justine to the front of Elders Hall, where they sit in folding chairs. Ella still wears the dress from her job as an auditor in north Jersey; in jeans, running shoes, and ponytail, Justine looks more ready for double-dutch than a deposition. With the mother and daughter walk Sarah Plowden and Yvonne Ziegler, who is the director of women's ministries, invited here by Reverend Youngblood to provide comfort to the Redmonds and insight to the board.

"Justine, how you doin'?" Reverend Youngblood begins. He sits several feet to the girl's side, bends over in his chair so his height will not intimidate.

"Okay," she says, composed.

"We wanna talk to you about what happened the Sunday you were here, the thing that happened with Mr. Naulls."

She tells a story that, except for a few finer details, most of the listeners already know. "My stomach started hurting.... I went to the bathroom and it didn't stop.... I went to sit by the window.... Mr. Naulls said I couldn't sit there.... He took me to Elders Hall.... Before I had a chance to sit, he was on me.... Squeezin' my butt and huggin' on me and kissin'." Then she adds one more point, one that flushes faces around the room. "When I got up to leave, he said, 'Are we still friends? Gimme five.' I didn't."

Not a breath stirs the air. Only from the hallway, beyond the closed door, come sounds—a phone ringing untended, the creak of shoe leather on linoleum. After a long moment Reverend Youngblood speaks, leading Justine back through the incident in a voice as soft as flannel, and only then allowing others to ask questions.

"Justine," Melvin Jones says, "when Mr. Naulls brought you in the room here, did he close the door?"

"He closed the door."

Elias Singleton asks how far he took her. Justine points to a chair about two feet inside the door. Other questions slowly emerge, Justine answering each without hesitation. "Where was he kissing you?" "On the neck." "More than once?" "Yes." "Were you crying when you left the room?" "Yes." "Did you run or walk out?" "I moved kind of fast."

"Justine," asks Rochester Blanks, "you know how Uncle Rocky hug you?" She nods. "He hug you like I hug you?"

"No."

Rocky folds his arms across his chest, lifts his eyes toward the ceiling, in contemplation or pain.

"Was it intentional when he felt you?" Elias asks. Then he demonstrates two motions, one of a hand accidentally brushing against buttocks, as it might on a crowded subway, the other of the fingers cupping flesh.

"He deliberately did it."

Another silence settles over the room. Reverend Youngblood stares at the tabletop. Rocky brings his open palm to his forehead, as if testing for fever. Ella Redmond lightly touches her neck.

"Any more questions?" the pastor asks, lifting his gaze. "No? Okay."

The three women and the girl leave, Ella and Justine for home, Sarah and Yvonne for the office next door.

"You ever had one of those days you just didn't want to go to work?" Reverend Youngblood says, not moving from his chair. "This is one of those days." He shakes his head in a slow, low curve. "'Are we still friends? Gimme five.'"

"And she was crying when he said that," adds Frank Kinard, a retired police detective.

"She was believable," says Charles Lewis, and nobody disagrees.

Yet Carter had appeared believable, too. He never denied approaching Justine, escorting her to the room, hugging and kissing her. The two versions are almost identical and yet irreconcilable. The actions exist in bold colors, their meanings in vague pastels of nuance, intent, implication. And though a court can issue a verdict without worrying about meeting the antagonists ever again, the elders will not have succeeded in this mission of healing if their decision drives anyone away. Now pens rest on pads. Arms dangle over chair backs. More than one Bible lies open.

"Oh, Lord," Reverend Youngblood says, wearily. "This is a precedent case for us, gentlemen. Because we're not just dealing with Justine and we're not just dealing with Carter. We're dealing with men and children and a hugging, kissing kind of congregation." He pauses.

"Clarence told me on Sunday he went to hug somebody, and ..." The pastor mimes Clarence catching himself, freezing in place, throwing up his arms like a criminal surrendering. "So how do we structure a village where we're trying to bring in men and teach them they're responsible for raising children, and there's this 'good touch, bad touch'?"

The question unanswered, hovering like low smoke, he sends for Sarah and Yvonne. Many of the elders, it is true, are fathers to young daughters, attuned to the danger of abuse. Still, the pastor believes, even that understanding has its limits. His men need not only to hear evidence, but to be edified by two women whom they trust.

"Tell us the things you think we've really got to consider," Reverend Youngblood entreats Sarah and Yvonne. As they demur, in confusion or caution, he explains: "To be a little facetious, it's like when you leave for school and your momma asks, 'Do you have your hat? Your lunch? Your galoshes?' That's kind of what we need. One of the reasons the ministry to women exists for us is because it's said men can lack sensitivities. So if we need to be made sensitive to some things, tell us."

"I'm struggling with this," Yvonne says. "I just have to go with my gut feeling. Which is that she told the truth. Speaking in front of a room full of men." She averts her eyes, gathers herself. "To me, she was credible."

"What makes her credible?" Elias asks.

"She didn't stutter. She wasn't nervous. She was clear. When she didn't understand a question, she said so." With each sentence, she slices the air with an open palm. "She's *ten years old*."

Sarah, in her custom, saves her thoughts for last.

"For any woman who hears a case like this," she says, "it becomes part of them. The reason we teach our daughters about 'good touch, bad touch' is because you can line us up and hear each one's incident." She regards the elders. "There's no way you can be sensitive to that. You've got to do what you have to do. I don't want Carter to be guilty. I don't want Justine to be scarred. Whether it happened or whether she imagined it." She echoes Yvonne, almost word for word. "She came into this room, answered all the questions. She's ten years old. I'm not sure I could've done that."

As the women depart, Frank Kinard slides back in his chair. Elias

Singleton narrows his eyes, stares at the side wall. Reverend Youngblood lists the disparities yet to be resolved: Was Justine sitting or
standing? Was she kissed on the lips or the neck? Was the door open or
closed? Lights off or on? Other girls watching or not? And what, what,
what was the meaning of "Are we still friends? Gimme five."?

"Well, men," he says as the meeting concludes, "I'll check your
knees before we make our decision. Anybody whose knees aren't dusty
and dirty can't have a say."

Just before dinner early on a Thursday evening, Reverend Youngblood
summons Larry Johnson and Monica Moody into his study. For this,
the second session of premarital counseling, the pastor also invites
Myrtis Brent, by title the church's prayer intercessor and in practice a
fount of life experience and common sense.

"So how were the Poconos?" Reverend Youngblood asks her, and
Myrtis's face crinkles with girlish giggles. At the age of sixty-two, she
just took a weekend with unspecified company.

Monica, meanwhile, removes from her purse one sheet of stationery from an electronics company, covered in a tight scrawl. On the
table before him, Larry places a legal pad, its top page marked in script
as clean as a draftsman's. These are their responses to the pastor's
assignment to list their favorite and least favorite qualities in each
other.

"Let's get the mushy stuff outta the way first," he says. "Monica?"

"He helps me with my son," she begins reading. "He tells me
good things. He tells me that he loves me. He's a good provider. I feel
he knows God. He's not cheap. He helps out around the house. He's
my ideal."

"Let's give him a standing O," Reverend Youngblood says, starting to rise from his chair.

Then Larry enumerates his favorite qualities in Monica, from
intelligence to independence, from religious faith to familial loyalty to
beauty of body and soul.

"And the thing is," the pastor says, "maybe you should tack that
list up somewhere to remind you. Let's go to the other list now. One
by one."

He draws a deep breath, balls and then straightens his fingers.

Larry and Monica each hesitate, waiting for the other to start. What looms is the sort of truth-telling easily omitted in the rapture of impending wedlock. But better to find the fault lines now, Reverend Youngblood believes, than to discover them only after the earthquake, when the damage may not be reparable.

"To me," Monica says, "he reads more into things than he should. He takes things very literally. Sometimes he'll fly off the handle and I just have to wait for him to come back to his senses."

Reverend Youngblood draws his left hand slowly down his beard, pinching a few chin whiskers.

"You have a five-year age difference," he says. "Larry's got five years more experience. And then he's got street in him. Where'd you grow up?"

"Queens."

"You know where he grew up?" He answers his own question, firmly. "Brownsville. Off Belmont. The projects."

"I understand that," Monica says.

"No, you don't," the pastor rejoins. "Listen to your language: 'I gotta wait till he comes back to his senses.' That's like saying he's crazy."

"But he *is*."

Monica lowers her eyes. Larry stews, angry or ashamed.

"Think of where you grew up," Reverend Youngblood reiterates. "Queens." The noun brings to a Brownsville mind images of ease and privilege—the expansive, groomed ballfields in Howard Beach, only miles from ruined Linden Park, or the mock Tudor architecture of Forest Hills, separated only by Cypress Hills cemetery from tenements and projects, or the frame homes and modest yards in the black middle-class districts like Springfield Gardens, where Monica grew up.

"But I hated Queens," she insists.

"It doesn't matter," Reverend Youngblood answers. "You made a *choice* to hate Queens. Larry *had* to grow up and survive in Brownsville, and he brings Brownsville to the rest of the world. He can change, but you can't browbeat him."

As Monica nods in agreement, the pastor turns to Larry.

"Is there any truth to what she says?"

"I know I get mad, but when I do, I know enough to get out of the house till I cool out."

"Would you say you're eligible for violence?"

"Yes."

"Did you know that?"

"Yes."

Reverend Youngblood looks now to Monica.

"Does it frighten you?"

"Yes," she says.

"Larry," the pastor resumes, "did you know that?"

"No," he says, remorse in his tone.

"When you get mad, are you mad at her?"

"No. It's always something else."

As an example, he talks about an argument they had this morning. Larry had expected to buy wedding rings on Long Island; Monica instead drove to downtown Brooklyn to get a marriage license. They scrapped over where to park. Monica resented always having to drive because Larry feared it. Larry was hurt that Monica didn't appreciate that the phobia arose from his father's severe injury in a car accident. He could still remember the pool of blood. Even now, in the retelling, they raise voices notch by notch, to the threshold of shouts.

"Okay," Reverend Youngblood says sharply. He had hoped they would catch, and halt, their own escalation. Instead he must play both coach and referee. "Y'all got to synchronize your watches," he says. "Because what I see here is misplaced anger. Monica, you don't want to be the victim of misplaced anger. And, Larry, you don't want to be the agent of it. You probably don't even *like* being angry." Larry nods. "You have a part in this, too. You have to learn how you come off. You have to learn how to tell her, 'Monica, you got the story wrong.' Without goin' off." He levels his gaze at Larry. "Please remember that your anger makes you eligible for things you don't want. Like the police. You're black, you're a man, and a woman has called the cops in danger."

He pauses, lets Larry imagine the rest of the scenario—handcuffs, fingerprints, a stationhouse beating.

"So y'all work on that," he says, voice lifting in levity. "Because I'll be looking Sunday morning"—he mimes craning his neck from the pulpit—"and seein', has Larry been mad this week? Has Monica been hurt this week?"

They continue through the lists, from her tardiness to his procrastination, from her casual housekeeping to his obsession with detail. Sometimes Reverend Youngblood retraces with them a pattern of expectations and misapprehensions; sometimes he instructs on the importance of tone as well as content in conversation.

"What've y'all heard here today?" he asks, bringing the session toward its close.

"Be more specific with each other," Monica says.

"Work on this stuff," Larry adds.

Myrtis, who has listened without comment until now, softly asks, "Do you ever read together?"

"She doesn't like to read," Larry says with disdain.

"I read so much in college," Monica answers defensively. "And I lost so many friends in public school because I skipped a grade."

"And I love to read," Larry continues. "Histories. Black literature."

The volume is rising again. The grievances are being toted and tallied. Reverend Youngblood, for one last time, whistles the scrimmage to a halt.

"Would you let Larry read to you?" he asks Monica.

She smiles, turns her eyes to his.

"Oh, yeah," she purrs. "He could do that. I think that'd be very nice. Very romantic."

Having guided the session to a sweet conclusion, Reverend Youngblood reminds Larry and Monica to make an appointment for one final meeting. It will be devoted primarily to a discussion and walk-through of the ceremony. Then all that will remain is the Saturday afternoon of August 18, that and the thousands of afternoons to follow.

As the couple leaves, Reverend Youngblood swivels his chair toward Myrtis, grinning with mischief.

"All right, you can tell me about the Poconos now," he says. "Might need to take you into the confessional. Give you some absolution."

When the elders convene for the last time on the matter of Justine Redmond and Carter Naulls, they find their meeting room arranged with a difference. Before the lectern, facing Reverend Youngblood, sit two chairs, one for Carter and one for Justine's mother, Ella. Behind the lectern rests the communion table, equipped with a small bottle of holy water and the silver dishes of the Lord's Supper. And on the lectern lies a portfolio containing the board's findings. "Oh, boy," the pastor says, withdrawing the document for a final inspection.

Nearly two months have passed since the encounter between the ten-year-old girl and the fifty-nine-year-old usher. The board has devoted weeks to determining which handful of children, from the hundreds in the congregation, had been waiting in the lobby with Justine that morning. By that time, some of them were out of Brooklyn, visiting relatives. When the interviews were finally held, several youngsters offered the same recollection: The door to Elders Hall was open when Justine and Carter were inside; Justine was not crying or visibly distraught when she emerged. The mothers of these girls, who also were interviewed by the board, said they had instructed their daughters about bad touch, and that the girls would have recognized any molestation against a peer. As for Carter, he was recalled to explain the meaning of "Are we still friends? Gimme five." It was, he readily said, just a pet phrase of his, offered to Justine in the same avuncular spirit as the buss on her cheek. For good measure, Reverend Youngblood plumbed his sources in the congregation for any whisperings about Carter and children. He found none.

Even then, with the investigation complete, neither the pastor nor the elders could consider the incident entirely clarified. Guilt or innocence seemed artificial polarities. Between them, in the gray zone of reasonable doubt, the board wrestled. The result consumed two single-spaced typed pages, with space at the bottom for the signatures of Carter Naulls and Ella Redmond.

Before they arrive, Reverend Youngblood, subdued in a dark blazer and a paisley tie, issues an invocation. "Father," he says, "it may be tension, but I just know I haven't looked forward to this. I don't want to be judge and jury tonight." He exhales heavily, like a man battling nausea. "Lord, I just want to be Your servant, if You will bless us with wisdom and compassion. We lift up Justine to You. We lift up Ella. We lift up Carter. And if we think about the easy way out, if we feel sorry for ourselves, then forgive us. We talk about the cross, Lord, but we don't always mean for ourselves. You've moved through us as men, Lord. You've done remarkable things. We come now at this particular time for his particular purpose. We make ourselves available. Have Thine own way."

Then the pastor reaches for a song he has known since childhood. Those gathered around the tables recognize it from worship service, where its insistent rhythm drives the sanctuary to celebration. Tonight, though, Reverend Youngblood slows the meter, and leads in the tender voice of a lullaby.

Jesus is a way maker
Jesus is a way maker
Jesus is a way maker
One day he made a way for me.

Clarence Davis taps a felt-tipped pen in cadence against the open pages of his Bible. Raymond Thompson removes his glasses and massages the skin around his eyes. From around the table, voices fasten in harmony.

In the song's wake, Charles Lewis leaves the room, returning momentarily with word that both Carter and Ella have arrived. Clad in a blue shirt and navy tie, Carter enters first, settling into a seat at the far end of the table. Leroy Howard points him to the front. Then Yvonne Ziegler brings Ella to the chair beside Carter's. As Frank Kinard reads from Romans, hands join around the room. For the circle to be closed, Carter and Ella must bring palm to palm. Their eyes do not meet.

Reverend Youngblood recapitulates the original allegation and the various stages of the investigation. Several elders bow their heads in private prayer. Carter and Ella, both seated now, rivet their vision to the pastor, as he begins to read the board's resolution.

1. Elder Naulls admitted to hugging and kissing Ms. Redmond on the forehead as a consoling act. He did not at any time intentionally touch her improperly.
2. There is no record or rumor of Mr. Naulls's ever being even accused of such proclivity.
3. The mothers of other children who were said to be present or to have witnessed the alleged incident stated that they taught their daughters to be aware of and alert to incidents of "bad touch" and that had the incident occurred as described by

Ms. Redmond their children would have responded. However, the children had not so much as hinted of such an incident, even to keep as a secret.

4. Mr. Naulls was engaged in the carrying out of his responsibilities as an usher; that is, he was seeing to it that no worshipers—especially children—are to be outside of the sanctuary at preaching time....

... We therefore conclude that Mr. Naulls is innocent of said charges. We believe Mr. Naulls's actions to be well intended and Ms. Redmond to be mistaken as it pertains to Mr. Naulls's intentions.

Both Carter and Ella are thanked for their cooperation. Carter is formally restored to the Board of Ushers. And the elders recommend that, as a matter of policy, when children are to be cared for or reprimanded during a worship service, an usher of the same gender be involved.

Removing pen from pocket, Reverend Youngblood says that he will sign the document as presiding elder, and he asks Carter and Ella to ratify it with their signatures. If there is a moment when the fragile construction that is human trust will crumble, this is it. Two people submitted a dispute of rare intensity to arbitration—acting out of faith in their pastor, in their church, in the tradition of racial self-governance known as "black law." And also, it was true, because each felt certain to be confirmed. Now only one of them has been. Things could still wind up in court; things could still tear the church apart.

Carter turns to glance at Ella, begins to lift off his chair, as if to make a gesture of comfort. Reverend Youngblood, with a glare, warns him back. Slowly, Ella nods assent. She and Carter rise, step forward, sign. In the hushed, anxious air can be heard the rustle of paper, the skitter of pen, the beep of a single digital watch, marking eight o'clock, the end of a long hour.

Now Reverend Slaughter moves between the lectern and communion table. "In Jesus," he prays, "we can agree to disagree and still be one." The elders stand, link arms in a circle. Within it, Carter and Ella and Yvonne clasp hands. Insistently, Carter's eyes search out Ella's, but her sight travels on a separate path, and tears spill down her cheeks.

"We thought it was right to celebrate communion tonight," Reverend Slaughter says in the soothing drawl of his native Virginia. "To remind ourselves that we are joined in the community of believers."

He raises the silver dish several inches above the table, then crumbles the crackers it holds into fragments. The plate moves around the room. Behind it comes a tray with tiny plastic cups of juice. Someone begins singing, "I was healed by the wound in His side."

"This is the body that was broken for us," Reverend Slaughter says. He lifts a cracker in his right hand, then a cup of juice in his left. "This is the blood that was spilled for the remission of sin." As he eats and drinks, the others follow.

Communion finished, community affirmed, Ella and Yvonne leave wordlessly. Charles Lewis shoos away several boys whom the opening door finds crouched outside in the posture of spies. Carter stands, blinking as if from a sudden light. "I just wanna thank you guys," he says haltingly. "For having trust in me. I missed you."

"To be honest, Carter," Reverend Youngblood says, "there was no friendship in this. We just believe that morning Justine misunderstood." He pauses. "Tonight, when you wanted to reach over and hug Ella, I might've saved your life by stopping you. She's gonna need time, and it's our job as a congregation to minister to her and her family. I don't know exactly how Ella feels. I'm not a woman and I'm not a mother. But I know she has a right to be angry. She has a right to mourn. She has a right not to want to be touched." Carter nods, less in understanding than obedience. "Now is a time for God to show Himself. It's up to God to honor this decision. Carter, stay cool, and the Lord will break this in His own time."

Zipping a clerical robe over his brown business suit, Reverend Youngblood peeks from his study door toward the lobby, checking on the final preparations for the wedding of Larry Johnson and Monica Moody. A fair number of the church staff have been deputized for the event. Eli Wilson pages through a fake book entitled *Everything for the Wedding Soloist*. Emily Walton hands out programs to the arriving guests. Rose Stokes and Greta Young, having decorated the sanctuary with lilies and mums, will supervise the procession. Leroy Howard has arranged with the police to post an officer outside the church during the ceremony, just in case the ex-boyfriend appears. And the pastor, who will lead the service and sign the license, has moved his car, leaving its reserved space for the white marital limousine.

Now Reverend Youngblood walks through his study and into the sanctuary. He quickly inspects the four carved chairs flanking the pulpit, each draped with a strip of *kente*. These are called the "ancestor chairs," and in a Saint Paul wedding they represent the spirits of forebears, whose names will be invoked during the ceremony. Returning to his study, the pastor finds Rose Stokes waiting with a list of those names, and they double-check every pronunciation, every relation.

A knock at the door interrupts. Larry Johnson enters, wearing a black tuxedo with a bow tie, pocket square, and cummerbund made of matching *kente*. At his side hovers Greta Young, trying to pin a boutonniere on the moving target that is his left lapel.

"You still got five minutes to change your mind," Reverend Youngblood says, deadpan. "After that ..." He lets the sentence trail off. "What's your number-one thought?"

"Get it over with."

The pastor laughs hard and raspingly.

"A common thought."

The organ flourishes in the sanctuary, signaling the guests to take seats. The light of flashbulbs presses through the seams of the study door. Larry pulls the marriage license from his vest pocket.

"Monica Moody," Reverend Youngblood reads. "No middle name?" Larry shakes his head. "Too bad. I usually have fun with those." Then he looks quickly at a photocopy of the vows. "You know your part?"

"Yeah."

"Blessings on you, man," Reverend Youngblood says, entering the sanctuary.

Eli strikes up the processional, "Bless the Lord, O My Soul," his organ chords vibrating the pews. Then they march, the ushers and the bridesmaids, the best man and the maid of honor. All eyes focus on the double doors, expecting the bride and groom, but the next person through is Rose, laying down the runner, as Greta coaxes the flower girl into action. Only when Eli shifts to the swooning rhythm of "I Surrender All" does Monica enter in veil and gown, followed a moment later by Larry.

After the opening prayer, after the proclamation of the ancestors,

Reverend Youngblood preaches. His topic is less the day's marriage than the counseling that has preceded it.

"I enjoy looking for hope and joy," he says. "And as I was looking at the faces of people here, I thought I could see on everybody's lips the phrase, 'I can't believe Larry's gettin' married.'" He waits for the laughter to ebb. "But I told him when there was five minutes to go he could still back out." Again, laughter interrupts. "But he's not here with a shotgun. He's here because he wants to be here."

Now he narrows his field of vision from the worshipers to the man and woman before him.

"Neither of you are teenagers," he says. "You didn't marry like a lot of us did to get out of the house. And there's no such thing anymore as 'Got to get married.' These days, even guys with five children don't feel they got to get married. No, there's no pressure here. Neither of you are novices in life. Both of you, in different ways, been to hell and back. And thank God for round-trip tickets."

"Amen," someone shouts.

"You stand here today as two sane, sober, mature, willing, sensitive people who have come together to say, 'We believe we can make a difference, just as God has made a difference in our lives.' And you can give us all lessons in this thing called marriage. Larry, you know Monica; Monica, you know Larry. But be careful about 'Monica belongs to me' and 'Larry belongs to me.' There's some of that, but you *both* belong to God. The two of you are really held together by life. And life exists by the grace of God."

The pastor leads a prayer, then calls on the elders. Nine step forward, drawing into a tight circle around the couple, touching them, embracing them, praising God on their behalf. When the men withdraw, Larry and Monica join hands as Reverend Youngblood reads the vows. After the exchange of rings, he serves them communion, speaking so quietly nobody but the couple can hear.

"Ladies and gentlemen, brothers and sisters," he then declares, "presenting to all of you, Mister and Missus Larry Johnson."

With hands that once robbed and beat and shot junk, hands that have been redeemed, Larry delicately pinches the hem of Monica's veil, lifts it as slowly as sunrise, to savor each inch of flesh being revealed. Then he almost falls forward into a kiss that lasts well into the first verse of Mendelssohn's march.

10

⬡

MORNING AT MIDNIGHT

VEN AT NOON, only slivers of sunlight reach Randy Murphy's room. He lives in the basement of his mother's house, a place of lumpy linoleum tile and wood paneling weakened by dripping water and three windows that look out on the hubcaps of passing cars. When Randy first moved here three years ago, as a man of twenty-two, he thought of the cellar as "my own little piece of life." Certainly it offered more freedom and privacy than his childhood bedroom upstairs. Here he could hang his posters of Luther Vandross and Leontyne Price. Here he could fix himself oatmeal and hot chocolate in the tiny rear kitchen. Here he could install the double bed he called "my ace."

And here, as he sweeps the floor on a Saturday off from work, he can dream of escape. He has his boxes lined against one wall—a dinner service for four, a set of sixteen glasses, a can opener, an iron, a matching set of soap dish, tissue box, and toothbrush stand. He has a black table and four chairs on layaway. He has a secondhand china cabinet filled with secondhand books. The title of one is *On Your Own*.

Randy moves through the damp air, through the muffled sounds, bringing order with a broom. He is a stickler for order, order and records. He keeps his records in a series of envelopes locked in a metal strongbox. There is an envelope for dry-cleaning tickets and an envelope for medical records and an envelope for pay stubs from his job. *I gotta get these alphabetical,* he tells himself, though he means chrono-logical. The money he makes, four dollars and fifty cents an hour, must be husbanded and budgeted with care. It must pay for contact lenses and dentures and voice lessons and, most of all, an apartment of his own. Rochester Blanks has been helping Randy with the numbers, and every week Randy saves twenty-five dollars, just like Rocky said. When he gathers a thousand or so, enough for a month's rent, a secu-rity deposit, and a small surplus, he can find a little place of his own. Then he can really get started on opening his flower shop. And prac-ticing for Amateur Night at the Apollo.

Which gets Randy to thinking. He leans the broom against the wall, inserts a tape into his cassette deck. A voice emerges, singing show tunes. It belongs to Jim Nabors, who played the impossibly good-hearted Marine in "Gomer Pyle, USMC." Randy lends his own formidable baritone to Nabors's, and their duet echoes. Though Randy really favors Simon Estes, the opera star, he loves this tape for its origin. Reverend Youngblood gave it to him, partly because Randy reminded the pastor of Gomer, and partly because of the song Nabors and Randy now share, "The Impossible Dream."

It is two o'clock, and the sunshine has disappeared. The only light comes from a fluorescent bulb, loosely held to a bare beam. Randy, however, is accustomed to the shadows. Shadows have shaped the condition of his life—the shadows of mental retardation, special edu-cation, a murdered father, an overprotective mother, a former fiancée, a breakdown, a mental hospital, stupefying medication, a security-guard job alone overnight, this basement room. "Nobody knows," Randy says, "all the hell I been through."

But Randy has solutions for shadows. He denies them. He ignores them. He tears them down like flimsy curtains. The people of Saint Paul have seen much of his will, from Reverend Youngblood and Rochester Blanks to Missus Mendez in the basic-skills program to Joe Dudley and Phil White in Eldad-Medad. What none of them quite knows, though, is what might happen when Randy's hopes collide with Randy's limits, for his survival has depended on seeing morning at midnight.

When Randy Murphy was a child, his mother taught school in the family basement. There were chairs, a table, and even a blackboard;

there were books by the carton. Deborah Murphy considered her five children "stair steps" for the way she conceived them, one after the other, but in her early lessons it became clear that more than age set them apart. Randy had been born with crossed eyes and needed glasses by age five to correct an astigmatism. His kindergarten teacher confirmed Deborah's sense that he was "slow." Tests and more tests arrived at the diagnosis "educable mentally retarded," and Randy vanished into the netherworld known as special education.

Eager, sensitive, and mannerly, Randy touched many of his instructors. One of them, Molly Donahue, arranged for him to attend sleep-away camp free for two summers, and sent him Christmas cards for years to come, even after she retired to Florida. Another introduced him to opera. More typical, however, was the teacher who made only one written recommendation during an entire year: that Randy watch "The Electric Company" on what she misspelled as "Channell 13." Despite a state law mandating that each special-education student be evaluated every three years—for intellectual capacity, current performance, and appropriate placement—Randy went from second grade to eleventh without being checked. And at that point, tests showed, his academic skills were those of a third-grader.

In social ways, too, school failed Randy. His crossed eyes, his thick glasses, his big feet, his gentle spirit all made him a pariah to his peers. They slapped him, beat him, pelted him with leftovers. When he dared flirt with a girl, her friends surrounded him in a hallway, chanting, "Randy is retarded, Randy is retarded." Deborah grew so exasperated she wrote to one teacher, asking how Randy was expected to maintain his self-respect. The letter went unanswered.

But the problems followed Randy into his home, too. His father, an occasional housepainter with a weakness for gambling, left the family in Randy's early childhood; his stepfather proved to be a stifling disciplinarian. On many nights, Randy fell asleep to the sound of an older brother being beaten for violating household curfew. With the immediate world so uncertain, and the outer world so cruel, Randy clung to the one sure bulwark, his mother, helping her scrub and wash and cook. Even then, he had to endure a brother, a younger brother at that, teasing, "You always in the house cleanin' up, and I'm out havin' fun. You a mama's boy."

On such infirm footing, Randy entered Tilden High School, the last stage before legal adulthood. His special-education teacher, Lloyd Abrams, could hardly believe the gaps in Randy's records, the years between evaluations. And when he compared Randy to classmates, those with violent dispositions or documented brain damage, he asked himself a question of terrible implications: Was Randy actually retarded, or had he just fallen to the level of a decade's worth of special-education classes, classes he might never have needed?

Abrams never resolved the question because he had neither the time nor the means. In the early 1980s, special education aimed at preparing students for menial employment and limited independence, teaching them how to fill out job applications and pay utility bills by check. Only in classes like music and woodworking could Randy move alongside normal students. His own academic courses relied on outdated textbooks, pitched at the aptitude of a seven-year-old. Worse still, after fifteen years as a special-education teacher, Abrams felt his energy and idealism expiring. One Friday afternoon he staggered into his house after work and slumped asleep on the carpet.

When the Class of 1983 graduated from Tilden, Randy, like the rest of the special-education students, did not receive a diploma. A new state rule barred the school from giving even the "completion certificates" that in prior years had let those students save a semblance of face. Randy's portrait did not appear in the yearbook. Nor was he listed in the section entitled "Camera Shy." By most formal measures, he seemed to have not existed.

Inside his skin, though, he existed almost too deeply. The definitive statement on his education, on his childhood, had been pronounced by the school psychologist who evaluated him at the start of his junior year:

> Randolph has an ardent desire to achieve. In effect, when unable to accomplish a task or answer an item, he would show harsh frustration and feel compelled to come up with an alibi such as: "Nobody's perfect"; "I know the answer"; "I don't know what's happening to me." In some instances, Randolph would almost beg the examiner to help him remember some responses; he would hit his forehead, tap the floor, twist his arms and desperately adopt a fetal position....
>
> He is a frustrated boy whose emotional state is worsened

by the awareness of his incompetence. He strives for autonomy and wants to perform beyond his limits.

One Sunday in 1984, during the men's Bible study classes that pre-dated Eldad-Medad, Reverend Youngblood asked for volunteers. He was going to Buffalo to help Reverend Glenn DuBois, a longtime mentor, clean his church from cellar to steeple. Among the five or six listeners who assented was a relatively new member of Saint Paul named Randy Murphy.

He had joined the church in 1983, after attending with his mother. She had come out of curiosity about the handsome building; he had stayed out of admiration for the preacher. In Reverend Young-blood's drive and authority, Randy heard the resonance of his grandfa-ther, Walton Jones, a church deacon whom he loved more than almost anyone else in the world. At Saint Paul, Randy could live free from his past and its stigma, perfecting what Rochester Blanks would later call "the art of camouflage." He carried a briefcase, wore suits and bow ties. He conversed with assurance—even the eleventh-grade evaluation had found his oral skills nearly three times as advanced as his written ones. And when it came to working, Randy never said no. Why, he had worked since age twelve, passing out flyers for the Muslims, mak-ing hamburgers at McDonald's, delivering packages for a hospital. Deborah Murphy often wished her other, more gifted children could have been blessed with Randy's motivation.

Reverend Youngblood, though, wondered that Sunday if he should turn down this particular volunteer. With his clumsy move-ments and hyperactive moods, Randy had struck the pastor as some-how awkward, off, wrong. But he swallowed his doubts, counted Randy among his contingent, and drove off to Buffalo and Jordan Grove Baptist Church.

The next day, Reverend Youngblood was hauling old furniture from Jordan Grove's attic to a Dumpster outside when John Barber, Saint Paul's custodian, rushed to him, saying, "You better come get Randy. He done gone crazy."

"What's he done?"

"He done *everything*," John answered. "He's throwin' people's stuff out. I can't stop him."

At the Dumpster, Reverend Youngblood found Randy depositing

hymn books, the pulpit Bible, and the radio equipment for Jordan Grove's Sunday broadcasts. Back inside the sanctuary, the wires hung like hacked vines. And Randy, filled with the unnatural energy Reverend Youngblood had noticed in him before, was returning for another load.

"Randy," the pastor said with deliberate restraint, "have you been sleepin'?"

"No, man," he declared, arms raised in triumph. "I feel so good, I don't have to sleep."

Reverend Youngblood moved toward him, step light and palms extended, so he would not present a threat.

"Randy, stop, calm down. Don't do anything else. Go and get something to eat. Then sleep."

"But I'm all right."

"Just do what I want you to do, and you'll be more all right."

So Randy ate and slept and relaxed. Reverend Youngblood returned the holy books and reconnected the radio equipment. The whole mess could now be forgotten. But the following Sunday, as the pastor shared a selective account of the Buffalo trip with the men's group, John Barber called out, "Don't forget about Randy."

Reverend Youngblood brought his fingertips to his temples. He felt the eyes upon him, Randy's more than most. Should he lie? Patronize? Tell a hurtful truth?

"Y'all," he began slowly, "Randy scared the shit outta me. Randy went off. While we were cleanin' up, Randy was cleanin' *out*."

Then he watched closely. Randy's jaw tensed; his forearms tightened; the pastor felt unnerved by the intensity. And then, as the men around him laughed easily, Randy joined them, enjoying the joke on himself, and savoring the thing he had always wanted most—to be treated like everybody else.

"I know I was buggin'," he said to Reverend Youngblood. "I hope I didn't embarrass you."

"No," the pastor replied. Candor, in this case, was not worth the cost.

Even with his flaws unmasked, Randy felt more accepted at church than anywhere else. Over the next months he became so ubiquitous, in fact, that Reverend Youngblood had to invent a word for the quality: *there-ness*. Randy tithed. He studied in the men's Bible class. He volunteered with the youth ministry. He brought roses to women on the staff. He rehearsed testimonies with Rocky, and when he delivered them to the congregation he held a handwritten text before him, so only his closest friends would know he was speaking from memory, not reading the page.

No friend became closer than Joe Dudley. They had met glancingly in high school, on opposite sides of a gospel choir competition—Joe playing the congas and singing first tenor with Brooklyn Tech's ensemble, Randy covering baritone and bass parts and wearing one of Tilden's trademark peach tuxedoes. A casual acquaintance grew into phone calls three or four times each day, enough to irritate Joe's mother, and frequent visits. Joe was attending Long Island University, his first step toward a master's degree and a profession teaching learning-disabled children, and Joe was a body-builder with a steady girl. He stood, for Randy, as a model of manhood.

Joe started him lifting weights. Joe taught him some self-defense. Joe fielded questions, including the one that was most often repeated: How do you treat a girlfriend? "Like a queen," Joe answered. "Like your queen."

But neither Joe nor Rocky nor Saint Paul could fill the holes in Randy's life as he neared his twenty-first birthday in early 1985. His mother and stepfather broke up. He lost his guard's job at La Guardia Airport in a strike. His father, absent so many years, reentered his life through tragedy—beaten to death with a pipe for the money he had just won on the numbers. And his beloved grandfather, the one who always blessed the house on Thanksgiving and then carved the turkey, died of cancer. In the last months, Randy had bathed him by hand.

The rupture occurred on the Sunday morning of June 9, 1985. Deborah awakened to find Randy sitting on the front stoop, a packed suitcase beside him. He was preaching that morning at Saint Paul, he told her. Reverend Youngblood was on the way to pick him up. He had already cooked the pastor a breakfast of bacon and eggs, set cups of orange juice all through the house.

Deborah slipped back into her bedroom, called the church, and asked for Leroy Howard, whose name she recalled. "I think Randy is getting sick," she told him. "He thinks he's coming to preach."

How'm I gonna talk to this brother? Leroy asked himself. *Is he gonna be violent? What's he capable of?*

He settled his wife and children in the sanctuary, then drove to the Murphy house. He found Randy pacing the sidewalk frenetically, literally frothing at the mouth.

"Let's go get something to eat," Leroy offered, opening the passenger door of his car.

"I don't want to eat."

"Then let's just get a cup of coffee," Leroy said, and Randy agreed.

They drove to a McDonald's four blocks from the church, and Randy vented for nearly an hour. In spurts and jagged fragments, he told of the recent deaths, the derision of his siblings, the way his mother kept him down, wouldn't let him be a man. "No pain, no gain," he declared at intervals, borrowing the phrase from a recent sermon by Reverend Youngblood.

Leroy prayed with Randy about the losses. He reminded him his mother was protecting him out of love. And he told him not to listen to anyone who ridiculed his faith. "If you have a personal relationship with the Lord," he said, "let that be your guide. Not your brother or sisters. Someday they'll come to you for advice."

With that, Randy appeared composed enough for Leroy to drive him home. His parting advice was not to worry about Saint Paul. As day gave way to evening, Deborah tried to talk Randy into entering a hospital. Not until he saw Reverend Youngblood, he insisted. The impasse dragged on for hours. Finally, Deborah picked up the receiver, dialed seven random numbers, and said, "Okay, Reverend, we'll meet you there." At three o'clock in the morning she took Randy to Kings County Hospital, where he was admitted into Building G, the psychiatric ward.

During his eleven days there, Randy walked around the dayroom, blessing other patients, laying on hands. When Elizabeth brought him chocolate-chip cookies, his favorite, he crumbled them like wafers and served communion. He was released with a program of psychotherapy and a prescription for Navane and Cogentin.

Navane is normally given to patients suffering hallucinations and delusions. But its side effects, a combination of extreme enervation and extreme restlessness, have driven some users to suicide. Cogentin, usually employed to counter those side effects, causes its own problems, including sedation. After he began taking the drugs, all Randy and those around him knew was that his hands often shook uncontrollably and he felt so slowed down, so wasted, he could not work for a year. Never had independence seemed so distant, so impossible.

One afternoon in the summer of 1986, as Randy Murphy was struggling to resume the rudiments of his life, he visited a friend who assisted Eli Wilson in Saint Paul's music program. He noticed a girl typing, a small, slender girl with glasses and a ponytail. So he started talking to her about church, and he brought her a glass of water. And after a while she asked if he could walk her home to a housing project two blocks away.

"Ma, come and look," Valerie Neal said to her mother, as she entered the apartment. "I got company. Look who I brought home."

Oh, shit, Celeste Neal thought to herself. As a frequent volunteer at Saint Paul, she knew Randy Murphy and parts of his story.

And watching him and Valerie chat and snack and play music for several hours, she could not dislodge the dread. Anyone could see the mismatch. Valerie was bound for college, a young woman who preferred reading Maya Angelou to washing dishes, an aspiring author whose short stories had already been published in a citywide student magazine. And Randy was—well, with a master's degree in education, Celeste could tell Randy was in some way impaired. What shook Celeste most, though, was that she could also see the match. Valerie was as needy as she was brilliant. An only child left by her father at eight, a loner ashamed of her secondhand clothes, she poured her heartache into poems with titles like "Death" and "Suicide" and "You Make Me Feel Stupid." Here was a young woman, Celeste knew, as desperate to get love as Randy was to give it.

"Do you really like this guy?" Celeste asked Valerie about a week later.

"Yes."

"You know," she said, choosing words with care, "he's special."

"What do you mean, 'special'?"

"He has some learning disabilities."

"You don't know what you're talking about," Valerie insisted. "He can read, he can learn like anyone else."

Valerie was perhaps the first person in Randy's life to believe in his possibilities as fiercely as he himself did. She spent hours showing him arithmetic, sounding out sentences from the Bible, teaching words from an illustrated dictionary. They did what all other couples did, too, gabbing for hours on the phone, necking like mad during movies, gazing at Manhattan's glitter from atop the World Trade Center. Randy bought her teddy bears, and Valerie sent him cards covered with lipstick kisses. And when the time came for sexual intimacy, Randy took them both to a clinic for checkups and contraceptives. The day Celeste asked diplomatically about "protection," Randy reached into his pocket for a handful of condoms.

Saint Paul watched the romance with a mixture of amusement and concern. "Val," people would say, lightly touching her sleeve, "do you know what you're doin'?" Seeing the couple pass, teenagers burst into laughter. Deborah Murphy eavesdropped on their phone calls, warned Randy that the girl was running his life. But none of those doubters ever saw the essay Valerie wrote as part of her application to Hunter College:

> How did Randolph change my life? ... Perhaps it was his personality. He always has a comical, but sincere smile on his face, which often serves as a "pick me up" after a long, tiresome day. He tells me he loves me almost ten times a day, encourages me and supports me in anything that I do, allows me to confide in him when something is troubling me and is always, absolutely, all the time, giving me something or taking me someplace.
>
> Randolph, unlike some men his age, is not caught up with his girl's wearing of flirtatious clothing or flouting a superficial, bombastic attitude. He has always told me that those things "tick him off"; it is a kind heart that attracts him the most.

In June 1988, marking two years together, Randy and Valerie made themselves a candlelight dinner of chicken, Rice-a-Roni, and wine coolers. Before dessert, Randy dropped to his knees and produced a gold ring. Valerie had admired it once, in a display case at Woolworth's, and Randy had saved for six months to pay its hundred-dollar price.

"You make my life full of happiness and joy," he said. "Will you marry me?"

"Yes," answered Valerie.

They planned, for the wedding, for an apartment, for Randy to support them while Valerie pursued a master's degree. And then, as the reality of their marriage drew nearer, Valerie and Randy started to fight.

There were times, on double dates with Joe Dudley and his girl-friend, when Valerie would say, "Randy, you should be more sure of yourself, like Joe is." Her comments, however mild, pierced to Randy's marrow. And, worse, events seemed to confirm them. A crowd of teenagers surrounded Randy and Valerie outside her building one night, spitting in her face, knocking off his glasses, rendering him instantly helpless. A few months later, as Randy and Valerie walked home from a revival service at Saint Paul, a group of children attacked them with snowballs, hardly a fatal weapon, except to Randy's self-esteem. He grew so distraught at his failure to protect Valerie that Celeste Neal had to call his brothers to escort Randy home.

Some months earlier, before their problems began, Randy had introduced Valerie to a friend on his block, a middle-aged man named Willsten, who worked as a contractor. When they visited him now, it seemed to Randy, Willsten was determined to destroy the engagement. With all the impact a surrogate father would wield on a young woman without her own, he would say, "Val, there's some things I need to talk to you about, and Randy wouldn't understand." And Randy would have to wait alone, as they spoke in a separate room.

Searching for ballast, Randy went to his friends in Eldad-Medad, who advised him to act like "a strong man of God." But Valerie only railed at Randy for sharing their squabbles with others, and she bridled at his attempts at assertion. Forbidden by him to visit Willsten again, she replied, "I'm the leader now, I'm gonna run the show."

The end came with an argument at Valerie's apartment, a few final kisses, a ring tossed on the bed. Some time later, Valerie Neal married Willsten's son.

They wondered, Randy's friends, how he would survive. Some days he barely spoke. Other times he hid behind bravado, crowing about all the women "who be givin' me the eye." Mostly, though, he prayed, over the phone and in Eldad-Medad and during Sunday worship. He would search out his comrades in the sanctuary, clutch them in a circle, and plead to God with a passion untainted by doubt. Randy was, as Rocky put it, "a man about prayer." He spent hours, too, in Joe Dudley's weight room, moving without pause from press to curl to squat, doing sit-ups until his stomach was as taut as a timpani. In training fifty people over the years, Joe had never seen another endure like Randy, singing to block out the pain. His favorite was Jennifer Holiday's curtain number from *Dreamgirls,* a cry of defiance entitled "And I Am Telling You I'm Not Going."

The cinder-block confines of Frank Taylor Hall had been transformed with linen and china into a stylish supper club. The occasion in June 1989 was a roast of Reverend Youngblood, and the man at the microphone was not only a church member but a part-time comedian, who went even in real life by his stage name, Phil White. First he mimicked Reverend Youngblood with the same perfect pitch he had brought in the old days to imitations of Billy Eckstine and Arthur Prysock. Then he played the Devil, scolding a sexy young woman. "I send this fine young thing out to corrupt Pastor," he shouted at the punch line, "and you bring me back Jim Bakker."

The listeners howled, none more than Randy Murphy. And when Phil left the podium, Randy seized on him. Phil dressed so well; Phil spoke so smoothly; how could he fail to impress a young man with designs on the stage? Randy talked about his singing and his job, about his plan to move out and live as his own man, and beneath all the words Phil could sense "the loneliness, the void," feelings he knew too well from his own life.

For years, Phil had put his vigor and spare hours into community groups, believing all the rhetoric about "working within the system." And, indeed, he had helped to build a gymnasium in a housing project and to create an industrial park with hundreds of new jobs. But one night, as he was introduced at a political fund-raiser, Phil saw the Democratic boss of Brooklyn, Meade Esposito, reach to rub his head "like I was his boy." Phil grabbed Esposito's wrist and glared, then stalked out. His career in the system had just ended, and for a time he considered leaving New York altogether. Only after joining Saint Paul in 1988 did he dare risk ideals again.

What struck Phil most in Randy's litany was his plan to stop taking Navane and Cogentin. He had always noticed in Randy "the way he was there but he wasn't there," and whatever prescription drugs so deadened him seemed to Phil no better than the dope that had junkies nodding on the corners.

"Get rid of that crutch," he said as the evening concluded.

Randy hugged him.

"This isn't just something I'm sayin' today," Phil continued. "If you want me, I'm available."

Randy called him nearly every day, and they met often for lunch. The subject of drugs rarely emerged, but Randy had in fact acted on Phil's words. With the consent of his psychiatrist, he dropped from five milligrams daily of each medication to three and then two. He told nobody else, because whenever he grew emotional, even when he had been using the full dosage, others instantly accused him of not taking his medicine.

There were times when all the obstacles, all the unfulfilled dreams pushed Randy to the edge of a second collapse. If Rocky drove a Volvo, he wanted a Volvo. If Joe Dudley went to college, he wanted to go to college. Awake and alone on his night shift, Randy routinely called people at three or five in the morning, until even his friends complained he was a "pain in the ass." Some Tuesday evenings, Randy would sit in Eldad-Medad, listen and wait and stew, and then burst into testimony, voice coiling and spiraling, leaping in desperate haste from idea to idea, unable to wait one more second for all that life had denied him.

"Don't be too loud, Randy," Phil counseled one night, moving to his side. "Don't get nervous. We're here for you."

Then Rocky rose from his pew and said, "C'mon, men, let's pray for Randy."

Every crisis passed, and gradually, secretly, Randy stopped taking the drugs at all. He waited several months, then told both Phil and his psychiatrist. And to answer any skeptic, he had the doctor write a letter, confirming that "he has been doing well and remains in remission" and "shows good self-care." He placed the letter in his briefcase, alongside the lists he made to guide his new life:

Discipline

Keep in mind *discipline,* is practice Time & aloT oF hard work & *sacrifice.*

Consistency—No matter how hard iT may get joy comes in The morning.

Private devotion—Prayer Time, devotion, bible study Time, mediTaTion, Think positive good ThoughTs
   "Read good books"

The search for books, and the ability to read them, led Randy to Gloria Mendez. A stout woman given to hair bows and high-collar dresses, Gloria Mendez directed the Youngblood-Odom Skills Development Center at Saint Paul. Whether tutoring a child with homework or teaching a grandfather to read, she insisted on the level of commitment that sent her own children to Princeton and MIT. And Mrs. Mendez—there was no calling her anything else—laid down a line of demarcation, even for her peers. "You're not my friend," she would say. "You're my student."

Randy tested the boundary more than most. Sometimes he spent his whole hour telling Mrs. Mendez about his mother or Valerie. Sometimes he asked her help in writing Christmas cards or learning a song's words from the sheet music. Once he arrived with a bouquet for a young woman who volunteered at Youngblood-Odom, and Mrs. Mendez saw the wound in Randy's eyes when the object of his ardor stuck the flowers in a corner. It took weeks before Randy could speak about it, and Mrs. Mendez knew better than to ask.

Whatever the interruptions, Mrs. Mendez taught Randy, too. He arrived with skills that had slipped since high school to a second-grade standard, and over more than two years Mrs. Mendez raised them two notches. Together they would lean over workbooks about phonics and spelling and reading comprehension, Randy's glasses only inches from the page, Mrs. Mendez's feet lifting out of her shoes. He might read a condensed version of *Sleeping Beauty*, laboring over words like "invited" and "fairies" and "grumpy." She might nudge him through a lesson on "Cause and Effect Pronouns." They might disassemble the word "distinguishing" into syllables.

It was painstaking and incremental work, and Randy often lost patience. If he discovered his skills remained in the elementary-school range, he insisted the calculation was wrong. Damn it, he was going to college, to study psychology. He even left the program once, enrolled in a different basic-skills center. A few weeks later he returned, explaining, "Mrs. Mendez, that place isn't like here."

She could not judge him harshly. Perhaps Randy would never

reach college. Perhaps Randy would struggle for a high school equivalency diploma. Still, Mrs. Mendez had no doubt that Randy deserved more than the tattered education with which the school system had thrust him out into the world. Instead of working as a security guard, she thought, he could learn enough to become a supervisor. Or even something better.

So she opened a dictionary one day this fall and indicated a word and asked Randy to read.

"Entepeneur," he said.

"Entrepreneur," she corrected.

Then she pointed to the definition and had him read again: "A person who organizes a business or industrial undertaking."

"What's that mean?" Randy asked.

"Remember when you told me you wanted to open a shop?"

"A flower shop," Randy put in.

"That's the word for you, then," Mrs. Mendez explained. "That's what you want to be."

Randy poised a pencil against a sheet of blank paper, and slowly copied the word and its meaning. When he finished, he said, "Beautiful."

"This flower shop, Randy, is this another one of your dreams?"

He nodded and smiled, ear to ear.

"Keep on dreaming, Randy," said Mrs. Mendez. "Without dreams, you are dead."

At the edge of the warehouse district, where the asphalt gives way to the cattails, Randy Murphy stands in his security guard's booth, surrounded by the immensity of night. A space heater rests atop two empty milk crates. A radio plays a religious station's talk show. Occasionally, Randy will call.

Not much else, after all, interrupts these nocturnal hours. Once a week, at one o'clock on Friday, Randy opens the gate for the truck delivering paychecks. Every other week, a tractor-trailer drops a load of supplies. Otherwise all Randy sees are the drag racers and the crack whores, against whose manic outbursts he maintains Mace and a club.

Every hour from midnight to eight, Randy leaves the booth to inspect the perimeter of this phone company facility. He makes sure nobody has breached the razor-wire fence, tried to steal a repair truck or break into an office. He punches a clock called a Detex at several locations, just to prove he has made the inspection, and then he writes on a legal pad the hour and the words "all secure."

On this shift, he is studying for his driver's license exam. He is reading an article about Danny Glover, the actor. The article says he was born with a reading problem and once saw letters upside-down. Now he is a star. Randy sees the story as a parable. He has written a note for himself: "Take your time and think and focus on one thing at a time get to the point."

Randy has a date book and calendar in his briefcase. He has his voice lesson in Manhattan later today. He has an appointment to be fitted for contact lenses. After that, he will get a haircut for Sunday. This is payday, so he will also deposit twenty-five dollars in the bank toward his own apartment.

Past seven o'clock, the world starts to stir. Commuter buses move past Randy on their way into Manhattan. Garbage trucks lumber through their rounds. The sky above turns turquoise. Purple clouds hug the horizon. Beneath the fading stars, seagulls wheel in flight. Randy starts to pack his things. Even here in East New York, in a glass booth outside a brick building tucked between an auto junkyard and a swamp, there is nothing so gorgeous as daybreak, morning light.

11

◉

In Caesar's Household

I N A RED BRICK ROW HOUSE the living room lights burn. Company is expected, a party of twelve, and yet the usual signs of welcome cannot be found. No shade covers the bulbs. No rug brightens the floor. No curtains flutter in the windows, open to the twilight of an August evening. In a space large enough for a couch and stereo and china hutch sit a folding table and metal chairs, and on the wall behind them hangs the sole decoration. It is an unlikely adornment, a photograph of one city block, enlarged from a tiny negative to the size of a poster. In the background of the picture hunch several apartment houses, windows plugged with plywood and doors sealed with concrete. Before them stretches a field of scrub grass and saplings, as tall as Iowa corn. In the entire panorama, not one person appears.

The photograph was taken ten years earlier on Blake Avenue, only a quarter-mile away. It captures Brownsville and East New York in the years before this row house and two thousand like it, the Nehemiah homes, rose from an urban landscape so depleted that a visiting mayor once pronounced it "the beginning of the end of our civilization." The houses down the block and around the corner, those occupied by bus drivers and nurse's aides and the like, boast all the details of domesticity, patios and front gates and even satellite dishes. Only this one, the headquarters of East Brooklyn Congregations, remains in its original state, sturdy but barren, a reminder to those who will enter tonight that there can be no rest when there is work to be done.

That work amounts to nothing less than the revival of EBC, from recruiting and grooming a new generation of leaders to defining and winning a new set of battles. Approaching its tenth year, the group has fallen naturally enough into metaphors about a "wedding anniversary" and the "renewal of vows." Those phrases, in turn, have raised the question of what sort of marriage EBC will embody in its second decade, the static or the dynamic, the one that falls asleep watching television or the one that makes love on the kitchen table.

The evening's host, Dave Nelson, distributes a one-page agenda to each arriving guest. He is the lead organizer for EBC, they the members of its "strategy team." There is Vincent Hall, a postal supervisor who lives in one of the last two houses standing on his block. There is Father John Powis, a balding and bilingual priest with activist credentials back to the school decentralization crisis of 1968. There are, from Saint Paul, Reverend Douglas Slaughter and Reverend Johnny Ray Youngblood. Men and women, laity and clergy, immigrants and natives, Catholics and Protestants, whites and blacks and Hispanics, these dozen are bound by a history stronger than their differences. All learned the community organizing gospel of the late Saul Alinsky in the immersion program known simply as "ten-day training." And all put that gospel into action during EBC's first decade. Beginning with issues as elemental as missing street signs, they ultimately built the Nehemiah homes and won guarantees of college scholarships and entry-level jobs for graduates of Brooklyn's most troubled high schools. From personal obscurity and political impotence, they vaulted onto television's "20/20" and into the *Congressional Record*.

Then reality interrupted. The Nehemiah program, at least in Brooklyn, is stalled by the city's refusal to condemn land that is virtually unoccupied. Hundreds of the jobs and scholarships have gone unclaimed because so few students could fulfill the minimum requirements—a diploma and reliable attendance. Neither the election of a black mayor nor the selection of a Puerto Rican, Joseph Fernandez, as chancellor of the public school system has changed much here in farthest Brooklyn. Children are shot almost daily. Emergency rooms serve as family doctors by default. Reading scores sag. In such ways the people of Bushwick and Brownsville and East New York are told every day they are worthless, much as they were told in the early 1980s that their neighborhoods did not deserve clean new houses, that their neighborhoods were meant only to wither and die in a process euphemistically called "planned shrinkage."

The war, then, is the same war, if the fronts have changed. The limited success of the scholarship and jobs program, for instance, has convinced the EBC leaders that incentives alone will not improve the local high schools, Bushwick and Thomas Jefferson. The group now proposes opening an "enrichment academy" in collaboration with the City University of New York for the ninth graders who would otherwise enter Bushwick and Jefferson. Only by physically removing students from those schools, EBC has argued, can the culture of academic failure be broken. Chancellor Fernandez practically invited the plan by daring EBC in an early encounter to "see just how radical I can be." Lately, though, he has left the matter to assistants, who stall and stupefy EBC with memos about "liaisons" and "planning committees" and "shared decision making."

"Maybe we ought to send this back," Dave Nelson tells the strategy team. Arm extended, he holds the latest memo like a spoiled fish. Then he indicates the photograph on the wall. "We need to say to Fernandez that Bushwick and Jefferson are the educational equivalent of those lots." Now he turns, points through the rear window, into the yards of the Nehemiah homes, where laundry hangs and grapevines grow. "If you want to make the vacant lot look like those houses, we can talk."

Spurred by the amens around him, Nelson reads the draft of a letter to Fernandez. It ridicules the "boilerplate" responses from his staff. It reiterates the proposal for an "educational Nehemiah." And it invites the chancellor to resume "creative discussion"—provided he speak to EBC personally instead of through underlings, and that the meeting occur not in his own office but in a Nehemiah home.

Such is hardball of the Alinsky school. Protected by a favorable press and the powerful teachers' union, Fernandez is enjoying a political honeymoon in New York. His pet program, "school-based management," reigns as the educational panacea of the moment. He has successfully attacked and even unseated principals, superintendents, and community school board members. He has muted several of the fiercest critics of New York's school bureaucracy by appointing them to it. Yet EBC is demanding that Fernandez compromise, that *he* come to *them*.

"Is it too much?" Nelson asks the strategy team, conducting one final check. "Is it okay to send that letter?"

"He knows we can gab," Reverend Youngblood says. "Now he'll find out we can jab."

Nelson proceeds to the next item on the agenda, community policing, asking Reverend Youngblood to brief the others. His story is one of unfulfilled expectations. When Lee Brown served as police commissioner in Houston, he collaborated closely with the Metropolitan Organization—like EBC an affiliate of the Industrial Areas Foundation—on a plan for community policing. The success of that plan, in fact, largely led to Brown's being chosen as commissioner in New York. Expecting Brown to be an ally, EBC flew Reverend Youngblood to Houston to meet with him, and the pastor returned impressed. So EBC approached Brown with a plan for community policing in several areas of East Brooklyn, a plan designed to provide residents with the public safety they desired without the adversarial posture that incidents like the Steve Kelly shooting had taught them to fear. Under the proposal, the police department would provide more officers and move them out of patrol cars onto the streets; EBC, in turn, would broker the relationship between officers and residents, arranging meetings and rewarding good work. Then, surprisingly, Brown refused, propounding instead a plan of his own, which used the same title without the comparable detail or personnel.

Now, as with Fernandez, the time has arrived for a private showdown. Should such pressure prove futile, a public confrontation will follow. Reverend Youngblood explains how he recently invited Brown to worship at Saint Paul. During the ceremony, the pastor oozed hospitality. But afterward, in his study, he delivered a blunt assessment. "People are starting to see you in a reactionary posture," he told the commissioner. "When there's a crisis, you're there. But you haven't been initiating anything." Then he handed Brown a personal letter, a copy of which he now reads to the strategy team. It castigates the commissioner for being "passive," assails his "inaction," and closes by saying, "My disappointment in you is profound."

Applause and hoots fill the air.

"Oh, you think that was fierce?" Nelson says. "You should've seen the first draft."

"I have to smile," Vincent Hall says. "That was a right-on letter. We oughta fry his butt. He came here with high plans, and he did nothing. Same with Dinkins. If we don't start now, in three years we'll be fighting the same battles, only bigger. We gotta get up in his face."

"We've put hope in them because they're black," adds Ingrid Moore, a middle manager for the telephone company, here representing a Catholic church in East Flatbush. "We've almost held them up to be gods. But they haven't done what they said."

Her words make Reverend Youngblood wince. Even reading the letter aloud, he had sounded subdued, almost pained.

"I get a lot of phone calls from newspapers for my opinion on Dinkins and Brown," he says. "And I've held back. Because we, EBC, haven't made up our minds on them. And because their blackness affects me." Mutterings of agreement come from several listeners. "We waited years before we started confronting Koch. And we should give them time." He pauses, again torn by the tug-of-war between racial solidarity and personal experience. "But they have *not* been responsive. And that's an affront."

Nelson leans forward on the table. His broad shoulders, barrel chest, and shag haircut bring to mind a flamboyant football star like Mark Gastineau more than the Middlebury-educated Lutheran minister he actually is.

"The last thing we said to Lee Brown was 'Negotiation is over,'" he reminds the strategy team. "He hasn't given us anything. We said we would polarize if we couldn't negotiate. I think we should stick to our word."

Tomorrow night the Nehemiah Homeowners Association is scheduled to meet with the police commander for this section of Brooklyn. The members will be instructed to ask him only one question: When will we have community policing? If the strategy does not bring results, EBC may release Reverend Youngblood's letter to the press. A major black minister attacking a black police commissioner—that's good copy.

By now, an hour into the meeting, only one matter remains. The line item calls it "Local Issues Campaign." As every veteran around the table knows, those words mean starting all over again, doing what they did ten years ago, organizing the unorganized, discovering what galls them, forging anger into activism.

"We need some fights," Nelson says. "We're like a sluggish heavy-weight. Remember when Tyson was good? When he was fighting every month. We need some victories, on the local level, things we can win in ninety, a hundred days. Action is oxygen."

"I like that 'oxygen,'" Reverend Youngblood says. Then, turning to Reverend Slaughter, he adds, "I swear he's a Baptist."

Nelson, hearing the compliment, grins briefly, then continues. An EBC meeting abides by its timetable, and this one must conclude before nine o'clock, only fifteen minutes away. Within a month, Nelson says, EBC will hold a rally for its 125 most proven members, its "action team." The object will be to launch formally the next decade of organizing.

"Start working," he tells Reverend Youngblood, "on the keynote address."

For two days, as rain fell without cease, Mike Gecan stared out the windows of a Brownsville church at the most staggering expanse of rubble he had seen in his life. It was late March 1980, and he had come to Brooklyn at the behest of thirty ghetto churchmen of various races and denominations, all seeking the organizing genius of the Industrial Areas Foundation, Gecan's employer. Slums did not shock him; he had worked in plenty, from Chicago's Lawndale to East Baltimore. Still, gazing across Stone Avenue at the loose bricks and charred beams and shattered cornices, he could summon only images of wartime, shelling, evacuation.

Yet somehow people lived in Brownsville, ruled by a government as distant as any imperial regime, plagued by guerrilla attacks from muggers, junkies, and thieves. Nowhere had Gecan seen doors with more locks. "Our church doesn't meet at night," one woman told him, knowing no explanation was required. Driving to a meeting with the residents of one block in East New York, Gecan found watchmen patrolling each corner. When he asked the hostess why, she replied, "Everybody's here. And if everybody's here, then nobody's home to guard our houses."

Only the strange chemistry of desperation and undying hope

could have brought IAF to Brooklyn at all. For twenty years the borough's poorest neighborhoods had served as test sites for philosophy after philosophy, program after program, from Model Cities to Operation Breadbasket, from the Office of Economic Opportunity to the Comprehensive Employment and Training Act. And after the experiments in white largesse and black empowerment had expired—a few, it was true, leaving pockets of renewal—the larger deprivation remained. So a few local priests and ministers and pastors reached back in time, back forty years, to the teachings of Saul Alinsky.

Until his death in 1972, Alinsky had swaggered through public life as an American original, educated in sociology at the University of Chicago, tutored in street life by a Capone mob enforcer, descended in spirit from such radical patriots as Tom Paine and John Brown. He aspired to "restore the democratic way of life" by creating an active citizenry, assembled into "People's Organizations." The first and most famous of these, born in 1939, was the Back of the Yards Neighborhood Council, based in the immigrant quarter beside Chicago's slaughterhouses. Alinsky united the community's famously fractious bands of Poles, Slovaks, Bohemians, and Lithuanians by bending their anger against a common enemy in the meat-packing industry and toward such practical goals as recreation, disease control, and collective bargaining. And by involving partners ranging from labor unionists to Catholic priests, Alinsky dressed dissident ideas in Main Street clothes.

The nation took note. Seven years later, Alinsky's political manual, *Reveille for Radicals,* became a bestseller. A new generation of People's Organizations formed in the burgeoning black ghettos, rising against opponents as powerful as Kodak and the University of Chicago. Through the Industrial Areas Foundation, which he had founded in 1940, Alinsky trained such protégés as Nicholas von Hoffman, later to become famous as a journalist, and Cesar Chavez, who would ultimately lead the United Farm Workers.

In theory or practice, the alpha and omega of Alinskyism stayed simple. Organize around the genuine institutions of a neighborhood. Find "specific, immediate, and realizable" issues. Then win the battles over them with "the constructive use of power," in the form of people, money, and actions. Not only can the poor beat City Hall, Alinsky maintained, they can "have a ball doing it." His groups picketed slumlords at their suburban homes and dumped uncollected garbage on the doorsteps of lazy ward bosses; in one confrontation with Chicago Mayor Richard J. Daley, Alinsky threatened to tie up every toilet in O'Hare Airport with a "shit-in." "Someone once asked me whether I believe in reconciliation," Alinsky observed at one point. "Sure I do. When our side gets the power and the other side gets reconciled to it."

As the 1960s arrived, however, Alinsky discovered the limits of permitting his "people's organizations" to be governed by local mores as much as by moral precepts. The Back of the Yards Neighborhood Council, once a progressive force, fiercely opposed integration. The Woodlawn Organization, based in a black district on Chicago's South Side, collaborated with street gangs to the point of storing their guns in a member church. In the national arena, too, Alinsky's influence waned. The New Left embraced his style of political theater but ignored his attention to pragmatism; the Civil Rights Movement paralleled his brand of grassroots organizing but depended almost wholly on a single charismatic leader, whose assassination crippled the crusade. Alinsky grew so despondent that he wrote shortly before his death, "The world as it stands is ... no evil dream of the night; we wake up in it again forever and ever."

It fell to Ed Chambers, the founder's heir, to revive the Industrial Areas Foundation. Through the 1970s he extended IAF into Texas, Maryland, and California, raising salaries for organizers to a middle-class level. Most important, he aligned the local groups almost exclusively with churches and synagogues, the sources of both moral values and stable members. The key publication of the reborn IAF was entitled *Organizing for Family and Congregation*.

One of Chambers's tendrils reached New York, where the Queens Citizens Organization was founded in 1977. Although the group claimed 47,000 families as constituents, it was, in fact, on the verge of disbanding by early 1978. Only a thousand members showed up for a meeting with Mayor Edward I. Koch in a parochial school auditorium the evening of February 27. And then everything changed. In office for less than two months, Mayor Koch had already become a municipal hero for his energetic, combative style; white ethnics, especially, revered him for "standing up" to black protesters. So when the mayor asked for two minutes to address QCO—an organization at that time rooted in mostly white, politically moderate Catholic parishes—he could hardly have anticipated the reaction. Stick to *our* agenda, he was told. Refusing, he was offered one minute. "I'm not here under sub-poena," Mayor Koch proclaimed, and he marched out to a round of boos. Days later, still seething, he compared the meeting to "the way it was when Stalin tried the Jewish doctors."

By the time the mayor retracted the allegation of anti-Semitism and granted QCO leaders a private audience, it was too late. His temper had transformed a ragtag militia into a fearsome army. Television newscasts feasted on the controversy. *The New York Times* devoted almost ten articles to the legacy of Alinsky in Queens, two appearing on the front page of the Metropolitan section and one in the prestigious "About New York" column, beneath the headline "Thumbs Down on the Emperor."

Among those who read and watched admiringly was a Lutheran pastor in Brownsville named John Heinemeier. A few years earlier, when he was based elsewhere in Brooklyn, Reverend Heinemeier had taken several days of IAF training. He knew a Lutheran minister and a Roman Catholic monsignor who were involved in QCO, and considered the group "a good demonstration of churches using their power." Lacking much in the way of alternatives, he had been thinking of inviting IAF to Brownsville. The way QCO had defied the mayor only confirmed his instincts.

Reverend Heinemeier gathered about fifteen clerics and church members for a meeting on April 6, 1978. At a subsequent session, they heard from QCO leaders. And then, on June 8, 1978, Ed Chambers blew into their lives. Their neighborhood, he declared, was "a bunch of rubble," "a garbage heap." This barely qualified as a unique insight, especially to Reverend David Benke, the pastor of Saint Peter's Lutheran Church. He had driven to the meeting straight from a hospital, where he had visited a parishioner who had been tied up, robbed, raped, and set afire in her apartment by two intruders. "On that night," Reverend Benke would later recall, "I didn't need Chambers to talk about garbage."

Chambers talked with equal bluntness about money. He would not bother with the nascent group until it accumulated $300,000 in assets, 150 leaders, and thirty member churches, each paying dues of five hundred to three thousand dollars per year. As an incentive, though, Chambers culled $45,000 in seed money from the United

Church of Christ's Board of Homeland Ministries. And on January 15, 1979, seven congregations officially formed East Brooklyn Churches.* Six more joined by year's end. Thirteen people attended ten-day training in Baltimore, another eighty-five went through a twelve-hour version in Brooklyn. It was clear that EBC would be able to meet Chambers's challenge. It was clear, too, that EBC already had a problem. For an organization created to uplift black and Hispanic slums, its leaders were overwhelmingly whites.

One of the few black pastors involved, Reverend Clarence Williams of the Southern Baptist Church, knew Reverend Youngblood from preaching circles, and in early 1979 visited him on a mission of persuasion. He failed. To Reverend Youngblood, the mere mention of "community" conjured a decade's worth of bad memories. From college and seminary through Bethany Baptist, he had seen scores of committees and coalitions and task forces created under the rubric "community," and few had produced more than a certificate of incorporation and some newspaper clippings. At best, such groups arose in reaction to events they were too late to influence. *Ambulance chasers,* the pastor thought them, *ambulance chasers.* And, Reverend Williams's presence aside, there was the matter of race. The 1960s and 1970s had left Reverend Youngblood suspicious of any program for blacks led by whites. Whites were never angry enough to fight the system, never genuine enough to work as equals, never brave enough to hold blacks accountable.

Still, Reverend Williams persisted. More out of clerical courtesy than actual interest, Reverend Youngblood agreed to delay his final decision. But the next salesman for EBC looked even more unlikely.

Perhaps because Father Leo Penta was only twenty-six, newly ordained, a scholar by training and temperament, he was just too green to realize his cause was hopeless. Even his superiors seemed to doubt Father Penta's grasp of the real world; they had assigned him to Saint Malachy's parish in East New York "to see if I could stick," as he would later recall. From Catholic University and the University of Innsbruck, from studies of Hannah Arendt and Johann-Baptist Metz, he plunged into a neighborhood where worshipers got mugged on the church steps, where gang beatings and drug deals greeted the faithful

---

* The name was amended to East Brooklyn Congregations in 1988, when a synagogue joined.

after mass. Father Penta joined EBC because it seemed the only vehicle for enacting all he had learned about piety and political engagement. And when a black parishioner told him, "There's this pastor, Reverend Youngblood, he's somebody we have to get," the young priest spent months angling for an appointment.

Finally consenting, Reverend Youngblood promised himself to make the meeting both brief and decisive.

"Where were you in the sixties?" he asked his short, bearded guest. It was a question in the grand tradition of blacks "woofing" whites, a question that assumed guilt just as surely as, "Still beating your wife?" Leaning back in his chair, the pastor waited for the priest to stammer, blush, and slink away.

"Personally, I was in high school in the sixties," Father Penta answered. "But I'm here now. And we have to deal with now."

Naïveté had saved Leo Penta. It had never occurred to him he should have been involved in the Civil Rights Movement, that he should apologize now for his absence then. He just answered the question literally. And his ingenuous honesty left Reverend Youngblood disarmed.

They talked a bit longer, the pastor and the priest, and they arranged another meeting. Reverend Youngblood began to appreciate a certain tenacity in Father Penta, an absorbent quality to his gaze. He still resisted joining EBC, but when the priest asked for Saint Paul's best lay people to attend ten-day training, Reverend Youngblood sent Sarah Plowden and Icie Johnson. They returned to Saint Paul afire, even Sarah with her guarded nature.

"It's gonna happen, Pastor," she said of EBC. "I've been in Brownsville a long time, and somethin's gonna happen."

"And it ought not happen," Icie added, "without us."

So in July 1980 Reverend Youngblood journeyed to suburban Chicago to learn the ways of Saul Alinsky. The spirit of ten-day training reminded him of a dormitory bull session, with all the talk about righting wrongs, changing the world. The difference was that the IAF people seemed capable, in street parlance, of talking that talk *and* walking that walk.

In one session, a leader sketched on a blackboard two columns, one headed "World as it is" and the other "World as it should be." Then he elicited from the trainees the attributes of each. Finally he explained, in concrete ways, how IAF was moving the actual toward the ideal. Reverend Youngblood heard how an IAF group in Chicago had uncovered both a drug-dealing ring outside a Catholic school and the corrupt police who tolerated it; he heard how an affiliate in San Antonio had brought the first storm drains to a Chicano neighborhood where children routinely drowned during floods.

Two teachings especially appealed to the pastor. The first was IAF's "iron rule": "Never do for others what they can do for themselves. *Never.*" Those words allayed his fear that EBC would be just another exercise in missionaries saving savages. Second, IAF taught that anger was not only acceptable, but a useful basis for organizing. The word *anger,* he learned, derives from the Norse word *angr,* meaning grief—grief, as IAF literature put it, "for all the opportunities lost and to be lost, for all the careers stunted and shortened, for all the hopes and dreams denied." Finally, Reverend Youngblood realized, he had found some white folk who weren't always asking blacks, "Why are you so angry?"

What the pastor harbored was more than any black man's rage at racism and poverty and "the system." His was a moral contempt rooted in Scripture. When he quoted Paul inveighing "against principalities, against powers, against the rulers of the darkness of this world, against spiritual wickedness in high places," he meant City Hall, the State Capitol, the White House. And when a member of Saint Paul worked for a public agency, as many did, Reverend Youngblood dubbed that person "a saint in Caesar's household."

During those ten days outside Chicago, though, the observation went two ways. As Reverend Youngblood took the measure of IAF, Mike Gecan was doing the same of Reverend Youngblood. He admired the self-sufficiency of black Baptist churches, but he also worried about the capacity of their pastors, each a bishop under his own roof, to share power, especially across lines of religion and race. Gecan saw in Reverend Youngblood a rare combination of leadership and fellowship, an ease with the white Catholics and Lutherans around him. Not long after IAF training ended, in the late summer of 1980, the two men spoke at length. Several Sundays later, at the pastor's invitation, Gecan worshiped at Saint Paul for the first time.

"You may have noticed the presence of one of our white brothers," Reverend Youngblood announced from the pulpit. Every eye searched out Gecan, a ruddy man in glasses, with a distance runner's build. "I need y'all to know he's not a bill collector." The congregation roared. "This is Mike Gecan. You need to get used to him. He'll be around a lot."

Gecan felt relief at the punctured tension, and as the service proceeded he felt something more, a kind of instant respect. In the hundreds of times he had attended black churches, rarely had he heard a sermon so intelligent, energetic, and witty, or seen a preacher project such personal rapport across a huge congregation. "Did you have a good time?" people asked Gecan as the service ended. "Come again. Bring your family." Their kindness, he realized, was more than a gimmick. It was a culture.

In his succeeding visits, Gecan took more than goodwill away from Saint Paul. Impressed by its tithing system, he engaged Sarah Plowden and Icie Johnson to teach it to EBC members from other churches. Even a few Catholic congregations, accustomed to living on dispensations from the diocese, began supporting themselves. Gecan also listened to a particularly stirring sermon that fall, one with consequences to come. Reverend Youngblood had lately been inspired by Howard Thurman's account of visiting Mohandas Gandhi. It was during the campaign to free India from British rule, yet Gandhi, leader of the independence movement, had withdrawn to a retreat, and Thurman could not fathom why. The reason was not fear, Gandhi told his visitor; the reason was self-esteem, or its absence. Until the Indians turned inside themselves, repaired their own souls, realized they were *worthy* of liberation, they could not win it. To Reverend Youngblood, sitting amid the ruins of East Brooklyn, the message rose off the page: To rebuild oneself was to rebuild the community, and to rebuild the community was to rebuild oneself. The text he selected, the text Gecan heard him preach, was the Book of Nehemiah.

Fall blustered into Brooklyn this afternoon, five days early, and by now, an hour past sunset, the winds have wiped the streets nearly clean. Sometimes a child scrambles past, collar upturned, shivering. Rap music drifts, disembodied, from the deeper reaches of a park. Two separate sirens pierce the air like drill bits. But, for once, most of the noctural action unfolds indoors, in this case within the gymnasium of Our Lady of Good Counsel Church in Ocean Hill, where the EBC action team is assembling.

Beneath basketball hoops and crepe-paper streamers they gather, 135 in all, nuns in habits, men still in work shoes, women with berets pulled over chilled ears. The aura is of parents' night at the parish school. In the Saint Paul contingent, Butch Carr kids Mavora Spruill about her birthday. No presents, he says, until she reveals her age.

"Forty-seven," she says without hesitation. "Now what do I get?"

"You get what you done got," Butch replies. "Forty-seven years of work."

The meeting begins, as always, punctually and with a prayer. A representative from each congregation next announces its presence and numbers, as a nun translates the words into Spanish, the favored language for more than half of EBC's members. Then a series of speakers briskly detail EBC's ongoing campaigns—the enrichment academy; a parental audit of Bushwick schools; training for potential City Council candidates; a proposal for several hospitals elsewhere in Brooklyn to open a primary-care clinic in East New York—and in the audience pens dutifully make notes.

The last spokesman is Leroy Howard, a man transformed by EBC. He had grown up in South Carolina, quick with curses and fists, but when he moved to New York at eighteen, he adopted reserve as a survival technique. Keeping quiet kept him out of trouble with the gangs he feared; and, he later realized, it opened professional doors sealed to more assertive blacks. After enough years, though, the persona consumed the person. "To think people would listen to me was unbelievable," Leroy put it, "because I thought I was a nobody." Even as Reverend Youngblood relied on Leroy's talents as church administrator, he unknowingly intimidated him with college degrees and confident oratory. Only with ten-day training in 1983 was the latent force in Leroy mined and minted into an organizer's instrument. Thrust into public speaking, he discovered, to his amazement, that people actually listened.

Tonight, explaining the impasse between EBC and Commissioner Brown on community policing, he stokes the crowd with practiced passion. But he is more than merely performing. Having seen the merchants' association rise and collapse, having witnessed the mayor's feeble appearance at the Seventy-fifth Precinct, having heard the police brass offer excuses for the crime on Stanley Avenue— remember Zito, the beat patrolman nobody had ever seen on his beat?—Leroy knows the feeling of disgust. He knows, too, the necessity of change.

After reiterating EBC's proposal for community policing, he says softly, "I don't need to tell you what the answer was." And then, playing tension and release, he booms, "NO!" The floor fairly quakes.

"I think the time has come," he continues, "to go public, to turn up the heat."

"Turn it up," shouts a woman in the third row.

"I'm tired of seeing our children killed on the street," declares Leroy, the father of two. "I'm tired of more innocent people being shot." Then, again, he winds down the volume. "But I need to know what you think."

"Turn it up!" comes the answer, in a husky chorus. "Do it! Keep the pressure on!"

As the applause eddies and swirls, Leroy surrenders the podium to Reverend Youngblood, who has flown back from a preaching assignment in Buffalo to deliver the keynote address. The text is outlined on six sheets from a legal pad; the subtext, though, appeared earlier this week in *Time* magazine. "The Rotting of the Big Apple," read the cover headline, spread across an illustration of stabbings, muggings, and pornographic bookstores. The article inside centered on a recent poll of New Yorkers, in which nearly sixty percent said that, given the choice, they would rather move away than remain. At once capturing and reinforcing the city's shaken psyche, *Time* has dominated conversation from talk show to dinner table for days.

It is no surprise that EBC's rejoinder will come from Reverend Youngblood. In a decade with the group, the pastor has emerged as its most striking speaker, capable of putting across a political message with preacherly charisma. He stands now with hands locked at the waist, eyes on his notes, barely stirring.

"Ten years ago," he says simply, "many of us did not know each other's names. Then years ago, our communities were valleys of despair, and we stood on the brink of a bankrupt faith."

Five or six more times, he invokes the same phrase, "ten years ago," evoking the East Brooklyn of 1980 with its unmarked streets and vacant lots and distance from both power and hope. "Ten years later," he then says, "here we are." He paints the religious and racial spectrum of EBC, and then he intones the names to prove it, moving

from Margaret Smyth to Elda Peralta to Kofi Hormeku as assuredly as
in childhood he had delivered from memory verse after verse of biblical "begats." "We're all in this thing together," he says, voice rising,
and he asks each listener to turn to a neighbor and repeat the words.
In this room of linoleum and cinder blocks and plywood, voices renew
EBC's wedding vows.

"And you know how it is when you get married," Reverend
Youngblood says, leaving some open air for laughter. "Somebody's
always betting. 'They ain't gonna make it.' Or 'You crazy to stay
together.' They sayin' the same thing about New York now. 'Ain't
gonna make it.' 'Gotta be crazy to stay.' There are some mandates
loose out there. Thou shalt run. Thou shalt move. Thou shalt buy
more alarms. Thou shalt put wrought-iron gates over your windows.
Thou shalt buy a gun. Thou shalt change schools. Thou shalt change
cities."

The room buzzes. Reverend Youngblood stops, lets out the slack
of silence. Quieting now, people lean forward in their chairs, as if to
snatch his next sound.

"I've come tonight from my own Mount Sinai," he says, "and I
say we have another mandate before us. The mandate is EBC. The
mandate is IAF. The mandate is, Thou shalt organize. Thou shalt
organize, disorganize, and reorganize."

He repeats the phrase two, three, four times, like a gospel singer
spiraling into ever greater rapture. The crowd answers, burying his
voice under its own.

"If you believe the city is worth saving," he shouts above the din,
"say amen."

"*Amen!*"

"If you believe the city can be saved, say amen."

"*Amen!*"

"If you believe we are the saviors of the city, say amen."

"*Amen!*"

"Remember," he says, drawing on Woody Guthrie and Abraham
Lincoln, appealing to the populist patriotism that was essential to Alinsky, too. "This land is our land. This city is our city. Of the people. For
the people. By the people." Then, at the last, he utters the words of
Thomas Jefferson, extending them to listeners the Founding Fathers
would have enslaved. "We the people."

* * *

On January 24, 1981, nearly two years after its founding, East Brooklyn Churches broke cover in a deliberately grand manner. Putting aside its emphasis on organizing by home and block and congregation, the obscure group dispatched a delegation of twenty ministers to meet with Brooklyn Borough President Howard Golden. There was no agenda for the session, but there was most certainly a goal, one less practical than psychological.

In his months with EBC, Mike Gecan had noticed the deference, even awe, that its leaders afforded politicians they knew to be hacks. Reverend Heinemeier, for instance, had pleaded with Gecan to invite some public official to an early EBC assembly "or we won't get a turnout." Gecan refused, and the event drew a standing-room crowd. "*You're* the legitimate leaders," he insisted in an evaluation after the rally. "You don't need celebrities. You don't need crutches. You don't need shortcuts. People follow *you*, not some star."

But only through experience, Gecan felt, would the EBC leaders ever understand. And until they understood, they could not act. So twenty of them settled around three sides of a conference table that afternoon, leaving the remaining edge to Golden and Edolphus Towns, a loyal member of the political organization then serving as deputy borough president and ultimately to represent East Brooklyn in Congress.

"What is your vision for Brooklyn?" Reverend Youngblood asked.

Golden appeared confused.

"Vision?" he asked. "What do you mean, vision?"

"Vision," Reverend Youngblood repeated. "How do you see the future of Brooklyn?"

Golden turned to Towns, his racial interpreter.

"What is this? Vision? Is this some religious thing?"

Towns had no answers, so Golden again faced Reverend Youngblood.

"We have plans for the waterfront," the borough president offered.

"We don't live on the waterfront," Reverend Youngblood cut in. "What's your vision for *us*?"

"You want to talk about services?" Golden said, reverting to a ward heeler's reflexes. "You want some garbage cans?"

"No," Reverend Youngblood said firmly. "We want to know what your vision is. Because we're going to be here for a long time."

Golden's patience expired. "I don't have a vision," he snapped.

"Then thank you very much for coming today," said Reverend Clarence Williams.

"That's it?" Golden asked.

"Yes."

Still baffled, Golden remained seated. So all twenty ministers stood up to leave. Only then did the borough president storm toward the door. He would later describe the encounter as "the worst meeting in the history of Brooklyn."

Much as Mayor Koch's pique had vested the Queens Citizens Organization with power, so Howard Golden's exasperated exit convinced EBC to have confidence in itself. Gecan put that confidence to work immediately. Several EBC members resigned from the community boards controlled by Golden. Under the tutelage of a second organizer, a black veteran of the United Farm Workers named Stephen Roberson, EBC embarked on a drive of one hundred "house meetings." In each one, an EBC leader would ask a roomful of residents their major concerns about life in East Brooklyn. What sounded like disparate bitching sessions amounted, in fact, to a reckoning of local issues, issues EBC hoped it could address and win. Crime topped the list, with housing second, and both struck the EBC leaders as too massive, too amorphous to confront. But the third issue, involving local markets and groceries, had potential. It offered specific and reparable grievances—short-weighting, overpricing, spoiled goods, abusive managers. It touched the lives of almost every family in East Brooklyn. And it supplied visible villains, from Arab to Hispanic to Jewish to African-American, a rainbow coalition of rogues.

From an initial list of eighteen "problem stores," an EBC team identified the ten worst offenders. For an extra measure of fairness, EBC arranged for the director of a grocers' trade association to make unannounced, incognito visits to the East Brooklyn stores; he pronounced them "intolerable by both industry and public standards." Father Penta and several parishioners meanwhile wrote an inspection survey form and studied the agencies charged with regulating food stores, gauging whether they could be pressured into a more active role. Finding the system toothless at best and corrupt at worst, EBC chose to step outside it. Father Penta, no longer a virgin to the brutal ways of Brooklyn, designed a campaign of public humiliation.

On several Saturdays in the late spring of 1981, in the prime marketing hours of early afternoon, scores of churchgoers descended on the ten stores armed with clipboards and survey forms; each wore a badge identifying himself or herself as an "EBC Shopper Inspector." Trawling the aisles, every one filled a shopping cart with sour milk, moldy fruit, rusty cans. Other customers gleefully served as their Sherpas, pointing out rat droppings behind refrigerators, week-old meat on shelves, heads of wilted lettuce.

"What're you getting *that* for?" one manager asked, looking at the curious cornucopia moving down the checkout line. "Let me get you something good."

"Oh, no," the inspector replied. "This is what we want."

In another store, the owner threatened to call the police.

"Don't worry," the inspector answered. "We already did."

Before leaving each store, an EBC inspector presented the owner with a list of violations and a contract to correct them. For those who declined to sign, the unspoken threat of a boycott loomed, although EBC was less interested in protracted struggle than instant victory. Seven owners rapidly agreed, with one ultimately installing thirty thousand dollars' worth of new refrigeration equipment. Three resisted, and kept resisting, until the July night they were summoned to Saint Paul. Thinking, perhaps, they would be facing just a handful of blowhards, the owners consented to appear.

Instead, four hundred people packed a recreation room beneath the sanctuary, lining the walls and spilling into the hallway. Father Penta, standing at the podium, recounted for them EBC's dealings with the three stores. Then he asked the owners to step forward. Halfway up the aisle, they found themselves surrounded. The crowd held a trained silence, more unsettling than any verbal abuse. Shakily, the owners reached a table before the podium.

"You're the only three in this community who refuse," Father Penta said. "Refuse to do not exceptional things, but decent things, normal things."

A woman, by design, rose and strode to the microphone.

"I move these managers be put on probation in the community," she announced. "All in favor, stand."

Seconds later, the only three sitting were the owners.

Then Father Penta dictated the terms of surrender. Within two weeks each owner would rectify his store's problems. Or else EBC would pursue all legal means to close it.

"And now," the priest said, as if addressing three naughty schoolboys, "you are dismissed."

They withdrew, all to sign the agreement by the deadline, and a collective sigh filled the room. Those petty tyrants, who poked into women's handbags on the pretext of stopping theft, who slapped surcharges on checks, who jacked prices up so high people rode the bus to Canarsie just to shop—they had been sent packing. Then the laughter began. In a black pastor's church, a white priest had shown his solidarity. And a congregation of the powerless, of what Howard Thurman would have called the disinherited, had discovered it was no longer bereft.

From food stores they turned to other finite, visible, and winnable issues, wringing response from a bureaucracy accustomed to repose. Under EBC pressure, local officials installed three thousand missing street signs, completed the long-overdue renovation of a park and swimming pool, and demolished three hundred vacant and irreparable buildings, shells suitable only for drug deals and sexual assaults. And when the blocks across Stone Avenue from Our Lady of Mercy Church had been cleared, somebody floated an idea at a strategy team meeting: Why not build a new Brownsville atop the ruins of the old?

A splinter of moon hangs above Hendrix Street. Metal gates guard the stores of Christ Square. Mothers peer out windows from the projects, worrying their children home. By now, the third week of November, the sky darkens well before dinner, and only the foolish or felonious or brave dare venture out until dawn. Two of this last group, Reverend Youngblood and Glinnie Chamble, hesitate at the corner of Stanley Avenue.

"We ain't gonna cross that park, Pastor," says Glinnie, a Saint Paul member especially active in EBC. She indicates the lot between them and their goal, a high-rise in the Linden Houses. There they will hold a "house meeting," the same sort that led to the grocery store action, as part of EBC's tenth-anniversary campaign.

"Why not?"

"Because it's dark," Glinnie answers, "and you always tellin' me I look near white. And you wearin' that crazy hat."

Reverend Youngblood removes the baseball cap, embroidered with the insignia of Ohio Wesleyan University, cups it in both hands like a furry pet.

"That's from Benny Rutherford," he says, referring to a member in his freshman year at the school. "I'm gonna have these from all the kids in college. Cover my wall."

Taking her arm, he guides Glinnie across the street, and follows the longer route along the sidewalk that borders the lot. Broken glass sparkles beneath street lamps. Garbage bags lie split open like overripe melons, having been searched for deposit bottles and edible scraps. A Chevy Vega slumps in a parking space, shorn of tires and doors.

"How's Jaral?" Reverend Youngblood asks about Glinnie's son, a freshman at a small college upstate.

"Supposed to be comin' home tonight," Glinnie says, and her eyes moisten. "Don't know if he can go back."

"The work?"

"The money."

"Lady," Reverend Youngblood says as they move briskly down Van Siclen, "if he takes care of the work, I think we can deal with the money."

They near the corner of Wortman, cut diagonally into the building. Two tenants, bundled in winter coats, patrol the lobby, its windows shattered and locks gouged loose. One elevator is broken. The other, into which the pastor and Glinnie step, smells of the ceaseless battle between urine and ammonia. At their floor, the wall is scrawled with the word "SPIT."

Down the hall, though, a door opens on an apartment as wholesome as the building is wretched. Reverend Youngblood and Glinnie trail their hostess, Rebecca Walsh, through a kitchen perfumed with cinnamon and sweet potato and into the living room, where ten women await. There are a seamstress, a domestic, a hospital attendant, a retired factory worker, all gathered around a coffee table set with fresh flowers. Lace curtains grace the windows, and plastic sheets protect the sofa and chairs. Glinnie sits near the corn plants and aquarium, Reverend Youngblood across the room, beside the graduation photos.

"We thank you," Glinnie says, "for giving us this opportunity to meet with you. We don't want to give you the idea it's a complaint session, but we want your ideas. Of how the neighborhood used to be when you moved in. And what can make it better now."

"We're interested," Reverend Youngblood adds, "in results."

By way of proof, he recounts the history of EBC and the Nehemiah homes. He talks about the current campaign. All over EBC's territory, in fact, the two months since the "action team" meeting have seen great bustle and ferment. Members have held several hundred house meetings. Twenty congregations have identified winnable local issues: a dangerous corner that needs a traffic light, a vacant building that can be turned into a community center, a tobacco store, actually a front for drug deals, that should be shut down.

At a higher level, too, the pace has quickened. Building its pressure on Lee Brown, EBC fed a compliant *Newsday* reporter a story assailing the commissioner for inaction on community policing. The article, which covered nearly a full page, prominently featured a quote from Reverend Youngblood: "We give Commissioner Brown an A-plus in rhetoric and an F in reality." Of five local hospitals EBC has approached about opening a primary-care facility in East Brooklyn, Saint Mary's has emerged as the likeliest partner. In the Alinsky tradition of "relational politics," a priest who serves on both EBC's "action team" and the hospital's governing board has been playing matchmaker. Chancellor Fernandez, meanwhile, recently met with EBC leaders in a Nehemiah home, as commanded, and officially approved the enrichment academy plan. Not that he was happy with EBC for returning his aide's "boilerplate" memo. But because the group's members last year had produced four thousand letters supporting three of Fernandez's controversial reforms, he quite simply owed them.

And such political arithmetic derives, firstly and finally, from meetings like this one.

"Miss Maybelle," Reverend Youngblood asks a graying woman who wears a winter jacket atop her house dress, "how many years you been in this community?"

"Twenty-one," she says.

Quickly the pastor polls the remaining women. None has lived in

East New York for less than thirteen years, long enough to make safety and cleanliness feel like vague memories. Then he returns to Miss Maybelle, asking simply, "What's on your mind?"

"Drugs," she says. "In the building."

"You see the crack caps in the staircase," says a woman named Dolores McCowan.

"And every night," puts in another, Helen Griggs, "you hear pop-pop-pop. You're scared to go outside. I say, 'Lord, I'm in Your hands.'"

"Ain't that the truth," someone adds.

"About two, three months ago," Griggs continues, "I saw two folks shot right down on the benches." She rises, walks to the windows, and points.

"Did you ever report it to Housing?" Glinnie asks.

"You call Housing, they don't do nothing," McCowan says, picking up the communal narrative. "They say they know. They call a big meeting. Nothing's ever followed up. Even with Mr. Griffith."

She means Ed Griffith, the neighborhood's state assemblyman, and a long-standing foe of EBC and Saint Paul. Just two months ago, in fact, he was scheduled to address the church's annual Political Awareness Night. By the time he turned up, a half hour late, he found an empty sanctuary. Unwilling to wait obediently for him, the congregation had marched homeward, en masse.

"You deal with Mr. Griffith?" Reverend Youngblood asks, betraying none of this history.

Two women simply double over in laughter.

"Priscilla Wooten?" he adds, referring to the City Council member who is Griffith's political ally.

"You only see them," says Hattie Thomas, a woman in a Las Vegas sweatshirt, "at election time."

"Well, we're interested in results," Reverend Youngblood says for the second time. "I'm sure you heard enough talk."

"Amen."

Reverend Youngblood's problem is to address two immense and related issues, drugs and crime, in a personal way. He can hardly promise to eradicate their scourge. He needs to find one front, one front where success is possible, before these women consign him and

EBC to their scornful laughter. He reaches back to a moment from the meeting between the merchants' association and the precinct police, fully seven months ago.

"The cops," he says, "consider this side of Linden Boulevard *low* crime."

"I don't know where they get that," Hattie says, instantly indignant. "We can't go out. If you go out, you're boogyin' right back."

"You can't go to a movie," Dolores adds. "You can't have dinner. You can't come home late. You just can't."

"You mad, ain't you?" Reverend Youngblood says.

"Too mad to talk about," says Ann Hudley, who is seated beside him.

"Oh, no," Reverend Youngblood answers, almost teasingly. "We want you to talk. Talk and more."

Now the anger born of grief, the ore of Alinsky's "iron rule," fills the room, and the examples turn specific and hard. On a pad, Reverend Youngblood scribbles the list: no heat in one wing, the failed security system, an old incinerator left in the lobby, rampant drug use in the nearby park. Then he hears the grievance he has been waiting for, the grievance so intimate and well defined and winnable it can transform victims into victors.

"They changed the bus stops," Hattie says, "'bout three months ago."

"So we have to get off at Pennsylvania," adds Dolores, once again finishing someone else's sentence, "and walk through that park with shooting and everything."

"I saw six mens there smokin' crack," comes another voice. "Broad daylight."

Reverend Youngblood lifts pen from pad, makes eye contact around the room.

"Could you lay out a map," he asks, "and choose an area where the bus ought to stop?"

"Where it used to be, for eighteen years!" shouts Cheryl Clark, silent until now. "At the corner of Vermont."

"The people who make the decisions don't ride no buses," Miss Maybelle adds. "Even the drivers didn't know. I worked at Transit for twenty-one years, and I *know* how it works."

Reverend Youngblood proposes a strategy. Write a petition, get two thousand signatures, send a delegation with it to the Transit Authority. Forget the Community Board. Forget Ed Griffith and Priscilla Wooten.

Scanning the room, Reverend Youngblood measures the response. Women lean forward, elbows on thighs, fists starting to clench. One rocks an impatient granddaughter on her lap, tells her they cannot leave yet. The pastor moves from his spot on the sofa to the arm of Miss Maybelle's chair.

"Now, you what we call feisty," he says. "You're the kind of person we think can be a leader. So when we go down to Transit, you doin' the talking."

"I got my pension," she says worriedly.

"They can't take that away," Reverend Youngblood reassures her.

"Can't touch this," Ann Hudley adds, quoting the hit song by M.C. Hammer. The room explodes with laughter. Ann runs in place without leaving her chair.

Nearly an hour has passed. Reverend Youngblood and Glinnie must go. An EBC "house meeting" puts a premium on brevity, one more way of stressing results over rhetoric.

"I know you been through tryin' before," the pastor says as he reaches for Benny Rutherford's hat. "I know you been through politicians and bureaucrats. But things can change. That's what I'm here to tell you. We can do things our way, a different way." Then he pronounces, in his own words, the "iron rule." "We'll be there to work with you. But it's got to be *your* organization. Y'all know the rule of life. Ain't nobody gonna do nothin' for you. Got to do it for yourself."

From its first utterance, the idea of rebuilding Brownsville struck Mike Gecan as both thrilling and treacherous. Saul Alinsky's disciples were a nomadic lot, developing issues and leaders in Memphis or Tucson or Jersey City and then moving on to organize somewhere else. Overhead was low, flexibility was high, and reliance on public funds was a cardinal sin, eroding the virtue of self-help. Gecan had learned these lessons most indelibly in watching the Woodlawn Organization stray from them to become a virtual development corporation, "in love with the glamour of brick and mortar."

And yet. And yet. The arc of EBC's ascent called for a larger, more galvanizing campaign. Housing had placed second among issues in the East Brooklyn house meetings. Prices for private homes, even in slums, exceeded what a letter carrier or bus driver could afford. And the Reagan administration had stanched federal aid for new construction.

Reverend Youngblood, among other EBC ministers, put the crisis in palpable, human terms. He could talk about Geraldine Jenkins, a nurse in her thirties, still living with her mother. Or Nell and Melvin Jones, she the church clerk and he a loader at United Parcel Service, ready to flee the projects for their native Virginia. Or Theressa Jordan, a postal worker, whose landlord snuck into her apartment in her absence. "Move," the pastor had told her. "Where?" she had answered. "Anyplace else, rent is too high."

Gecan found himself recalling a sermon from months ago, Reverend Youngblood's exegesis of Nehemiah, the prophet of a Jewish nation staggering home from forced exile. The organizer opened his Bible and read the scriptural account for the first time since his days at Saint Ignatius High. The words spoke to him in present tense about the Brooklyn before his eyes, particularly two verses:

> And they said unto me, The remnant that are left of the captivity there in the province are in great affliction and reproach: the wall of Jerusalem also is broken down, and the gates thereof are burned with fire....
>
> Then I said unto them, Ye see the distress that we are in, how Jerusalem lieth waste, and the gates thereof are burned with fire; come, and let us build up the wall of Jerusalem, that we be no more a reproach.

As the unwitting originator of what was instantly dubbed "the Nehemiah plan," Reverend Youngblood reacted to the evolving proposal with passion. There were so few ways in which poor people could control their own lives, least of all living in tenements owned by absentee landlords or projects presided over by distant bureaucracies. And yet, as he often said, "Nobody keeps a cleaner house than poor folk." He thought of his maternal grandmother, sweeping her dirt yard every morning, or his father, building a shotgun house with leftovers, or his mother, scrubbing it back to a shine after the flood had deposited mud two feet deep. What his congregants needed were homes where they could put values and muscles to work.

One elemental question remained: How to build them? It carried Gecan back more than a year, to a conversation with Ed Chambers. The IAF director had handed Gecan a folder of articles by a retired builder named I. D. Robbins. "This is a guy," Chambers had said, "who knows what New York is all about." In the flurry of EBC organizing, Gecan had not opened the folder for eight months. And only now did its contents matter to him.

Robbins had been writing since 1971 about New York's lack of affordable housing—and his plan for building it. One article in the *Daily News*'s Sunday magazine declared in its headline, FOR THE $12,000-A-YEAR INCOME: BLUEPRINT FOR A ONE-FAMILY HOUSE, and was accompanied by floor plans for a brick row house. Robbins offered repeatedly to build one for $36,000, at his own expense, if only the city would give him a single slice of land. (Which mayor after mayor refused to do.) If this was boasting, it was boasting with cause. During the heyday of his construction career, Robbins had erected 1,700 homes in a single year. He held deep ties to the "good government" movement, having run once for mayor on a reform line. And he possessed a blunt, irreverent, irascible demeanor that Alinsky himself might have appreciated; Robbins once upbraided a reporter for misquoting him as calling a politician an idiot, when what he had actually called him was a *fucking* idiot.

Gecan arranged to meet the maverick at Big Six Towers, an apartment complex for union members that Robbins had erected in 1963. Arriving early, the organizer proceeded to ride the elevators, knock on the walls, check the foundation for cracks. Satisfied by the workmanship, he turned his attention to the workman, eavesdropping in the lobby as tenants warmly greeted him as "Robby." Finally, Gecan introduced himself.

"What do you really want to do?" Robbins asked.

"I want you to build housing for us."

"Sure," Robbins said in his urban drawl. "A lotta people do. What're you gonna use for money?"

"We could raise it," Gecan said.

"How much?"

"Twelve million."

Gecan had no reason for choosing the figure, except that it had a great many zeros. All that counted, and urgently so, was that Robbins believe EBC to be credible, not just some do-gooders with big ideas and little wallets.

"Then what," Robbins answered, "are we waiting for?"

Acting nothing but confident about finding the fortune, Gecan brought Robbins into a series of intense discussions with Chambers and the EBC strategy team, and together they framed five inviolable rules for the Nehemiah program. First, it would produce only single-family homes, to create a clear sense of accountability. Second, the houses would be owned rather than rented, so every resident had an emotional and financial stake in the experiment's success. Third, they would be attached to one another, to hold construction costs below fifty thousand dollars per unit. Fourth, they would be built by the thousand, rather than in the small numbers of most pilot projects, to foster a renewed sense of neighborhood. And finally, they would not rely on any gifts or grants from the public sector. All EBC sought from the city or state were the rights to land that was virtually vacant; low-interest mortgages under an existing program; a ten-year deferral of property tax on land that was yielding few taxes anyway; and a ten-thousand-dollar, interest-free loan on each home, which would be repaid when it was sold. For the city and state, slipping into recession, such a deal would cost almost nothing. For EBC, wary of Caesar's household, it would ensure control.

Paying for construction appeared simple. A revolving loan fund would advance the money, then be replenished as each row house was sold. And hadn't Mike Gecan vowed to raise twelve million dollars?

The truth, of course, was that Gecan had not yet scraped together twelve. Nor, in six months of concerted effort, did he show any sign of being able to. First he and the EBC leaders approached nine banks and insurance companies with notably deep pockets. All turned down Nehemiah, saying, "It'll never work," "Start small," "That's *our* business." Then EBC tried the "God Box," the Manhattan office building that served as the Vatican for several progressive Protestant denominations. Some pled poverty. Others complained the Nehemiah homes would not be aiding "the poorest of the poor."

The next gambit seemed the most hopeless of all. Two of EBC's mainstays, Reverend David Benke and Reverend John Heinemeier, appealed to their denomination, the Lutheran Church–Missouri Synod, one of the most politically and religiously conservative in America. Not for the Missouri Synod Lutherans were liberation theology or the social gospel. They believed in the inerrancy of the Bible and the detachment of the church from all worldly issues except abortion. But the two Brooklyn pastors, analyzing the synod's leadership, found five potential allies, officials with power, access to money, and sympathetic values.

Two of them—Norman Sell, the treasurer, and Ed Westcott, the director of missions—came from their St. Louis offices to East Brooklyn on December 16, 1981. Awaiting them was an itinerary elaborately scripted by EBC as a mixture of Christian fellowship and shock therapy. The Nehemiah program, after all, was running out of chances.

From Reverend Benke's church in East New York, the two visitors traveled by van into the blighted core of Brownsville. "If you compare this to Dresden after the fire-bombing," the pastor said as they drove, "it would be the same." In the rearview mirror, he watched their jaws fall slack. Then he heard them gasp.

The tour complete, Reverend Benke led Sell and Westcott into the basement of his church. There, amid the tangle of exposed pipes, waited six members of local Missouri Synod congregations. As if intoning a liturgy, each described families trapped in housing projects, made homeless by arson, doubled and tripled up with friends, families that could live instead in Nehemiah homes. Speaking last, his voice quaking, Reverend Benke told of Marie Schmidt, the elderly parishioner who had been robbed and raped and set afire in her own apartment. "We have people, as you can see, who live in hell on earth," he concluded. "We need to have a little bit of heaven. God's people deserve a little bit of heaven."

The room now silent, Reverend Benke let the image penetrate. Then he turned from the moral to the practical, summarizing Robbins's five-point plan and stressing that the Nehemiah project would function as a mission, a way of spreading the Gospel and strengthening local churches. Finally he uttered the words he had memorized early that morning before the shaving mirror: "We are here to request from the Missouri Synod an interest-free loan for up to five years in the amount of one million dollars."

As they had rehearsed, every person in the room swiveled to face the synod officials. Westcott stared down at the table. A moment passed. He lifted his eyes to the rest.

"All I can tell you," he said, "is that I will put every ounce of weight I possess behind the proposal. You have my commitment."

Buoyed by success, EBC took its campaign to the Roman Catholic Diocese of Brooklyn, appealing directly to Bishop Francis J. Mugavero. A bald, bespectacled man of sixty-seven, Bishop Mugavero was a prince of the church with the heart of a peasant. He had grown up in Bedford-Stuyvesant, living in the apartment above his father's barbershop. Rising through the Catholic hierarchy, he had hurled himself into charities and social causes, following a "pro-life" philosophy that included not only vigorous opposition to abortion but also to the Vietnam War, capital punishment, and racial or religious bias. Through it all, he remained approachably common, calling himself "Kojak" with children, answering to the nickname "Muggsy," telling those who saluted him as "Excellency," "I'm not excellent."

From that first meeting in the diocese's chancery, Bishop Mugavero grasped the logic of the Nehemiah plan. His Italian values told him, "You take care of what you own," and on the blueprints he could see the three bedrooms, the kitchen, the driveway, even the backyard that stirred a childhood memory of fig trees. He knew EBC's priests personally, and respected Father Powis so greatly he later recommended that Rome elevate him to monsignor. The only problem, as the bishop saw it, was that these admirable people with their admirable plan wanted the impossible: two or three million dollars.

They're wackos, he thought, celebrating mass after the meeting. *Where am I going to get that money?*

Two days later, climbing the chancery stairs, Bishop Mugavero realized the answer. It was common for the diocese to request that religious communities supply chaplains or parish priests or parochial school teachers. Why not trade on his reputation to ask those communities for loans? Two of them, the Pallottines and the Redemptorists, committed $500,000 apiece. Then, using the connections he had built twenty years earlier as head of the diocese's Office of Catholic Charities, Bishop Mugavero culled another $1.5 million. (The diocese's total contribution to the revolving loan fund would ultimately reach $5 million.)

And the bishop provided EBC with more than money. He

became the latest linchpin in Alinsky-style "relational politics," giving the group access to the highest levels of government. From his days with Catholic Charities, he had known Mario Cuomo, like him the son of an Italian immigrant shopkeeper, then practicing law in downtown Brooklyn. With a single meeting, Bishop Mugavero won from Governor Cuomo an agreement to write state-subsidized, 9.9 percent mortgages for Nehemiah homeowners. And on June 8, 1982, the bishop brought Gecan, Chambers, Robbins, Reverend Youngblood, and several others into the lair of their enemy, Mayor Edward I. Koch.

Without the bishop, a friend sometimes invited to dine at Gracie Mansion, the mayor would never have entertained such a delegation. He disdained Robbins, an outspoken political foe. He considered EBC rabidly radical. And surely the mayor, by now at the zenith of his popularity and arrogance, harbored a grudge from his embarrassment by the Queens Citizens Organization three years earlier. Even friends of Gecan's had insisted that the chance of convincing Mayor Koch was so small, so absolutely infinitesimal, that EBC would be wiser to wait for a new mayor to be elected. Nor was EBC acting from a position of strength. That very morning, like a conscience-struck altar boy, Gecan had told the bishop, "About the twelve million dollars, we don't have it." Only $2.5 million, in fact, was in hand. "You worry too much," the bishop responded. Still, Gecan and the rest bowed their heads outside Mayor Koch's office and prayed.

Once inside, Bishop Mugavero did the talking. He emphasized the middle-class value of home ownership. He noted the affordable price—$48,000, and even less with city loans. Mayor Koch knew well enough that the city, obliged as it was to bid all contracts and hire union labor and follow federal pay guidelines, could never compete. The handful of ranch houses it was building in the South Bronx cost $120,000 apiece.

"Well, Ed," the bishop concluded, "we've got twelve million dollars, and we're ready to build."

Gecan and Reverend Youngblood exchanged looks of shock. What if Koch asked for proof? Gecan had lain awake nights lately, dreading that very question.

Clearly impressed by the fallacious number, the mayor turned to Anthony Gliedman, his housing commissioner, and asked, "Has anyone ever come to us with this kind of money?"

"Never, Mr. Mayor."

Then Bishop Mugavero put forward EBC's request for the land condemnation, the tax deferral, and the interest-free loans, ideally $10 million worth, enough for one thousand Nehemiah homes.

"If we could get money from you, Ed," the bishop was saying, when Mayor Koch cut in, "There's no money."

"Then steal it," Bishop Mugavero calmly resumed, "and I'll give you absolution."

"You got it," the mayor promised.

Just to make certain, EBC held a Manhattan press conference three weeks later, announcing its readiness to start construction, and forcing the absent Mayor Koch, reached by reporters at City Hall, to commit himself publicly to the project. Even so, the next time Gecan, Reverend Youngblood, and Bishop Mugavero met with him, the mayor announced the city would provide land and loans for only one hundred houses. "You don't know what you're doing," he complained. "You've never built housing before." Only when the delegation rose to walk out did the mayor relent. Eleven days later, on July 25, one of his deputies announced to a huge rally in Brownsville that the city would give the Nehemiah program tax deferrals for a decade, thirteen blocks of land, and $10 million in loans, enough for one thousand houses.*

On the blustery and overcast afternoon of October 31, 1982, the circle came full. Across the street from Our Lady of Mercy, atop the same rubble Mike Gecan had first seen more than two years earlier, sat a bulldozer. A hundred yards before it stood a stage, bedecked with an EBC banner. And between them pressed nearly six thousand members from forty-two churches. By city bus and gypsy cab and shoe leather they had traveled, still wearing the suits and heels of Sunday-morning worship, streaming down the blocks, astounding the part of Brownsville that was waxing its cars or buying its groceries or drinking its malt liquor with no greater dream than hitting the number.

The keynote address belonged to Reverend Youngblood, and he

---

* Mayor Koch's account of the Nehemiah negotiations differs in several respects from those of virtually all the other participants interviewed for this book. He maintained, for example, that it had been his idea—not EBC's—to provide the ten-thousand-dollar loan for each home. He also said that he had refused to release any city money for the project until EBC had raised several million dollars for construction. And he denied that the EBC press conference affected his decision to support the project.

had been preparing it for days. This would not be a sermon derived from Scripture; it would be a statement of political will, a cry of triumph and vindication. Yet he had to resist the temptation to gloat. He thought of something Reverend J. Pius Barbour, a mentor of Martin Luther King's, had once told him: "Your task as a pastor is to keep your friends and win your enemies." He thought of the true meaning of the term *public servant*. And he thought of a phrase Gecan had dropped in a discussion earlier that week, *grass roots*.

"Contrary to popular opinion," Reverend Youngblood proclaimed from the stage, "we are not a 'grassroots' organization." Listeners leaned up on tiptoes. Clenched fists spiked the air. "Grass roots grow in smooth soil. Grass roots are shallow roots. Grass roots are tender roots. Grass roots are fragile roots. *Our* roots are deep roots." Now came the cries of "All right!" and "Praise God!" Tears welled in the eyes of Francis Mugavero, the Italian Catholic bishop; "amen" rose from the throat of John Heinemeier, the Lutheran minister reared in West Texas. "Our roots are tough roots. Our roots are determined roots. The roots of EBC have fought for existence in the shattered glass of East New York, in the blasted brick and rubble of Brownsville, in the devastation of central Bushwick. Our roots are deep in this city." Then he turned one shoulder slightly, swept his eyes from the audience to one man on the dais. "And so we say to you, Mayor Koch, 'We love New York!'" The crowd thundered back the words, transforming a tourism slogan into a mantra of self-worth. "*We* love New York!" they chanted after Reverend Youngblood. *"We."*

Then the bulldozer bit into the earth. Twenty months later, on June 14, 1984, a couple named Herbert and Leolin Schleifer moved into 668 Mother Gaston Boulevard, the first Nehemiah home. Nearly 2,300 were ultimately built in East Brooklyn, supported by more than $7 million in loans, $100,000 of that from Saint Paul alone.* Geraldine Jenkins, Theressa Jordan, and Nell and Melvin Jones, whose frustrations had helped inspire the program, all bought Nehemiah homes, as did thirty-five families from Saint Paul. Like the Joneses, nearly half of the new homeowners moved directly from housing projects, and the income for a Nehemiah household averaged only $25,000.

With success came some ironic side effects. Politicians who had

---

* Besides Saint Paul, the Brooklyn Diocese, and the Missouri Synod, the Episcopal diocese of Long Island loaned $1 million.

fought EBC took credit for the Nehemiah program, even as they refused any more land for it. Congress passed a bill to fund similar initiatives nationwide, but only after adding enough loopholes to turn the reform into a pork-barrel bonanza. The advocacy press, having championed Nehemiah as a theory, attacked it in practice for displacing residents and building shoddily. All the hypocrisy was, in Alinsky's phrase, "the world as it is." But so were the front gates and patios, the laundry lines and satellite dishes, and the red brick row houses to which they were tethered.

Dave Nelson stands in the basement auditorium of Saint Barbara's School in Bushwick. It is a clean room, but one too long between repairs, the consequence of its parish's privation. Paint flakes off the ceiling. Holes pock the structural columns where plaster has fallen by the chunk. The clock reads an eternal one-thirty-two. Yet as he sweeps his arms from raised stage to rear door, across rows of empty chairs, Nelson speaks of multitudes.

"If they're hangin' from the rafters," he tells the dozen EBC leaders around him, "then we've got eleven hundred, twelve hundred. If it's full, a thousand. Three-quarters full, then ..." His eyes narrow like a navigator's. "Still a thousand."

His listeners laugh. They need a standing-room crowd tonight, when nearly a year of effort, effort that began even before the formal opening of the tenth-anniversary campaign, reaches its climax. EBC has invited to its podium leaders from the police force, the education establishment, the medical community, and the local political apparatus, demanding they say yes or no to its initiatives. At eight o'clock, less than two hours from now, Nelson and Reverend Youngblood and the rest will hear the answers, and with them the verdict on EBC's viability.

As little as possible will be left to spontaneity. Nelson guides the evening's speakers through the agenda, line by line. He reminds the floor leaders when to cheer and boo, when to make and second motions. And he beams with the news that four principals of nearby elementary schools have been barred by the district superintendent from attending. "Principals can't meet with parents," he says. "This is great. This is just great."

By seven-thirty the church vans start moving toward Bushwick, beneath the clattering El, past the liquor stores and *cuchifrito* stands, down the gap-toothed blocks of tenements, unreconstructed from the arson of a decade ago. From EBC's fifty-four churches and synagogues, delegates pour into the auditorium, clad in *kente* and *khaffiyeh*s, Giants caps and Task Force jackets. The Saint Paul contingent, nearly four hundred strong, arrives in identical yellow sweatshirts emblazoned "He Is Lord," the same ones worn for the Palm Sunday prayer walk around the eighty-block area considered "redemptive turf." In the introductory rounds, Leroy Howard announces the congregation's presence. "We want to know," he adds, "the results of everything that's gone on for the last year."

His words bring Reverend David Benke to the mircophone. He has thinning hair, tortoiseshell glasses, an off-the-rack suit, and the bile to belie so mild an appearance.

"We have been negotiating, EBC and the powers that be, for fifty weeks," he says. "And in fifty weeks we've discovered that the meaning of negotiating is meeting. Planning the meeting. Arranging the meeting. Setting up the meeting. And when it finally gets to the meeting, the agenda is the next meeting. I can't say those meetings were unproductive; they were *re*productive. They gave birth to little baby meetings."

He surveys the audience, packed four deep at the rear wall and up the back stairs, stirred by his sarcasm. Then he reaches inside the lectern for a wall clock he has secreted there, and holds it aloft.

"We say tonight, powers that be, listen up. The clock is done ticking. Time has run out. We are way past the deadline on negotiating for empty promises from empty suits. At eight-fifteen tonight, you're either with us or against us. And I say to you, EBC, we're either in action with those who can and do, or we're in active battle against those who can't and won't. Are you ready?" People stand and whoop and shake their fists. Reverend Benke reprises his words in Spanish, switching to English for the addendum, "We want results we can touch."

He yields the podium to a black woman in a paisley head wrap, Vanessa Dixon. She reiterates EBC's proposal for a primary health-care center, and she underlines it with the story of having her daughter delivered by doctors she had never met before, doctors whose impersonal manner "violated and stripped and raped me of my pride."

After her testimony, with the whole room abuzz, a balding white man with horn-rim spectacles moves gingerly from a chair on the stage to the microphone. His name is Tom Hall, and he is the assistant executive director of Saint Mary's Hospital. He announces the hospital will open a primary-care facility on Atlantic Avenue in East New York, capable of handling twenty thousand visits annually by 1992. He receives applause, but impatient applause, applause that wants to know what comes next.

It is Genevieve Wright, a tall, slender woman with cornrows. She reprises EBC's first attempt at reform, the program of college scholarships and entry-level jobs for graduates of Bushwick and Jefferson. It was, she says bluntly, a failure. It proved EBC could not make radical change within the existing schools. So EBC must create its own school.

"It is my privilege now," she says, "to introduce a new ally to you." She indicates behind her a middle-aged woman with pearls and a pleated skirt, Ann Reynolds, the chancellor of the City University of New York. Then she reads Reynolds's complete vita, down to scholarly articles.

The chancellor herself announces the basis for alliance, a commitment to house the enrichment academy on the campus of Medgar Evers College in Crown Heights, a branch of the City University. She speaks of the rigorous college preparatory courses the academy will offer, and she also sounds the politically expedient notes of "multicultural curriculum," "dignity and self-esteem," "strong parental involvement." As if to underscore those sentiments, she shares the microphone with Edison Jackson, the black who is president of Medgar Evers, and Robert Diaz, a Hispanic attorney for her office. "Education is the fastest elevator to the top," Jackson says, "and we're just foolish enough to believe we can do it." Then Diaz translates the vow into Spanish, setting off a second round of cheers.

The rally proceeds in its well-drilled fashion. One speaker delivers the latest tally of Nehemiah homes in Brooklyn, and the word that, after years of dickering with the city, ground can be broken for more in the South Bronx. Another speaker wrings from school officials onstage a schedule for repairing broken roofs, fire doors, playground equipment, and toilets in Bushwick's public schools. All the while Nelson works the auditorium, chatting with a reporter, checking positions on stage, covering a legal pad with notes.

Margaret Smyth, a nun and educator from East New York, assumes the microphone. "After such good news," she says, "I give you the next part of our program: silence." She explains that Lee Brown, the police commissioner, has skipped tonight's meeting, the latest in a series of snubs. "You can't talk when there's nobody to listen," she says. "But EBC and QCO won't let this issue die. Will they?"

"No," the throng replies in unison.

Father John Powis, the monsignor of Saint Barbara's, has the penultimate spot on the program. He is nominally speaking about the battle between a group of Bushwick parents and the local school board, which is firmly under the influence of Councilman Victor Robles. But his words address a theme far larger, as old as the Back of the Yards Neighborhood Council.

"We won't beg Victor Robles or any other politician for anything," Father Powis proclaims. "You shouldn't have to beg any politician to get bathrooms and windows fixed in a school." Then he slows for emphasis. "I ... beg ... only ... *God!*"

An ovation rises less from lungs than guts, less from minds than souls. As it subsides, a former member of EBC's "strategy team" named Nereida Bati nudges aside Father Powis. Severely ill with cancer, she has been inserted into the program as a special kindness, and in a lusty Spanish that denies her disease, she introduces the final speaker, "Yonnie Rey Jong Blood."

Reverend Youngblood faces the audience, smiling broadly. He has delivered many speeches like this since that afternoon in October 1982. They no longer frighten him, and they no longer draw from his listeners the naïve, beatific stares of hope abruptly reawakened. The difference is not that the orations have become routine, but rather that Reverend Youngblood and his EBC listeners understand by now that social change will not come either easily or quickly. Mike Gecan sometimes talks about the one time he saw Martin Luther King preach. It was in 1965, the year King carried his crusade from the segregation laws of the South to the economic injustice of the North. There the enemy did not loose dogs and fire hoses, did not bomb churches and burn crosses. There, it seemed to Gecan as he sat in a half-filled church on an especially dark night, King looked weary and small and almost defeated. But it was his determination to hurl himself back into battle, to take the existential leap, that convinced Gecan of the man's genuine heroism.

"We have great endurance," Reverend Youngblood says near the end of his address. "We're not going anywhere. We got no moving vans outside. These are our roots." He draws breath. "And we are angry. If we were not church people, you might say we were mad as hell. At people who are all lips and no labor. At the bureaucrats who would diminish us into beggars. At the weavers who turn red tape into red cable. At those who attack our self-esteem. It must be known that we are the fairest fighters in town. We never ask for what cannot be done. We only ask for what is our due as citizens."

A few moments later, his comments completed, Reverend Young-blood leads the 1,200 in singing "The Battle Hymn of the Republic." And at the juncture when the verses switch from English into Spanish, the program having provided a translation, he thrusts a fist skyward, and shouts in a frayed voice the single word, "Work!"

12

◎

PASSAGE TO THE PAST

Slowly the plane descends, riding the warm wind called the *harmattan*. Somewhere below, the savanna unfolds, the brown rivers run, the stone forts bear witness to commerce in slaves. Below wait Accra, and Ghana, and Africa. Reverend Johnny Ray Youngblood, peering through his window, sees only night, night and the reflection of a boy across the aisle, wearily knotting his tie.

Turning his gaze back into the cabin, he sees the Ghanaians beginning to stir. Most sleep beneath wool overcoats, the clothing of diaspora in Brixton or the Bronx. Now they are returning home, to *kente* and palm wine, to families and villages they support from abroad. That indistinct land outside a dark window, the pastor knows, is supposed to feel like home to him, too.

He has come here, after all, for Saint Paul to seal a compact with its past, in the form of a mission in the village of Asafo. But there are connections he represents beyond those of brick and mortar. On his way to the airport yesterday, the second of December, Reverend Youngblood found a woman waiting outside his study door. She pressed an envelope into his hands, and when he opened it hours later, between planes in Amsterdam, he discovered a plea: "If you, Pastor, possibly could pay homage, for so many of us, to the memories of our lost ancestors. Surely their souls cry out for our presence."

The words made him feel both proud and unworthy. It is Osei

Yaw Akoto, his partner on this trip, who has made the pilgrimage before, who has traced his lineage back to a ship's log. The pastor was reared with the Africa of Tarzan. The nuns of his grammar school would scold a naughty black child, "You wild little African." Even the blues song counseled, "If you're white, you're all right. If you're brown, stick around. If you're black, get back. Get way back." And nothing in Reverend Youngblood's adulthood—not *Roots*, not Malcolm X, not *Before the Mayflower*—could repair all the damage. He thinks now of Countee Cullen's question, "What's Africa to me?" Then he reaches into his shoulder bag, retrieves a sheet of shirt cardboard and a pen, and begins to write with the title, "The Middle Passage 371 Years Later."

> *Not by ship of wood,*
> *But by ship of metal.*
> *Not by water.*
> *But by air.*
>
> *Is this The Return?*
> *So desired and so despaired about*
> *By those who took the original trip?*
>
> *O, Lord, have You now decided*
> *That You will remember and respond*
> *To the prayer of our fathers?*
> *That You will remember Your covenant with them?*
>
> *Am I a participant?*
> *If so*
> *Open mine eyes that I might see glimpses*
> *of the truth Thou hast for me.*

At noon on his first day in Africa, real Africa, Reverend Youngblood sits to lunch in a Chinese restaurant. Christmas tinsel dangles in loops from the ceiling, and a pop group, the Carpenters, sings carols on tape. The pastor shares the table with Osei and two Ghanaian friends, a genial pharmacist named Victor Aphreh and Kwame Charles, a son of Asafo now parking cars in New York. It is Kwame, home for his first visit in five years, who has arranged a meeting after lunch with the village's chief, a lawyer during the week with an office in Accra.

"Sometimes I'm embarrassed," Reverend Youngblood says to Victor and Kwame. "Because you African brothers think of us as being *here*." He raises a hand above his head. "And we're not." He drops his palm back to the table. "What do *I* have to say to African people? This is my first time. If this is home for me, I have to admit some of home is strange."

He awakened at daybreak on the outer edge of the city, in the brick and mahogany home of a friend of Victor Aphreh's. Cinderblock houses covered the low land, and the once-green hills to the west had been shaved down to stubble. Still, the pastor thought he could feel Africa there—in the *harmattan* blowing, in thonged feet padding down roads, in the rhythmic thump of yam and plantain being pounded into *fufu*, the sound that Osei has called "the heartbeat of Ghana."

More than anything else, it was the soil that seemed to link Africa with his own life. He saw himself as a child, during Mississippi summers, playing in a yard of that selfsame red clay. He saw his Grandma Inola eating the rich dirt for health, and mixing it with water to apply to burns as a balm. He saw her walking from the fields, a basin of cucumbers balanced on her head, just like these women this morning carrying laundry or palm fronds.

But once Victor arrived and drove him deeper into Accra, the pastor's sense-memory grew quickly confused. He passed the Bronx Hair Salon and a theater called the Apollo, running the very same Schwarzenegger film that Joel and Jernell had seen only months ago in New York. Standing in line to change money, he heard the radio play "We're All in This Together," a song by David Peaston, a member of Saint Paul. And when he submitted his visa form to the immigration office, as all visitors must, the inspector corrected his answer on the "nationality" line. He left intact the word *American*, then drew his pen through its predecessor, its companion, *African*.

Duality, though, was the inescapable truth. "One ever feels his two-ness," Reverend Youngblood had read in W. E. B. Du Bois. "An American, a Negro; two souls, two thoughts, two unreconciled strivings; two warring ideals in one dark body." Du Bois himself had journeyed to Ghana, to celebrate its independence and ultimately to die.

He had finally found the identity toward which the pastor still gropes, with his sermons on how a village raises its children, with the "ancestor chairs" at Larry Johnson's wedding, with the bust of black Jesus in "the listening post." Perhaps Asafo would be where Africa met him halfway.

The chief, Barima Asante Abedi III, practices law above a bridal shop downtown. He wears wire-rimmed glasses and a blue suit that hangs limply in the heat. He has just returned from court, and the office is harried. Four piles of legal papers mount beneath metal weights. A secretary clatters out a brief on a manual typewriter. Two graying men in tribal robes arrive to discuss a land dispute, as bicycle bells and diesel fumes rise from the street.

Waiting his turn with Osei, Kwame, and Victor, Reverend Youngblood has already reached one decision. Saint Paul will not build a church in Asafo, for religion seems one resource in which Ghana abounds. Not a jitney rumbles through Accra without "The Name of God" on the windshield or "Deliver Me" above the bumper. There are businesses called Christ the King Motors and Psalm 106 Pipe Fittings. A single crossroads bears signs for churches led by Baptists, Presbyterians, Seventh-Day Adventists, and Assemblies of God, so many the pastor joked to Osei, "It's like we never left Brooklyn." No, whatever Asafo needs from Saint Paul might have more to do with the children darting through traffic, peddling sticks of gum, or the women lighting cooking fires next door to hotels, or the open sewers and open sores. The missionaries' message, Christianity as cure-all, was a failure and a lie.

Chief Abedi now welcomes the visitors into his office, thanks the pastor for previous donations of money and clothes. Reverend Youngblood, reciprocating, says, "I have come as a student. I have come looking. I am honored and I am humbled to come." He asks question after question, about customs of greeting and burial, about the easy way men walk holding hands, about the political legacy of Kwame Nkrumah, Ghana's founding father.

The chief belongs to the generation that was to build modern Ghana, but has seen progress move with maddening leisure. Educated in law and economics in England, he presides over a village that only last year received electricity and still lacks enough medicine for its clinic or a high school within a fifteen-mile radius. "We are still ninety percent illiterate," he tells Reverend Youngblood.

"In Asafo?" the pastor asks.

"The whole country," Chief Abedi cries, throwing his hands toward the ceiling. "The whole country."

"Well, what if we could change that?" Reverend Youngblood says. "Even in one village?"

The chief nods, intrigued.

"I know there's been talk about a church," the pastor continues. "But one thing I do not want to do is build a church." He waits for objection; none comes. "Isn't it more important to have a school you've never had than one more church full of folk who can't read?"

"The concern of all Africa," Chief Abedi replies, "is to be better educated."

"Then this is the beginning."

But first, the chief insists, the pastor must visit Asafo. This Sunday the village will hold a *durbar,* a festival, in his honor. There will be dancing and eating and singing and ceremony. And when the revelry ends, there will be daylight enough left to find a site for a school.

> *I look for some click,*
> *Some reminder, some moment of déjà vu.*
> *Some all-focusing, resurrecting, cataclysmic birth*
> *That answers all questions, fills all the gaps.*
> *I hope, I wish, I hallucinate.*

Once Victor Aphreh's car pushes free of Accra, bound east on the Cape Coast Highway, the face of Africa softens from corrugated tin to palm thatch. Fishing villages perch on the oceanside bluffs, and in the surf shirtless men hoist nets heavy with the day's catch. Yet here, where the foreign hand seems most absent, white men first came to shore. They called this land "The Mine" for its abundance of gold, a commodity soon supplanted by prisoners of war. And indeed, as the car turns into the town of Elmina, the columns and louvers of Europe appear. Past the church with its bell tower and across the softly arched bridge stands the reason for this settlement, the Castle of St. George.

Its double moat dry, its cannons long silent, the castle now serves as a museum alone. But for more than four centuries its purpose was profit. In its most efficient years, St. George warehoused and shipped ten thousand slaves, nearly fifteen percent of the continent's annual total. So lucrative was business that the Dutch, having captured the castle from its Portuguese founders, erected a second fortress to protect their investment. Britons, Swedes, Germans, French, Danes—all competed in the trade, building castles of their own along a 150-mile coast.

"Every time I come here, I get something deeper," says Osei, who has visited twice before, as he steps from the car. "Something that fills a void that's been in me for a long time."

"I can't figure how I'm supposed to feel," Reverend Youngblood says. "I'm more than a tourist. This is history. Our history. But how do you get angry at something so huge?"

"Wait till you get inside," Osei says as they walk toward the gate. "Inside is rough."

They enter a stone plaza surrounded by thick whitewashed walls. It resembles, fittingly enough, a medieval village square, for the fortress once housed its own masons and tailors, coopers and blacksmiths. Even a priest practiced here, in the castle's private church, above whose door was inscribed a verse from Psalm 132: "For the Lord hath chosen Zion to be a habitation for himself: It is his dwelling place forever."

A series of unlit tunnels leads to the cells where the captives were held. Hearing voices, Reverend Youngblood and the rest follow down one, joining the castle's sole tour guide, who is already leading a few Europeans. Just now he is pointing into a windowless room, adorned by the portrait of a man wearing *kente* and an unrepentant glare. He is Prempeh I, the Ashanti king who mounted a rebellion against Ghana's British rulers in the late 1800s. Slavery being illegal by then, the British punished him with prison, followed by exile, only to see the Ashanti queen take the insurrection's reins.

Around a corner and through an archway, the guide comes to a square room, perhaps twelve feet by thirty, the dungeon that held up to two hundred women. They received food through an iron gate and air from a single two-foot-square hole. They had neither toilets nor sleeping pallets. The routine varied only for the most mutinous women, who were beaten in a courtyard and then chained to cannonballs. From a terrace above, officers chose their sexual victims.

"Remember that boy yesterday?" Osei asks Reverend Young-blood.

He refers to a child they had passed in Accra, whose tawny skin and loose curls had puzzled the pastor, here in a pure-blooded black nation.

"Now you know why," Osei says with dry disgust.

Behind the guide, they now squeeze through a tunnel and into the chamber that held men. It is a damp and nearly lightless room with an upward-curved ceiling that suggests a wine cellar. But the place carries a harsh and bittersweet smell, as if the scent of black bodies had worked its way forever into the mortar and stone.

"This is the sole exit," the guide says. He indicates a window as tall as his waist, as wide as his arm from elbow to wrist. Through it can be viewed a cove and the pilings left from a pier. The captives, it is clear, could see the ships that would take them away. "The Portuguese built it small so no one could escape," the guide continues. "When the boats were ready, they were pushed through, one at a time."

Reverend Youngblood asks a question about resistance or rebellion. And the guide, by way of answer, leads the group across the plaza. He halts outside a single cell, ten feet high and wide and deep, marked above its entrance with a skull and crossbones. "This was for the leaders," he explains. "They would starve them to death."

Only a few strides from the cell stands a church, built for worship by the Portuguese but used as a slave market by the British and Dutch. Here victorious tribes sold their prisoners into bondage on an altar transformed into an auction block; here money was counted in what had been confessionals. "It's enough," Reverend Youngblood says to Osei, "to turn you against religion."

They climb from the plaza to an apartment inside the west bastion of the castle. By the standards used for Africans, these rooms could have housed hundreds; but only a handful lived here, the colonial governor and his family. They had beds and chairs and wide windows overlooking the surf, trappings that even today evoke a resort.

Afterwards, atop the battlement, nobody speaks. Reverend Youngblood leans forward, regarding the ocean and the palm-shaded beach, the last piece of Africa the captives ever saw. The sound of chirping laughter suddenly rises from below. In a rocky tidal pool, three village boys are playing, splashing each other with sea water until their naked bodies gleam. Reverend Youngblood spots them and waves.

For all its massive scale, genocide was a deeply personal crime—one kidnapping, one murder, committed millions of times. The sight of those boys reminds the pastor of a family story. Generations back on his mother's side, seven brothers had mistakenly cut wood on a white man's property. Over days they were hunted down, left to die in the fields, only one escaping barefoot down the road to New Orleans. And from the time Ottie Mae told him, at the age of thirteen, Johnny had never asked her another question about Reconstruction or slavery. Until today, in a sense, disbelief and helplessness and fear have conquered memory.

Without words, Reverend Youngblood and the others walk to the museum's office. There, covered with sweat and salt spray, they sign the visitors' register. In the column headed "Impressions," a Dane has written, "Have a good day," followed by a Swiss with the comment, "I would not mind having a bedroom view like the governor."

Reverend Youngblood reads their words, struck but not surprised at the lack of compassion. He remembers the aftermath of the racial murders in Howard Beach and Bensonhurst, when whites questioned about bigotry told reporters, "My family never owned slaves." So he writes of his day at the Castle of St. George: "Though horrible and hateful, it keeps the history alive." And he says to Osei, as they return to the car, "To survive all this shit, it must have been for *something*."

> *If you're my real folk, resonate for me.*
> *Home seems strange when you've been away,*
> *Family seems different when you've been apart.*
> *Is there no place like home?*
> *Is home where the heart is?*
> *Do I have a heart?*
> *Or was it lost in the Middle Passage?*

Five miles off the main road from Accra to Kumasi, surrounded by palms and banana groves, the village of Asafo sits hunched on a hilltop. It appears, amid the greenery, as a palette of earth tones—the red-brown of rusting tin roofs, the burnt orange of ferric soil, the pale mustard of mud walls, the beige of bamboo fences, protecting every precious cashew tree.

The town seems nearly deserted as Reverend Youngblood and Osei arrive late on a Saturday afternoon. Three boys shoot marbles. Two barefoot girls sell mirrors and locks from a wood stand. A bush taxi bounces through town, past the Otargo Trading Agency and the Looking Cute Beauty Base, kicking up clouds of red dust.

"Hey, Rasta man," someone calls to Osei, indicating his dreadlocks. An old man with a walking stick recognizes him from a past visit, and he moves toward the car, giggling children in his wake. Osei dips into his backpack for the snapshots from his last trip, and he flips through the pile, giving a copy of each print to its subject, playing the returning brother for the gathering crowd.

"*Akwaba,*" says a graying man in green *kente,* the village captain, greeting the visitors in the regional language of Twi.

"*Medasi,*" says Reverend Youngblood, thank you. He has been practicing for this moment all week.

Most of the people, the captain explains, are attending a funeral on the outskirts of town. Reverend Youngblood and Osei will be taken to the ceremony, formally introduced to the chief and his court. But first there are rituals to be observed, of welcome and return.

The captain, whose name is Edward Bismarck Adjebemj, leads Osei and the pastor through a gap between two stores, down a gulley, across a creek, and onto the back porch of his home. Kwame Charles joins them, bare-chested, wrapped in cloth from waist to shin, only his camera carried over from New York. He will serve as Reverend Youngblood's "linguist," the interlocutor who in Ghanaian culture represents any man of position. Two boys enter the yard lugging an iron pot of palm wine and a calabash cup. As the captain speaks in Twi, the other men adding words of concurrence, he ladles wine from pot to calabash, deliberately spilling several drops on the ground. He is "pouring libation," in the Ghanaian phrase, beseeching the ancestors to intercede with the divine.

"Kwame," Reverend Youngblood whispers, "tell me some of what he said."

"He prays to God and Mother Earth for your safe arrival," Kwame explains. "It is good you have come to Asafo to see things for yourself. God should help you. And if bad spirits try to stop you, then the ancestors should punish them. The ancestors should always protect you."

A boy brings the calabash to Osei. He spills a drop, touches the wine to his sober lips without swallowing, spills a bit more. Then Reverend Youngblood, to applause, drains the vessel. The wine tastes like sour orange juice, and it is covered with foam that must be wiped free of flies. None of that matters now. "Come," the captain says, pointing the way toward the funeral. "Let us rise."

At the dirt crossroads that marks the center of town, the men turn west into the setting sun. As they pass the rural bank and the lottery kiosk and the children peddling groundnuts and brown eggs, the raucous pulse of high-life music reaches toward them. Its source is the funeral, an affair not of sorrow but celebration, and an occasion when ancient and modern easily mesh.

The man who died, Okyeane Kwaku Ottum, was at eighty-five the most senior and esteemed of Chief Abedi's four linguists. Hundreds of villagers have gathered in tribute, the dignitaries on a raised concrete platform, the families beneath a palm-thatch pavilion. Highlife pours from two speakers and a tape deck, all cooled by a whirling fan. Across a clearing sit four drummers, awaiting their time, each with a crooked staff at the ready. Some villagers dance in the open space, while others carry money to collectors seated on the podium. Half will be given to the linguist's survivors and half held for the donor's clan association in two parallel expressions of mutual aid.

"I got thirty million questions in my head," Reverend Youngblood says to Kwame, but the funeral is beginning to surrender to twilight. Its joyous spirit reminds him of the phrase he employs at Saint Paul, not "funeral" but "homegoing celebration." The syncopated procession, as it heads back into town, resembles nothing so much as the New Orleans jazz funerals of his childhood, with their "second-line" meter and swaying umbrellas, just like the one the chief carries now. It was one thing to study and speak about "African retentions," another to see one march before your eyes.

Asafo, it is clear, works as Accra never will. Whatever its material wants, it is an African place with a time-honored logic, not a European imposition struggling to adapt. Even Chief Abedi, who looked so beleaguered and put-upon in his law office, exudes a kind of radiance here. Gone are the glasses, the suit, the yellowing papers. He wears ebony *kente* with a red sash across one shoulder, and a string of cowrie shells. His body looks supple, muscular, young.

Although the *durbar* will not be held until tomorrow, Reverend Youngblood will be officially announced now. Kwame leads him into the courtyard of the chief's palace, a weathered brick building two stories tall. The pastor shakes hands with the courtiers, then, through his linguist, addresses the chief.

"Osei Yaw, my brother, came to Ghana and Asafo last year in a search for his roots," he says. "And he returned to us with the message that there were needs we could meet as African-Americans and Christians. So this trip is for me, so I can go home and tell my people what we can do."

There is applause as Kwame translates.

"In the five days I have been in Ghana, I have seen enough churches. At this point, I am not interested in a church, but more so a school. It is our desire to build a secondary school in Asafo."

Kwame translates again, adding at the end the Twi words for "Education first."

When the clapping subsides, Chief Abedi speaks.

"The people of Asafo thank you for your speech and your happiness," he says. "When we look at your face, we know you are not from America. You are from here."

Later in the evening they talk more, and more privately. They sit in folding chairs on the porch of the chief's house, lit by kerosene lamps. From his *parrain* in New Orleans to William Jones in Brooklyn, all of Reverend Youngblood's elders had known his unquenchable curiosity. Now, amid the sounds of crickets and rustling leaves, Chief Abedi fields the first of those thirty million questions, all of which add up to one question: "What is my reason for being?"

"I remember about twenty-five years ago," the chief says, "Louis Armstrong came here. And when he played trumpet, a woman started dancing, and Louis Armstrong said she looked like his mother. He hugged her. So when we see American blacks, we see our brothers and sisters. You look like us. It is a chain."

But the chain, if not broken, was strained and warped by abduction. And as a Christian, a black Christian familiar with the unsparing analysis of Malcolm X, the pastor wonders aloud if he is practicing "the religion of the oppressor." The other day in Accra, in fact, he had laughed bitterly at the cartoon painted on a truck's tailgate. Two mice were regarding a trap set without cheese. "And they call themselves Christians," one muttered.

"When the white missionaries first came," Chief Abedi replies, "they gave us the idea our beliefs were no good, paganism. They made us discard them. They made us swallow their religion." He clears his throat. "But now we vomit. We have African theologians, and we are fashioning a Christianity to suit our conditions. We remember and honor the dead ancestors. For what they have achieved and what they have set aside for us. We want to keep our bond."

"Have you ever forgiven the white man?" Reverend Youngblood asks, thinking not only of enforced Christianity but of the Castle of St. George.

"Slavery was heinous, but we also think in retrospect, we, too, are partly to blame. We should not have sold our own people, captured our own brothers, for cloth or rum. We, too, are morally culpable."

The talk turns to the proposed school. And the more Chief Abedi speaks of the need for practical training, particularly in agriculture and public health, the more Reverend Youngblood thinks of Booker T. Washington's Tuskegee. Finally they reach the subject of money. To build a facility for six hundred children, the chief says, would cost fifteen thousand dollars. Reverend Youngblood, shocked, tells him that in New York fifteen thousand dollars might purchase one child one year of college.

"If I know my people," he says, "unless things have changed a lot since I left, you've got your fifteen thousand dollars."

In the amber lamplight, Chief Abedi's hands move, palm striking palm in soft, sincere thanks.

Am I a Joseph,
Part of a providentially orchestrated affair?
Am I a Bedouin, a wandering Aramean?
Am I a prodigal son of a type,
Who remembers the assets of home,
While in the pig pen of a far country?
Am I a Moses? God, help!

Late on Sunday morning, the drums sound. They converse, rhythms weaving, timbres from treble to bass joining in a harmony like song.

They call up the streets and down the hills and into the fields, inviting the village to assemble. Men dressed in the hand-me-downs of Western pop culture, shirts stenciled with "Georgia Bulldogs" or Garfield the cat or even "Same Shit, Different Day," shed those skins for *kente*. Reverend Youngblood buttons his dress shirt and tightens his navy tie, packed by Joyce in case he went to church. He, too, is being summoned in the traditional way, by the drums that plantation masters forbade so slaves could not conspire, the drums that blacks in New Orleans played in the lot called Congo Square, keeping Africa alive.

Reverend Youngblood enters the palace courtyard to find Chief Abedi ensconced atop an ebony throne. On the concrete steps before him crouch two criers, and at the chief's left shoulder stands his praise-singer, trumpeting a fanfare through an elephant-tusk horn. Linguists, drummers, and courtiers arrange themselves beneath a colonnade, and the pastor shakes hands with each one. The somber attire of yesterday's funeral has given way to teal and turquoise and scarlet and orange, to crossing stripes and paisley swirls. This is a day doubly graced, first because it is a *durbar* and second because it is unique. Normally the village celebrates the festival only twice in a year, to honor the chief in July and give thanks for the harvest in October. With the coming of Reverend Youngblood, the religious calendar for 1990 has been expanded by half.

The drumming ceases, and two lines of girls stride into the courtyard, their voices lifted in lilting melody, part lullaby, part hymn. Then the drummers resume, the air rippling with percussion, and the girls begin their dance. It is called a *kantata*, used in the Ewe tribe as a ritual of welcome. They lean forward slightly, shuffle two paces left, then two right, swishing a handkerchief with each step. A taller, older girl in the back declares a verse, and the rest chant in the call-and-response pattern that survived in America as work songs and ring shouts.

Ten minutes later, with the girls gleaming with sweat, a linguist holds aloft a staff, and the dance halts. The staff is topped with a carving of three faces, symbolizing the wisdom of consensus. This very morning, Chief Abedi heard petitioners in the hearings called *nsiesie*, the tribal alternative to the adversarial law he practices in Accra. Sitting on his front porch in sandals and tennis shorts, he settled disputes ranging from overdue debts to familial succession. Here, Reverend Youngblood felt, was the same kind of "black law" he had applied in the awful business between Carter Naulls and Ella Redmond.

Now, on the chief's behalf, the linguist opens a small bottle of schnapps and makes an invocation. He speaks in insistent bursts, rapid and directed, sprinkled with words Reverend Youngblood can follow—"Osei Yaw," "America," "Reverend Doctor." Time after time, the linguist pours libation, the wet circle on the ground spreading eighteen inches in diameter. When he displays the empty glass, the court applauds.

Then the village captain leads the pastor and Osei into the center, facing the chief. With Kwame as his linguist, Reverend Youngblood repeats his remarks from Saturday, tracing the stages from Osei's initial visit to the decision that Saint Paul would build Asafo a high school. Within six months, he adds, the money will arrive, and Osei will accompany it to help supervise construction. Then he offers one last joke about how much he enjoyed the palm wine and tells the court, *"Medasi."*

Rising from his throne, Chief Abedi says, "God has given us our school." He steps within inches of Reverend Youngblood, holding aloft a sword, its iron blade curved, its handle covered in gold leaf.

"There is not much time," he says through Kwame. "Now we are going to give you a native name. And you swear your name will last for all your time."

"I swear," Reverend Youngblood says in a hushed voice.

"You are Kwaku, 'Wednesday-born.' God gave you to us, so we call you Nyamekye, 'God's gift.' According to your speeches, everything you say, you give help. Anybody comes your way, you give help. So, Boafo, 'helper.' "

Children gather at the palace gates, watching. A woman places handfuls of mashed yam at several stations in the courtyard, begging a blessing from God. Chief Abedi passes the sword to Reverend Youngblood, who now must swear his oath.

"I, Kwaku Nyamekye Boafo, promise," he says, repeating Kwame's translation of the chief's words, "that in the rain, in the storm, in the cold, whatever happens, I will be present anytime I'm invited, unless I am sick. May God, Mother Earth, and the ancestors help me."

Then he kneels like a young knight. Chief Abedi drapes him with a *kente* strip and a necklace of sandstone beads.

"Today, Sunday, December 9, 1990," he says, "the village of Asafo and you and your congregation over there, in the rain or the sunshine, we are all one."

And instantly the courtyard bursts into dance. First the Queen Mother, then three, five, eight women waving handkerchiefs as if in flirtation, and finally the linguist with his staff and the courtiers with raised swords—they whirl around Reverend Youngblood, swaying and shimmying. For a moment he stands frozen, amazed, his smile a wide ivory seam. *Just like Saint Paul,* he tells himself, *when folk get happy.* Just like Tom Carter, hearing "Lazarus and the Black Man," punching the air and shouting, "We got church today!"

There is more dancing and more singing and an appeal by the chief for everyone with relatives abroad to solicit money for the school. And finally, as the rest of the celebrants scatter for home or the fields, Chief Abedi leads Reverend Youngblood on a brief tour.

They ride by pickup truck to Asafo's medical clinic, erected twenty years ago by a government that was overthrown by a military regime that cannot or will not pay to maintain it. The roof leaks. Torn blankets cover beds. The medicine cabinets open onto nearly empty shelves.

"Do people use this every day?" Reverend Youngblood asks the chief.

"People are sick every day," he replies.

They stop next at the junior high school. On the porch and in the classrooms the concrete has buckled like streets during an earthquake. Window shutters have broken or fallen off their hinges altogether. The desks resemble sawhorses, and the rooms have no lights. And this place is the terminus of education in Asafo.

In a moment, Chief Abedi will show Reverend Youngblood a more hopeful spot, an expanse of flat scrubland that could be cleared for the high school. But these images from the clinic and junior high have brought the pastor's trip to a chastening, challenging end. He will fly back to New York tomorrow knowing that Africa mirrors black America in disturbing as well as comforting ways. If slavery had not succeeded in defeating history, sundering past from present, then it had nonetheless left ruins across two continents that centuries could not heal. Thirty-one years have passed since Chief Abedi returned from law school in England to build a new nation, and the effort seemed never to end. It has been sixteen since Reverend Youngblood accepted the call to "God's Alcatraz," and there, too, resurrection remained unfinished, a work in progress.

"Chief," Reverend Youngblood asks as they climb into the truck, "do you ever think about giving up?"

"No," he says, chuckling. "We want to keep trying. To please our ancestors."

How sweetly have I heard your name pronounced—
Africa.
The awe, the honor intoned by the speaker—
Africa.

Your womb held the world.
Your breast suckled us all.
We are indebted to you.
Mama, I'm home.

EPILOGUE

◉

AGAINST THE GATES

I T IS DECEMBER 23, 1990, the Sunday before Christmas, and the yuletide spirit is less of celebration than of struggle. In the deserts of Saudi Arabia, more than a quarter-million American soldiers gather for war against the Iraqi forces that have seized and occupied Kuwait. In the offices and factories back home, layoffs mount into the hundreds of thousands as the nation sinks ever deeper into recession. And in the streets and shops of New York, twelve people are murdered in a single weekend, as the most violent year in the city's history nears its end.

All of this matters to Reverend Johnny Ray Youngblood and Saint Paul Community Baptist Church. The cliché about economics says that when white America has a cold, black America has pneumonia, and if that is so, then the victims have always looked to the black church as their emergency room. A woman of twenty-two named Sonia Clark-Murray, like a dozen other members of Saint Paul, suddenly finds herself stationed in the Persian Gulf, within range of Saddam Hussein's Scud missiles and chemical weapons. Betty Howard, Leroy's wife, has lost her job in a Wall Street bank after sixteen years, instantly dropping the family out of the fragile black middle class.

As both a church and a community, Saint Paul must provide. One morning, Reverend Youngblood places an empty chair beside the pulpit, and tells the congregation to imagine the Almighty sitting there.

Then he invites those with family and friends in the war zone to shout out their anger and fear, to get up in the face of God. A group drawn largely from Eldad-Medad and taking the title Fifty Black Churchmen raises a pool of eighty thousand dollars for starting small businesses. Their first investment allows an elder, Bob Wilson, to open a soul-food restaurant on Christ Square. Bob, in turn, hires Betty Howard to work the counter. And her wages allow her and Leroy's son, Trevor, to remain in college.

So there is a reason for wreaths on the door and poinsettias in the windows of Saint Paul. There is a reason for the choir to sing "Go Tell It on the Mountain." There is a reason for the staff members to post their Christmas cards to the congregation on the lobby bulletin board. The reason might be called tradition or mutual aid or simply survival.

In the choir, Tom Approbato sings. He is sweating his way through Hebrew in seminary, serving informally as a hospital's chaplain, drawing nearer to ordination as a minister. In the first row, as usual, Osei Yaw Akoto listens. He will return to Ghana in just a few weeks with the fifteen thousand dollars for Asafo's school and the construction skills to help build it. A few rows behind him, Inez Simpkins claps in time, but without her usual partner. Annie Nesbitt left yesterday to visit her parents in North Carolina, and Inez saw her off at the airport with the words, "Don't be sad." Toward the back, among the teenagers, Ali Nurse shows off the letter announcing his admission to Norfolk State University. Kathleen Wilson, knowing not to intrude, worships a discreet distance away. And in the folding chairs of the sanctuary extension, the place claimed almost exclusively by men, Randy Murphy seals the envelopes containing his two-dollar offering and twenty-five-dollar tithe. "Put it this way," he often says. "Life is sacrifice, doctor."

The service proceeds with Eli Wilson singing a passage of Handel's *Messiah* and his brother, Darryl, soloing on a spiritual entitled, "It Was the Blood." Reverend Youngblood reads aloud several children's report cards and salutes an elder who has been named Businessman of the Year by a Panamanian social club and officially welcomes back from a hospital stay Rose Stokes, whom he calls "Rosiella Stokes of Hickory Valley, Tennessee." Rochester Blanks and Robert Nix make separate appeals for members to bring one hundred dollars apiece to the worship service on Watch Night, as New Year's Eve is known, so the last debts on the sanctuary expansion can be retired.

After all that, after the prayers and the sermon, the elders distribute the grape juice and crackers that form the Lord's Supper, and Reverend Youngblood moves one final time to the pulpit.

"Last night," he says, "I was having a go-round with God. And I asked Him, 'Why must I feel the compulsive urge to preach all these different angles on the gospel? Why do I have to make this church a Church Unusual? Why can't I just run with it the way I heard it as a child?' And the Lord didn't answer."

He pauses.

"But I know He answers in His own time. And I got my answer when Eli sang that aria this morning. It was a change for us. And I know you're open to change."

Now he raises both arms, his robe stretching like open wings.

"So we celebrate the Lord's sacrifice. We receive the emblems of his broken body and his shed blood. And I feel there's power in them."

He brings the cracker toward his mouth and says, "Let's eat together."

He touches the grape juice to his lips and says, "Let's drink together."

Then Reverend Johnny Ray Youngblood, himself and his people once again redeemed, turns to face Eli at the organ. And against bigotry and poverty and murder and war, against the gates of hell, he says, "Mr. Wilson, let's go down, singing."

BIBLIOGRAPHY

Anderson, James. "Crazy for Kente Cloth: The Tradition Behind the Trend." *Emerge*. October 1990, 68, 69.

Ashenburg, Katherine. "Rochester in Bloom." *The New York Times*, 5 May 1991.

Attinger, Joelle. "The Decline of New York." *Time*, 17 September 1990, 36–52.

Baker, Russell W. "The Land of the LuLu: Nine Reasons the Council Isn't the Senate." *7 Days*, 8 November 1989.

Baldwin, James. *Go Tell It on the Mountain*. New York: Alfred A. Knopf, 1953.

Barone, Michael, and Grant Ujifusa. *The Almanac of American Politics 1990*. Washington: National Journal, 1990.

Barrett, Wayne. "High Noon in Brooklyn." *The Village Voice*, 29 November 1983.

———. "Stalking Sam Wright: Five Years in Brownsville." *The Village Voice*, 11 April 1977.

Benke, Rev. David H. *The Nehemiah Plan: New Jerusalem in East Brooklyn*. New York: New York Theological Seminary, 1983.

Berger, Joseph. "School Boards Said to Pad Their Payrolls." *The New York Times*, 14 March 1990.

Bernal, Martin. *Black Athena: The Afroasiatic Roots of Classical Civilization*. New Brunswick: Rutgers University Press, 1987.

Berry, Jason, Jonathan Foose, and Tad Jones. *Up from the Cradle of Jazz: New Orleans Music Since World War II*. Athens, Ga.: University of Georgia Press, 1986.

"Blockbusting: A Report on an Unethical Practice." New York: City Commission on Human Rights, 1963.

Boyte, Harry C. *CommonWealth: A Return to Citizen Politics*. New York: Free Press, 1989.

Branch, Taylor. *Parting the Waters: America in the King Years 1954–63*. New York: Touchstone, 1989.

Brozan, Nadine. "Mourners of Brooklyn Girl Rail at Latest Casual Killing." *The New York Times,* 25 September 1990.

Calvocoressi, Peter. *Who's Who in the Bible.* New York: Viking, 1987.

Chira, Susan. "Black Churches Turn to Teaching the Young." *The New York Times,* 7 August 1991.

Clines, Francis X. "Thumbs Down on the Emperor." *The New York Times,* 18 May 1978.

Cone, James H. *A Black Theology of Liberation.* New York: Lippincott, 1970.

———. *Black Theology and Black Power.* New York: Harper & Row, 1969.

———. *Martin & Malcolm & America: A Dream or a Nightmare.* Maryknoll, N.Y.: Orbis, 1991.

Davis, Gerald L. *I Got the Word in Me and I Can Sing It, You Know: A Study of the Performed African-American Sermon.* Philadelphia: University of Pennsylvania Press, 1985.

DeParle, Jason. "For Some Blacks, Social Ills Seem to Follow White Plans." *The New York Times,* 11 August 1991.

———. "Suffering in the Cities Persists As U.S. Fights Other Battles." *The New York Times,* 27 January 1991.

Didion, Joan. "New York: Sentimental Journeys." *The New York Review of Books,* 17 January 1991, 45–55.

Dolkart, Andrew S. *This Is Brooklyn: A Guide to the Borough's Historic Districts and Landmarks.* Brooklyn: The Fund for the Borough of Brooklyn, 1990.

Du Bois, W. E. B. *The Souls of Black Folk.* New York: New American Library, 1982.

Egan, Timothy. "A Choirboy, Crossfire, And Tragedy Comes Again." *The New York Times,* 16 October 1990.

Farrell, Bill, and Joseph McNamara. "Farewell to a Father; Pastor Calls for Equal Justice." *New York Daily News,* 31 January 1989.

Felder, Cain Hope. *Troubling Biblical Waters: Race, Class, and Family.* Maryknoll, N.Y.: Orbis, 1989.

Flesher, John. "Young Blacks in Trouble." *New York Daily News,* 27 February 1990.

Foner, Philip S. *Business and Slavery: The New York Merchants and the Irrepressible Conflict.* Chapel Hill: University of North Carolina Press, 1941.

Forbes, James. *The Holy Spirit and Preaching.* Nashville: Abingdon, 1989.

Frazier, E. Franklin, and C. Eric Lincoln. *The Negro Church in America, the Black Church Since Frazier.* New York: Schocken, 1974.

Garrow, David. *Bearing the Cross: Martin Luther King, Jr., and the Southern Christian Leadership Conference.* New York: Morrow, 1986.

Genovese, Eugene D. *Roll, Jordan, Roll: The World the Slaves Made.* New York: Pantheon, 1974.

Giordano, Mary Ann. "Cop Law: Rewards, Anguish." *Manhattan Lawyer,* 7 June 1988, 1.

Gittings, Jim. "Churches in Communities: A Place to Stand." *Christianity and Crisis,* 2 February 1987, 5–11.

Goell, Milton J. *East New York Must Have Public Housing.* Brooklyn: Brownsville

Neighborhood Council and East New York Dispensary, 1951.

Goldfield, David R. *Black, White, and Southern: Race Relations and Southern Culture, 1940 to the Present.* Baton Rouge: Louisiana State University Press, 1990.

"Good Old East New York." (Commemorative magazine.) Brooklyn: East New York Savings Bank, 1943.

Goss, Linda, and Marian E. Barnes, eds. *Talk That Talk: An Anthology of African-American Storytelling.* New York: Touchstone, 1989.

Graham, Judith. "The Slave Fortresses of Ghana." *The New York Times,* 25 November 1990.

"Groundbreaking." *The New Yorker,* 25 March 1991, 26–27.

Hancock, LynNell. "The Cookie Monster of P.S. 224." *The Village Voice,* 7 February 1989.

Harris, Reverend William. "Why Most Black Men Won't Go to Church." *Upscale,* April–May 1990, 22–23.

Hedges, Chris. "Wild Shooting on Street Hits Girl, 9, in Car." *The New York Times,* 23 July 1990.

Heidenreich, Frederick J. *Old Days and Old Ways in East New York.* Brooklyn: Heidenreich, 1948.

Hiss, Philip Hanson. *Netherlands America: The Dutch Territories in the West.* New York: Essential, 1943.

Hoffman, Paul. "Unrest in Brooklyn: The Causes." *The New York Times,* 23 July 1966.

Hornblower, Margot. "Homes, Hope Rising from N.Y. Rubble." *The Washington Post,* 12 July 1985.

Horwitt, Sanford D. *Let Them Call Me Rebel: Saul Alinsky, His Life and Legacy.* New York: Alfred A. Knopf, 1989.

Hurston, Zora Neale. *The Sanctified Church: The Folklore Writings of Zora Neale Hurston.* Berkeley: Turtle Island Foundation, 1981.

Hyland, Tony. *The Castles of Elmina.* Accra, Ghana: Ghana Museums and Monuments Board, 1971.

Jaynes, Gerald David, and Robin M. Williams, Jr., eds. *A Common Destiny: Blacks and American Society.* Washington, D.C.: National Academy Press, 1989.

Johnson, Paul. *A History of the Jews.* New York: Harper & Row, 1987.

Jones, William A., Jr. *God in the Ghetto.* Elgin, Ill.: Progressive Baptist Publishing House, 1979.

———. *Responsible Preaching.* Morristown, N.J.: Aaron Press, 1989.

Kifner, John. "Koch and Queens Group. In Standoff." *New York Times,* 1 March 1978.

Koch, Edward I. "The Lonesome Death of Stephen Kelly." *The New York Voice,* 11 February 1989.

Kotlowitz, Alex. *There Are No Children Here: The Story of Two Boys Growing Up in the Other America.* New York: Doubleday, 1991.

Krebs, Albin. "Brooklyn Sniper Kills Negro Boy in Race Disorder." *The New York Times,* 22 July 1966.

Landesman, Alter F. *A History of New Lots*. Port Washington, N.Y.: Kennikat Press, 1977.

Lee, Felicia R. "East New York, Haunted by Crime, Fights for Its Life." *The New York Times,* 5 January 1989.

Lemann, Nicholas. *The Promised Land: The Great Black Migration and How It Changed America*. New York: Alfred A. Knopf, 1991.

Lincoln, C. Eric, and Lawrence H. Mamiya. *The Black Church in the African American Experience*. Durham: Duke University Press, 1990.

Loeb, Penny. "Mitchell-Lama Violations Persist; Despite Regulations, Officials Haven't Moved." *New York Newsday,* 11 October 1988.

Lynn, Frank. "Koch Offers Apology on Queens Remarks." *The New York Times,* 10 March 1978.

Marriott, Michel. "Afrocentrism: Balancing or Skewing History." *The New York Times,* 11 August 1991.

Mauer, Marc. *Young Black Men and the Criminal Justice System: A Growing National Problem*. Washington: The Sentencing Project, 1990.

Mbiti, John S. *African Religions and Philosophy*. 2nd edition. Portsmouth, N.H.: Heinemann Educational Books, 1990.

McAllister, Bill. "The Menaced Lives of Black Men." *New York Newsday,* 3 January 1990.

McAllister, Jared. "100G to Project for New Homes." *New York Daily News,* 17 September 1984.

McKinley, James C., Jr. "Teen-Ager Arrested in Shooting of Girl, 3." *The New York Times,* 23 August 1990.

Moehringer, J. R. "Slain Father's Six Sons Reuniting in Grief." *The New York Times,* 28 January 1989.

Muwakkil, Salim. "Living fast, dying young in America's inner cities." *In These Times,* 26 December 1990, 7.

———. "More are going back to the future with Farrakhan." *In These Times,* 21 March 1990, 6, 10.

Mydans, Seth. "Blacks' Identity vs. Success and Seeming 'White.'" *The New York Times,* 25 April 1990.

———. "Homicide Rate Up for Young Blacks." *The New York Times,* 7 December 1990.

Navarro, Mireya. "After a Stray Shot: A Girl's Family Seeks Meaning in a Random Loss." *The New York Times,* 26 August 1990.

Newfield, Jack. "Sam Wright: Why Brownsville Looks Like Beirut." *The Village Voice,* 13 September 1976.

Nouwen, Henri J. M. *The Wounded Healer: Ministry in Contemporary Society*. New York: Doubleday, 1972.

Ostling, Richard N. "Strains on the Heart." *Time,* 19 November 1991, 88–90.

Ottley, Roi, and William J. Weatherby, eds. *The Negro in New York: An Informal Social History*. New York: The New York Public Library, 1967.

Perry, Cynthia. *IAF 50 Years: Organizing for Change*. Franklin Square, N.Y.: Industrial Areas Foundation, 1990.

Plan for New York City. New York: City Planning Commission, 1969.

Population Characteristics and Neighborhood Social Resources. Vol. 1. New York: Bureau of Community Statistical Services, Research Department, Community Council of Greater New York, 1959.

Powell, Michael. "Alliance Blasts Brown." *New York Newsday,* 17 October 1990.

Protestant Council of the City of New York, *East New York ... and Neighboring Communities.* New York: 1956.

Raboteau, Albert J. *Slave Religion: The "Invisible Institution" in the Antebellum South.* New York: Oxford University Press, 1978.

Rainone, Nanette, ed. *The Brooklyn Neighborhood Book.* Brooklyn: The Fund for the Borough of Brooklyn, 1985.

"Report to the Mayor: 'Implementing the Laws in Behalf of Equality.'" New York: City Commission on Human Rights, 1963.

Rieder, Jonathan. *Canarsie: The Jews and Italians of Brooklyn against Liberalism.* Cambridge: Harvard University Press, 1985.

Robbins, I. D. "Blueprint for a One-Family House." *New York Daily News Sunday Magazine,* 21 January, 1980, 33–35.

Robertson, Nan. *Getting Better: Inside Alcoholics Anonymous.* New York: Morrow, 1988.

Schanberg, Sydney H. "Bricks and Local Power." *The New York Times,* 21 February 1984.

Sheehy, Maura. "The Hands of Reverend Youngblood." *Details,* June 1991, 13–18.

Sleeper, Jim. "East Brooklyn's Nehemiah Opens Its Doors and Answers Its Critics." *City Limits,* June–July 1984, 14–15.

———. "East Brooklyn's Second Rising." *City Limits,* December 1982, 12–16.

———. *The Closest of Strangers: Liberalism and the Politics of Race in New York.* New York: Norton, 1990.

Smith, Bennett W., Sr. *Tithing as Taught by the Holy Scriptures.* Elgin, Ill.: Progressive Baptist Publishing House, n.d.

Smith, Michael P. *A Joyful Noise: A Celebration of New Orleans Music.* Dallas: Taylor Publishing Company, 1990.

Sorin, Gerald. *The Nurturing Neighborhood: The Brownsville Boys Club and Jewish Community in Urban America, 1940–1990.* New York: New York University Press, 1990.

"Standing for the Whole." Franklin Square, N.Y.: Industrial Areas Foundation, 1990.

Steele, Shelby. *The Content of Our Character: A New Vision of Race in America.* New York: St. Martin's Press, 1990.

Stern, Michael. "Mayor Pays Visit to Family of Boy." *The New York Times,* 22 July 1966.

Stokes, Henry Scott. "Alinsky's Theory of Protest as Applied in Queens." *The New York Times,* 7 March 1978.

Telander, Rick. *Heaven Is a Playground.* New York: Fireside, 1988.

Thurman, Howard. *Jesus and the Disinherited.* Nashville: Abingdon, 1949.

Vanderbilt, Gertrude. *The Social History of Flatbush.* Brooklyn: Frederick Loesser & Co., 1909.

Washington, James Melvin, ed. *A Testament of Hope: The Essential Writings and Speeches of Martin Luther King, Jr.* New York: HarperCollins, 1991.

———. *Frustrated Fellowship: The Black Baptist Quest for Social Power.* Macon, Ga.: Mercer University Press, 1986.

Weiss, Samuel. "Ethnic Plan for a School Seen Fading." *The New York Times,* 5 July 1991.

West, Cornel. "Nihilism in Black America: A Danger that Corrodes from Within." *Dissent,* Spring 1991, 221–26.

Wilkerson, Isabel. "Middle-Class Blacks Try to Grip a Ladder While Lending a Hand." *The New York Times,* 26 November 1990.

Wilkinson, Ed. "Praise Bishop's Role in Rebuilding Brownsville." *The Tablet,* 10 August 1985.

Wilmore, Gayraud S. *Black Religion and Black Radicalism: An Interpretation of the Religious History of Afro-American People.* 2nd edition. Maryknoll, N.Y.: Orbis, 1983.

———, and James H. Cone. *Black Theology: A Documentary History, 1966–1979.* Maryknoll, N.Y.: Orbis, 1979.

Winnick, Louis. *New People in Old Neighborhoods.* New York: Russell Sage Foundation, 1990.

Wood, Forrest G. *The Arrogance of Faith: Christianity and Race in America from the Colonial Era to the Twentieth Century.* New York: Alfred A. Knopf, 1990.

Woodson, Carter G. *The History of the Negro Church.* Washington, D.C.: The Associated Publishers, 1972.

Woodward, Catherine. "The Shadow of AIDS: East New York Fighting Fear, Drugs, Looming Threat of Virus." *New York Newsday,* 24 March 1991.

Woolf, Craig. "Guns Offer New York Teen-Agers A Commonplace Deadly Allure." *The New York Times,* 5 November 1990.

Wright, Lawrence. "The First Church of Rednecks, White Socks, and Blue Ribbon Beer." *Rolling Stone,* 13 December 1990.

Wycliff, Don. "Bricks, Mortar, Hearts, Minds." *The New York Times,* 27 August 1985.

X, Malcolm. *The Autobiography of Malcolm X.* New York: Grove Press, 1965.

Young, Henry J. *Major Black Religious Leaders: 1755–1940.* Nashville: Abingdon, 1977.

ACKNOWLEDGMENTS

No AMERICAN, HOWEVER WELL-INTENTIONED, can live unencumbered by our country's tragic history of race relations. The enslavement of Africans was indeed a kind of original sin. Generations and generations later, even the innocent are implicated. My point is neither that black Americans enjoy an innate moral superiority nor that white Americans must flog themselves with guilt. It is, rather, that any encounter across the line of race occurs both in its own discrete moment and as part of that larger continuum, making trust hard to earn and suspicion easy to arouse.

Reverend Johnny Ray Youngblood took a leap of faith nearly three years ago when he agreed to allow me to write a book about himself and his church. Far from being a scholar of African-American Christianity, I was a double outsider—a white and a Jew—possessed only of curiosity and the desire to learn. "Sam's *tabula*," the pastor told the congregation during the first Sunday worship service I attended, "is a whole lotta *rasa*."

Having accepted the risk of my presence, Reverend Youngblood granted me complete access to Saint Paul, its members, and his own family. He spoke to me, at length and for publication, about deeply personal subjects. And in any situation in which I was met with understandable resistance—from East Brooklyn Congregations' confidential planning sessions to the church elders' inquiry into the matter of Carter Naulls and Justine Redmond—he put his own reputation at stake in vouching for my fairness, accuracy, and sensitivity. He often told me he wanted this book to convey Saint Paul's struggles and tensions as well as its triumphs. I only hope he feels his faith has been rewarded.

Of the dozens of members of the Saint Paul congregation whom I interviewed seven opened their lives most generously of all. So I bear a special debt to Tom Approbato, Osei Yaw Akoto, Annie Nesbitt, Inez Simpkins, Kathleen Wilson, Ali Nurse, and Randy Murphy. The Youngblood family—Joyce, Joel, and Jason in Brooklyn; Palmon, Ottie Mae, and Jernell in New Orleans—accepted my intrusions and many questions with goodwill. With unfailing finesse, Thenia Brandon, Reverend Youngblood's administrative assistant, fitted the innumerable interviews I required into the pastor's schedule. Eli Wilson taught me much about gospel music, and Rochester Blanks, Leroy Howard, and Shirley Raymond did the same in the area of church finance. Allie Smith, the widow of Reverend Adolphus Smith, shared with me the original manuscripts of several hundred of his sermons. Helen Parilla, Monica Walker, and Charles Lewis made me feel welcome in the tight confines of Saint Paul's media department office, the closest thing I had to a home base during fifteen months of day-to-day research. Charles, in particular, became far more than an obliging host—a sounding board, a fellow journalist willing to share his own copious files, and, ultimately, a friend.

In subliminal ways, this book had its inspiration both in the night in 1978 when Richard Boyce took me to a storefront church in Newark, where he was playing bass with his cousin's gospel group, and in the many conversations about their Bronx church that I overheard two friends, Mary Moore and Bertie Leonard, engaging in during the mid-1980s. Still, I might never have found Saint Paul at all were it not for two guides. At the outset of this project in October 1989, knowing virtually nothing about the multitude of black churches in New York, I sought the help of Marjorie Moon, artistic director of the Billie Holiday Theater in Bedford-Stuyvesant, and Frank DeRosa, director of information for the Roman Catholic Diocese of Brooklyn. In separate meetings each told me the same thing: "You've got to check out Johnny Ray Youngblood's church."

Through the year I spent writing the manuscript of *Upon This Rock,* I read innumerable passages over the telephone to Michael Shapiro, who analyzed them as acutely, honestly, and patiently as only an old and trusted friend possibly could. August Wilson, Ari Goldman, Tom Morgan, and Caren Thomas read the completed draft and offered both confirmation of its strengths and, more important, remedies for its weaknesses. Prof. David J. Garrow and Dr. James H. Cone brought their expertise in black theology and black church history to bear on the draft's sections about those topics. Working with me for the second book in a row, Jude Hayes proved again to be a researcher without peer. On the days when I was unable to attend the Stephen Kelly murder trial, Sara Lomax covered it on my behalf, producing voluminous and invaluable notes.

For favors too numerous to list here, I also wish to thank Jim Duggan, Berlencia Davis, Jim Sleeper, Lou Winnick, Wayne Barrett, LynNell Hancock, J. J. Hornblass, Dick Blood, Maura Burnett, Jessica Siegel, Darren Haber, Dr. Lisa Dixon, Dr. Irwin Redlener, Leonard Rutkowitz, Tim Mulligan, Carol Freedman, Frank Vardy, Joan Bacchus, Victor Aphreh, George Vecsey, Harvey Fisher, Arthur Tullman, Wilborn Hampton, Dick Shepard, and Terrie Williams.

The people of HarperCollins stayed closely involved with this book from its beginning. I feel grateful for the efforts of William Shinker, Rose Carrano, Sheila Gillooly, and, most of all, Rick Kot, an editor whose syllable-by-syllable scrutiny of a manuscript gives the lie to the truism that there are no more Maxwell Perkins types in the publishing industry.

Barney Karpfinger is a writer's dream of an agent—part advocate, part literary critic, part therapist. It has been a pleasure, and an honor, to have worked with him for six years now.

Finally, and with an abundance of love, I thank my wife, Cynthia. She encouraged me to pursue this project, knowing that it would take me away for scores of Sundays in addition to all the long hours during the week. As my own fascination with Saint Paul grew, she accompanied me to the church on a number of occasions, read each chapter as it was written, and opened our home to Reverend Youngblood, Charles Lewis, and other guests from Saint Paul. May she savor whatever further joy *Upon This Rock* brings.